RESIDENTIAL PATTERNS IN AMERICAN CITIES: 1960

by

Philip H. Rees
The University of Leeds

THE UNIVERSITY OF CHICAGO
DEPARTMENT OF GEOGRAPHY
RESEARCH PAPER NO. 189

1979

Published 1979 by The Department of Geography
The University of Chicago, Chicago, Illinois

Library of Congress Cataloging in Publication Data

Rees, Philip H., 1944–

Residential patterns in American cities, 1960.

(Research paper–University of Chicago, Department of Geography; no. 189)
Bibliography: p. 391

1. Residential mobility–United States. 2. Cities and towns–United States.
3. Social classes–United States. 4. United States–Social conditions–1960.
5. Sociology, Urban. I. Title. II. Series: Chicago. University. Dept. of Geography.
Research paper; no. 189.

HD7293. R37 1978 301.36′1

78-12169

ISBN 0-89065-096-9

Research Papers are available from:

The University of Chicago
Department of Geography
5828 S. University Avenue
Chicago, Illinois 60637
Price: $8.00 list; $6.00 series subscription

PREFACE

This dissertation has been a long time in gestation from original draft to its present form. The author must bear the responsibility for this overlong delay, having been seduced into pastures new before completing the harvest in the old fields. As a result the monograph has slipped from being a report on the socioeconomic geography of contemporary American cities to being a snapshot view of American urban populations at one date, 1960. Readers will obviously want to look elsewhere for a more contemporary view based on the 1970 U.S. Census (Association of American Geographers, 1976a, 1976b and 1976c), and for more sophisticated multivariate analyses. However, it is hoped that this monograph will provide readers with an interesting picture of the mid-century American city, as seen by a temporary immigrant to one particular city.

The debts that one accumulates in the course of a piece of research are many. The first and foremost is the one that I owe to Brian Berry who as my advisor during four years of graduate study was a constant source of ideas, advice and encouragement. He pointed me in the direction of urban residential studies, encouraged me to undertake a comparative study of many cities and provided, in connection with other research projects at the Center for Urban Studies, University of Chicago, the substantial amount of computer time this work required.

The second debt I owe is to my student colleagues at Chicago, in particular Yehoshua Cohen, David Meyer and Philip Lankford, who made graduate study an exciting and stimulating period. My thanks are also due Marvin Mikesell for providing a scholarly environment in which to research, and to Peter Goheen for his comments on many of my embryonic ideas. My stay at Chicago was financed through a Richard King Mellon Fellowship in Urban Studies and an Economic Development Administration Fellowship in Urban and Regional Studies. This generous support by an American Foundation and the American Government made possible this monograph.

The bulk of this study was written at the School of Geography at the University of Leeds. I owe my thanks to Bill Birch and to Alan Wilson for their support. Gordon Bryant, Geoff Hodgson and Tim Hadwin gave valuable help in converting my many illustrations into finished form.

However, without the love, support and encouragement of my wife through many a long year this research would never have seen the light of day.

Philip H. Rees

Leeds, Britain, 1977.

TABLE OF CONTENTS

Chapter Page

Chapter Page

LIST OF TABLES

Table		Page

Table | Page

Table | Page

LIST OF ILLUSTRATIONS

Figure Page

Figure Page

Figure | Page

CHAPTER I

REVIEW OF THE LITERATURE AND OUTLINE OF STUDY

Many of the activities of a city's population are spatially focused on the home. Much of the day is spent there and most trips to work, to shop and to visit friends begin and end there. It is therefore both interesting and important to ask what kinds of people live in what parts of the city and why? From this basic question stem a series of others. Where do the poor live and why? the rich? the young? the old? the black? the white? Are the residential areas of the inner city exclusively of low status, and are the suburbs of wholly higher status? How do the answers to these questions differ from city to city in the United States, and how are the differences or similarities observed related to the type of city? These are the kinds of questions which will be addressed in this monograph.

In this chapter the concept of residential pattern is defined. The study of residential patterns is placed in the wider context of studies of the residential sector and alternative approaches are briefly described. Previous work and findings on residential patterns in American cities are reviewed. Finally, a set of questions about residential patterns in U.S. cities are posed which are investigated in the chapters that follow.

Residential Patterns Defined

The residential portion of the urban system is made up of homes, the people who live in them and the people who supply them. Residential patterns are the regularities or relationships that characterize the residential subsystem. For example, a distinctive pattern — clustering in a few inner city neighborhoods — may be present in a map of the distribution of a particular population group over the residential areas of the city. At a more complex level several different characteristics of residential area populations may be observed to co-vary across the city. This clustering of population characteristics can be regarded as a residential pattern. The clustering so observed may in fact be open to interpretation in a social as well as a spatial sense: the spatial co-variation of people in poverty and people belonging to a particular ethnic group suggests that the distribution of income within that group might be different from other groups. Pattern will here be used in one of these four senses:

(i) a map pattern of a variable

(ii) a spatial co-variation of variables

(iii) a spatial co-variation of variables with social implications

(iv) an association between variables at an aggregate level.

The variables may be numbers, ratios or more complex indexes that describe the spatial distribution of different kinds of people.

The Residential Subsystem

It is useful, before considering studies of people living in their homes in detail, to stand back and look at the residential subsystem in a wider context. This is attempted in Figure 1.

The residential subsystem is represented at the heart of the diagram. Processes, events and outcomes in the residential system are affected by what goes on in the other four parts of the urban system identified. The demographic subsystem affects housing demand by supplying larger or smaller numbers of new households through formation and in-migration and by withdrawing larger or smaller numbers of households through dissolution or out-migration.

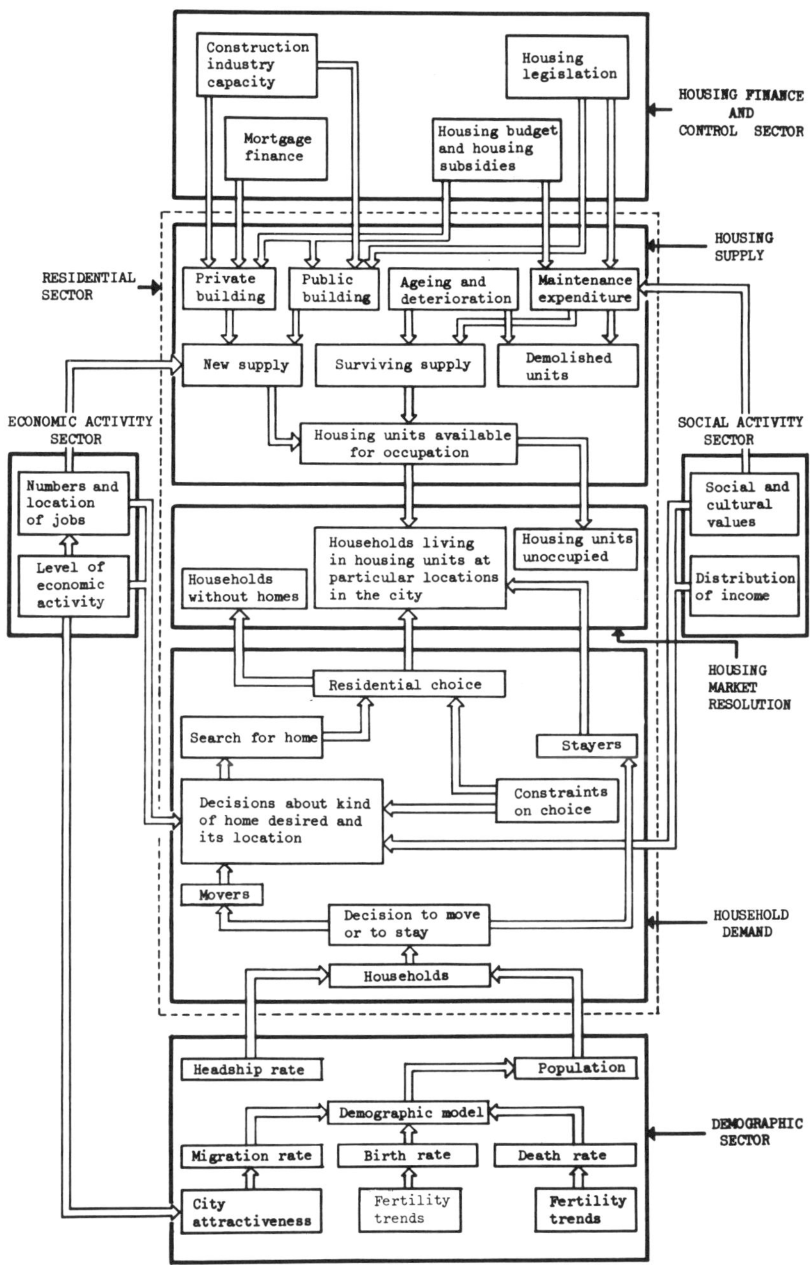

Fig. 1.--Processes at Work in the Residential Sector of the Urban System

The economic activity subsystem affects the residential sector by determining the numbers and types of jobs available and so the occupational composition of the city's working population. The location of employment also affects critically many household location and housing supply decisions.

Social and cultural values generated in the social activity subsystem also affect residential choice: the kind of home sought, the kind of neighbors preferred and the kind of residential area desired are all intimately bound up with the social values that a particular population holds.

Finally, the housing finance and control subsystem is important in determining the volume and type of housing that has been and is being constructed through factors like the availability of mortgage finance, housing subsidies, public housing funds, and construction industry capacity.

The residential subsystem proper can be divided into three parts shown on Figure 1: firstly, that concerned with the demand for houses, with the choice and location decisions of housing consumers; secondly, that concerned with the supply of houses, with the choice and location decisions of housing suppliers; and thirdly, that concerned with the resolution of demand and supply in a spatial context.

We conceive that the outputs of the residential subsystem, namely, people living in homes in residential areas in the city, are located in the central part of the residential subsystem box. These outputs are the principal objects of study in this monograph. We will be principally concerned with describing the patterns characteristic of these outputs. Conclusions reached about processes going on in other parts of the residential subsystem (for example, Simmons, 1968, Brown and Moore, 1970) about the links between the residential and other subsystems will aid interpreting the patterns described. Conversely, it is hoped that the analysis of residential patterns will help to put the work on individual or entrepreneur decision making in a proper context.

A Classification of the Studies of the Residential Subsystem

A simple classification of studies of the products of the residential subsystem is proposed in Figure 2. The classification serves to place the analyses in this monograph in the wider context of work on the residential system at the aggregate level (that is, work located in the central box of Figure 1).

In the section that follows, the nature of the links between studies in the Figure 2 classification is discussed; each type of study is briefly described and the conclusions of residential pattern studies of American cities are reviewed in detail.

The studies classified in Figure 2 have in common a basic data matrix of population, housing and environmental information (Table 1). This basic data matrix, derived from the national census, business directories, *Who's Who* or sample surveys, consists of rows which are the small areal subdivisions of the city, and columns which are the groups or classes or traits that go to make up the city's population, housing stock or environment. The cells in the table contain the raw numbers of group members falling in particular subareas of the city. Most analyses of residential pattern involve analysing this basic set of data. Most residential location modelling involves using some of the information in the matrix, such as the housing distribution or employment distribution to predict other parts of information, such as the population distribution and the city. In Figure 2 these relationships are represented by arrows going from the appropriate boxes in the central data box to the outer boxes. There are no returning arrows from the pattern study boxes but the model boxes do return arrows to the population cell in the central box.

Residential Pattern Studies: Cross-sectional

Cross-sectional pattern studies analyze patterns at a point in time. Three techniques of pattern analysis are listed in Figure 2: social area analysis, multivariate analysis, and segregation index analysis.

Social area analysis, originally proposed by Shevky and Williams (1949), is a technique for constructing indexes that summarize the characteristics of small areas within cities. The indexes were computed for each census tract in the city and the variation among tracts in social area scores was examined. The indexes were regarded by their authors as summarizing the social variation among the neighborhoods in American cities.

Extensive use has been made of multivariate techniques such as factor analysis or cluster analysis to examine the co-variation of many small area population and housing characteristics. This arose from a disatisfaction with the Shevky-Bell indexes.

Practitioners of both social area analysis and multivariate analysis examine the basic data matrix (Table 1) from a "row" point of view. Concern is focused on the way in which the component areas of the city differ with respect to their social group or housing type composition. In segregation index analysis (Duncan and Duncan, 1955a and 1955b, Taeuber and Taeuber, 1965) a "column" point of view is adapted in which attention is concentrated on the ways in which population groups or housing types differ in terms of their locational distributional or areal composition. Computation of an index of segregation of two groups, or a group and the rest of the population is one of the common ways in which the comparative distribution of social groups has been examined.

Residential Pattern Studies: Dynamic

Residential pattern investigation has been extended in a temporal direction (Murdie, 1969; Goheen, 1970; Salins, 1969 and 1971; Brown and Horton, 1970), though much remains to be done.

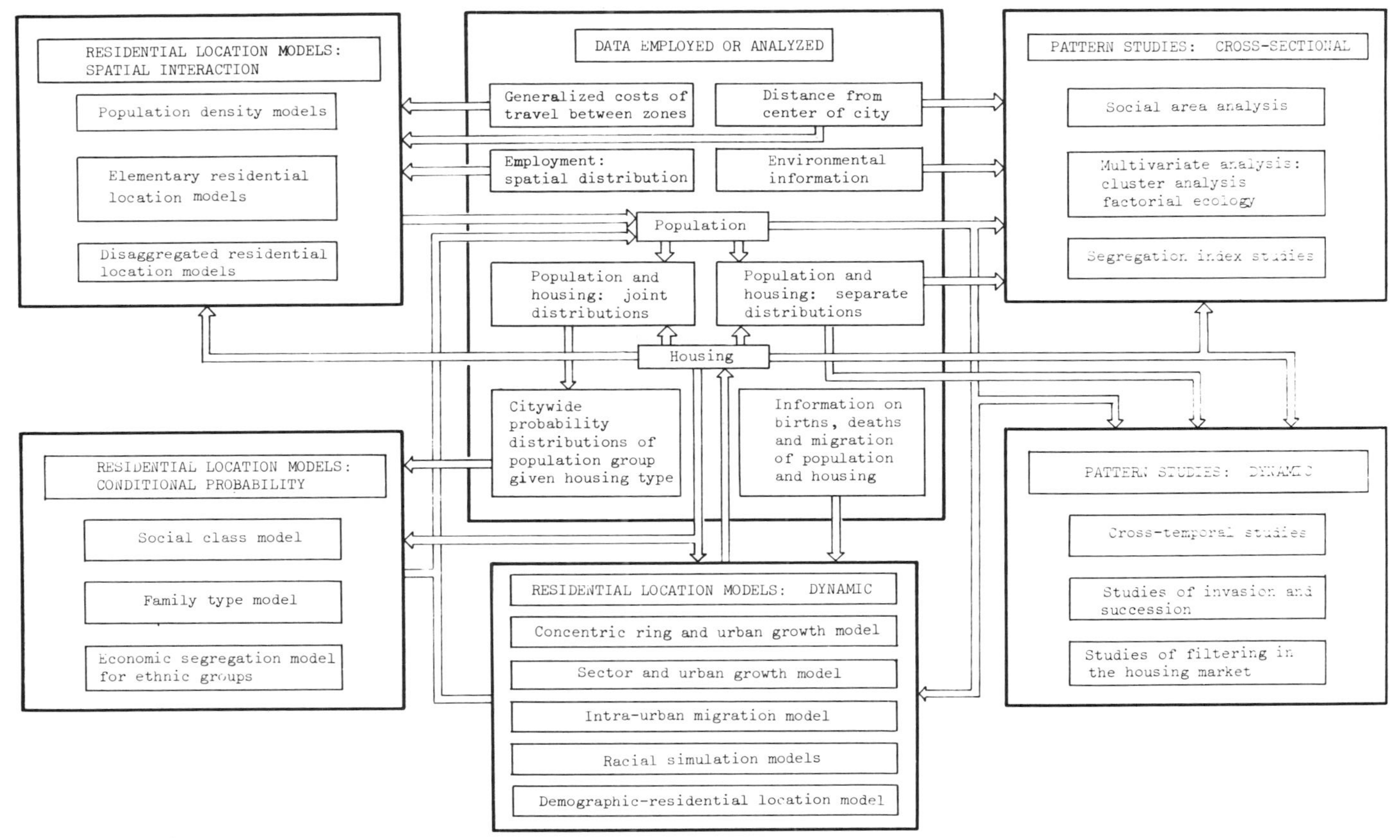

Fig. 2.-- A CLASSIFICATION OF STUDIES OF THE RESIDENTIAL SUBSYSTEM

TABLE 1

THE BASIC DATA MATRIX

		Population groups			Housing types			Environmental features		
		1	2 ...	g	1	2 ...	v	1	2 ...	z
	1	N_{11}	N_{12} ...	N_{1g}	U_{11}	U_{12} ...	U_{1v}	X_{11}	X_{12} ...	X_{1z}
	2	N_{21}	N_2 ...	N_{2g}	U_{21}	U_{22} ...	U_{2v}	X_{21}	X_{22} ...	X_{2z}
	.	.	.	.	.	.	.	.	.	.
	.	.	.	.	.	.	.	.	.	.
	.	.	.	.	.	.	.	.	.	.
Subareas of the City	i	N_{i1}	N_{i2} ...	N_{ig}	U_{i1}	U_{i2} ...	U_{iv}	X_{i1}	X_{i2} ...	X_{iz}
	.	.	.	.	.	.	.	.	.	.
	.	.	.	.	.	.	.	.	.	.
	.	.	.	.	.	.	.	.	.	.
	m	N_{m1}	N_{m2} ...	N_{mg}	U_{m1}	U_{m2} ...	U_{mv}	H_{m1}	H_{m2} ...	H_{mz}

Terms

N_{ig} = number of persons or families or households of population group g living in area i of the city

U_{iv} = number of housing units of housing type v located in area i of the city

X_{iz} = variables indexing the magnitude of environmental feature in area i of the city.

Such studies involve the comparison of map or factorial patterns at different points in time or the computation and analysis of key indexes of change. In relation to the volume of population movement between permanent residences that takes place over time in the city and in relation to the considerable social and economic changes that take place in the nation and the world, the gross socio-spatial pattern of city remains remarkably stable over periods of several decades (Simmons, 1968) though in certain critical periods, like the third quarter of the nineteenth century in Toronto (Goheen, 1970), it can change dramatically.

Residential Location Models: Cross-sectional

In Figure 2, pattern studies, mainly empirical and inductive in character, are contrasted with studies using explicit residential location models. A proper understanding of the nature of residential patterns requires, however, that models of the way in which people come to reside where they do in the city and how neighborhoods come to contain the kinds of people they do be constructed and tested.

Urban population density models (Casetti, 1969; Newling, 1969; Rees, 1970a) are very simple kinds of residential location models which various economists (Muth, 1969; Mills, 1968) have attempted to link to microeconomic theory. The population density of a residential area is modelled as a function of the distance the area is from the main employment and shopping focus of the city, the Central Business District. This location model has been generalized by Lowry (1964) who postulated that the residential population of an area within the city was a function of its accessibility to all employment locations. Wilson (1969 and 1970b) has shown that Lowry's residential location model is an elementary form of a spatial interaction model, and can be more consistently expressed using entropy, maximizing methods. The population density models, the Lowry model, and the elementary residential location model proposed by Wilson consider only population in aggregate, or population disaggregated by place of employment. Wilson (1970a and 1970b) has suggested, however, that the elementary residential location model can be disaggregated by wage level of employee or income level of household. A start has thus been made (Senior,1973; Cripps and Cater, 1972; Wilson and Senior, 1972) on designing models that capture the variety of dimensions that pattern study has shown to be present in cities. Other simple kinds of cross-sectional residential location models are described and tested later in this study.

Residential Location Models: Dynamic

The concentric ring theory of Burgess (1925 and 1929) and the sector theory of Hoyt (1939) are essentially verbal models of how the city grows and how its social status map changes as a result. Though not precisely formulated their validity has been extensively tested by examination of the spatial pattern of social status in cities at single points in time. In original conception, however, both studies were models of how spatial patterns of social status evolved over time.

Other dynamic models include that of Morrill (1965a) who simulates the way in which the Negro residential area expands in Seattle, and the proposals of Wilson (1972) and Rees(1972b) concerning the use of demographic and migration models as dynamic residential location models. Dynamic residential location models accept the spatial pattern of a population or social group at the starting point in time as fixed. Like dynamic pattern studies they do not replace their cross-sectional equivalent but add to them the dimensions of change through time.

Residential Patterns in American Cities

Before we can begin to construct and test effective models of residential location models, however, we need to be clear what it is that we are attempting to model. There are a number of problems and issues in cross-sectional pattern analysis that still require careful elucidation. In this section we describe the development of cross-sectional pattern analysis, present the major findings to-date on residential patterns in American Cities and outline what questions still remain to be answered. There have been a fair number of detailed reviews of this field (Robson, 1969; Abu-Lughod, 1969; Timms, 1971; Johnston, 1971b; Rees, 1970b and 1972a; Herbert, 1972) and the reader is referred to them for greater detail. We begin with a consideration of social area analysis.

Social Area Analysis

The inventors of social area analysis (Shevky and Williams, 1949; Shevky and Bell, 1955) put forward the proposition that there were some three basic constructs that described the way in which social characteristics varied from place to place across the city. These three indices (standardized to a 0 to 100 range) were:

(1) an Index of Social Rank (or Economic Status) made up of one education and one occupation variable;

(2) an Index of Urbanization (or Family Status) made up of the variables fertility, the proportion of women in the labor force and the proportion of single family dwellings in the housing stock; and

(3) an Index of Segregation (or Ethnic Status) made up of combined proportions of minority groups (Negroes, Other Races, Foreign Born Whites from Eastern and Southern Europe, Foreign Born from the Rest of the World Besides Europe).

Values of these indices are calculated for each census tract. The tract is thereby located in a particular position in a three dimensional space whose axes are the Social area indices. Tracts are classified according to their locations in this space by dividing the space formed by the first two indices into sixteen classes. The first two indices are arranged at right angles to each other (Shevky and Bell, 1955), and the ranges of both indices are divided into four equal parts, yielding the sixteen classes, which were called "social areas." Use of the index of segregation to divide the sixteen social categories further into those with a higher and those with a lower than average proportion of minority group members was made an optional feature of the classification. Generally, the two dimensional classification has been used in further research, and the third dimension dealt with by examining the distribution of ethnic groups populations among portions of social space (Shevky and Bell, 1955).

In the studies of Los Angeles and San Francisco of Shevky and his associates considerable attention is paid to the location of particular census tracts or collections of tracts making up neighborhoods in social space. Little, however, is said about the location of types of census tract or social area class in the geographical space of the city, despite the fact that the maps included in the monographs show considerable evidence of spatial pattern (Shevky and Lewin, 1949). The task of describing the social *geography* of the city is left to city planners, geographers and human ecologists (Shevky and Bell, 1955, p. 43).

From the work of Shevky and his collaborators has stemmed a considerable volume of subsequent effort. The development of this effort is charted in Figure 3, and surveyed in the paragraphs that follow.

Criticisms of Social Area Analysis

Social area analysis has been criticized both on theoretical grounds and for empirical reasons. The theory underlying the index construction proposed by Shevky and Bell (1955) was described by Hawley and Duncan (1957) as

> look[ing] suspiciously like an *ex post facto* rationalization for their choice of indexes ...one searches in vain among these materials for a statement explaining why *residential areas* should differ one from the other or be *internally* homogeneous. (Hawley and Duncan, 1957, pp. 339-340).

Subsequent researchers have moulded the theory into a different and more reasonable form: it is proposed that societies differing in modernization will also differ in the significant dimensions that

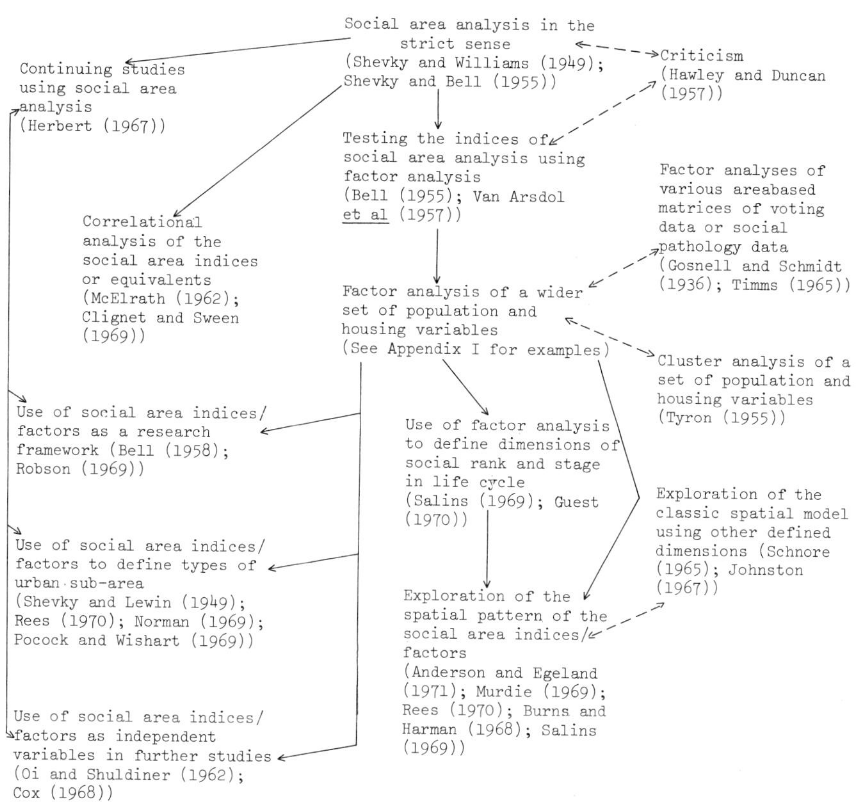

Notes

The references in parentheses are a selection of the more important papers classified under the heading above. Full citations may be found in the Bibliography.

⟵ Developmental sequence

⟵ - - - - - - ⟶ Related research

Fig. 3. -- THE DEVELOPMENT OF STUDIES IN THE SOCIAL AREA TRADITION are needed to describe the residential patterns of their cities and that as societies modernize the nature of these dimensions changes (Abu-Lughod, 1969). Some suggestions have also been made about a theory of residential area differentiation (Abu-Lughod, 1969) but these are best dealt with in a later section of the chapter.

The method of index construction has also been criticized on the grounds the measures employed to index each construct were assumed, without careful testing, to be highly associated with each other and disassociated with measures used to index other constructs.

The assumption that the three Shevky indices were _the_ dimensions underlying the social geography of the city was subsequently tested through use of factor analysis by Bell (1955) for two cities and by Van Arsdol _et al._ (1958) for ten.

Bell (1958) performed a centroid grouping form of factor analysis coupled with oblique rotation. The original variables that were used to construct the Shevky indices were used as inputs to the factor analysis. Bell found that Shevky's constructs were each matched by one factor (that is, the constructs were unidimensional) but that there was association between pairs of factors, particularly between economic status and ethnic status (Table 2).

Van Arsdol _et al._ (1958) found that two of the ten definitely did not conform to the Shevky model, and that alternative models did better for some five out of the ten cities.

These findings suggested that the validity of Shevky's proposed dimensions should not be accepted uncritically but rather should be decided empirically by examining the patterns of association of the variables across tracts. One extension of this argument was that many more variables detailing the way in which urban subareas differ according to the characteristics of their populations and housing stocks should be included in the analysis. Multivariate analysis of some form should be used to isolate the fun-

TABLE 2

INTERCORRELATION BETWEEN FACTORS, BELL (1955)

	Los Angeles, 1940		San Francisco, 1940	
	Family Status	Ethnic Status	Family Status	Ethnic Status
Economic Status	-0.50	-0.73	-0.33	-0.62
Family Status		0.15		-0.21

Note

The numbers in the table are coefficients of correlation (Pearson's r) as measured by comparing factor scores of the census tracts.

damental patterns of variation in the data, whether or not they were Shevky-like dimensions.

Multivariate Analyses and the Resulting Dimensions

In a spate of studies in the late 1950's, the 1960's and early 1970's students of the city have subjected matrices of tracts and their characteristics to a welter of different forms of multivariate analysis — linkage analysis, cluster analysis, principal components analysis, and common factor analysis in the narrow sense.

What were the results of this considerable effort? The following kinds of factors (using the term in the broadest sense) or dimensions emerged in most of the North American studies.

(1) Socioeconomic status dimensions. If variables of known relevance in social stratification in the particular city were included in the analysis, a socioeconomic status dimension, and usually only one, emerged in the analysis. Labels such as "socioeconomic status," "social rank," "social class," "social status," "economic achievement," "economic status," and "affluence " were

applied to this dimension. Occasionally, the factor was interpreted as "prestige value of neighborhood" (Anderson and Bean,1961). Variables that were highly associated with this factor were measures of the educational attainment of the tract's population, measures of its occupational mix, measures of income received, value of home owned or rent paid, measures of the material possessions of the households in the subarea, and density of occupance of housing space.

(2) Family status dimensions. Among the studies there was less broad agreement on how to label what I have called family status dimensions. Some studies revealed more than one dimension associated with measures of family type, age structure or marital status (Guest, 1970). Typical labels for this factor were "family status," "age structure," "stage in life cycle," "progeniture," "familism," and "the aged." Measures that tended to be associated with this dimension were age of the population measures, size of household measures, fertility indices, marital status variables, family type categories, housing type categories, and measures of housing age.

(3) Minority group or ethnic dimensions. If variables measuring the proportion of a subarea's population that belong to one or other distinct group in the society were included in the analysis in most cases a dimension associated with that group emerged from the analysis. The groups might be regarded as distinctive on grounds of race, national origin, regional origin (within the same country) or language. Where the groups included in the analysis were racial, a dimension associated with the racial group variable usually emerged. This was variously labelled "segregation," "ethnic status," "racial status," "race and resources," "the minorities factor," "non-white ethnic status," "race," or "Negro segregation." Other ethnic variables were included in the analysis less often. Where they were dimensions with labels like "Jewish ethnic status,"

"Immigrants and Catholics," "Jews and Russians," "Irish and Swedes," "New Canadians," "Ethnic Differences," "Swedish Language," "Irish middle class," or "foreign population" emerged from the factor analysis. This sort of dimension arranges tracts in a continuum, at one end of which are concentrations of the particular ethnic group referred to in the label for the factor and at the other end of which the tracts contain relatively few of the ethnic group.

(4) A mobility dimension. The first three sets of dimensions correspond, at least in part, to the constructs originally proposed by Shevky. Several authors have suggested that a residential mobility dimension should also be regarded as a fundamental basis of variation among subareas of the city. Where variables that index movement rates, or movement classified by origin, or population change are included in the analysis, a "mobility-stability" dimension emerges. Tracts are distinguished one from another in terms of the proportion of movers or stayers in their population.

(5) Other dimensions. Among the most common other dimensions are dimensions incorporating distance from the city center with other variables, dimensions including size of tract variables, dimensions including variables relating to change and various land use dimensions. Each of these sorts of dimensions is either a source of confusion in the analysis or is irrelevant if the focus of the research is the social geography of the city. Inclusion of distance in a multivariate analysis biases any subsequent description or test of spatial pattern; the size of census tracts is a product of decisions by census takers and is of no theoretical relevance; admixture of cross-temporal and cross-sectional variables is to be avoided if factor structures are to be interpreted clearly; and finally the pattern of land uses in the city is worthy of a study in its own right and inclusion of such variables in a multivariate analysis serves only to confuse.

So much for the existence of particular dimensions. What

about their specific nature, their variation from city to city and their interrelations? And how do these North American dimensions compare with the results of studies in other parts of the world? These two sets of questions are best considered together.

Interrelationships Among Dimensions

In her review, Abu-Lughod (1969) proposed that studies of cities employing correlational or factor analytic techniques to analyze the basic matrix of tracts and their characteristics could be arrayed on a scale in terms of the degree to which social status and family status were found to be related.

Most studies of cities located in the northern and western portions of the U.S. and in Canada have found that social status and family status emerged as independent dimensions. Some association between variables indexing the two concepts was found by Van Arsdol _et al_. (1958) in the southern cities of their sample of ten. The factor model in which fertility loaded on the Social Rank factor was found to be superior to the Shevky-Bell structure in which fertility loaded on Family Status for Atlanta, Birmingham, Kansas City and Louisville. Further along the scale is Rome in which fertility and female labour force participation are moderately associated with socal rank (McElrath, 1962). In her own study of Cairo, Egypt Abu-Lughod (1969) found that her first factor, labelled "style of life," was a dimension in which class and family patterns were inextricably linked. In the African cities studied by McElrath (1968) and by Clignet and Sween (1969) neither family status nor socioeconomic status were important residential dimensions.

In the majority of North American studies at least one factor was found that indexed the relative segregation of a population group (usually a minority group racially different from the majority of the population or one consisting of fairly recent immigrants). In a large proportion of these studies some degree of association was revealed between socioeconomic status and racial status. This might be in the form of some primary and many secondary loadings of social status indicators on the racial status factor, or in more extreme cases the racial status variable may load most highly on the socioeconomic status factor. In the latter case, however, the minority racial group usually remains highly segregated from the rest of the city's population.

Spatial Patterns of the Major Dimension

Examination of the spatial patterns displayed by the major dimensions (Anderson and Egeland, 1961; Berry, 1965; Murdie, 1969; Salins, 1971) has suggested that each dimension has its own characteristic spatial structure. Socioeconomic status is said to display a predominantly sectoral pattern, family status a predominantly concentric pattern, and racial status a clustered pattern. There are exceptions to this generalization: Rees (1970b) found that both socioeconomic status and family status displayed mixed spatial patterns though the sectoral component was more significant than the concentric in the socioeconomic status map and the concentric pattern was more important than the sectoral in the family status map. It was suggested (Rees, 1970b) that a mixed spatial pattern might well be commoner than hitherto supposed, and might be most characteristic of the largest metropolises.

Questions to be Addressed

Our review of findings on residential patterns in American cities has revealed a number of questions to which definitive answers have not been given. These questions are now discussed and the ways in which answers will be sought are outlined.

Comparative Factorial Dimensions

The generalizations made in the preceding section about the

kind of factorial dimensions characteristic of American cities were based largely on a survey of individual city studies. The differences amongst studies in variables selected, factor analytic method employed and study area chosen make firm generalization difficult. Comparative city studies to date suffer from deficiencies in the number and type of variables used (Van Arsdol et al., 1958), small number of cities (Salins, 1971), restricted variable set (Guest, 1970) or restricted residential area studied (Meyer, 1970), though all have contributed greatly to our knowledge of American city residential patterns. In Chapters III and IV an attempt is made to make firm statements about the factorial dimensions characteristic of American cities through a set of principal component analyses of data sets for a sample of some 12 cities.

The Spatial Patterns

The generality of the Berry (1969) and Murdie (1969) conclusions on spatial patterns is assessed using a set of social dimension indexes. Comparative study of the map and spatial variance patterns of major dimensions demands that fixed definition indexes be designed. The design of the indexes builds on the factor analytic results of Chapter III, the theory of social stratification and the theory of the life cycle. The indexes are described in Chapter V. In Chapter VI the spatial patterns of socioeconomic status for the sample cities are described; in Chapter VII the family status spatial patterns of the cities are outlined; and in Chapter VIII detailed consideration is given to the spatial patterns of racial and ethnic groups.

The Relative Strengths of the Dimensions

None of the analyses so far described enables us to judge how strong each dimension is as a residential "sorter" of people. The factorial dimensions and social dimension indexes are all similarly scaled. One way in which we can assess the relative strength of each dimension is to measure the residential segregation of groups classified by each of the dimensions. Chapters VI, VII, and VIII therefore include a discussion of how spatially segregated are socioeconomic status groups, family status groups and racial/ethnic status groups.

Interrelationships Among Dimensions

A number of questions concerned with the relationships between dimensions need to be answered. The independence of socioeconomic status and family status dimensions as inferred from a factor analysis has been recently challenged (Johnston, 1971a and 1971b). We need therefore to establish without ambiguity what the relationship among dimensions in American cities is. This is done in Chapter IX.

A second set of relationships which need to be explored are those between racial status and socioeconomic status. To what extent are associations based on factor analysis of small area socioeconomic characteristics indicative of the social relationships in the population as a whole? This question is explored through analysis of S.M.S.A. crosstabulations of socioeconomic status indicators and color in Chapter IX.

A Theory of Residential Patterning

We still lack a proper theory of how the residential areas of the city come to be differentiated in the ways they are. We can, on the one hand, recognize that the role of change through time must play a part in such a theory, and that this monograph, concentrating on cross-sectional analysis at one point in time, cannot say very much on that score. The small amount of dynamic evidence that we do present (in Chapters VI and VIII) tends to show that the American city in recent decades has been characterized by rather stable gross residential patterns.

On the other hand, we still need a theory that will explain

the pattern at a point in time as a function of the conditions at that time (static equilibrium theory, that is). In Rees (1970b) a model of the residential location process was proposed that translated a household's position in social space into a choice of house in housing space, community space and physical space. This model was supported by work on the residential choice process reviewed by Simmons (1968) and by the factor analyses carried out for Chicago SMSA.

The many household characteristics that affect the choice of household residence can be boiled down to two sets of related characteristics: the socioeconomic status of a household and its family status. These two macro-attributes of households can be used as the two axes of a graph to form a two-dimensional space labelled "Social Space: Households" (Figure 4). Any household will occupy a unique position in this space. The many characteristics that describe housing units can be similarly reduced to two complex dimensions: that of housing unit value, and that of housing unit type. A housing unit can be located in two-dimensional graph using these macro-attributes as axes (Figure 4). The graph is called "Housing Space: Housing Units." Social space can be mapped onto housing space in an orderly fashion, or in other words the position of a household in social space will determine its choice of dwelling unit in housing space. If we were to plot the distribution of households in a confined portion of social space in housing space we would expect the resulting distribution to be clustered in housing space.

If the hypotheses formulated at the household scale are well founded, then we should expect to find the same pairs of dimensions characteristic of the variation among the small areal units of the city in population and housing attributes, as long as the different kinds of housing were segregated spatially at the small area scale employed. In factor analyses of population variables for census

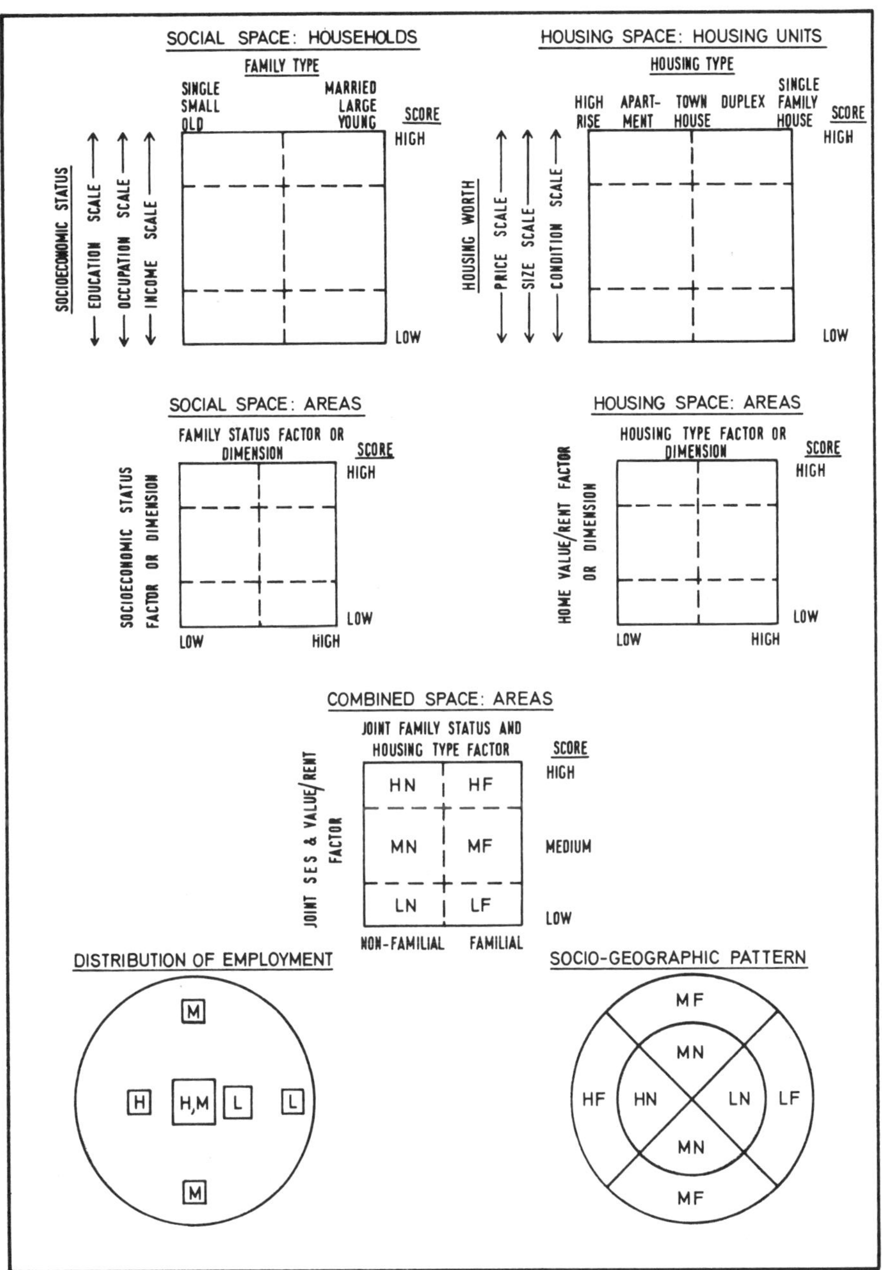

Fig. 4. -- A Model of Residential Location Decisions and Consequent Residential Patterns

tracts we should observe dimensions of socioeconomic status and of family status; in factor analyses of housing attributes of census tracts we should expect to observe housing value and housing type factors; in joint analyses of population and housing characteristics we should expect joint socioeconomic status/housing value factors and joint family status/housing type factors.

We can translate these two hypothesized relations into two simple but explicit residential location models. The first involves socioeconomic status groups, the second family status groups.

We might hope to predict the social class composition of a small residential area within the city if we knew the value and rent distributions of the housing located there, and the propensity of households in different social classes to live in housing of different value or rent. In equation form this model, specified for income groups, might be

$$H_i(y) = \sum_{v} U_i(v)\, P_*(y,v) \tag{1}$$

where $H_i(y)$ is the predicted number of households of income y in tract i, $U_i(v)$ is the observed number of housing units in value/rent category v and $P_*(y,v)$ is the city-wide conditional probability of finding a household of a particular income group y given that the housing unit occupied is in value/rent category v. It did not prove possible to test the model in this monograph but evidence of the strong relationship between income and value/rent is presented in Chapter VI.

A second residential model seeks to predict the number of households of different sizes living in a residential zone from the number of housing units of different tenure type without zone. It is described and tested in detail in Chapter VII.

One serious distortion of this theory of residential patterning which has been noted in previous studies is the influence of ethnicity. Ethnic factors can either persuade a household to choose a home not in the position in housing space corresponding to the household's position in social space, or can force this situation upon the household as a result of housing market discrimination. In Chapter VIII a model is presented which attempts to predict the distribution of racial groups on the basis of ability to pay for housing, and an attempt is made to determine the reasons for its poor performance.

Relationship of Residential Pattern to City Type

A final, and largely unexplored question which is addressed in the final chapter on the monograph is how the general characteristics of a city — its size, regional location, population, composition, site topography — affect the residential patterns it displays.

In the next chapter the process by which the sample of cities was selected for study is outlined together with a brief resume of their salient features. The study areas used for each city are justified, the variables selected for factor analysis are described and the methods of factor analysis briefly specified.

CHAPTER II

CITIES STUDY AREA, VARIABLES AND FACTOR ANALYSIS METHOD

General Characteristics of the Data Used

The most comprehensive source of data for residential areas in American cities is the decennial census. Information on the population and housing composition of census tracts is provided by the Bureau of the Census in the published metropolitan area reports (U.S. Bureau of the Census, 1962b) and on magnetic tape. This is the data source utilized here. All analyses refer to April 1, 1960, the last census date for which information on tracts was available at the time that the bulk of the research reported in this monograph was carried out. Substantial analyses have now been completed on census data from the 1970 census (Association of American Geographers, 1976a, 1976b, and 1976c).

Cities Chosen[1]

In 1960, the U.S. Bureau of the Census defined and provided census tract statistics for 212 Standard Metropolitan Statistical Areas (hereafter usually referred to as SMSAs). Given the time and resources available it was decided to select a sample of 12 SMSAs from the 212 available. A stratified random sample was selected that ensured good regional coverage and a wide variety of types of city. The strata used were the SMSA classes identified by Berry and Neils (1969). These classes had been defined through a multivariate grouping analysis of all SMSAs using as attributes in the process the factor scores for each SMSA that were the product of a

[1]In this monograph, the words "city" and "cities" are used very generally to refer to functional urban regions. The term "central city" will be used when the major and central urban administrative unit within an SMSA is referred to.

factor analysis of an extensive set of social, demographic and economic statistics describing SMSAs. Some 12 major classes of SMSA emerged from the analysis. One SMSA was chosen randomly from the SMSAs in each of the 12 major classes in the Berry and Neils typology (Table 3), with two exceptions. No SMSA was selected from class C, Mining towns, and two SMSAs were selected from class D, Cities of the agricultural Midwest and Plains.

The grouping of SMSAs in the Berry and Neils analysis turned out to be regionally clustered, so that the sample of cities chosen covers a good deal of the U.S. (Figure 5). The type of city that is missing from the sample is the very large national metropolis (New York, Los Angeles, Chicago, Philadelphia, Boston, Washington). The task of studying just one of these cities is great in itself and was not undertaken in this monograph. However, these large metropolises have been extensively studied and where possible the results for the sample cities are compared with similar analyses for the larger urban areas.

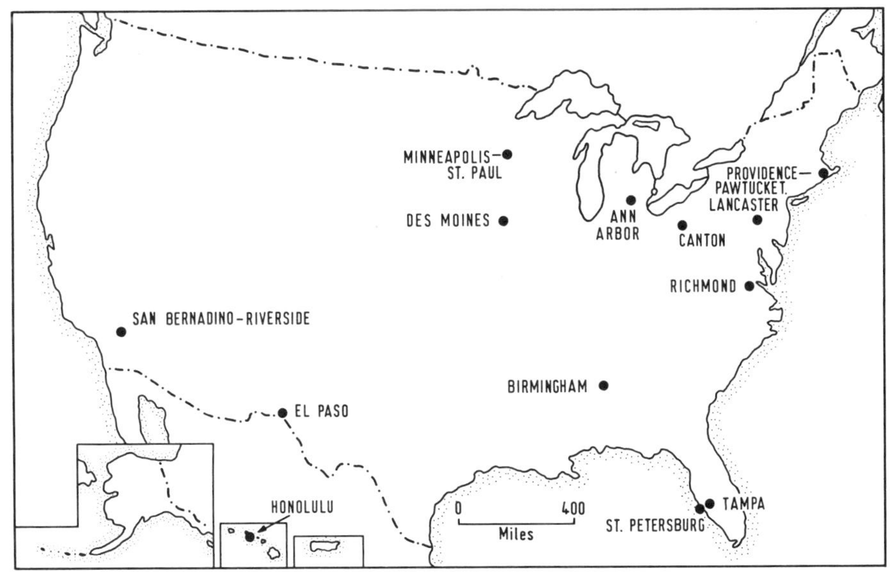

Fig. 5. -- THE CITIES SELECTED FOR STUDY

TABLE 3

SMSA TYPOLOGY AND SAMPLE CHOSEN

SMSA Type and Salient Characteristics[a]	SMSA Chosen
A. New England, eastern New York and New Jersey cities Intermediate to higher SES, older and/or larger, slow growth 1950-60, substantial commercial orientation, foreign-born population, substantial use of public transport and cross-commuting	Providence-Pawtucket, Rhode Island
B. Manufacturing belt cities Older and/or larger, industrial, slow growth 1950-60, high density, substantial foreign born, use of public transport	Canton, Ohio
C. Mining towns Low SES, older populations, substantial use of group quarters, public transport	
D. Cities of the agricultural Midwest and Plains Younger populations, slow growth 1950-60, commercial orientation, relative isolation, little use made of public transport	Des Moines, Iowa Minneapolis-St. Paul, Minnesota
E. Smaller towns of Pennsylvania, Ohio, Southern Indiana and Border South Average or modest on all factors, few foreign born, somewhat older population, weaker commercial bases	Lancaster, Pennsylvania
F. Larger Mason-Dixon line cities, plus Atlanta, Richmond, Roanoke Some manufacturing, younger populations, slower growth, fewer foreign born	Richmond, Virginia
G. Southern cities Low SES, young populations, growing, weak commerce, few foreign born, substantial Negro population	Birmingham, Alabama

TABLE 3--Continued

SMSA type and Salient Characteristics[a]	SMSA Chosen
H. Florida Older populations, rapid growth, commercial, many foreign born, relatively isolated, low density	Tampa-St. Petersburg, Florida
I. Texas and Arizona	
J. Mountain States cities Young cities, young populations, commercial, few Negroes, relatively distant (El Paso also has some of the characteristics of type Ib. Mexican border towns: very low SES, very young populations, commercial, many foreign born, many institutional, military)	El Paso, Texas
K. West Coast cities Higher SES, commercial, substantial military involvement	San Bernadino-Riverside-Ontario, California
L. Other groups Ld. Honolulu High SES, high Other Non-white population	Honolulu, Hawaii

[a]Adapted from Berry and Neils (1969), Table 2, pp. 291-292.

Table 4 lists some of the aggregate characteristics of the sample cities. They vary in size from Minneapolis-St. Paul's population of over one million to Lancaster's population of under 100,000. Median family incomes vary from $3664 (Tampa, St. Petersburg SMSA) to $6890 (Ann Arbor SMSA), spanning most of the median family income range of U.S. metropolitan areas. The median income of families living in the urbanized area portion of the SMSAs in the sample is significantly higher than that of the SMSA as a whole.

TABLE 4

AGGREGATE CHARACTERISTICS OF THE SAMPLE CITIES

Sample City	SMSA			Urbanized Area	
	Population	Median Income: Families	Per Cent White	Population	Median Income: Families
Ann Arbor	172,440	$6,890	92.40	115,282	$7,086
Birmingham	634,864	$4,452	65.37	521,330	$5,143
Canton	340,345	$5,591	94.56	213,574	$6,209
Des Moines	266,315	$5,479	95.90	241,115	$6,529
El Paso	314,070	$4,180	96.62	277,128	$5,208
Honolulu	500,409	$4,946	35.74	351,336	$6,994
Lancaster	278,359	$5,101	98.66	93,855	$6,272
Minneapolis-St. Paul	1,482,030	$5,806	98.15	1,377,143	$6,890
Providence-Pawtucket	816,148	$4,935	98.04	659,542	$5,688
Richmond	408,494	$5,035	73.60	333,438	$6,037
San Bernadino-Riverside-Ontario	809,782	$4,970	95.28	377,531	$6,185
Tampa-St. Petersburg	772,453	$3,664	88.46		
St. Petersburg				324,842	$4,332
Tampa				301,790	$4,749

Source: U.S. Bureau of the Census (1961) and (1962a)

The income of families living in the rural fringe included in the SMSA defintion but excluded from the Urbanized Area area definition is considerably lower than the metropolitan average.

Study Area

The following criterion was used in selecting the study area definition for the sample of cities. It was felt that the study area should be that region which most closely approximated the functional housing and labor market of the city. This was the region in which lived enough people working the the SMSA's central city to make the local area's housing market part of the wider metropolitan market. There were two possibilities: the SMSA and the Urbanized Area (hereafter referred to as the UA). The SMSA includes most of the people who commute to work in the central city (Berry, Goheen and Goldstein, 1968). However, on its periphery the SMSA includes many households, such as those headed by farmers, involved only in the local economy and local housing market and not in the metropolitan housing market. The UA avoids this overcounting problem but omits many households, members of which commute to the central city. There is little, then, to choose between the two study area definitions. On balance it was decided to adopt the UA as the study area to be used as this avoided the inclusion of extensive rural areas which occur in three of the SMSAs in the sample (Ann Arbor, Lancaster, San Bernadino-Riverside).

Since UAs are not defined precisely in terms of census tracts by the Bureau of the Census the UA study area used was delimited by map inspection as that minimum set of census tracts that included all of the Bureau's urbanized area as drawn on the relevant maps in the State volumes of the 1960 Census.[1] The number of cities

---

[1]The UA definition adopted will generally be clear from the sets of residential pattern maps included in Chapters VI, VII and VIII.

studied expands from 12 to 13 when the urbanized area is adopted as study area since Tampa-St. Petersburg is split into two urbanized areas. The differences between the two urbanized areas proved sufficiently interesting to make retention of two study areas in the Tampa-St. Petersburg SMSA worthwhile.

Variables Selected

The population variables selected for the factor analysis carried out are listed in Table 5 and the housing variables are given in Table 6.

Population variables were chosen as indicators of three major concepts — socioeconomic status, family status, and ethnic status — on *a priori* grounds. These major concepts were broken down into constituent subconcepts: education, occupation, income, household size, female labor force participation, racial status, nativity and national origin. Variables were selected to describe the distribution of the residential area's population along scales corresponding to the subconcept. For example, the income status of families in a residential area was indexed by a central value, *Median Income: Families*, and by the proportions at the two ends of the income distribution, *Per Cent* of Families with Incomes of $*10,000* per year *or More* and *Per Cent* of Families with Incomes per year *Under $4,000*. Or, where a central value was not appropriate (for subconcepts measured using nominal variables rather than ratio), the proportions in each of the distinct groups involved in the subconcept were used. These principles of variable selection were applied to each of the subconcepts. In the case of the national origin indicators, 8 of the 13 possible variables were chosen for each city, the 8 groups selected being the eight largest in the particular SMSA.

The same principles were applied to the selection of housing variables to index the concepts housing worth, housing type and

TABLE 5

POPULATION VARIABLES

Variable Set	Variable Subset	Variables
Socioeconomic Status	Education	Median School Years Pct Grade School Pct College
	Occupation(1)	Pct White Collar Pct Blue Collar
	Income	Median Income: Families Pct Under $4,000 Pct $10,000 or More
	Occupation (2)	Pct Professional Pct Managerial Pct Clerical Pct Sales Workers Pct Craftsmen Pct Operatives Pct Service Workers Pct Laborers Pct Unemployed
Family Status	Age	Median Age (Male) Pct Under 15 Pct 65 and Over
	Household Size	Population per Household Pct 1+2 Person Households Pct 6+ Person Households
	Women in the Labor Force	Pct Women in the Labor Force
Ethnic Status	Racial Status	Pct Negro Pct Other Non-white
	Nativity	Pct NBFMP Pct Foreign Born
	National Origin	Pct U.K. Pct Ireland Pct Norway Pct Sweden Pct Germany Pct Poland Pct Czechoslovakia Pct Austria Pct Hungary Pct Russia Pct Italy Pct Canada Pct Mexico

TABLE 6

HOUSING VARIABLES

Variable Set	Variable Subset	Variable
Housing Worth	Housing Value	Median Home Value Pct Less than $10,000 Pct $20,000 or More
	Housing Rent	Median Rent Pct Under $40 Pct $100 or More
	Housing Size	Median Rooms Pct 2 Rooms or Less Pct 7 Rooms or More
Housing Type	Structure Type	Pct One Unit Pct 3 or More Units
	Age of Structure	Pct Built Before 1940 Pct Built 1950-1960
	Tenure	Pct Owner Occupied Pct Renter Occupied
Housing Quality and Occupance Density	Condition	Pct Sound Pct Deteriorating Pct Dilapidated
	Occupance Density	Pct 1.01 or More (Persons Per Room) Pct 0.50 or Less (Persons Per Room)

housing quality via the subconcepts value, rent, size, structure, age of structure, tenure, condition and occupance density (Table 6).[1]

The population variables (36 per city) and the housing variables (20 per city) are used in the factor analyses reported in Chapters III and IV separately and jointly.

---

[1]Detailed definitions of the construction of the variables are not given here. They should be familiar to users of the 1960 or 1970 census or to the reader of the urban literature.

Method of Factor Analysis Employed

Factor analysis is a mathematical technique for discovering the broad patterns of association in a matrix of observational units and their characteristics.[1] The matrix of observational unit characteristics is, in our case, the matrix of census tracts as observational units and the ratio variables described in the preceding section, which refer either to the population living in a census tract or to the housing stock in a tract or to both at the same time.

This data matrix was subjected to R-mode principal components analysis using the University of Chicago Computation Center Program "Mesa 85." The matrix of factor loadings so produced was converted through a process of rotation into a set of more easily interpretable set of loadings. In this study all the tables of factor loadings presented are the products of principal component analysis subject to orthogonal rotation according to the normal varimax criterion. All factors which had eigenvalues of one or more were rotated. At least as much variance was associated with these factors as with one input variable in standardized form. The factor loadings tables which were produced for each city could therefore contain a varying number of rotated factors, but each of the tables was produced using the same criterion.

Some researchers have argued that oblique rotation is a more appropriate technique that enables one to measure the degree of association between dimensions identified in the factor analysis. However, when we know a great deal about the likely clustering of variables we can derive the same information from an orthogonal

---

[1]For a detailed description of the factor analysis procedure the reader is referred to Harman (1968) and Rummel (1970). Here we describe very simply the techniques used to produce the tables interpreted in Chapters III and IV. The term "factor analysis" is employed as descriptive of the technique in general rather than of a particular model.

factor loadings table. We can measure the proportion of the variance of a conceptually defined variable cluster, the variable sets and subsets in Tables 5 and 6, for example, that loads on a factor:

$$v_k^S = (\sum_{j \epsilon S} a_{jk}^2)/m^S \tag{2}$$

where v_k^S is the proportion of the variance of variable set S loading on factor k, a_{jk} is the factor loading of variable j, a member of set S, on factor k, and m^S is the number of variables in set S. We use this statistic in Chapter III to measure the association between variable sets based on particular concepts and the factors that emerge from the principal component analysis with orthogonal rotation.

In the next two chapters attention is devoted to the factorial dimensions that emerge from a comparative analysis of a sample of American cities, and the evidence they offer for the theory of residential patterning described in Chapter I is assessed.

CHAPTER III

FACTORIAL DIMENSIONS: POPULATION

Factor Structure Types

From the survey of previous analyses made in Chapter I it would appear that there are four important factor structures exhibited by American cities, and these are set out in their simplest form in Table 7. The structure originally assumed by Shevky and Bell (1955), of unidimensional, independent constructs, forms the basis of Type 1. What this subtable and the others that follow show is the association between variables classified on theoretical grounds (spelled out in Chapter V) into a smaller number of sets (three in the case of Table 6, rather more in the later empirical analyses) and the factors that emerge from the factor analysis. The numbers in the subtables are the per cents of the total variance of the variables in each variable set accounted for by given factors. Their formal definition was given in equation (2) in the preceding chapter. The figures used for the hypothesized associations of variable sets and factors are meant to be illustrative only: very few analyses will exhibit as simple a structure as those shown in Table 7.

A second form of factor structure is that displayed in Type 2. Here a measure of association is exhibited between the socioeconomic status set variables and the racial or ethnic status variable or variables through the association of factor three with both sets to a greater (in the case of racial status) or to a lesser (in the case of socioeconomic status) degree. Association between the socioeconomic status and racial status concept sets is even closer in Type 3 in which all the variance of the racial status variable is associated with the factor on which the socioeconomic status

TABLE 7

ORTHOGONAL FACTOR STRUCTURE TYPES

Type 1: Unidimensional, Independent Factors

Variable Set	Factor 1	Factor 2	Factor 3
Socioeconomic Status	100[b]		
Family Status		100	
Racial Status[a]			100

Type 2: Association between Socioeconomic Status and Racial Status

Variable Set	Factor 1	Factor 2	Factor 3
Socioeconomic Status	75		25
Family Status		100	
Racial Status			100

Type 3: Socioeconomic Status and Racial Status Form One Factor

Variable Set	Factor 1	Factor 2	Factor 3
Socioeconomic Status	100		
Family Status		100	
Racial Status	100		

Type 4: Two Family Status Dimensions

Variable Set	Factor 1	Factor 2	Factor 3	Factor 4
Socioeconomic Status[c]	100			
Family Status		50	50	
Racial Status[c]				100

[a]Only the subconcept racial status is considered here, rather than all the subconcepts inherent in ethnic status.

[b]Per cent of total variance of the variables in the variable set accounted for by given factors; it equals the sum of the squared factor loadings divided by the number of variables in the variable set.

[c]Or, Socioeconomic Status and Racial Status may be associated as in Type 2 or Type 3, giving rise to two other versions of Type 4.

variables load most highly. In other words socioeconomic and racial status form one factor. Previous work (Cohen, 1968) has suggested that cities of the Deep South may exhibit this kind of factor structure and that other cities in the U.S. would probably show factor structures which approximated to a greater or lesser degree to Type 2.

A final type set out in Table 7 is not really one separate and distinct from the first three, but rather a variant which could occur in combination with any of them. In this type, two rather than one family status dimensions emerge from the analysis, though previous work is not conclusive about the nature of the separate life cycle related dimensions. Thus, each of the first three types could have a second version in which two family status dimensions were identified, making possible six types in all, rather than the four shown in Table 7. Given that family status variables are, in the American context, rarely associated with those in the socioeconomic status or racial status sets, it was decided to consider the issue of the dimensionality of family status separately from that of the assoication of socioeconomic and racial status.

In order to assess the relevance of these factor structure types, a number of steps of analysis were undertaken:

(1) a principal components analysis of the population variable data matrix for each urbanized area was carried out;

(2) an interpretation of the nature of the factors that emerge from the analysis was made;

(3) calculations of the associations between factors and variable sets were performed; and

(4) comparison of the resulting tables with the types of Table 7 was undertaken.

The chapter describes the nature of the factors and factor structures for all the cities in the sample in a comparative fashion and attempt some generalization based on this comparative analysis. A number of key questions concerning the relationship between the dimensions described are raised and the reader is pointed forward to Chapter IX where these interrelations are considered in more detail.

Explanations for the factor structures based on population variables are considered in the next Chapter, Chapter IV. The evidence for the theory of residential patterning proposed in Chapter I is assessed through comparison of the population factors described earlier with dimensions derived from factor analysis of housing variable data matrices for the sample cities.

The Major Factor Related to Socioeconomic Status

Listed in Table 8 are the first principal components of each urbanized area analysis. In each case this first component was the one most closely identified with socioeconomic status. The nature of this first factor is clearly defined by the high loadings of the three education variables, the two general occupational variables and the three income variables. These variables can be regarded as the basic indicators of socioeconomic status, the spatial patterns of which are largely caputred by this first component. The figures in Table 8 show that from 49.89 to 84.08 per cent of the variance of these basic socioeconomic status indicators is associated with the first factors. All these indicators have signs on their loading values which behave in a consistent fashion: the higher status indicating variables load in one direction (positively)[1] and the lower status indicating variables are loaded in the opposite direction (negatively). Thus, Median School Years, Per Cent College, Per Cent White Collar, Median Income of Families, and Per Cent Incomes $10,000 or More are all loaded positively; Per Cent Grade School, Per Cent Blue Collar and Per Cent Incomes Under $4,000 are

---

[1]In 11 out of 13 cases this was how the loadings were arranged in the computer program output. In the case of Minneapolis-St.Paul and St. Petersburg the signs were reversed, but have been switched around in Table 14 for the purposes of easier comparison.

TABLE 8

THE MAJOR SOCIOECONOMIC STATUS FACTORS
FOR 13 URBANIZED AREAS

Variable	Ann Arbor	Birming-ham	Canton	Des Moines
Median School Years	0.963	0.831	0.872	0.843
Pct Grade School	-0.936	-0.868	-0.869	-0.859
Pct College	0.972	0.577	0.968	0.952
Pct White Collar	0.901	0.839	0.938	0.879
Pct Blue Collar	-0.886	-0.840	-0.939	-0.883
Median Income: Families	0.367	0.678	0.837	0.905
Pct Incomes Under $4000	-0.100	-0.783	-0.647	-0.650
Pct Incomes $10000 Plus	0.431	0.458	0.928	0.959
Pct Professional	0.930	0.423	0.881	0.919
Pct Managerial	0.291	0.515	0.915	0.965
Pct Clerical	0.137	0.895	0.579	0.169
Pct Sales Workers	-0.052	0.802	0.752	0.782
Pct Craftsmen	-0.630	0.325	-0.341	-0.472
Pct Operatives	-0.796	-0.672	-0.852	-0.669
Pct Service Workers	-0.411	-0.797	-0.601	-0.479
Pct Laborers	-0.428	-0.654	-0.617	-0.502
Pct Unemployed	-0.705	-0.716	-0.684	-0.545
Pct Negro	-0.439	-0.811	-0.383	-0.388
Pct Other Non-white	0.491	-0.019	-0.305	-0.179
Pct NBFMP	0.612	0.361	0.224	0.464
Pct Foreign Born	0.403	0.210	-0.370	-0.127
Pct U.K.	0.144	0.341	0.424	0.193
Pct Ireland	—	0.229	—	0.489
Pct Norway	—	—	—	0.195
Pct Sweden	—	—	—	-0.086
Pct Germany	0.055	0.366	0.167	0.374
Pct Poland	0.558	0.145	0.104	—
Pct Czechoslovakia	—	—	-0.268	—
Pct Austria	0.536	0.214	-0.099	—
Pct Hungary	0.083	—	-0.085	—
Pct U.S.S.R.	0.526	0.015	0.207	0.792
Pct Italy	0.079	0.092	-0.104	0.077
Pct Canada	0.503	0.345	—	0.706
Pct Mexico	—	—	—	—
Median Age (Male)	-0.072	0.538	0.189	0.157
Pct Under 15	-0.267	-0.278	0.010	0.006
Pct 65 and Over	-0.132	-0.129	-0.072	0.063
Population Per Household	-0.299	-0.403	0.056	0.078
Pct 1-2 Person Households	0.120	0.057	-0.110	-0.103
Pct 6+ Person Households	-0.476	-0.717	-0.360	-0.172
Pct Women in Labor Force	-0.394	0.133	-0.180	0.015

Notes

0.959 Loading greater than or equal to |0.700|

-0.650 Loading less than |0.700| but greater than or equal to |0.400|

TABLE 8--Continued

Variable	El Paso	Honolulu	Lancaster
Median School Years	0.852	0.785	0.914
Pct Grade School	-0.884	-0.771	-0.934
Pct College	0.660	0.893	0.905
Pct White Collar	0.745	0.909	0.904
Pct Blue Collar	-0.723	-0.912	-0.945
Median Income: Families	0.518	0.818	0.946
Pct Incomes Under $4000	-0.763	-0.571	-0.854
Pct Incomes $10000 Plus	0.346	0.809	0.930
Pct Professional	0.796	0.869	0.879
Pct Managerial	0.286	0.756	0.912
Pct Clerical	0.852	0.298	0.095
Pct Sales Workers	0.478	0.498	0.491
Pct Craftsmen	-0.193	-0.623	-0.389
Pct Operatives	-0.783	-0.709	-0.906
Pct Service Workers	-0.152	-0.339	-0.724
Pct Laborers	-0.794	-0.756	-0.773
Pct Unemployed	-0.379	-0.318	-0.506
Pct Negro	0.034	-0.096	-0.571
Pct Other Non-white	0.806	-0.411	-0.076
Pct NBFMP	-0.891	-0.135	0.270
Pct Foreign Born	-0.771	-0.518	-0.260
Pct U.K.	0.613	0.617	0.579
Pct Ireland	0.322	0.451	0.109
Pct Norway	—	—	—
Pct Sweden	—	0.472	—
Pct Germany	0.821	0.142	-0.240
Pct Poland	0.311	0.183	0.317
Pct Czechoslovakia	—	—	—
Pct Austria	—	—	0.292
Pct Hungary	—	—	—
Pct U.S.S.R.	0.016	0.214	0.417
Pct Italy	0.853	0.416	-0.502
Pct Canada	0.747	0.426	0.457
Pct Mexico	-0.895	—	—
Median Age (Male)	0.258	0.021	-0.195
Pct Under 15	-0.314	-0.062	-0.193
Pct 65 and Over	-0.347	-0.043	-0.103
Population Per Household	0.335	0.065	0.055
Pct 1-2 Person Households	-0.115	0.064	-0.128
Pct 6+ Person Households	-0.623	-0.281	-0.321
Pct Women in Labor Force	-0.195	0.012	-0.734

Notes

0.959 (underlined) Loading greater than or equal to |0.700|

-0.650 (broken underline) Loading less than |0.700| but greater than or equal to |0.400|

TABLE 8--Continued

Variable	Minneapolis-St. Paul	Providence-Pawtucket	Rich-mond
Median School Years	0.850	0.909	0.834
Pct Grade School	-0.857	-0.881	-0.828
Pct College	0.942	0.966	0.932
Pct White Collar	0.969	0.948	0.744
Pct Blue Collar	-0.972	-0.951	-0.742
Median Income: Families	0.804	0.876	0.638
Pct Incomes Under $4000	-0.579	-0.616	-0.531
Pct Incomes $10000 Plus	0.874	0.927	0.644
Pct Professional	0.850	0.871	0.885
Pct Managerial	0.846	0.905	0.531
Pct Clerical	-0.057	0.266	0.394
Pct Sales Workers	0.756	0.728	0.304
Pct Craftsmen	-0.461	-0.425	-0.327
Pct Operatives	-0.845	-0.880	-0.839
Pct Service Workers	-0.556	-0.152	-0.338
Pct Laborers	-0.675	-0.576	-0.564
Pct Unemployed	-0.601	-0.573	-0.624
Pct Negro	-0.291	-0.164	-0.376
Pct Other Non-white	-0.191	-0.124	-0.159
Pct NBFMP	-0.036	-0.331	0.404
Pct Foreign Born	-0.252	-0.418	0.269
Pct U.K.	0.412	-0.010	0.201
Pct Ireland	–	0.148	0.346
Pct Norway	-0.009	–	–
Pct Sweden	-0.010	0.341	–
Pct Germany	-0.295	0.469	0.152
Pct Poland	-0.231	-0.253	0.368
Pct Czechoslovakia	–	–	0.113
Pct Austria	-0.200	–	–
Pct Hungary	–	–	–
Pct U.S.S.R.	0.129	0.429	0.327
Pct Italy	–	-0.212	0.006
Pct Canada	0.285	-0.307	0.159
Pct Mexico	–	–	–
Median Age (Male)	0.012	0.033	0.036
Pct Under 15	0.014	0.009	-0.023
Pct 65 and Over	-0.224	-0.108	-0.061
Population Per Household	0.147	0.113	-0.238
Pct 1-2 Person Households	-0.201	-0.110	0.116
Pct 6+ Person Households	-0.035	0.021	-0.429
Pct Women in Labor Force	-0.197	-0.553	-0.149

Notes

0.959 Loading greater than or equal to |0.700|

-0.650 Loading less than |0.700| but greater than or equal to |0.400|

TABLE 8--Continued

Variable	San Bernadino-Riverside	St. Petersburg	Tampa
Median School Years	0.492	0.914	0.865
Pct Grade School	-0.487	-0.900	-0.872
Pct College	0.674	0.956	0.951
Pct White Collar	0.762	0.805	0.915
Pct Blue Collar	-0.681	-0.810	-0.917
Median Income: Families	0.927	0.892	0.938
Pct Incomes Under $4000	-0.662	-0.883	-0.889
Pct Incomes $10000 Plus	0.939	0.904	0.827
Pct Professional	0.854	0.755	0.919
Pct Managerial	0.542	0.678	0.792
Pct Clerical	0.179	0.380	0.649
Pct Sales Workers	0.139	0.573	0.780
Pct Craftsmen	-0.463	-0.419	-0.427
Pct Operatives	-0.573	-0.766	-0.781
Pct Service Workers	-0.193	-0.546	-0.622
Pct Laborers	-0.388	-0.553	-0.666
Pct Unemployed	-0.502	-0.545	-0.715
Pct Negro	-0.115	-0.467	-0.486
Pct Other Non-white	-0.091	-0.110	0.242
Pct NBFMP	0.044	0.426	0.165
Pct Foreign Born	0.076	-0.017	-0.211
Pct U.K.	0.236	0.200	0.636
Pct Ireland	—	0.189	0.381
Pct Norway	—	—	—
Pct Sweden	0.068	-0.007	0.299
Pct Germany	0.257	0.130	0.442
Pct Poland	0.034	0.019	0.290
Pct Czechoslovakia	—	—	—
Pct Austria	—	—	—
Pct Hungary	—	—	—
Pct U.S.S.R.	0.286	0.306	0.523
Pct Italy	0.062	0.052	-0.125
Pct Canada	0.176	0.293	0.312
Pct Mexico	-0.235	—	—
Median Age (Male)	0.235	0.152	0.197
Pct Under 15	-0.138	-0.149	-0.089
Pct 65 and Over	-0.082	-0.004	-0.052
Population Per Household	0.033	-0.071	-0.133
Pct 1-2 Person Households	-0.186	0.020	-0.037
Pct 6+ Person Households	-0.200	-0.347	-0.425
Pct Women in Labor Force	0.064	-0.387	-0.186

Notes

0.959 (underlined) Loading greater than or equal to |0.700|

-0.650 (underlined with dashes) Loading less than |0.700| but greater than or equal to |0.400|

TABLE 9

ASSOCIATIONS BETWEEN VARIABLE SETS AND THE MAJOR SOCIOECONOMIC STATUS FACTORS FOR 13 URBANIZED AREAS

Variable Set and Subset	Urbanized Area						
	Ann Arbor	Birmingham	Canton	Des Moines	El Paso	Honolulu	Lancaster
Education	91.61	59.23	81.75	78.49	64.77	66.94	84.23
Occupation (1)	79.84	70.48	88.07	77.42	53.89	89.90	85.51
Income	11.02	42.75	66.01	72.04	32.34	54.99	82.97
Basic SES set	58.44	55.86	77.43	75.85	49.89	66.45	84.08
Occupation (2)	32.67	44.68	50.73	42.94	34.64	37.13	46.72
SES set total	44.27	49.94	63.30	58.43	41.81	50.93	64.30
Age	3.13	12.78	1.37	0.96	9.52	0.20	2.86
Size	11.01	22.66	4.83	1.54	17.12	2.91	4.08
Women in Labor Force	15.24	1.77	3.24	0.03	3.80	0.01	53.88
FS set total	8.28	15.44	3.12	1.07	11.96	1.34	10.67
Racial Status	19.27	65.77	14.67	15.05	0.12	9.22	32.60
Nativity	26.85	8.72	9.35	11.57	69.42	14.33	7.03
National Origin	15.63	5.53	5.04	18.06	44.30	20.43	13.68
ES set total	17.80	11.08	6.56	16.72	44.80	14.38	14.15

Notes

[a]The variable composition of the variable sets is given in Table 5.

[b]SES – Socioeconomic Status
FS – Family Status
ES – Ethnic Status

TABLE 9--Continued

Variable Set and Subset	Minneapolis-St. Paul	Providence-Pawtucket	Richmond	San Bernadino-Riverside	St. Petersburg	Tampa
Education	78.14	84.52	74.99	31.12	85.31	80.43
Occupation (1)	94.19	90.02	55.21	52.22	65.21	83.91
Income	58.18	66.87	36.79	72.64	79.75	78.47
Basic SES set	74.67	79.31	55.72	51.97	78.20	80.57
Occupation (2)	45.17	42.41	32.73	22.85	35.17	51.50
SES set total	59.05	59.77	43.55	36.55	55.42	65.18
Age	1.68	0.43	0.18	2.70	1.51	1.65
Size	2.11	0.84	8.47	2.52	4.20	6.66
Women in Labor Force	3.88	30.58	2.22	0.41	14.98	3.46
FS set total	2.18	4.91	4.03	2.30	4.58	4.05
Racial Status	8.47	2.69	14.14	1.32	21.81	23.62
Nativity	3.24	14.21	11.78	0.39	9.09	3.59
National Origin	5.39	8.45	5.43	3.42	3.19	15.15
ES set total	5.28	8.93	7.22	2.73	5.73	13.93

Notes

[a]The variable composition of the variable sets is given in Table 5.

[b]SES — Socioeconomic Status
FS — Family Status
ES — Ethnic Status

loaded negatively.

What does the remarkable consistency in size and sign of the loadings of the basic socioeconomic status indicators across 13 very different U.S. urbanized areas mean in terms of the ecological structure of the American metropolis? This consistency implies that socioeconomic status is a universal sorting principle in American cities. People of like social rank tend to live together and apart from those of unlike rank. Residential areas in American cities are clearly arranged in a consistent fashion along a common and unidimensional scale of socioeconomic status.

Deviant Cases

There are a number of instances in which some of the basic socioeconomic status indicators load only moderately on the first component.

Only 11 per cent of the variance of the income variables in the case of Ann Arbor, for example, is accounted for by the first principal component. The income variables have their highest loadings on Ann Arbor's fourth factor. This factor structure implies that educational and economic status are not closely associated in the residential area populations of Ann Arbor. The correlation between Median School Years and Median Income of Families is only 0.385 compared with an average of 0.771 for the other urbanized areas. The reason for this is clear when we examine the scatter diagram for these two variables (Figure 6). Those tracts with much lower incomes than their median education would seem to indicate are those in which there are large concentrations of graduate students and junior staff connected with the University of Michigan and Eastern Michigan State University. These persons and families have yet to translate their educational investment into dollars, and in a college town such as Ann Arbor this delay reveals itself in the town's ecological structure.

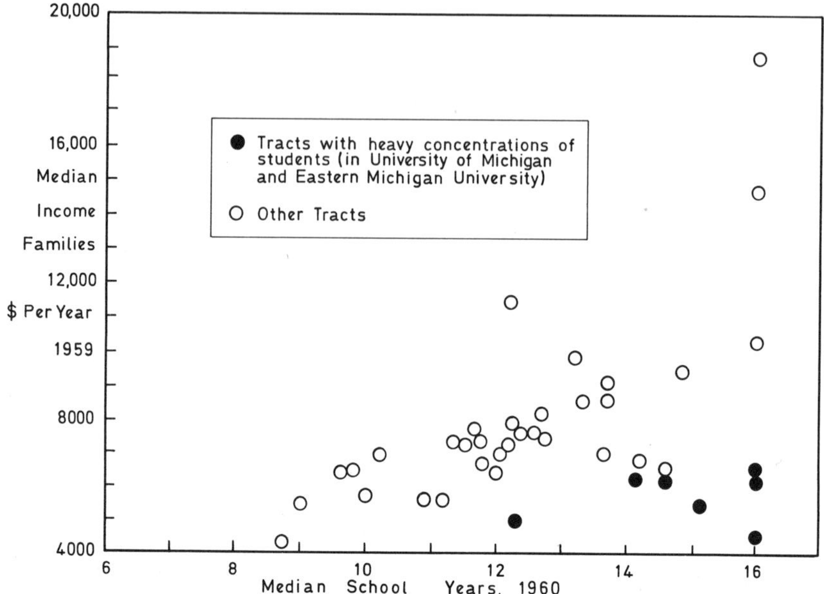

Figure 6--The relationship between the median income and the median education of tract populations, Ann Arbor, 1960

Other cases of low loadings of the basic socioeconomic status indicators are the income set in the Birmingham analysis and the education set in the San Bernadino-Riverside analysis. In these analyses there are other factors with high loadings of socioeconomic status indicators. We examine these other factors a little later in the chapter.

The Occupational Variables

The variables which index the more detailed breakdown of occupations were not included among the basic socioeconomic status indicators because they do not display as consistent a pattern of loadings on the first factor of each analysis. There is, however, a general consistency about the loadings in terms of sign. The first four occupational groups listed in Table 8 tend to have positive loadings; the second four together with the Per Cent Unemployed tend to have negative signs. This reflects the average status of these occupations in general.

The most consistently loading occupational variables were Per Cent Professional and Per Cent Operative with average loadings over the 13 urbanized areas of 0.833 and -0.775 respectively. The occupational groups Clerical and Craft recorded low loadings, and often loaded most highly on factors other than the first. In the Des Moines factor structure, for example, the Per Cent Clerical and Per Cent Craftsmen variables loaded on a factor which was interpreted as sex-related occupational status. Other occupational variables also exhibited high loadings on factors other than the first.

Association between the Major Socioeconomic Status Factor and Family Status Indicators

The loadings of the age and size indicators on the first factor in each analysis were usually very small, and the signs were not consistent (Table 8). An average of only 5.69 per cent of the variance of the family status set variables was accounted for by the first principal component for the 13 urbanized areas. So, overall, the association between socioeconomic status and family status dimensions, as we have defined them here, is very small. In terms of the review of the relations between these two dimensions carried out in the first chapter, the dimensions are largely orthogonal and independent. This means that at every social status level there are a range of tract populations at different stages in the life cycle, and that there is a wide range of social status among communities at all stages in their populations' life cycle. Despite the clearcut nature of this factorial evidence Johnston (1971a, 1971b) has suggested that the socioeconomic status dimension and the family status dimension may be partially related. A careful test of their independence is performed in Chapter VIII when relationships between dimensions are examined in more detail.

Of course, there are exceptions to this generalization in the form of some occasional high loadings of family status indicators on the first factors. In Birmingham and in El Paso the variable indexing the presence of large sized families, Per Cent 6 or More Person Households loads -0.717 and -0.623 respectively on the first factor, principally identified with socioeconomic status. The implication is that the tracts which contain the poorest people also contain, in these cities, the largest families. The sign of the loading of this variable is negative in all but one analysis and the average fraction of the variance accounted for is about an eighth, so that this may be a general though not very strong relationship.

Another indicator included in this group which has a number of high loadings on the first factor is Per Cent Women in the Labor Force, suggesting that, areally speaking, in some urbanized areas (e.g. Lancaster) lower status areas will tend to have a higher proportion of working women than higher status areas. The pattern of other urbanized areas' loadings, however, suggests that this may not be a general pattern.

The Association between the Major Socioeconomic Status Factor and Racial and Ethnic Group Variables

When the loadings of the racial and ethnic variables are examined (Table 8) it is clear that many of them have high associations with the principal socioeconomic status factor. The high loading ethnic indicators may be grouped into those with negative loadings (Per Cent Negro, Per Cent Mexican), those with mixed signs (Per Cent Other Non-white, Per Cent Italian) and those with positive loadings (Per Cent British, Per Cent Russian, Per Cent Canadian). We focus attention here on the association between the variables indexing disadvantaged minority groups, Per Cent Negro and Per Cent Mexican, and the major socioeconomic factor.

The meaning of the negative loadings of the Per Cent Negro variable would appear to be as follows: that those tracts which score highly on the first factor and which tend to be of higher than average socioeconomic status will tend to contain less than the average proportion of Negroes and that those tracts which have low scores on the first factor, will tend to be of lower than average socioeconomic status, will tend to contain more than the average proportion of Negroes. This is a statement related explicitly to areal rather than social patterns, but it does imply that Negroes are in all probability, though not necessarily, socioeconomically disadvantaged vis a vis the rest of the population. We investigate the extent of this socioeconomic disadvantage in the cities in our sample in Chapter IX.

The association between racial status and socioeconomic status is revealed not only in the major socioeconomic status factors but also in other factors of the type which were labelled "Race and Resources" factors in an earlier analysis (Rees, 1970b).

Race and Resource Factors

Factors which include moderate or high loadings of the Per Cent Negro variable and socioeconomic status indicators are listed in Table 10 and the associations between the variable sets and these factors are given in Table 11. These factors are associated with factor structures of type 2 (Table 7). The loadings are characteristically as follows: loading in the same direction and in the same order of magnitude as the Per Cent Negro variables are the variables Per Cent Service Workers, Per Cent Laborers and Per Cent Unemployed. The variables Per Cent Managerial, Per Cent Clerical, Per Cent Sales Workers and Per Cent Craftsmen all load in the opposite direction to the Per Cent Negro variable. Also consistent in loading within the first group of urbanized areas is the variable Per Cent Incomes Under $4,000: this loads in the same direction as the Per Cent Negro variable. These loadings all imply that tracts in the urbanized areas concerned contain greater than average proportions of service workers, laborers and families with low incomes, and less than average proportions of managers, clerical and sales workers and craftsmen.

This kind of factor can be interpreted as one of "Race and Resources" in the following way. The rewards of the social system (good jobs, income and so on) can be viewed as being distributed according to two criteria in the American city: cumulative merit in an achievement system, and according to the color of one's skin. Black Americans have to work in lower status occupations in far greater numbers than their share of the total population or indeed their educational attainment would suggest: in service work, including private household service and in laboring. The variably signed and very low loadings of the Per Cent in Professional occupations variable suggest that blacks have been able to enter this occupational group more easily.

The other variables included in the analysis load rather more erratically on the factors listed in Table 10. The signs of the loadings of Median School Years, Per Cent (with only) Grade School education, Per Cent in White Collar occupations, Per Cent in Blue Collar occupations and Median Income of families are all consistent with the interpretation proposed above except in the case of Honolulu. The family status indicators' loadings are low and variable in sign: this implies that there is little relation between racial and family status. The ethnic group indicators are similarly variable in loading sign and level except that the native born of foreign or mixed parents load opposite in sign to the Negro variable implying that they are concentrated in different areas of the city.

TABLE 10

RACE AND RESOURCES TYPE FACTORS

Variable / Factor →	Ann Arbor 5	Canton 3	Honolulu 2	Providence-Pawtucket 3
Pct Negro	0.648	0.802	0.740	0.803
Median School Years	-0.087	-0.341	0.104	-0.028
Pct Grade School	0.178	0.335	-0.321	0.068
Pct College	0.046	-0.051	0.166	0.042
Pct White Collar	-0.215	-0.275	0.028	-0.084
Pct Blue Collar	0.205	0.288	-0.015	0.082
Median Income: Families	-0.064	-0.251	-0.396	-0.309
Pct Incomes Under $4,000	0.559	0.511	0.451	0.537
Pct Incomes $10,000 or More	-0.066	0.002	-0.396	-0.133
Pct Professional	0.087	-0.168	-0.088	0.101
Pct Managerial	-0.106	0.009	-0.144	-0.136
Pct Clerical	-0.495	-0.609	-0.056	-0.110
Pct Sales Workers	-0.793	-0.385	0.542	-0.188
Pct Craftsmen	-0.467	-0.479	-0.632	-0.204
Pct Operatives	0.003	-0.002	-0.116	-0.107
Pct Service Workers	0.597	0.540	0.687	0.773
Pct Laborers	0.313	0.691	-0.048	0.134
Pct Unemployed	0.380	0.558	0.703	0.452
Pct Other Non-white	0.100	0.462	-0.774	0.781
Pct NBFMP	-0.326	-0.265	-0.848	-0.617
Pct Foreign Born	0.092	0.189	-0.105	-0.186
Pct U.K.	0.018	-0.493	0.178	-0.309
Pct Ireland	—	—	0.156	0.167
Pct Norway	—	—	—	—
Pct Sweden	—	—	0.147	-0.050
Pct Germany	-0.382	-0.636	0.215	-0.077
Pct Poland	-0.115	0.090	0.301	-0.004
Pct Czechoslovakia	—	-0.280	—	—
Pct Austria	-0.015	-0.308	—	—
Pct Hungary	-0.065	0.182	—	—
Pct U.S.S.R.	0.057	0.023	-0.071	0.121
Pct Italy	0.100	0.212	0.503	-0.261
Pct Canada	0.071	—	0.272	-0.241
Pct Mexico	—	—	—	—
Median Age (Male)	-0.097	-0.069	-0.341	-0.065
Pct Under 15	-0.083	0.109	0.186	-0.088
Pct Over 65	0.106	-0.010	-0.400	0.223
Population Per Household	0.090	0.191	-0.212	-0.243
Pct 1-2 Person Households	0.089	-0.077	0.079	0.328
Pct 6+ Person Households	0.286	0.535	-0.321	0.085
Pct Women in Labor Force	0.054	0.096	-0.779	-0.216

Notes As in Table 8.

TABLE 10--Continued

Variable	Factor →	Rich-mond	San Bernadino-Riverside	St. Petersburg	Tampa
		3	4	3	3
Pct Negro		0.800	0.837	0.724	0.796
Median School Years		-0.408	-0.370	-0.297	-0.313
Pct Grade School		0.381	0.349	0.349	0.292
Pct College		0.058	-0.268	-0.008	0.078
Pct White Collar		-0.420	-0.166	-0.299	-0.267
Pct Blue Collar		0.427	0.411	0.319	0.265
Median Income: Families		-0.163	-0.192	-0.136	-0.036
Pct Incomes Under $4,000		0.665	0.339	0.318	0.331
Pct Incomes $10,000 or More		-0.078	-0.121	0.107	0.174
Pct Professional		0.068	0.081	-0.184	0.090
Pct Managerial		-0.063	-0.196	0.122	-0.121
Pct Clerical		-0.730	-0.305	-0.623	-0.483
Pct Sales Workers		-0.411	-0.127	-0.399	-0.439
Pct Craftsmen		-0.831	-0.203	-0.701	-0.798
Pct Operatives		0.037	0.056	0.011	-0.028
Pct Service Workers		0.812	0.835	0.764	0.709
Pct Laborers		0.685	0.417	0.504	0.621
Pct Unemployed		0.528	0.637	0.035	0.097
Pct Other Non-white		0.035	0.044	-0.072	-0.016
Pct NBFMP		-0.324	-0.071	-0.533	-0.053
Pct Foreign Born		-0.118	-0.130	-0.422	-0.084
Pct U.K.		-0.123	-0.303	-0.465	-0.374
Pct Ireland		-0.331	–	0.068	-0.197
Pct Norway		–	–	–	–
Pct Sweden		–	-0.235	-0.566	-0.267
Pct Germany		-0.214	-0.234	-0.502	-0.479
Pct Poland		-0.216	-0.159	-0.219	-0.213
Pct Czechoslovakia		-0.599	–	–	–
Pct Austria		–	–	–	–
Pct Hungary		–	–	–	–
Pct U.S.S.R.		-0.086	-0.044	0.089	0.197
Pct Italy		-0.177	-0.111	-0.420	0.121
Pct Canada		-0.070	-0.238	-0.512	-0.507
Pct Mexico		–	0.083	–	–
Median Age (Male)		-0.084	-0.050	-0.177	-0.029
Pct Under 15		0.118	0.027	0.138	-0.052
Pct Over 65		0.059	0.065	-0.122	-0.055
Population Per Household		0.081	-0.110	0.129	-0.064
Pct 1-2 Person Households		0.177	0.173	-0.096	0.177
Pct 6+ Person Households		0.507	-0.069	0.508	0.218
Pct Women in Labor Force		0.021	0.057	0.647	0.678

Notes As in Table 8.

TABLE 11

ASSOCIATIONS BETWEEN VARIABLE SETS AND RACE AND RESOURCES FACTORS[a]

Variable Set	Ann Arbor	Canton	Honolulu	Providence-Pawtucket	Richmond	San Bernadino-Riverside	St. Petersburg	Tampa
Factor →	5	3	2	3	3	4	3	3
Education	1.39	7.70	4.71	0.24	10.50	11.25	7.00	6.11
Occupation (1)	4.41	7.93	0.05	0.69	17.94	9.82	9.56	27.08
Income	10.70	10.80	17.83	18.38	15.83	5.55	4.37	4.70
Basic SES set[b]	5.63	8.92	8.24	5.28	14.36	8.34	6.65	5.82
Occupation (2)	19.00	20.24	18.96	10.54	31.22	16.39	21.30	22.05
SES set totals	12.71	14.91	13.91	8.07	23.84	12.60	14.45	14.41
Age	0.92	0.56	10.36	2.06	0.82	0.25	2.18	0.22
Size	3.26	10.95	5.14	5.80	9.83	1.56	9.46	2.76
Women in Labor Force	0.29	0.92	60.68	4.67	0.04	0.32	41.86	45.68
FES set total[b]	1.83	5.07	15.31	4.03	4.57	0.82	10.97	7.85
Racial Status	41.99	64.32	54.76	64.48	64.00	70.06	52.42	63.36
Nativity	5.74	5.29	36.71	20.76	5.95	1.10	23.11	0.49
National Origin	2.14	12.46	12.73	9.81	6.90	3.41	14.36	9.28
ES set total[b]	6.06	15.58	20.19	16.19	11.50	8.58	18.99	12.33

Notes

[a] The variable composition of the variable sets is given in Table 5.

[b] SES — Socioeconomic Status; FS — Family Status; ES — Ethnic Status

Secondary Socioeconomic Status Factors

The factor structures of Birmingham and El Paso do not exhibit "Race and Resources" type factors. Birmingham's first factor is the socioeconomic status factor most closely associated with racial status. The second factor (Tables 12 and 13) has moderate to high loadings of socioeconomic status indicators such as Per Cent with College Education, Median Income of Families, Per Cent with Incomes of $10,000 or More, and Per Cents in Professional and Managerial occupations, and this suggests that the factor is picking out areas of highest status in the city irrespective of racial composition. The high loadings of the variables indexing concentrations of Poles, Austrians, Russians and Canadians on this second factor implies that these groups cluster at the upper end of the status ladder. The factor structure produced in the Birmingham analysis implies an association between racial status and socioeconomic status stronger than that implied by factor structures that include a "Race and Resources" type factor.

The El Paso and San Bernadino-Riverside factor structures differ from those of the other urbanized areas in that a second deprived and discriminated against minority group is present in substantial proportions in those Southwestern cities. The Per Cent Mexican variable loads highly on El Paso's factor one (Table 8) and on San Bernadino's factor three (Table 12). The third factor from the El Paso analysis picks out a pattern of Jewish ethnic concentration associated with high income and managerial status, and the fourth factor suggests that the lowest status occupational groups have a distribution all of their own. San Bernadino's third factor (Table 12) implies far less association between areas of Mexican concentration and areas of lowest social status than in El Paso, except in terms of educational status. However, the moderate positive loadings of Median School Years and Per Cent with Grade School education only on this factor together with the negative loading of Per Cent Mexican, Per Cent Foreign Born and Per Cent Native Born of Foreign or Mixed Parents imply that Mexican dominated tracts contain the poorest educated population but that this disadvantage disappears at later stages of the status system.

It will be clear from the discussion so far in this chapter that there is a complex set of relationships between the socio-economic status of residents of American cities and their ethnic status. We explore further these relationships in Chapter IX.

The Family Status Factors

The rotated principal components which could be interpreted as factors which differentiated among tracts within urbanized areas in terms of their age and family structures have been extracted from the individual urban area analyses and are listed in Table 14. The associations between the variable sets and family status factors are set out in Table 15.

The loadings of the age and family size variables are remarkably consistent in sign and level across the 13 sample urbanized areas. Median Age (male), Per Cent 65 and Over and Per Cent 1 and 2 Person Households all load positively and Per Cent Under 15, Population Per Household and Per Cent 6 or More Person Households all load negatively. Thus, tracts which score highly on this factor contain populations of older than average age structure and smaller than average household size; these are populations at later stages in their life cycle or occasionally concentrated populations of young single persons. Tracts which score negatively on this factor tend to contain younger than average populations of larger than average household sizes; these are populations at younger stages in the life cycle.

Relatively high percentages (from 50 to 85) of the total variances of the basic family status indicators (the age and household

TABLE 12

SECONDARY SOCIOECONOMIC STATUS FACTORS FOR BIRMINGHAM, EL PASO AND SAN BERNADINO-RIVERSIDE

Variables	Birmingham	El Paso	El Paso	San Bernadino - Riverside
Factors →	2	3	4	3
Pct Negro	-0.213	-0.117	0.278	-0.040
Median School Years	0.503	0.263	-0.353	0.617
Pct Grade School	-0.449	-0.306	0.310	-0.652
Pct College	0.743	0.624	-0.325	0.326
Pct White Collar	0.457	0.347	-0.430	0.314
Pct Blue Collar	-0.456	-0.369	0.445	-0.092
Median Income: Families	0.655	0.631	-0.558	0.062
Pct Incomes Under $4,000	-0.359	-0.313	0.499	-0.138
Pct Incomes $10,000 or More	0.815	0.781	-0.459	0.062
Pct Professional	0.677	-0.451	-0.228	0.130
Pct Managerial	0.744	0.508	-0.704	0.217
Pct Clerical	0.003	-0.005	-0.172	0.418
Pct Sales Workers	0.159	-0.042	-0.244	0.080
Pct Craftsmen	-0.138	-0.700	-0.312	0.271
Pct Operatives	-0.476	-0.469	0.192	-0.134
Pct Service Workers	-0.246	0.180	0.832	0.014
Pct Laborers	-0.122	-0.199	0.236	-0.365
Pct Unemployed	-0.320	-0.165	0.820	-0.004
Pct Other Non-white	0.027	-0.182	0.309	-0.017
Pct NBFMP	0.611	-0.183	0.248	-0.736
Pct Foreign Born	0.505	-0.151	0.418	-0.810
Pct U.K.	0.314	0.236	-0.252	0.199
Pct Ireland	0.419	-0.056	-0.071	—
Pct Norway	—	—	—	—
Pct Sweden	—	—	—	0.040
Pct Germany	0.488	0.163	0.048	0.216
Pct Poland	0.864	0.816	0.070	0.148
Pct Czechoslovakia	—	—	—	—
Pct Austria	0.661	—	—	—
Pct Hungary	—	—	—	—
Pct U.S.S.R.	0.839	0.837	-0.203	0.059
Pct Italy	-0.015	0.042	0.228	-0.138
Pct Canada	0.717	0.551	0.150	0.172
Pct Mexico	—	-0.263	0.285	-0.862
Median Age (Male)	0.270	0.367	-0.166	-0.080
Pct Under 15	-0.113	-0.264	-0.203	0.120
Pct Over 65	0.065	0.089	-0.007	-0.066
Population Per Household	-0.103	-0.171	0.028	-0.031
Pct 1-2 Person Households	0.000	0.041	0.020	-0.091
Pct 6+ Person Households	-0.137	-0.185	0.150	-0.046
Pct Women in Labor Force	-0.137	-0.126	-0.399	0.067

Notes As in Table 8.

TABLE 13

ASSOCIATION BETWEEN VARIABLE SETS AND SECONDARY SOCIOECONOMIC STATUS FACTORS FOR SELECTED URBANIZED AREAS

Variable Set	Birmingham	El Paso	El Paso	San Bernadino-Riverside
Factors →	2	3	4	3
Education	33.56	18.41	10.88	30.40
Occupation (1)	20.84	12.83	19.15	5.35
Income	40.74	36.87	25.70	0.89
Basic SES set	33.07	23.94	18.50	13.07
Occupation (2)	17.14	14.14	24.35	5.22
SES set total	24.64	18.75	21.60	8.92
Age	3.00	7.08	2.29	0.84
Size	0.98	2.17	0.79	0.38
Women in Labor Force	1.88	1.59	15.92	0.45
FS set total	1.97	4.19	8.39	0.59
Racial Status	4.57	1.37	7.73	0.16
Nativity	31.42	2.81	11.81	59.89
National Origin	32.39	10.66	4.09	10.06
ES set total	29.90	16.08	5.68	17.54

Notes

[a] The variable composition of the variable sets is given in Table 5.

[b] SES — Socioeconomic Status; FS — Family Status; ES — Ethnic Status

size variables) are associated with the family status factors (Table 15). Given the relatively low associations of the family status indicators (from 1 to 15 per cent of their variances) with the principal socioeconomic status factors this means that there is very little association between the dimensions of socioeconomic status and family status.

The loadings of the variable indexing female participation in the labor force are a varied set ranging from a high positive one for Canton (0.811) to a negative one for St. Petersburg (-0.429). For Ann Arbor, Canton, El Paso, and Minneapolis-St. Paul, the Per Cent Women in Labor Force loading recorded in Table 14 is the

TABLE 14

FAMILY STATUS FACTORS

Variable	Ann Arbor	Birming-ham	Canton	Des Moines
Median Age (Male)	0.401	0.667	0.897	0.841
Pct Under 15	-0.891	-0.881	-0.969	-0.955
Pct 65 and Over	0.459	0.897	0.954	0.871
Population Per Household	-0.881	-0.816	-0.959	-0.884
Pct 1-2 Person Households	0.956	0.843	0.965	0.958
Pct 6+ Person Households	-0.502	-0.499	-0.623	-0.822
Pct Women in Labor Force	0.691	0.420	0.811	0.391
Pct NBFMP	0.246	0.189	0.244	0.166
Pct Foreign Born	0.222	0.485	0.290	0.349
Pct Negro	0.045	-0.231	-0.017	0.287
Pct Other Non-white	0.575	0.605	0.265	0.276
Pct U.K.	-0.014	0.173	0.363	0.258
Pct Ireland	—	0.606	—	0.507
Pct Norway	—	—	—	0.437
Pct Sweden	—	—	—	0.264
Pct Germany	-0.002	0.442	0.345	0.485
Pct Poland	0.383	0.047	0.061	—
Pct Czechoslovakia	—	—	0.040	—
Pct Austria	-0.005	0.043	-0.039	—
Pct Hungary	0.146	—	-0.096	—
Pct U.S.S.R.	0.379	0.236	0.177	0.230
Pct Italy	0.032	0.109	-0.144	-0.152
Pct Canada	0.065	0.257	—	0.144
Pct Mexico	—	—	—	—
Median School Years	0.097	0.061	-0.021	-0.065
Pct Grade School	0.049	-0.013	0.252	0.104
Pct College	0.070	0.076	0.002	0.194
Pct White Collar	0.067	0.238	0.186	0.119
Pct Blue Collar	-0.045	-0.236	-0.160	-0.090
Median Incomes: Families	-0.226	-0.156	-0.368	-0.292
Pct Incomes Under $4,000	0.404	0.214	0.508	0.556
Pct Incomes $10,000 or More	-0.135	-0.003	-0.135	-0.091
Pct Professional	0.046	0.257	0.201	0.183
Pct Managerial	-0.146	0.082	0.056	-0.016
Pct Clerical	0.137	0.238	0.241	0.233
Pct Sales	0.030	0.158	0.151	-0.084
Pct Craftsmen	-0.351	-0.065	-0.663	0.107
Pct Operative	-0.312	-0.210	-0.232	-0.509
Pct Service	0.476	-0.002	0.495	0.245
Pct Laborer	-0.060	-0.344	-0.086	-0.173
Pct Unemployed	-0.051	-0.019	0.122	-0.013

Notes As in Table 8.

TABLE 14--Continued

Variable	El Paso	Honolulu	Lancaster
Median Age (Male)	0.825	0.814	0.289
Pct Under 15	-0.780	-0.815	-0.910
Pct 65 and Over	0.870	0.721	0.870
Population Per Household	-0.888	-0.894	-0.958
Pct 1-2 Person Households	0.960	0.917	0.968
Pct 6+ Person Households	-0.673	-0.764	-0.645
Pct Women In Labor Force	0.742	0.396	0.538
Pct NBFMP	-0.075	0.081	0.246
Pct Foreign Born	0.192	0.655	0.607
Pct Negro	-0.032	-0.042	-0.248
Pct Other Non-white	-0.075	0.022	-0.013
Pct U.K.	0.380	0.386	0.213
Pct Ireland	0.681	0.164	-0.033
Pct Norway	—	—	—
Pct Sweden	—	0.170	—
Pct Germany	0.104	0.405	0.119
Pct Poland	—	0.221	0.088
Pct Czechoslovakia	—	—	—
Pct Austria	—	—	0.419
Pct Hungary	—	—	—
Pct U.S.S.R.	0.136	0.101	0.021
Pct Italy	-0.037	-0.190	0.284
Pct Canada	-0.034	0.265	-0.167
Pct Mexico	-0.010	—	—
Median School Years	0.206	-0.213	-0.116
Pct Grade School	-0.110	0.208	0.052
Pct College	0.065	0.097	0.170
Pct White Collar	0.319	0.041	0.264
Pct Blue Collar	-0.291	-0.016	-0.146
Median Incomes: Families	-0.070	-0.060	-0.182
Pct Incomes Under $4,000	0.070	0.041	0.256
Pct Incomes $10,000 or More	0.079	-0.076	-0.057
Pct Professional	0.105	0.133	0.270
Pct Managerial	0.268	0.205	-0.068
Pct Clerical	0.324	-0.208	0.399
Pct Sales	0.489	-0.056	0.186
Pct Craftsmen	-0.229	-0.234	-0.596
Pct Operative	-0.160	-0.240	-0.160
Pct Service	-0.156	0.264	0.230
Pct Laborer	-0.301	0.209	0.071
Pct Unemployed	-0.078	0.049	-0.089

Notes As in Table 8.

TABLE 14--Continued

Variable	Minneapolis-St. Paul	Providence-Pawtucket	Rich-mond
Median Age (Male)	0.824	0.863	0.655
Pct Under 15	-0.943	-0.926	-0.840
Pct 65 and Over	0.876	0.879	0.672
Population Per Household	-0.955	-0.806	-0.897
Pct 1-2 Person Households	0.944	0.824	0.898
Pct 6+ Person Households	-0.813	-0.753	-0.610
Pct Women in Labor Force	0.714	0.190	0.182
Pct NBFMP	0.531	0.189	0.204
Pct Foreign Born	0.613	0.535	0.293
Pct Negro	0.150	0.006	-0.118
Pct Other Non-white	0.439	0.309	0.054
Pct U.K.	0.285	0.137	0.233
Pct Ireland	—	0.428	0.219
Pct Norway	0.416	—	—
Pct Sweden	0.264	-0.003	—
Pct Germany	0.429	-0.053	0.206
Pct Poland	-0.033	0.152	0.079
Pct Czechoslovakia	—	—	-0.104
Pct Austria	0.095	—	—
Pct Hungary	—	—	—
Pct U.S.S.R.	0.155	0.277	0.065
Pct Italy	—	-0.024	0.281
Pct Canada	0.353	0.056	0.210
Pct Mexico	—	—	—
Median School Years	-0.280	-0.165	-0.015
Pct Grade School	0.367	0.227	0.044
Pct College	0.029	-0.008	0.026
Pct White Collar	0.058	0.053	0.258
Pct Blue Collar	-0.044	-0.028	-0.249
Median Income: Families	-0.287	-0.168	-0.051
Pct Incomes Under $4,000	0.649	0.340	0.038
Pct Incomes $10,000 or More	-0.121	-0.045	0.016
Pct Professional	0.058	0.126	0.244
Pct Managerial	-0.148	0.026	0.062
Pct Clerical	0.379	-0.025	0.184
Pct Sales	-0.178	-0.008	0.308
Pct Craftsmen	-0.705	-0.520	-0.235
Pct Operative	-0.165	0.054	-0.242
Pct Service	0.595	0.311	-0.096
Pct Laborer	0.197	-0.008	-0.158
Pct Unemployed	0.346	0.262	-0.063

Notes As in Table 8.

TABLE 14--Continued

Variable	San Bernadino-Riverside	St. Petersburg	Tampa
Median Age (Male)	0.896	0.932	0.903
Pct Under 15	-0.830	-0.947	-0.954
Pct 65 and Over	0.941	0.954	0.956
Population Per Household	-0.932	-0.964	-0.969
Pct 1-2 Person Households	0.862	0.965	0.952
Pct 6+ Person Households	-0.459	-0.712	-0.716
Pct Women in Labor Force	0.041	-0.429	0.412
Pct NBFMP	0.080	0.492	0.128
Pct Foreign Born	0.161	0.728	0.033
Pct Negro	-0.120	-0.384	-0.139
Pct Other Non-white	0.047	-0.035	0.077
Pct U.K.	0.597	0.689	0.417
Pct Ireland	—	0.714	0.643
Pct Norway	—	—	—
Pct Sweden	0.362	0.201	-0.036
Pct Germany	0.617	0.605	0.395
Pct Poland	0.008	0.206	0.145
Pct Czechoslovakia	—	—	—
Pct Austria	—	—	—
Pct Hungary	—	—	—
Pct U.S.S.R.	0.233	0.181	-0.014
Pct Italy	0.058	0.148	-0.001
Pct Canada	0.344	0.486	0.142
Pct Mexico	-0.214	—	—
Median School Years	0.015	0.101	0.084
Pct Grade School	0.080	-0.082	-0.018
Pct College	0.035	0.150	0.133
Pct White Collar	0.206	0.448	0.152
Pct Blue Collar	-0.163	-0.431	-0.140
Median Income: Families	-0.089	-0.292	0.101
Pct Incomes Under $4,000	0.234	0.250	0.059
Pct Incomes $10,000 or More	0.072	0.009	0.295
Pct Professional	0.228	0.220	0.253
Pct Managerial	0.090	0.422	-0.179
Pct Clerical	0.174	0.361	0.351
Pct Sales	-0.032	0.282	0.099
Pct Craftsmen	-0.140	-0.359	-0.159
Pct Operative	-0.222	-0.377	-0.131
Pct Service	0.179	-0.160	0.015
Pct Laborer	-0.167	-0.415	-0.171
Pct Unemployed	-0.005	0.003	-0.090

Notes As in Table 8.

TABLE 15

ASSOCIATION BETWEEN VARIABLE SETS AND FAMILY STATUS FACTORS

Variable Set	Ann Arbor	Birmingham	Canton	Des Moines	El Paso	Honolulu	Lancaster
Age	38.85	67.52	88.46	79.26	68.20	61.56	55.62
Size	64.74	54.18	74.63	79.16	72.10	74.13	75.69
Basic Family Status Indicators	51.79	60.85	81.55	79.21	70.15	67.84	65.67
Women in Labor Force	47.75	17.64	65.77	15.29	55.06	15.68	28.94
Family Status Set Total	51.21	47.84	79.29	70.08	67.99	60.39	60.41
Pct Negro	0.20	5.34	0.03	8.24	0.10	0.17	6.15
Nativity	5.49	13.35	7.18	7.47	2.12	21.78	21.45
National Origin	3.52	12.18	4.32	11.03	7.17	5.94	3.92
Ethnic Status Set Total	4.08	11.84	4.44	10.20	5.74	8.10	7.03
Education	0.56	0.32	3.46	1.76	1.96	3.27	1.50
Occupation (1)	0.33	5.62	3.01	1.12	9.32	0.10	4.55
Income	7.75	2.34	13.72	13.42	3.73	0.37	3.40
Basic Socioeconomic Status Indicators	3.20	2.40	7.20	5.97	3.08	1.39	2.97
Occupation (2)	5.52	3.57	9.83	5.06	6.96	3.72	7.98
Socioeconomic Status Set Total	4.42	3.02	8.59	5.49	5.13	2.62	5.62

TABLE 15--Continued

Variable Set	Minneapolis-St. Paul	Providence-Pawtucket	Richmond	San Bernadino-Riverside	St. Petersburg	Tampa
Age	77.85	79.16	52.87	79.24	89.18	87.98
Size	82.14	63.19	66.10	60.74	78.92	78.60
Basic Family Status Indicators	80.00	71.18	59.49	69.99	84.05	83.29
Women in Labor Force	50.98	3.61	3.31	0.17	18.40	16.97
Family Status Set Total	75.85	61.52	51.46	60.02	74.67	73.82
Pct Negro	2.25	0.00	1.39	1.44	14.75	1.93
Nativity	32.89	16.10	6.37	1.62	38.60	0.87
National Origin	9.55	4.49	3.24	12.14	19.17	8.80
Ethnic Status Total	12.83	6.05	3.61	9.49	22.04	6.91
Education	0.73	2.63	0.09	0.26	1.31	0.84
Occupation (1)	0.27	0.18	6.43	3.45	10.04	2.14
Income	17.27	4.86	4.86	2.26	4.93	3.36
Basic Socioeconomic Status Indicators	6.82	2.85	3.47	1.81	4.85	2.11
Occupation (2)	13.75	5.07	3.82	2.45	10.06	3.43
Socioeconomic Status Set Total	10.49	4.02	3.65	2.15	7.61	2.81

variable's highest; for Birmingham, Des Moines, Honolulu, Lancaster, St. Petersburg and Tampa the Table 14 loading is the variable's second highest, its highest loading being on either the principal socioeconomic status factor or a factor with high loadings of female dominated or male dominated occupations (e.g. the Des Moines factor structure).

Female labor force participation turns out to be a complexly determined phenomenon in the American city case. Its ecological associations suggest that the degree of femal participation in the labor force is in part a function of (1) ability (women with children tend to be tied to the home — hence its association with the family status factors in certain cases); (2) necessity (whether there is economic pressure on women to work or not); (3) cultural desire (whether women want to work and whether their husbands approve) and (4) opportunity (whether the economy offers female employment). As a simple indicator of family status it should probably be dropped.

Ethnic Factors

Each urbanized area analysis contains factors other than those already described; in the main these contain high loadings of ethnic group variables in combination with others (Table 16 and 17). A further set contain high loadings of other variables (mainly occupational) together with high loadings of one or two ethnic variables (Table 18), and a final group contain high loadings of mainly occupational variables (Table 19).

What the factors in Tables 16 and 17 are doing is picking out spatial patterns of ethnic groups that are separate and distinct from those associated with social class or family status. A number of the factors are fairly general in nature: several groups have similar spatial patterns and their pattern is coextensive with that of the foreign stock population in general. Ann Arbor's factor 3

(Table 17) is associated with foreign stock British, Italians, Germans and to a lesser extent Russians and Canadians (whose highest loadings are on other factors) as well as with the foreign born in general, and the native born of foreign or mixed parentage to a lesser degree. Honolulu's factor 4, Lancaster's factor 5, Richmond's factor 2 and San Bernadino-Riverside's factor 8 are all of this nature, including several ethnic groups which are spatially coextensive.

Other factors among the ethnic set identify ethnic groups or pairs of ethnic groups that have fairly distinct patterns in more than one city. Swedes and Norwegians load together highly on Des Moine's factor 6 (Table 16), together with the British and on Minneapolis-St. Paul's factor 3 (Table 16). Italians stand out on a unique factor in Canton (factor 5, Table 16), in Des Moines (factor 5, Table 16) together with the foreign stock in general, and in Tampa (factor 4, Table 16). In Providence-Pawtucket an Italian ethnic factor is also prominent (Table 17) but is associated with high loadings of opposite sign of the Canadian, British and Polish groups. This implies that tracts in which an above proportion of Italians is found will contain below average proportions of Canadians, Britons and Poles. Russians figure predominantly on Lancaster's factor 8 (Table 16) and together with Poles on Minneapolis-S . Paul's factor 4, Providence-Pawtucket's factor 7, Richmond's factor 5 and with Italians on St. Petersburg's factor 4. Urban Americans of Russian origin are largely of the Jewish faith and many of the country's Polish born or of Polish parentage are also Jews, particularly those Poles in cities outside of the Northern industrial metropolises. These factors therefore identify the unique spatial distribution of the Jewish population in many American cities.

The remaining factors tend to identify ethnic groupings particular to one city or to pick out groups identified as having unique

TABLE 16

FACTORS ASSOCIATED WITH ETHNIC GROUPS

Variable	Ann Arbor	Birmingham	Canton	Canton
Factor	7	5	4	5
Pct U.K.	0.029	0.539	-0.117	-0.082
Pct Ireland	—	0.028	—	—
Pct Norway	—	—	—	—
Pct Sweden	—	—	—	—
Pct Germany	0.331	0.230	0.041	-0.083
Pct Poland	0.103	0.129	0.338	0.120
Pct Czechoslovakia	—	—	0.022	0.027
Pct Austria	0.245	0.266	0.711	0.185
Pct Hungary	-0.850	—	0.788	-0.011
Pct U.S.S.R.	0.466	-0.003	0.651	0.306
Pct Italy	-0.118	0.853	0.147	0.880
Pct Canada	0.033	0.031	—	—
Pct Mexico	—	—	—	—
Pct NBFMP	0.232	0.630	0.363	0.680
Pct Foreign Born	0.030	0.531	0.456	0.577
Pct Negro	0.175	-0.198	-0.084	0.067
Pct Other Non-white	0.062	-0.121	0.114	-0.374
Median School Years	0.037	0.089	-0.056	-0.075
Pct Grade School	0.090	-0.076	0.054	0.104
Pct College	0.075	-0.040	-0.003	-0.020
Pct White Collar	-0.081	0.098	-0.007	0.024
Pct Blue Collar	0.060	-0.098	0.006	-0.012
Median Income: Families	0.119	0.056	-0.031	-0.015
Pct Incomes Under $4,000	-0.047	-0.140	-0.025	0.022
Pct Incomes $10,000 or More	0.076	0.054	-0.024	0.017
Pct Professional	-0.025	-0.039	0.016	-0.007
Pct Managerial	-0.062	0.065	-0.027	0.000
Pct Clerical	-0.155	0.217	-0.097	0.039
Pct Sales	0.030	0.039	0.097	0.239
Pct Craftsmen	0.022	0.146	0.075	-0.077
Pct Operative	-0.019	-0.067	0.042	-0.073
Pct Service	0.080	-0.113	0.122	0.008
Pct Laborer	0.156	-0.142	0.023	0.125
Pct Unemployed	0.040	-0.037	-0.003	0.119
Median Age (Male)	-0.291	0.172	0.129	0.091
Pct Under 15	0.000	-0.196	-0.045	-0.032
Pct 65 and Over	0.013	0.187	0.039	0.053
Population Per Household	0.019	-0.160	0.016	0.053
Pct 1-2 Person Households	-0.059	0.085	0.007	-0.039
Pct 6+ Person Households	0.024	-0.206	-0.013	-0.035
Pct Women in the Labor Force	-0.230	0.053	-0.118	-0.072

TABLE 16--Continued

Variable	Canton	Des Moines	Des Moines	El Paso
Factor	6	5	6	5
Pct U.K.	-0.057	-0.039	0.533	0.203
Pct Ireland	—	0.082	0.059	0.311
Pct Norway	—	0.121	0.574	—
Pct Sweden	—	-0.023	0.800	—
Pct Germany	0.216	-0.046	0.192	0.312
Pct Poland	-0.783	—	—	-0.054
Pct Czechoslovakia	-0.751	—	—	—
Pct Austria	0.081	—	—	—
Pct Hungary	-0.162	—	—	—
Pct U.S.S.R.	-0.333	0.005	0.034	0.038
Pct Italy	-0.019	0.960	-0.141	-0.075
Pct Canada	—	-0.110	0.032	-0.005
Pct Mexico	—	—	—	0.034
Pct NBFMP	-0.364	0.596	0.450	0.071
Pct Foreign Born	-0.180	0.858	0.160	0.097
Pct Negro	0.203	-0.181	-0.425	-0.862
Pct Other Non-white	0.119	-0.073	-0.129	0.167
Median School Years	0.044	-0.056	0.059	-0.015
Pct Grade School	-0.024	0.083	0.003	-0.005
Pct College	-0.075	-0.064	-0.012	0.048
Pct White Collar	0.030	0.021	0.082	0.134
Pct Blue Collar	-0.041	-0.006	-0.085	-0.177
Median Income: Families	-0.078	0.059	0.113	-0.002
Pct Incomes Under $4,000	0.074	-0.074	-0.146	0.063
Pct Incomes $10,000 or More	-0.083	0.027	0.047	-0.002
Pct Professional	0.162	-0.032	0.025	0.156
Pct Managerial	-0.088	0.092	0.081	0.179
Pct Clerical	-0.021	-0.009	0.096	0.043
Pct Sales	-0.005	0.022	0.065	-0.015
Pct Craftsmen	-0.131	-0.019	0.053	-0.160
Pct Operative	-0.110	0.031	0.051	-0.048
Pct Service	0.014	-0.008	-0.335	-0.349
Pct Laborer	0.131	-0.018	-0.079	0.105
Pct Unemployed	0.122	0.057	-0.052	-0.064
Median Age (Male)	-0.028	0.091	0.231	-0.068
Pct Under 15	0.085	-0.059	-0.086	0.234
Pct 65 and Over	-0.042	0.041	0.239	0.024
Population Per Household	0.054	0.057	0.007	-0.017
Pct 1-2 Person Households	-0.017	-0.003	0.014	0.074
Pct 6+ Person Households	0.207	-0.098	-0.006	0.040
Pct Women in the Labor Force	0.183	0.145	-0.096	0.051

TABLE 16--Continued

Variable / Factor	Honolulu 4	Honolulu 6	Lancaster 5	Lancaster 6
Pct U.K.	0.332	0.227	0.614	-0.036
Pct Ireland	0.605	-0.034	0.850	0.176
Pct Norway	—	—	—	—
Pct Sweden	0.634	0.036	—	—
Pct Germany	0.070	0.731	0.073	0.912
Pct Poland	0.131	0.767	-0.062	0.191
Pct Czechoslovakia	—	—	—	—
Pct Austria	—	—	-0.146	0.087
Pct Hungary	—	—	—	—
Pct U.S.S.R.	0.806	0.054	0.088	0.112
Pct Italy	0.197	0.111	0.537	-0.317
Pct Canada	0.603	0.123	0.211	-0.012
Pct Mexico	—	—	—	—
Pct NBFMP	-0.283	-0.159	0.522	0.667
Pct Foreign Born	-0.240	0.167	0.482	0.296
Pct Negro	-0.039	0.161	0.049	-0.257
Pct Other Non-white	-0.384	-0.170	-0.421	-0.277
Median School Years	0.196	0.085	0.021	-0.111
Pct Grade School	-0.273	-0.083	-0.029	0.097
Pct College	0.283	0.128	0.045	-0.042
Pct White Collar	0.257	-0.024	0.071	-0.018
Pct Blue Collar	-0.268	0.012	-0.009	0.053
Median Income: Families	-0.040	0.209	0.074	0.089
Pct Incomes Under $4,000	0.248	-0.468	-0.110	-0.121
Pct Incomes $10,000 or More	0.026	0.140	0.118	0.016
Pct Professional	0.239	-0.095	0.101	-0.045
Pct Managerial	0.265	0.200	-0.103	0.048
Pct Clerical	0.112	0.054	0.110	-0.150
Pct Sales	0.044	-0.269	0.114	0.176
Pct Craftsmen	-0.219	0.007	-0.027	0.073
Pct Operative	-0.043	-0.246	0.016	0.063
Pct Service	-0.280	0.263	0.019	-0.008
Pct Laborer	-0.150	-0.003	-0.110	0.018
Pct Unemployed	0.041	-0.095	0.078	0.272
Median Age (Male)	-0.108	0.196	-0.025	0.068
Pct Under 15	-0.089	-0.220	-0.061	-0.033
Pct 65 and Over	-0.116	0.246	0.105	0.043
Population Per Household	-0.280	0.008	0.013	-0.049
Pct 1-2 Person Households	0.310	0.068	-0.037	0.043
Pct 6+ Person Households	-0.180	0.089	-0.119	-0.202
Pct Women in the Labor Force	0.119	-0.168	0.175	-0.127

TABLE 16--Continued

Variable / Factor	Lan-caster 8	Minne-apolis-St. Paul 3	Minne-apolis-St. Paul 4	Minne-apolis-St. Paul 6
Pct U.K.	-0.142	-0.020	0.073	0.008
Pct Ireland	0.102	—	—	—
Pct Norway	—	0.804	0.132	-0.156
Pct Sweden	—	0.886	0.059	-0.030
Pct Germany	-0.010	-0.149	0.101	0.612
Pct Poland	0.139	-0.059	-0.745	0.292
Pct Czechoslovakia	—	—	—	—
Pct Austria	-0.056	-0.216	-0.153	0.743
Pct Hungary	—	—	—	—
Pct U.S.S.R.	0.813	-0.152	-0.825	-0.141
Pct Italy	-0.131	—	—	—
Pct Canada	-0.191	-0.235	-0.110	-0.109
Pct Mexico	—	—	—	—
Pct NBFMP	0.169	0.493	-0.400	0.363
Pct Foreign Born	0.013	0.197	-0.615	0.035
Pct Negro	0.328	-0.299	-0.006	-0.574
Pct Other Non-white	0.438	-0.091	0.046	-0.181
Median School Years	-0.026	-0.025	0.164	-0.140
Pct Grade School	0.044	0.053	-0.027	0.147
Pct College	0.161	-0.113	0.092	-0.138
Pct White Collar	0.109	0.005	0.002	-0.009
Pct Blue Collar	-0.022	-0.002	-0.011	0.008
Median Income: Families	0.108	0.042	-0.029	0.141
Pct Incomes Under $4,000	0.031	-0.113	-0.051	-0.219
Pct Incomes $10,000 or More	0.118	0.002	-0.053	0.073
Pct Professional	0.165	-0.115	0.096	-0.022
Pct Managerial	0.113	-0.016	-0.088	0.000
Pct Clerical	-0.117	0.084	0.085	0.088
PCt Sales	0.054	0.143	-0.149	-0.107
Pct Craftsmen	-0.253	0.214	0.105	0.199
Pct Operative	-0.015	0.016	-0.165	0.058
Pct Service	0.100	-0.142	0.079	-0.247
Pct Laborer	0.090	-0.113	0.033	0.032
Pct Unemployed	-0.086	-0.122	0.062	-0.069
Median Age (Male)	0.045	0.301	-0.086	0.194
Pct Under 15	0.041	-0.175	0.054	-0.107
Pct 65 and Over	0.190	0.175	-0.045	0.070
Population Per Household	0.101	-0.109	0.019	-0.040
Pct 1-2 Person Households	0.004	0.060	-0.016	0.015
Pct 6+ Person Households	0.161	-0.291	0.148	-0.045
Pct Women in Labor Force	-0.226	0.022	0.048	-0.054

TABLE 16--Continued

Variable	Minne-apolis St. Paul	Provi-dence-Paw-tucket	Rich-mond	San Bernadino-Riverside
Factor	7	7	5	8
Pct U.K.	0.557	-0.059	0.028	0.309
Pct Ireland	—	0.136	0.169	—
Pct Norway	-0.037	—	—	—
Pct Sweden	0.059	-0.408	—	0.085
Pct Germany	0.312	0.177	0.143	0.027
Pct Poland	-0.127	0.635	0.725	0.728
Pct Czechoslovakia	—	—	0.338	—
Pct Austria	0.071	—	—	—
Pct Hungary	—	—	—	—
Pct U.S.S.R.	0.121	0.526	0.808	0.608
Pct Italy	—	0.016	0.024	0.675
Pct Canada	0.233	0.124	-0.053	0.365
Pct Mexico	—	—	—	-0.251
Pct NBFMP	0.251	0.415	0.446	0.151
Pct Foreign Born	-0.056	0.305	0.419	0.039
Pct Negro	0.102	0.104	-0.023	-0.165
Pct Other Non-white	-0.696	0.039	0.540	-0.011
Median School Years	0.029	-0.096	0.105	0.166
Pct Grade School	-0.046	0.140	-0.122	-0.200
Pct College	-0.091	-0.062	0.096	0.025
Pct White Collar	0.074	-0.017	0.153	0.092
Pct Blue Collar	-0.070	0.026	-0.152	-0.115
Median Income: Families	0.182	-0.037	-0.100	0.112
Pct Incomes Under $4,000	-0.203	0.170	-0.014	-0.069
Pct Incomes $10,000 or More	0.167	0.017	0.061	0.130
Pct Professional	-0.351	-0.144	0.011	0.090
Pct Mangerial	0.206	0.092	0.023	0.159
Pct Clerical	0.227	-0.161	0.318	0.007
Pct Sales	0.303	0.178	0.091	-0.048
Pct Craftsmen	0.096	-0.139	-0.211	0.157
Pct Operative	-0.072	0.149	-0.144	-0.106
Pct Service	-0.153	-0.160	-0.063	-0.205
Pct Laborer	-0.027	-0.062	0.003	-0.144
Pct Unemployed	-0.044	0.211	-0.052	0.020
Median Age (Male)	0.157	0.030	0.100	0.128
Pct Under 15	0.029	0.038	-0.141	-0.169
Pct 65 and Over	0.164	-0.070	0.099	-0.010
Population Per Household	0.054	-0.083	-0.036	-0.074
Pct 1-2 Person Households	-0.048	-0.008	0.063	-0.053
Pct 6+ Person Households	0.016	-0.223	0.043	0.109
Pct Women in Labor Force	-0.161	0.011	0.351	-0.011

TABLE 16--Continued

Variable / Factor	St. Petersburg 4	St. Petersburg 5	Tampa 4
Pct U.K.	0.131	0.182	-0.297
Pct Ireland	0.314	-0.311	-0.315
Pct Norway	—	—	—
Pct Sweden	0.099	0.390	-0.271
Pct Germany	0.319	-0.043	-0.346
Pct Poland	0.723	-0.157	0.051
Pct Czechoslovakia	—	—	—
Pct Austria	—	—	—
Pct Hungary	—	—	—
Pct U.S.S.R.	0.725	0.015	0.133
Pct Italy	0.525	-0.126	0.941
Pct Canada	0.195	0.047	-0.333
Pct Mexico	—	—	—
Pct NBFMP	0.454	-0.060	0.884
Pct Foreign Born	0.393	0.086	0.739
Pct Negro	-0.138	0.161	-0.209
Pct Other Non-white	0.197	-0.778	-0.268
Median School Years	0.024	-0.052	-0.203
Pct Grade School	-0.058	0.069	0.215
Pct College	0.008	0.042	-0.125
Pct White Collar	0.193	0.021	-0.020
Pct Blue Collar	-0.185	-0.021	0.041
Median Income: Families	0.112	-0.016	0.040
Pct Incomes Under $4,000	-0.083	0.043	-0.055
Pct Incomes $10,000 or More	0.121	0.049	-0.010
Pct Professional	-0.068	-0.077	-0.051
Pct Managerial	0.143	0.078	0.044
Pct Clerical	0.212	-0.072	-0.069
Pct Sales	0.290	0.105	0.013
Pct Craftsmen	-0.126	-0.246	-0.040
Pct Operative	-0.182	-0.138	0.382
Pct Service	-0.097	0.055	-0.151
Pct Laborer	-0.139	0.268	-0.134
Pct Unemployed	-0.025	-0.295	0.172
Median Age (Male)	0.151	0.097	0.129
Pct Under 15	-0.126	-0.050	-0.188
Pct 65 and Over	0.023	0.069	-0.040
Population Per Household	-0.065	0.027	0.030
Pct 1-2 Person Households	0.072	0.013	-0.048
Pct 6+ Person Households	-0.061	0.096	-0.158
Pct Women in Labor Force	-0.015	-0.105	0.155

TABLE 17

FACTORS ASSOCIATED WITH ETHNIC GROUPS
AND SOME OTHER VARIABLES

Variable	Ann Arbor	Ann Arbor	Providence Pawtucket	Providence Pawtucket
Factor	3	6	4	5
Pct U.K.	0.881	0.158	0.471	0.294
Pct Ireland	—	—	0.120	0.665
Pct Norway	—	—	—	—
Pct Sweden	—	—	0.096	0.231
Pct Germany	0.622	0.227	0.120	0.096
Pct Poland	-0.199	-0.379	0.438	0.194
Pct Czechoslovakia	—	—	—	—
Pct Austria	-0.102	0.449	—	—
Pct Hungary	-0.016	-0.098	—	—
Pct U.S.S.R.	0.412	-0.169	-0.099	0.376
Pct Italy	0.848	-0.286	-0.860	-0.125
Pct Canada	0.377	0.539	0.737	-0.239
Pct Mexico	—	—	—	—
Pct NBFMP	0.430	0.285	-0.345	0.068
Pct Foreign Born	0.736	-0.123	-0.165	-0.015
Pct Negro	-0.217	0.143	-0.051	0.038
Pct Other Non-white	-0.055	-0.173	-0.003	0.024
Median School Years	-0.035	0.073	0.039	0.197
Pct Grade School	0.070	0.059	-0.024	-0.231
Pct College	0.020	-0.039	0.050	-0.062
Pct White Collar	0.203	-0.069	-0.019	0.255
Pct Blue Collar	-0.297	0.033	0.018	-0.241
Median Income: Families	0.001	-0.084	0.050	-0.143
Pct Incomes Under $4,000	0.129	0.197	-0.125	-0.084
Pct Incomes $10,000 or More	-0.072	-0.047	0.008	-0.160
Pct Professional	0.051	-0.023	0.070	0.119
Pct Managerial	0.263	-0.018	-0.080	-0.128
Pct Clerical	0.416	-0.146	0.022	0.833
Pct Sales	-0.285	0.005	-0.041	0.317
Pct Craftsmen	-0.275	-0.135	-0.047	0.012
Pct Operative	-0.135	-0.056	0.148	-0.266
Pct Service	-0.204	0.023	-0.078	-0.022
Pct Laborer	-0.272	0.628	-0.487	-0.196
Pct Unemployed	-0.344	0.080	-0.177	-0.221
Median Age (Male)	0.317	0.093	-0.025	-0.009
Pct Under 15	-0.130	0.019	0.056	-0.018
Pct 65 and Over	0.706	0.067	0.088	0.045
Population Per Household	-0.217	-0.057	-0.126	0.015
Pct 1-2 Person Households	0.084	0.049	0.272	0.082
Pct 6+ Person Households	0.413	-0.172	0.062	-0.156
Pct Women in the Labor Force	-0.093	-0.216	0.252	0.088

Notes As in Table 8.

TABLE 17--Continued

Variable	Providence-Pawtucket	Richmond	Tampa
Factor	6	2	5
Pct U.K.	0.085	0.884	0.065
Pct Ireland	-0.124	-0.046	-0.161
Pct Norway	–	–	–
Pct Sweden	0.458	–	0.630
Pct Germany	0.544	0.875	0.276
Pct Poland	0.086	0.094	0.705
Pct Czechoslovakia	–	0.063	–
Pct Austria	–	–	–
Pct Hungary	–	–	–
Pct U.S.S.R.	-0.035	0.127	0.464
Pct Italy	-0.027	0.854	-0.021
Pct Canada	-0.127	0.891	0.490
Pct Mexico	–	–	–
Pct NBFMP	-0.185	0.648	-0.012
Pct Foreign Born	-0.347	0.751	0.051
Pct Negro	-0.020	-0.281	-0.147
Pct Other Non-white	0.085	-0.049	-0.672
Median School Years	0.159	0.179	0.217
Pct Grade School	-0.172	-0.261	-0.258
Pct College	-0.032	0.082	0.081
Pct White Collar	0.067	0.385	0.218
Pct Blue Collar	-0.071	-0.386	-0.215
Median Income: Families	0.019	0.352	-0.137
Pct Incomes Under $4,000	-0.090	-0.354	0.073
Pct Incomes $10,000 or More	-0.011	0.492	-0.272
Pct Professional	-0.081	-0.105	0.041
Pct Managerial	0.078	0.729	0.417
Pct Clerical	0.183	0.037	0.043
Pct Sales	0.113	0.693	0.244
Pct Craftsmen	0.542	-0.094	-0.042
Pct Operative	-0.172	-0.296	-0.338
Pct Service	-0.209	-0.319	-0.021
Pct Laborer	-0.289	-0.241	-0.188
Pct Unemployed	-0.034	-0.256	-0.024
Median Age (Male)	0.141	0.456	0.039
Pct Under 15	0.138	-0.205	0.028
Pct 65 and Over	-0.060	0.606	0.033
Population Per Household	0.053	-0.243	-0.009
Pct 1-2 Person Households	-0.092	0.147	-0.019
Pct 6+ Person Households	0.007	-0.154	-0.226
Pct Women in the Labor Force	-0.477	-0.673	-0.281

Notes As in Table 8.

spatial patterns in only one city.

In Chapter VIII the spatial patterns of ethnic and racial groups in American cities are explored more thoroughly. It would be useful here to ask whether the factor analytic results summarized in this chapter anticipate the findings produced by the more detailed analyses of Chapter VIII.

The answer must be both yes and no. The later results confirm the existence of distinctive spatial patterns for Italians in Canton, Des Moines, Providence-Pawtucket and Tampa, for Russians and Poles in Minneapolis-St. Paul, Providence-Pawtucket, Richmond and St. Petersburg and for the Swedish-Norwegian duo in Des Moines and Minneapolis-St. Paul. However, the Russian pattern proves to be a feature of the social geography of all the urbanized areas studied, even in those areas in which the Russian group variable does not load on its own distinct factor in the present analysis.[1] And the factor analysis fails to identify one of the most important ethnic groupings identified in Chapter VIII, that of the WASP's (White Anglo-Saxon Protestants), comprising native whites of native parents, Canadian foreign stock, British foreign stock, German foreign stock and sometimes Scandinavian foreign stock.

The principal feature of the ethnic geography of American cities — the residential segregation of black Americans from white — is, however, clearly identified in the factor analysis of most urbanized areas, though most of the factors with high loadings of the Per Cent Negro variable have many socioeconomic status indicator loadings as well.

Occupational Factors

Since we are concerned in this monograph with generalizing

---

[1]In many cases the Russian variable loads on the principal socioeconomic status factor in the positive direction, implying a high social status for the group as a whole.

TABLE 18

FACTORS ASSOCIATED WITH OCCUPATIONAL AND ETHNIC GROUPS AND SOME OTHER VARIABLES

Variable	Ann Arbor	Des Moines	Des Moines
Factor	4	3	4
Pct U.K.	0.072	-0.618	-0.083
Pct Ireland	—	-0.134	0.280
Pct Norway	—	-0.411	0.035
Pct Sweden	—	0.066	-0.281
Pct Germany	0.214	-0.499	0.140
Pct Poland	-0.157	—	—
Pct Czechoslovakia	—	—	—
Pct Austria	0.400	—	—
Pct Hungary	-0.023	—	—
Pct U.S.S.R.	-0.079	-0.001	0.007
Pct Italy	0.021	-0.014	-0.061
Pct Canada	-0.359	-0.130	-0.054
Pct Mexico	—	—	—
Pct NBFMP	0.140	-0.371	0.103
Pct Foreign Born	-0.271	0.016	0.003
Pct Negro	-0.099	0.345	0.300
Pct Other Non-white	-0.416	-0.165	0.450
Median School Years	0.066	-0.326	-0.298
Pct Grade School	-0.092	0.341	0.316
Pct College	0.021	0.047	-0.140
Median Income: Families	0.822	-0.028	-0.102
Pct Incomes Under $4,000	-0.595	0.154	0.411
Pct Incomes $10,000 or More	0.851	0.137	-0.043
Pct White Collar	0.187	-0.401	-0.166
Pct Blue Collar	-0.183	0.401	0.173
Pct Professional	0.183	-0.147	-0.080
Pct Managerial	0.794	0.045	-0.050
Pct Clerical	-0.592	-0.895	-0.163
Pct Sales	0.074	-0.327	-0.310
Pct Craftsmen	-0.068	0.648	-0.534
Pct Operative	-0.208	-0.067	0.322
Pct Service	-0.060	-0.102	0.635
Pct Laborer	-0.142	0.179	0.746
Pct Unemployed	-0.342	-0.026	0.669
Median Age (Male)	0.691	0.157	-0.072
Pct Under 15	-0.012	0.149	0.034
Pct 65 and Over	0.408	-0.165	0.258
Population Per Household	0.163	0.346	-0.109
Pct 1-2 Person Households	-0.044	-0.123	0.124
Pct 6+ Person Households	0.279	0.210	0.351
Pct Women in the Labor Force	-0.198	-0.819	0.273

Notes As in Table 8.

TABLE 18--Continued

Variable	Lancaster	Lancaster	Lancaster
Factor	3	4	7
Pct U.K.	-0.072	0.140	-0.134
Pct Ireland	0.026	0.059	0.091
Pct Norway	—	—	—
Pct Sweden	—	—	—
Pct Germany	-0.078	-0.029	0.049
Pct Poland	-0.781	0.067	-0.062
Pct Czechoslovakia	—	—	—
Pct Austria	-0.037	-0.700	0.071
Pct Hungary	—	—	—
Pct U.S.S.R.	-0.150	-0.154	-0.035
Pct Italy	0.025	0.221	-0.104
Pct Canada	0.252	-0.315	0.615
Pct Mexico	—	—	—
Pct NBFMP	-0.206	-0.054	0.006
Pct Foreign Born	0.053	-0.115	0.196
Pct Negro	0.080	-0.555	-0.158
Pct Other Non-white	0.523	0.345	0.043
Median School Years	-0.249	-0.026	-0.048
Pct Grade School	0.175	-0.106	0.014
Pct College	-0.060	-0.242	-0.210
Median Income: Families	-0.272	0.052	0.058
Pct Incomes Under $4,000	0.226	-0.009	-0.098
Pct Incomes $10,000 or More	-0.111	-0.041	0.019
Pct White Collar	0.326	-0.204	-0.032
Pct Blue Collar	0.000	-0.228	-0.036
Pct Professional	-0.124	-0.109	-0.182
Pct Managerial	0.019	-0.211	0.189
Pct Clerical	0.412	0.629	0.176
Pct Sales	-0.599	0.128	0.304
Pct Craftsmen	0.254	0.496	0.075
Pct Operative	0.238	0.094	0.023
Pct Service	0.188	-0.346	-0.412
Pct Laborer	-0.154	-0.440	-0.011
Pct Unemployed	0.605	0.065	-0.028
Median Age (Male)	-0.152	0.162	0.853
Pct Under 15	-0.002	0.054	0.226
Pct 65 and Over	-0.100	0.032	0.103
Population Per Household	0.043	-0.058	-0.184
Pct 1-2 Person Households	-0.062	-0.065	0.010
Pct 6+ Person Households	0.491	-0.181	-0.151
Pct Women in the Labor Force	0.060	-0.044	0.005

Notes As in Table 8.

TABLE 18--Continued

Variable	Richmond	San Bernadino-Riverside	San Bernadino-Riverside
Factor	6	5	6
Pct U.K.	-0.059	-0.134	-0.093
Pct Ireland	0.509	—	—
Pct Norway	—	—	—
Pct Sweden	—	0.031	-0.694
Pct Germany	0.071	0.186	-0.027
Pct Poland	0.054	-0.306	0.052
Pct Czechoslovakia	-0.216	—	—
Pct Austria	—	—	—
Pct Hungary	—	—	—
Pct U.S.S.R.	0.213	-0.021	-0.057
Pct Italy	-0.077	0.316	0.012
Pct Canada	0.052	0.034	0.045
Pct Mexico	—	-0.112	0.098
Pct NBFMP	0.173	0.181	-0.154
Pct Foreign Born	0.068	-0.236	0.235
Pct Negro	-0.155	-0.213	-0.009
Pct Other Non-white	-0.065	-0.656	0.308
Median School Years	0.159	-0.043	-0.013
Pct Grade School	-0.102	0.076	-0.110
Pct College	0.245	-0.158	-0.051
Median Income: Families	0.095	0.137	0.032
Pct Incomes Under $4,000	-0.093	0.472	-0.065
Pct Incomes $10,000 or More	0.513	0.115	-0.012
Pct White Collar	-0.226	-0.415	-0.279
Pct Blue Collar	0.532	0.070	0.154
Pct Professional	-0.149	-0.039	0.077
Pct Managerial	0.353	0.126	-0.195
Pct Clerical	0.039	0.252	0.046
Pct Sales	0.081	0.094	-0.865
Pct Craftsmen	0.090	0.524	0.316
Pct Operative	0.033	0.420	-0.391
Pct Service	-0.193	0.040	0.226
Pct Laborer	-0.063	0.119	-0.580
Pct Unemployed	-0.011	0.161	0.183
Median Age (Male)	0.477	0.013	-0.033
Pct Under 15	-0.255	0.381	-0.067
Pct 65 and Over	0.155	0.027	-0.077
Population Per Household	0.101	0.078	-0.055
Pct 1-2 Person Households	-0.133	0.136	-0.227
Pct 6+ Person Households	-0.029	-0.615	0.001
Pct Women in the Labor Force	-0.110	-0.110	-0.027

Notes As in Table 8.

about residential patterns in U.S. cities not a great deal can be said about the somewhat unique patterns revealed by the factors listed in Tables 18 and 19. However, the occupational groups Clerical and Craftsmen figure in a number of factors as high loadings (opposite in sign) often in conjunction with the variable indexing female participation in the labor force. This was earlier identified in the case of Des Moines as connected with the proportion of males and females in those two particular occupations: clerical occupations are dominated by women, craft occupations by men. Hence the association of the clerical variable with Per Cent Women in the Labor Force. Why the distribution of craft workers should tend to be the mirror image of that of clerical workers is not clear. Perhaps craft workers like their wives to stay at home and can also afford for them not to go out to work.[1] Des Moines' factor 3, Birmingham's factor 4, Honolulu's factor 5, Minneapolis-St. Paul's factor 5 and San Bernadino-Riverside's factor 7 show some of these characteristics.

Conclusions

In concluding this chapter we summarize the basic findings of our factor analysis of the population variables, attempt an interim assessment of the role of factor analysis, and look forward to the analyses carried out in later chapters that grow out of the factor analyses.

Our first conclusion is that the set of principal component analyses of 13 urbanized areas confirmed the earlier proposition that socioeconomic status would emerge as a universal dimension in American cities, and that it would be associated, to a greater or lesser extent, with racial status.

---

[1]Table 37 shows that on average only managers and professionals have higher incomes than craft workers.

TABLE 19

FACTORS ASSOCIATED WITH OCCUPATIONAL GROUPS

Variable	Birmingham	Honolulu	Minneapolis-St. Paul	San Bernadino-Riverside
Factor	4	5	5	7
Pct U.K.	0.313	0.063	-0.086	-0.117
Pct Ireland	0.169	0.035	—	—
Pct Norway	—	—	-0.035	—
Pct Sweden	—	0.052	-0.063	0.028
Pct Germany	0.091	0.041	-0.020	-0.017
Pct Poland	-0.068	-0.086	-0.056	0.072
Pct Czechoslovakia	—	—	—	—
Pct Austria	0.107	—	0.072	—
Pct Hungary	—	—	—	—
Pct U.S.S.R.	-0.052	-0.246	0.081	-0.085
Pct Italy	-0.026	-0.267	—	0.037
Pct Canada	-0.025	-0.051	-0.235	-0.267
Pct Mexico	—	—	—	0.069
Pct NBFMP	0.063	-0.135	-0.111	0.114
Pct Foreign Born	-0.007	0.304	0.089	-0.075
Pct Negro	-0.387	-0.297	0.161	0.066
Pct Other Non-white	0.064	0.047	0.147	0.120
Median School Years	0.018	-0.380	-0.195	-0.285
Pct Grade School	0.012	0.354	0.151	0.268
Pct College	-0.250	0.048	0.036	-0.374
Median Income: Families	0.146	0.234	0.242	0.010
Pct Incomes Under $4,000	-0.362	0.155	0.053	0.245
Pct Incomes $10,000 or Over	0.081	0.259	0.297	0.016
Pct White Collar	-0.049	-0.273	-0.144	-0.281
Pct Blue Collar	0.048	0.251	0.138	0.166
Pct Professional	-0.097	-0.047	-0.072	0.120
Pct Managerial	0.098	0.362	0.363	-0.398
Pct Clerical	0.032	-0.846	-0.778	-0.542
Pct Sales	-0.197	-0.226	0.102	-0.078
Pct Craftsmen	0.826	-0.040	-0.135	0.010
Pct Operative	0.307	0.355	-0.034	0.161
Pct Service	-0.440	0.001	0.227	-0.011
Pct Laborer	-0.212	0.394	0.492	0.228
Pct Unemployed	-0.011	0.025	0.439	-0.042
Median Age (Male)	-0.116	0.263	0.163	0.007
Pct Under 15	0.140	-0.074	0.157	-0.075
Pct 65 and Over	-0.060	0.280	0.065	0.088
Population Per Household	0.260	0.085	0.105	0.187
Pct 1-2 Person Households	-0.453	0.055	-0.070	-0.189
Pct 6+ Person Households	0.045	0.253	0.221	0.486
Pct Women in the Labor Force	-0.805	-0.329	0.498	-0.917

Notes As in Table 8.

Our second conclusion is that a variety of different types of "racial status" factors characterize U.S. cities. In some the factor loadings table is characterized by a "race and resources" type factor found in previous work (Rees, 1970b, 1972); in others (Birmingham, Alabama and El Paso, Texas) the racial or ethnic variable loaded most highly on the dominant socioeconomic status dimension. The implication was that the association between socioeconomic disadvantage and minority group membership was extremely close in such cities. In Chapter IX we examine, in some detail, the associations between the socioeconomic, family and ethnic status variables as revealed in the crosstabulations of the whole population of each SMSA, and compare those associations with the evidence revealed in the area based factor analyses of this chapter and the next.

A third conclusion to emerge was that family status was revealed in all analyses to be a unidimensional concept with little or no association with the other statuses. Several general foreign stock factors appeared in the analyses together with some particular factors that picked out Swedes and Norwegians (together), Italians, and Russians (who were mainly Jewish). A number of occupational groups showed distributions that departed from the general association of these groups with socioeconomic status.

How then do we assess the utility of factor analysis as a tool in the investigation of the geography of social groups in American cities? Its basic role, I feel, must be as a learning device, and as a means of hypothesis generation. It will suggest that certain spatial patterns are present in the social geography of the city and that the city's social structure as expressed ecologically is characterized by particular relationships. Further work is required to validate these suggestions, however. Factor analysis cannot stand alone, as it so frequently does.

In this chapter the implications of a set of factor analyses of population characteristics of 13 cities have been examined for the geographic and social patterns they suggest. In the next chapter, a similar set of factor analyses of housing characteristics is described with a particular view to assessing the extent to which the housing dimensions parallel the population dimensions. In Chapter IV we also put all the selected variables together and examine the results of a joint population and housing attribute analysis.

CHAPTER IV

FACTORIAL DIMENSIONS: HOUSING, AND HOUSING AND POPULATION

The residential area characteristics which were used in the factor analyses reported in the previous chapter refer exclusively to the population living in those residential areas (census tracts). Explanations for the emergence of particular population factors have been based to a greater or lesser extent on the association of population characteristics with housing characteristics. Abu-Lughod (1969) has probably outlined this explanation best; it was amplified in Rees (1971), and put forward in revised form in diagramatic form in Figure 4 in Chapter I.

One way we can begin to test the propositions put forward earlier, in Chapter I, is to examine the factorial dimensions that emerge from an analysis of the housing attributes of residential areas. If these parallel the most important factors that are present in the population attribute factor analyses then we shall have evidnce for our "theory of residential patterning." Further support can be found if we observe stability in the factors that emerge from a joint analysis of both the population characteristics of residential areas and the housing characteristics. The results of the factor analysis of both housing characteristics alone, and population and housing characteristics jointly are reported in this chapter.

It may be objected, by the seasoned observer of studies under the "factorial ecology" umbrella, that in the joint population and housing factor analysis we have arrived at the point from which most other work on residential area factorial dimensions begins. In response to this comment, it can be said that by studying the two sets of variables both separately and jointly we will have demonstrated unambiguously the patterns present in each and their relationships, if any. Very often, in the interpretation of factor structures (and right from the beginning of social area analysis), people and their dwellings have been considered together in a rather entangled way. "Disentangled" analysis is preferable.

Housing Dimensions

Principal component analyses of 20 housing variables for each of the 13 urbanized areas contained in the sample were carried out. Those components with eigenvalues greater than one were rotated using the normal varimax criterion (as in the population variable analysis).

The factor loadings from the 13 urbanized area analyses have been reassembled, by factor type, in Tables 20, 21, 22 and 23. Each column of these tables refers to a particular vector of factor loadings for an urbanized area. The number that heads each column indicates the rank order of the factor concerned in terms of associated eigenvalue. The variables which make up the rows of the tables are arranged in three sets. Variables within each set covary with fellow members of the set. The figures in the tables are the loadings of variables on factors produced in the analyses (principal component analyses) of urbanized area data matrices. Loadings greater than or equal to 0.700 in absolute value are underlined with a full line. Loadings between 0.400 and 0.699 in absolute value are underlined with a pecked line. Loadings of less than 0.400 in absolute value are not underlined.

Some 20 variables are included in the factor analyses of housing characteristics. "Pct One Unit" indicates the percentage of the housing stock in structures of one unit only (that is, single family housing units); "Pct Three or More Units" measures the percentage of the housing stock in structures of three units or more (that is, apartment units). "Median Number of Rooms" is the number of rooms in the median housing unit in a distribution of units by number of rooms; "Pct 2 Rooms or Less" and "Pct 7 Rooms or More" give the percentages of housing units in the fewest rooms category and in the most rooms category. As in the factor analyses of the population variables, we use variables that indicate lower and upper ends of the distributions of relevant attributes.

"Pct Owner Occupied" and "Pct Renter Occupied" are the percentages of housing units of owner occupied tenure and renter occupied tenure respectively. "Pct Built Before 1940" and "Pct Built 1950-60" give the percentages of the housing stock built before 1940 and in the 1950s respectively. "Median Home Value" is the median in the distribution occupied-assessed values of owner occupied housing units; the ends of the distribution of home value are described by "Pct Less than $10,000" (per cent of owner occupied housing units assessed to be less than $10,000 in value) and "Pct $20,000 or More" (per cent of owner occupied housing units assessed to be equal to or more than $20,000 in value). "Median Rent" refers to the median rent of renter occupied housing units; "Pct Under $40" and "Pct $100 or More" index the percentages of renter units with low and high rents respectively. For certain census tracts the number of owner or renter occupied units is very low and the resulting variable values unreliable. They are used, nevertheless, in the analysis as being a better guide than the citywide average, which would be the alternative that could be employed.

"Pct Sound," "Pct Deteriorating" and "Pct Dilapidated" are variables which measure the percentages of housing units, assessed by the enumerator, to be in a "sound," a "deteriorating" or "dilapidated" condition, mainly on the basis of external appearance. "Pct 1.01 or More" and "Pct Less than 0.50" measure the density of occupance of a housing unit, and are the percentage of housing units with 1.01 or more persons per room and the percentage of housing units with less than 0.50 persons per room.

Three very similar factors emerge in all 13 urbanized area analyses and a fourth factor is characteristic of 9 of these 13 analyses. These factors are:

(i) a housing type, size and tenure factor (13 urbanized areas)

(ii) a home value and rent factor (13 urbanized areas)

(iii) a housing condition factor (13 urbanized areas)

and (iv) a housing age factor (9 urbanized areas).

Housing Type, Size and Tenure

The factor loadings for this factor are given in Table 20. This factor scales census tracts in terms of the structural type of housing they contain, the roominess of that housing and the tenure under which it is occupied. Tracts which score highly on this factor contain higher than average proportions of single family homes, of owner occupied homes and of large homes and a smaller than average proportion of apartment units, small homes and renter occupied dwellings. Tracts scoring low on this factor have the converse characteristics.

Housing age is associated with this factor, but only to a moderate degree in most of the sample urbanized areas, exceptions being El Paso, Providence-Pawtucket and St. Petersburg. The loading signs for the variables indexing rental levels in census tracts are consistent in a direction that suggests that the rental units in tracts at the single family, owner occupied end of the scale formed by this factor have higher than average monthly rentals.

Home Value and Rent

A second factor, the factor loadings of which are displayed in Table 21, in the housing variable analysis distinguishes tracts

TABLE 20

THE HOUSING TYPE, SIZE AND TENURE FACTORS

Variable	Ann Arbor	Birmingham	Canton	Des Moines	El Paso	Honolulu	Lancaster
Factor	1	2	2	1	2	1	1
Pct One Unit	0.956	0.933	0.803	0.932	0.875	0.913	0.892
Pct Three or More Units	-0.977	-0.936	-0.932	-0.956	-0.872	-0.938	-0.960
Median Number of Rooms	0.886	0.603	0.721	0.848	0.610	0.819	0.833
Pct 2 Rooms or Less	-0.928	-0.778	-0.904	-0.913	-0.582	-0.695	-0.940
Pct 7 Rooms or More	0.419	0.141	0.069	0.212	0.236	0.585	0.313
Pct Owner Occupied	0.945	0.731	0.764	0.886	0.829	0.884	0.720
Pct Renter Occupied	-0.945	-0.731	-0.764	-0.886	-0.829	-0.884	-0.720
Pct Built Before 1940	-0.383	-0.304	-0.378	-0.451	-0.696	-0.067	-0.397
Pct Built 1950-1960	0.334	0.364	0.310	0.396	0.580	0.184	0.366
Median Home Value	-0.069	-0.138	0.285	0.220	0.075	0.161	0.270
Pct Less than $10,000	0.167	0.279	-0.104	0.099	-0.034	-0.093	-0.165
Pct $20,000 or More	0.065	0.064	0.054	0.182	0.084	0.604	0.143
Median Rent	0.473	0.123	0.443	0.403	0.261	0.302	0.214
Pct Under $40	-0.550	-0.060	-0.699	-0.324	-0.349	-0.254	-0.345
Pct $100 or More	0.452	0.132	0.253	0.332	0.382	0.268	0.154
Pct Sound	0.071	0.170	0.309	0.183	0.310	0.094	0.722
Pct Deteriorating	-0.124	-0.071	-0.346	-0.265	-0.272	0.156	-0.669
Pct Dilapidated	0.064	-0.202	-0.161	-0.038	-0.295	-0.250	-0.791
Pct 1.01 or More	-0.409	-0.014	0.013	0.344	-0.023	0.044	0.042
Pct Less than 0.50	0.236	0.043	-0.235	-0.183	-0.049	0.213	-0.060

TABLE 20--Continued

Variable	Minneapolis-St. Paul	Providence-Pawtucket	Richmond	San Bernadino-Riverside	St. Petersburg	Tampa
Factor	1	1	3	1	1	1
Pct One Unit	0.770	0.862	0.845	0.924	0.963	0.944
Pct Three or More Units	-0.935	-0.779	-0.902	-0.634	-0.956	-0.965
Median Number of Rooms	0.852	0.259	0.636	0.182	0.859	0.750
Pct 2 Rooms or Less	-0.912	-0.178	-0.820	-0.467	-0.920	-0.882
Pct 7 Rooms or More	0.358	0.163	0.306	-0.488	0.073	0.093
Pct Owner Occupied	0.821	0.797	0.779	0.887	0.863	0.856
Pct Renter Occupied	-0.821	-0.797	-0.779	-0.887	-0.863	-0.856
Pct Built Before 1940	-0.324	-0.925	-0.432	-0.498	-0.793	-0.644
Pct Built 1950-1960	0.289	0.908	0.350	0.640	0.742	0.536
Median Home Value	0.136	0.284	0.013	0.190	-0.084	0.081
Pct Less than $10,000	-0.138	0.056	0.219	-0.029	0.091	-0.158
Pct $20,000 or More	0.157	0.174	-0.004	0.163	-0.062	0.048
Median Rent	0.470	0.377	0.301	0.476	0.487	0.401
Pct Under $40	-0.707	-0.220	-0.339	-0.343	-0.244	-0.491
Pct $100 or More	0.353	0.420	0.200	0.383	0.397	0.179
Pct Sound	0.345	0.281	0.111	0.086	0.265	0.310
Pct Deterioring	-0.317	-0.364	-0.063	-0.129	-0.313	-0.333
Pct Dilapidated	-0.325	-0.057	-0.177	0.009	-0.146	-0.176
Pct 1.01 or More	0.159	0.152	-0.081	0.211	-0.028	0.095
Pct Less than 0.50	0.090	-0.640	0.137	-0.165	0.134	0.113

with higher than average priced owned or rented property from those with lower priced units. The tracts at the higher end of this factor scale contain more than their average share of larger units (those with 7 rooms or more), although the other two housing size variables ("Median Number of Rooms" and "Per Cent of Housing Units with 2 Rooms or Less") load on the housing type, size and tenure factor.

Housing conditions

A third factor, the factor loadings of which are displayed in Table 22, is associated with housing condition and, in some urbanized areas, with degree of crowding of housing units. Areas with higher than average percentages of sound housing are distinguished from those with lower than average proportions and higher than average numbers of deteriorating or dilapidated dwellings. From 80 to 90 per cent of the housing in U.S. SMSAs was judged sound structurally by the 1960 Census enumerators and from 70 to 80 per cent was reported as sound with all plumbing facilities. So only a small number of tracts in any SMSA score at the bottom end of this housing condition factor.

Associated with housing condition are rent levels: the Median ent and Per Cent Renter Units with Rents of $100/month or More score negatively on this factor, and Per Cent Renter Units with Rents of $40/month or less score positively. Low rent goes with poor conditions. The rental variables are ones which load moderately on all three factors so far outlined: rental levels are functions of the type mix of housing for rent, the value of housing in an area (indexing in part its prestige value) and the condition of housing.

An Age of Housing Factor

Some 9 out of the 13 urbanized areas (Table 23) studied exhibit a factor with high or moderate loadings of the two housing

TABLE 21

THE HOME VALUE/RENT FACTORS

Variable	Ann Arbor	Birmingham	Canton	Des Moines	El Paso	Honolulu	Lancaster
Factor	4	3	1	2	3	5	2
Pct One Unit	0.014	-0.025	0.519	-0.011	-0.001	0.066	0.370
Pct Three or More Units	0.030	0.044	-0.288	-0.008	-0.051	-0.091	-0.214
Median Number of Rooms	0.395	0.398	-0.035	0.469	0.390	-0.108	0.095
Pct 2 Rooms or Less	-0.057	0.016	-0.166	-0.089	-0.207	0.172	-0.160
Pct 7 Rooms or More	0.726	0.861	0.077	0.729	0.903	0.064	0.077
Pct Owner Occupied	0.045	0.112	0.579	0.039	0.253	0.233	0.645
Pct Renter Occupied	-0.045	-0.112	-0.579	-0.039	-0.253	-0.233	-0.645
Pct Built Before 1940	-0.023	-0.119	-0.909	-0.195	0.192	-0.007	-0.823
Pct Built 1950-1960	0.175	0.233	0.927	0.174	-0.227	0.007	0.806
Median Home Value	0.837	0.845	0.712	0.889	0.728	0.619	0.890
Pct Less than $10,000	-0.345	-0.628	-0.726	-0.836	-0.529	-0.859	-0.896
Pct $20,000 or More	0.934	0.922	0.672	0.814	0.890	0.366	0.803
Median Rent	0.269	0.515	0.611	0.438	0.165	0.162	0.417
Pct Under $40	-0.216	-0.293	-0.073	0.124	-0.280	-0.220	0.021
Pct $100 or More	-0.084	0.630	0.638	0.577	0.107	0.167	0.584
Pct Sound	0.255	0.167	0.317	0.455	0.196	0.180	0.308
Pct Deteriorating	-0.297	-0.242	-0.367	-0.523	-0.172	-0.101	-0.368
Pct Dilapidated	-0.072	-0.019	-0.134	-0.293	-0.186	-0.184	-0.101
Pct 1.01 or More	-0.241	-0.392	-0.052	-0.696	-0.519	-0.240	-0.425
Pct Less than 0.50	0.388	0.513	-0.432	0.627	0.876	0.051	-0.091

TABLE 21--Continued

Variable	Minneapolis-St. Paul	Providence-Pawtucket	Richmond	San Bernadino-Riverside	St. Petersburg	Tampa
Factor	3	2	1	3	3	2
Pct One Unit	0.298	0.218	0.048	-0.046	-0.109	0.027
Pct Three or More Units	-0.108	-0.123	0.021	0.055	0.135	0.014
Median Number of Rooms	0.324	0.356	0.530	0.493	0.267	0.519
Pct 2 Rooms or Less	-0.035	0.144	0.020	-0.066	0.013	-0.111
Pct 7 Rooms or More	0.684	0.751	0.853	0.443	0.535	0.828
Pct Owner Occupied	0.253	0.196	0.277	0.265	0.083	0.179
Pct Renter Occupied	-0.253	-0.196	-0.277	-0.265	-0.083	-0.179
Pct Built Before 1940	-0.375	-0.114	-0.181	-0.101	-0.232	-0.242
Pct Built 1950-1960	0.322	0.170	0.212	0.336	0.296	0.376
Median Home Value	0.903	0.868	0.847	0.871	0.901	0.925
Pct Less than $10,000	-0.487	-0.548	-0.693	-0.744	-0.782	-0.784
Pct $20,000 or More	0.928	0.885	0.890	0.818	0.879	0.883
Median Rent	0.524	0.679	0.631	0.435	0.664	0.698
Pct Under $40	-0.041	-0.224	-0.255	-0.087	-0.201	-0.325
Pct $100 or More	0.517	0.710	0.631	0.531	0.681	0.747
Pct Sound	0.191	0.239	0.251	0.181	0.320	0.279
Pct Deteriorating	-0.261	0.282	-0.311	-0.164	-0.366	-0.331
Pct Dilapidated	-0.001	-0.087	-0.086	-0.159	-0.221	-0.104
Pct 1.01 or More	-0.411	-0.694	-0.552	-0.469	-0.180	-0.367
Pct 0.50 or Less	0.090	0.537	0.617	0.115	0.057	0.233

TABLE 22

THE HOUSING CONDITION FACTORS

Variable	Ann Arbor	Birmingham	Canton	Des Moines	El Paso	Honolulu	Lancaster
Factor	2	1	3	3	1	2	4
Pct One Unit	-0.017	0.082	0.095	-0.085	-0.397	-0.153	-0.002
Pct Three or More Units	-0.026	-0.105	-0.027	0.032	0.404	0.098	-0.003
Median Number of Rooms	-0.110	-0.549	-0.348	-0.135	-0.570	-0.436	-0.096
Pct 2 Rooms or Less	0.004	0.426	0.164	0.307	0.715	0.568	0.144
Pct 7 Rooms or More	-0.115	0.401	-0.212	-0.079	-0.139	-0.067	-0.005
Pct Owner Occupied	-0.156	-0.407	-0.126	-0.314	-0.076	-0.025	-0.149
Pct Renter Occupied	0.156	0.407	0.126	0.314	0.076	0.025	0.149
Pct Built Before 1940	0.249	0.159	-0.017	0.247	0.467	0.622	0.071
Pct Built 1950-1960	-0.231	-0.126	-0.020	-0.218	-0.496	-0.308	-0.021
Median Home Value	-0.473	-0.293	-0.363	-0.297	-0.360	-0.136	-0.084
Pct Less than $10,000	0.819	0.379	0.564	0.302	0.231	0.255	0.273
Pct $20,000 or More	-0.248	-0.017	-0.228	-0.118	-0.025	-0.063	0.144
Median Rent	-0.668	-0.531	-0.453	-0.648	-0.613	-0.364	-0.258
Pct Under $40	0.017	0.758	0.305	0.854	0.702	0.843	0.807
Pct $100 or More	-0.672	-0.221	-0.411	-0.537	-0.340	-0.215	-0.279
Pct Sound	-0.860	-0.768	-0.875	-0.821	-0.846	-0.843	-0.537
Pct Deteriorating	0.695	0.435	0.810	0.694	0.736	0.520	0.552
Pct Dilapidated	0.875	0.792	0.902	0.891	0.809	0.828	0.433
Pct 1.01 or More	0.278	0.761	0.878	0.267	0.687	0.133	0.564
Pct Less than 0.50	-0.051	-0.735	-0.728	0.180	-0.281	-0.026	-0.369

TABLE 22--Continued

Variable	Minneapolis-St. Paul	Providence-Pawtucket	Richmond	San Bernadino-Riverside	St. Petersburg	Tampa
Factor	2	4	2	2	2	3
Pct One Unit	-0.304	-0.063	-0.018	0.115	-0.099	-0.138
Pct Three or More Units	0.152	0.047	-0.095	-0.115	0.095	0.067
Median Number of Rooms	-0.240	-0.163	-0.367	-0.230	-0.131	-0.089
Pct 2 Rooms or Less	0.257	0.080	0.168	0.267	-0.024	0.048
Pct 7 Rooms or More	-0.075	0.026	-0.141	0.021	0.020	-0.067
Pct Owner Occupied	-0.309	-0.195	-0.346	-0.176	-0.436	-0.400
Pct Renter Occupied	0.309	0.195	0.346	0.176	0.436	0.400
Pct Built Before 1940	0.291	0.191	0.333	0.416	0.173	0.340
Pct Built 1950-1960	-0.274	-0.160	-0.214	-0.352	-0.209	-0.294
Median Home Value	-0.261	-0.230	-0.401	-0.292	-0.285	-0.293
Pct Less than $10,000	0.581	0.274	0.530	0.464	0.411	0.365
Pct $20,000 or More	-0.077	0.001	-0.017	0.003	-0.085	-0.039
Median Rent	-0.497	-0.113	-0.548	-0.561	-0.298	-0.386
Pct Under $40	0.493	0.233	0.630	0.475	0.681	0.460
Pct $100 or More	-0.487	-0.031	-0.433	-0.425	-0.288	-0.347
Pct Sound	-0.875	-0.875	-0.896	-0.932	-0.813	-0.867
Pct Deteriorating	0.792	0.646	0.833	0.835	0.732	0.736
Pct Dilapidated	0.823	0.836	0.816	0.836	0.889	0.836
Pct 1.01 or More	0.161	0.388	0.713	0.535	0.893	0.711
Pct Less than 0.50	-0.097	-0.061	-0.338	-0.016	-0.656	-0.253

age variables. This suggests that housing age and housing type are at least partially independent.

Other Housing Factors

Finally, in Table 24 are displayed other housing factors peculiar to individual urbanized areas in which particular variables load highly on a factor separate from the general ones described above. These appear to be fairly idiosyncratic in nature.

Population and Housing Dimensions

In Chapter I, it was suggested that the population and housing dimensions were linked in an orderly fashion. The components from the population analysis can be linked with those from the housing analysis as follows:

Population Factor	Housing Factor
(i) Socioeconomic status	(ii) Home value and rent
(ii) Family status	(i) Housing type, size and tenure
(iii) Racial status, associated with socioeconomic status	(iii) Housing conditions

If this correspondence of population and housing components is correct then we should expect them to merge into some three joint factors in a principal component analysis of both population and housing variables. The full tables of factor loadings to emerge from such analysis are given in Tables 25, 26, and 27. The factor loadings for the socioeconomic status and home value/rent factors are given in Table 25; those for the family status and home-type factor are given in Table 26; those for the factors in which racial or ethnic status is associated with socioeconomic status are shown in Table 27. Table 28 summarizes the findings of the combined population and housing factor analyses.

In the first type of factor (Table 25), both indicators of the socioeconomic status of a tract's population and indicators of the price and quality of its housing stock load on the same factor.

TABLE 23

THE AGE OF HOUSING FACTORS

Variable	Ann Arbor	Bir-ming-ham	Des Moines	Hono-lulu	Minne-apolis-St. Paul	Rich-mond	San Berna-dino-River-side	St. Peters-burg	Tampa
Factor	3	4	4	3	4	4	5	4	4
Pct One Unit	-0.180	-0.128	-0.299	-0.012	-0.378	-0.325	-0.077	-0.022	-0.176
Pct Three or More Units	0.020	-0.004	0.212	-0.063	0.193	0.108	0.295	-0.055	0.063
Median Number of Rooms	0.126	-0.333	0.109	-0.130	0.184	-0.040	-0.168	0.343	0.310
Pct 2 Rooms or Less	-0.056	0.176	0.045	0.053	-0.032	-0.171	0.089	-0.221	-0.201
Pct 7 Rooms or More	0.364	0.025	0.436	0.017	0.493	0.064	-0.011	0.719	0.450
Pct Owner Occupied	-0.113	-0.438	-0.312	-0.353	-0.314	-0.355	-0.125	-0.112	-0.135
Pct Renter Occupied	0.113	0.438	0.312	0.353	0.314	0.355	0.125	0.112	0.135
Pct Built Before 1940	0.846	0.833	0.824	0.648	0.789	0.761	0.562	0.478	0.584
Pct Built 1950-1960	-0.757	-0.836	-0.855	-0.851	-0.809	-0.823	-0.464	-0.505	-0.647
Median Home Value	-0.021	-0.327	-0.138	-0.370	-0.056	-0.187	0.061	0.117	-0.009
Pct Less than $10,000	-0.057	0.476	0.211	-0.053	0.036	0.218	0.129	-0.034	0.033
Pct $20,000 or More	-0.060	-0.142	-0.165	-0.446	-0.023	-0.098	0.224	0.189	0.148
Median Rent	-0.080	-0.455	-0.266	-0.543	-0.219	-0.145	0.033	-0.080	-0.193
Pct Under $40	0.498	0.221	0.001	0.133	-0.103	-0.368	-0.231	-0.182	0.021
Pct $100 or More	-0.054	-0.525	-0.218	-0.678	-0.276	-0.214	-0.098	-0.182	-0.287
Pct Sound	-0.277	-0.461	-0.189	-0.383	-0.057	-0.238	-0.029	-0.202	-0.026
Pct Deteriorating	0.445	0.604	0.227	0.492	0.138	0.306	0.005	0.231	0.062
Pct Dilapidated	-0.175	0.121	0.107	0.186	-0.124	0.061	0.061	0.087	-0.045
Pct 1.01 or More	-0.631	0.279	-0.372	0.120	-0.728	-0.058	-0.518	-0.252	-0.474
Pct Less than 0.50	0.791	0.077	0.655	-0.034	0.946	0.538	0.927	0.650	0.872

TABLE 24

OTHER HOUSING FACTORS

Variable	Canton	El Paso	Honolulu	Lancaster	Providence-Pawtucket	San Bernadino-Riverside
Factor	4	4	4	3	3	4
Pct One Unit	-0.046	-0.039	-0.066	0.010	-0.372	0.131
Pct Three or More Units	-0.019	0.093	0.091	-0.008	0.528	0.600
Median Number of Rooms	0.511	0.221	0.108	0.517	-0.826	0.748
Pct 2 Rooms or Less	-0.093	-0.104	-0.172	-0.133	0.846	-0.692
Pct 7 Rooms or More	0.932	0.098	0.064	0.879	-0.459	0.684
Pct Owner Occupied	-0.017	0.372	-0.233	0.010	-0.485	0.110
Pct Renter Occupied	0.017	-0.372	0.233	-0.010	0.485	-0.110
Pct Built Before 1940	0.081	-0.301	0.007	0.387	0.089	-0.304
Pct Built 1950-1960	0.021	0.468	-0.007	-0.431	-0.065	0.026
Median Home Value	0.483	0.464	-0.619	0.270	0.053	0.179
Pct Less than $10,000	-0.141	-0.711	0.859	-0.135	-0.035	-0.100
Pct $20,000 or More	0.622	0.060	-0.366	0.358	-0.108	0.161
Median Rent	0.239	0.645	-0.162	0.625	-0.419	0.177
Pct Under $40	-0.094	-0.329	0.220	-0.260	0.708	-0.548
Pct $100 or More	0.359	0.783	-0.167	0.438	-0.164	0.043
Pct Sound	0.090	0.261	-0.180	0.134	-0.239	0.142
Pct Deteriorating	-0.110	-0.395	0.101	-0.123	0.303	-0.234
Pct Dilapidated	-0.021	-0.061	0.184	-0.151	0.058	0.046
Pct 1.01 or More	-0.328	-0.430	0.240	-0.466	0.020	-0.095
Pct Less than 0.50	0.392	0.055	-0.051	0.836	-0.315	-0.081

The following factors emerge from the combined population and housing variable analysis:

(i) a socioeconomic status and home value/rent factor, characteristic of all 13 urbanized areas;

(ii) a family status and home type factor, characteristic of 10 of the 13 urbanized areas; and

(iii) a factor in which are associated racial or ethnic status on the one hand and deprived socioeconomic status and housing condition on the other. This factor is characteristic of some 9 urbanized areas.

Some of the variance of these two variable sets is associated with another factor (Table 27) that is characterized by a high loading of the Per Cent Negro or Per Cent Mexican variable. Some 9 of the 13 urbanized areas show this factor in which racial or ethnic status is associated with socioeconomic status and housing condition. As in the population variable analysis, Birmingham, Richmond, St. Petersburg and Tampa show particularly strong association between socioeconomic status and housing condition on the one hand and racial status on the other, and El Paso shows a similar association with respect to ethnic status (Chicano/Anglo distinction). The simple correlations between racial status (Per Cent Negro) or ethnic status (Per Cent Mexican) and the three housing condition indexes are given in Table 29 and confirm the suggested link between racial status and housing condition components for all urbanized areas except Honolulu where the associations are not as predicted and Lancaster and Minneapolis-St. Paul where they are rather weak.

A family status and house type factor (Table 26) characterizes most of the urbanized area analyses and confirms the residential location hypothesis put forward in Chapter I, and is explored in more detail in Chapter VII. Exceptions to this congruent pattern are discussed there.

To sum up the argument, then, the housing component analyses suggest that housing is distributed across the American metropolis in some three basic patterns of value/rent level, of home type and of condition, and that these patterns are linked with those characterizing the population through the process of residential choice. A variety of exceptions to this association between population and housing dimensions serve to emphasize that these areal associations may not hold in urban situations radically different from the American norm, in ethnically tolerant Honolulu or in the retirement city of St. Petersburg, for example.

We can examine the available cross-tabulations of population

TABLE 25

THE SOCIOECONOMIC STATUS AND HOME VALUE/RENT FACTORS

Variable / Factor	Ann Arbor 1	Birmingham 3	Canton 1	Des Moines 1	El Paso 2	Honolulu 1	Lancaster 1
Median School Years	0.924	0.546	0.701	0.798	0.272	0.564	0.839
Pct Grade School	-0.942	-0.491	-0.709	-0.802	-0.302	-0.627	-0.836
Pct College	0.921	0.797	0.919	0.967	0.613	0.869	0.874
Pct White Collar	0.935	0.517	0.813	0.834	0.400	0.809	0.832
Pct Blue Collar	-0.920	-0.516	-0.815	-0.836	-0.412	-0.816	-0.902
Median Income: Families	0.578	0.696	0.757	0.875	0.699	0.551	0.863
Pct Incomes Under $4,000	-0.311	-0.359	-0.458	-0.582	-0.355	-0.172	-0.706
Pct Incomes $10,000 +	0.640	0.878	0.928	0.966	0.822	0.590	0.910
Pct Professional	0.936	0.697	0.777	0.902	0.426	0.812	0.798
Pct Managerial	0.511	0.813	0.921	0.954	0.636	0.780	0.955
Pct Clerical	0.020	0.040	0.349	0.090	-0.028	0.122	-0.043
Pct Sales Workers	0.010	0.220	0.596	0.737	0.095	0.436	0.462
Pct Craftsmen	-0.570	-0.328	-0.436	-0.372	-0.533	-0.757	-0.486
Pct Operatives	-0.806	-0.518	-0.810	-0.716	-0.418	-0.642	-0.833
Pct Service Workers	-0.480	-0.234	-0.408	-0.475	-0.042	-0.227	-0.641
Pct Laborers	-0.510	-0.241	-0.435	-0.505	-0.232	-0.514	-0.599
Pct Unemployed	-0.805	-0.330	-0.487	-0.561	-0.305	-0.088	-0.512
Median Home Value	0.858	0.812	0.836	0.916	0.697	0.269	0.919
Pct Less than $10,000	-0.789	-0.554	-0.642	-0.711	-0.417	-0.138	-0.810
Pct $20,00 or More	0.739	0.919	0.936	0.910	0.851	0.234	0.885
Median Rent	0.661	0.517	0.645	0.616	0.162	0.537	0.533
Pct Under $40	-0.079	-0.256	-0.165	-0.285	-0.091	-0.263	-0.158
Pct $100 or More	0.474	0.674	0.781	0.689	0.225	0.494	0.593
Pct Sound	0.749	0.246	0.464	0.616	0.180	0.278	0.389
Pct Deteriorating	-0.667	-0.265	-0.493	-0.646	-0.236	-0.249	-0.443
Pct Dilapidated	-0.633	-0.124	-0.312	-0.485	-0.082	-0.215	-0.191
Pct 1.01 +	-0.269	-0.329	-0.517	-0.547	-0.321	-0.766	-0.618
Pct 0.50 -	0.159	0.430	0.266	0.391	0.496	0.849	0.319
Median Age (Male)	0.118	0.361	0.243	0.240	0.385	0.208	-0.054
Pct Under 15	-0.197	-0.167	0.007	-0.006	-0.239	0.303	-0.179
Pct 65 and Over	-0.047	0.060	-0.056	-0.011	0.119	0.144	-0.078

TABLE 25--Continued

Variable / Factor	Ann Arbor 1	Birmingham 3	Canton 1	Des Moines 1	El Paso 2	Honolulu 1	Lancaster 1
Population Per Household	-0.189	-0.200	-0.040	-0.113	-0.179	-0.468	-0.024
Pct 1+2 Person Households	0.036	0.062	-0.094	-0.028	0.081	0.406	-0.050
Pct 6+ Person Households	-0.360	-0.256	0.228	-0.239	-0.200	-0.546	-0.295
Pct Women in Labor Force	-0.443	-0.051	-0.166	-0.042	0.046	0.085	-0.669
Pct One Unit	-0.140	-0.037	0.186	0.053	0.152	-0.038	0.263
Pct Three or More Units	0.212	0.097	-0.105	-0.032	-0.135	0.056	-0.136
Median Number of Rooms	0.172	0.383	0.437	0.525	0.420	0.122	0.265
Pct 2 Rooms or Less	0.109	-0.051	-0.179	-0.208	-0.159	0.092	-0.151
Pct 7 Rooms or More	0.444	0.820	0.765	0.802	0.827	0.551	0.436
Pct Owner Occupied	-0.019	0.145	0.301	0.171	0.191	0.080	0.537
Pct Renter Occupied	0.019	-0.145	-0.301	-0.171	-0.191	-0.080	-0.537
Pct Built Before 1940	-0.212	-0.217	-0.418	-0.275	-0.074	-0.101	-0.538
Pct Built 1950-1960	0.300	0.301	0.504	0.249	0.098	0.062	0.502
Pct Negro	-0.504	-0.248	-0.201	-0.325	-0.125	-0.547	-0.085
Pct Other Non-white	0.316	-0.019	-0.225	-0.167	-0.226	-0.306	0.206
Pct NBFMP	0.618	0.584	0.122	0.419	-0.174	-0.279	-0.184
Pct Foreign Born	0.319	0.460	-0.279	0.097	-0.129	0.780	0.422
Pct U.K.	0.176	0.261	0.318	0.138	0.308	0.719	0.007
Pct Ireland	—	0.400	—	0.494	-0.034	—	—
Pct Norway	—	—	—	0.178	—	0.741	—
Pct Sweden	—	—	—	-0.038	—	0.229	-0.245
Pct Germany	0.128	0.485	0.048	0.340	0.103	0.210	0.293
Pct Poland	0.503	0.829	0.035	—	0.814	—	—
Pct Czechoslovakia	—	—	-0.267	—	—	—	0.534
Pct Austria	0.557	0.620	-0.098	—	—	—	—
Pct Hungary	0.093	—	-0.078	—	—	—	—
Pct U.S.S.R.	0.451	0.793	0.131	0.805	0.896	0.502	0.375
Pct Italy	0.122	-0.018	-0.078	-0.101	0.001	0.332	0.526
Pct Canada	0.336	0.722	—	0.682	0.427	0.722	0.576
Pct Mexico	—	—	—	—	-0.242	—	—

TABLE 25--Continued

Variable / Factor	Minneapolis-St. Paul 2	Providence-Pawtucket 1	Richmond 1	San Bernadino-Riverside 1	St. Petersburg 2	Tampa 2
Median School Years	0.716	0.866	0.764	0.542	0.822	0.575
Pct Grade School	-0.726	-0.826	-0.736	-0.551	-0.808	-0.613
Pct College	0.911	0.965	0.942	0.743	0.919	0.854
Pct White Collar	0.868	0.907	0.664	0.778	0.729	0.664
Pct Blue Collar	-0.871	-0.910	-0.662	-0.773	-0.730	-0.670
Median Indome: Families	0.806	0.856	0.758	0.874	0.862	0.756
Pct Incomes Under $4,000	-0.446	-0.530	-0.447	-0.625	-0.811	-0.586
Pct Incomes $10,000+	0.912	0.934	0.801	0.888	0.913	0.733
Pct Professional	0.767	0.834	0.714	0.802	0.633	0.794
Pct Managerial	0.897	0.915	0.637	0.574	0.733	0.751
Pct Clerical	-0.225	0.183	0.270	0.251	0.235	0.221
Pct Sales Workers	0.689	0.674	0.293	0.167	0.488	0.502
Pct Craftsmen	-0.567	-0.460	-0.366	-0.527	-0.530	-0.683
Pct Operatives	-0.855	-0.837	-0.757	-0.652	-0.758	-0.656
Pct Service Workers	-0.373	-0.107	-0.286	-0.238	-0.388	-0.277
Pct Laborers	-0.456	-0.540	-0.436	-0.422	-0.449	-0.281
Pct Unemployed	-0.379	-0.476	-0.490	-0.535	-0.452	-0.478
Median Home Value	0.873	0.886	0.864	0.726	0.922	0.880
Pct Less than $10,000	-0.482	-0.494	-0.712	-0.683	-0.841	-0.651
Pct $20,000 or More	0.888	0.901	0.842	0.575	0.878	0.886
Median Rent	0.551	0.804	0.613	0.686	0.646	0.610
Pct Under $40	-0.159	-0.360	-0.199	-0.282	-0.356	-0.274
Pct $100 or More	0.540	0.821	0.582	0.738	0.638	0.662
Pct Sound	0.373	0.394	0.380	0.454	0.455	0.240
Pct Deteriorating	-0.416	-0.441	-0.418	-0.477	-0.497	-0.260
Pct Dilapidated	-0.190	-0.173	-0.228	-0.293	-0.363	-0.133
Pct 1.01 or More	-0.444	-0.585	-0.532	-0.517	-0.387	-0.437
Pct Less than 0.50	0.178	0.372	0.563	0.240	0.232	0.239
Median Age (Male)	0.138	0.048	0.201	0.212	0.129	0.128
Pct Under 15	-0.046	-0.016	-0.122	-0.152	-0.130	-0.026
Pct 65 and Over	-0.091	-0.072	0.051	-0.103	-0.037	-0.134
Population Per Household	0.051	0.060	-0.197	0.017	-0.066	-0.053

TABLE 25--Continued

Variable / Factor	Minneapolis-St. Paul 2	Providence-Pawtucket 1	Richmond 1	San Bernadino-Riverside 1	St. Petersburg 2	Tampa 2
Pct 1-2 Person Households	-0.088	-0.067	0.126	-0.199	0.022	-0.036
Pct 6+ Person Households	-0.048	-0.002	-0.329	-0.159	-0.262	-0.201
Pct Women in Labor Force	0.237	-0.567	-0.212	0.151	-0.288	-0.043
Pct One Unit	0.319	0.466	0.075	0.106	-0.035	-0.055
Pct Three or More Units	-0.115	-0.366	0.009	-0.080	0.046	0.102
Median Number of Rooms	0.370	0.523	0.540	0.621	0.366	0.468
Pct 2 Rooms or Less	-0.080	-0.046	-0.046	-0.375	-0.047	-0.011
Pct 7 Rooms or More	-0.736	0.798	0.865	0.340	0.595	0.864
Pct Owner Occupied	0.271	0.440	0.293	0.266	0.205	0.102
Pct Renter Occupied	-0.271	-0.440	-0.293	-0.266	-0.205	-0.102
Pct Built Before 1940	-0.342	-0.380	-0.269	-0.142	-0.238	-0.108
Pct Built 1950-1960	0.271	0.415	0.306	0.299	0.284	0.218
Pct Negro	-0.181	-0.096	-0.324	-0.134	-0.334	-0.108
Pct Other Non-white	-0.108	-0.059	-0.078	-0.031	-0.107	0.154
Pct NBFMP	-0.058	-0.323	0.396	-0.054	0.350	0.073
Pct Foreign Born	-0.174	-0.370	0.273	-0.030	-0.051	-0.150
Pct U.K.	0.403	-0.037	0.189	0.316	0.122	0.321
Pct Ireland	—	0.116	0.477	—	0.202	0.129
Pct Norway	-0.036	—	—	—	—	—
Pct Sweden	-0.069	0.295	—	0.085	0.012	0.148
Pct Germany	-0.218	0.467	0.164	0.177	0.037	0.188
Pct Poland	-0.232	-0.205	0.275	0.105	0.020	0.191
Pct Czechoslovakia	—	—	0.010	—	—	—
Pct Austria	-0.143	—	—	—	—	—
Pct Hungary	—	—	—	—	—	—
Pct U.S.S.R.	0.147	0.420	0.316	0.334	0.349	0.605
Pct Italy	—	-0.203	-0.023	0.012	-0.008	-0.055
Pct Canada	0.256	-0.290	0.196	0.183	0.231	0.085
Pct Mexico	—	—	—	-0.208	—	—

Notes As in Table 8.

TABLE 26

THE FAMILY STATUS AND HOME TYPE FACTORS

Variable / Factor	Ann Arbor 2	Ann Arbor 3	Birmingham 3	Canton 2	Des Moines 2	El Paso 3	Honolulu 2	Honolulu 3
Median Age (Male)	-0.083	0.805	0.378	0.828	0.687	0.813	-0.041	0.824
Pct Under 15	-0.758	-0.493	-0.598	-0.911	-0.887	-0.775	-0.144	-0.507
Pct 65 and Over	0.081	0.744	0.548	0.947	0.794	0.892	-0.066	0.697
Population Per Household	-0.843	-0.401	-0.673	-0.900	-0.904	-0.860	-0.594	-0.451
Pct 1-2 Person Households	0.793	0.539	0.725	0.935	0.940	0.940	0.566	0.555
Pct 6+ Person Households	-0.639	-0.116	-0.356	-0.460	-0.698	0.641	-0.488	-0.287
Pct Women in Labor Force	0.491	0.301	0.551	0.808	0.538	0.691	0.033	0.207
Pct One Unit	-0.961	0.026	-0.900	-0.904	-0.950	-0.546	-0.921	-0.178
Pct Three or More Units	0.939	-0.154	0.905	0.883	0.953	0.481	0.924	0.137
Median Number of Rooms	-0.879	0.378	-0.602	-0.396	-0.751	0.212	-0.828	-0.412
Pct 2 Rooms or Less	0.875	-0.184	0.774	0.756	0.928	0.201	0.629	0.582
Pct 7 Rooms or More	-0.415	0.583	-0.116	0.112	-0.041	0.219	-0.672	0.002
Pct Owner Occupied	-0.948	0.081	-0.731	-0.856	-0.947	-0.278	-0.850	-0.094
Pct Renter Occupied	0.948	-0.081	0.731	0.856	0.947	0.278	0.850	0.094
Pct Built Before 1940	0.578	0.678	0.334	0.745	0.633	0.598	0.069	0.655
Pct Built 1950-1960	-0.512	-0.586	-0.376	-0.684	-0.590	-0.606	-0.235	-0.375
Median School Years	0.238	-0.024	-0.065	-0.332	-0.122	0.203	-0.210	-0.624
Pct Grade School	-0.090	0.095	0.092	0.381	0.149	-0.094	0.103	0.584
Pct College	0.271	-0.087	0.025	-0.077	0.085	0.054	-0.24	-0.171
Pct White Collar	0.112	0.079	0.070	0.051	0.064	0.300	-0.185	-0.330
Pct Blue Collar	-0.092	-0.082	-0.070	-0.024	-0.024	-0.282	0.214	0.339
Median Income: Families	-0.559	0.432	-0.312	-0.472	-0.370	-0.022	-0.723	0.006
Pct Incomes Under $4,000	0.710	-0.172	0.384	0.651	0.627	0.071	0.697	0.041
Pct Incomes $10,000 +	-0.481	0.475	-0.135	-0.197	-0.186	0.075	-0.707	-0.005
Pct Professional	0.148	0.039	0.181	0.091	0.106	0.080	-0.243	-0.201
Pct Managerial	-0.493	0.468	-0.010	-0.026	-0.089	0.263	-0.325	0.064
Pct Clerical	0.420	-0.265	0.051	0.079	0.272	0.326	0.021	-0.505
Pct Sales Workers	-0.123	0.053	-0.009	0.020	-0.154	0.446	0.128	-0.265
Pct Craftsmen	-0.403	-0.178	-0.324	-0.706	-0.049	-0.202	-0.128	0.072
Pct Operatives	-0.255	-0.231	-0.246	-0.152	-0.338	-0.141	0.167	0.055
Pct Service Workers	0.345	0.205	0.231	0.640	0.359	-0.182	0.299	0.265

TABLE 26--Continued

Variable / Factor	Ann Arbor 2	Ann Arbor 3	Birmingham 3	Canton 2	Des Moines 3	El Paso 3	Honolulu 2	Honolulu 3
Pct Laborers	-0.041	-0.043	-0.006	0.084	0.003	-0.284	0.220	0.583
Pct Unemployed	0.076	-0.216	0.062	0.278	0.143	-0.108	0.486	0.034
Median Home Value	-0.074	0.160	0.136	-0.387	-0.193	0.249	-0.173	-0.247
Pct Less than $10,000	-0.049	-0.048	-0.279	0.238	-0.082	-0.234	0.162	0.165
Pct $20,000 or More	-0.202	0.223	-0.059	-0.167	-0.124	0.284	-0.595	-0.165
Median Rent	-0.574	-0.033	-0.064	-0.454	-0.495	-0.052	-0.432	-0.314
Pct Under $40	0.681	0.211	0.018	0.473	0.444	-0.116	0.235	0.850
Pct $100 or More	-0.508	-0.176	-0.083	-0.295	0.372	-0.233	-0.393	-0.215
Pct Sound	-0.262	-0.169	-0.197	-0.149	-0.308	-0.036	-0.204	-0.756
Pct Deteriorating	0.334	0.281	0.122	0.213	0.354	0.117	0.063	0.311
Pct Dilapidated	0.013	-0.125	0.192	-0.041	0.197	0.062	0.247	0.857
Pct 1.01 or More	0.278	-0.582	-0.010	-0.288	-0.442	-0.381	0.189	-0.059
Pct Less than 0.50	-0.107	0.952	-0.044	0.686	0.421	0.676	-0.302	0.052
Pct Negro	0.025	-0.005	-0.004	0.152	0.227	-0.051	0.347	-0.095
Pct Other Non-white	0.792	-0.054	0.492	0.349	0.474	-0.134	-0.201	0.293
Pct NBFMP	0.153	0.248	0.086	0.127	0.101	-0.061	-0.232	0.175
Pct Foreign Born	0.390	0.001	0.362	0.331	0.269	0.153	0.230	0.808
Pct U.K.	-0.055	0.173	-0.107	0.215	0.211	0.371	0.039	0.026
Pct Ireland	—	—	0.304	—	0.499	0.661	0.120	-0.035
PCt Norway	—	—	—	—	0.336	—	—	—
Pct Sweden	—	—	—	—	0.000	—	0.121	-0.040
Pct Germany	-0.190	0.254	0.269	0.199	0.503	0.062	0.116	0.095
Pct Poland	0.416	-0.069	0.012	0.027	—	-0.016	0.080	-0.010
Pct Czechoslovakia	—	—	—	-0.062	—	—	—	—
Pct Austria	-0.081	0.276	-0.084	-0.097	—	—	—	—
Pct Hungary	0.099	0.089	—	-0.084	—	—	—	—
Pct U.S.S.R.	0.409	0.091	0.119	0.124	0.160	0.047	0.210	-0.142
Pct Italy	-0.005	0.108	0.166	-0.115	-0.141	-0.076	-0.012	-0.244
Pct Canada	0.363	-0.150	0.029	—	0.135	-0.063	0.244	-0.148
Pct Mexico	—	—	—	—	—	-0.006	—	—

TABLE 26--Continued

Variable / Factor	Lancaster 2	Minne-apolis-St. Paul 1	Providence-Pawtucket 2	Richmond 4	San Bernadino-Riverside 2	St. Peters-burg 1	St. Peters-burg 3	Tampa 3
Median Age (Male)	0.435	0.512	0.805	0.241	0.896	0.889	-0.341	0.858
Pct Under 15	-0.658	-0.785	-0.868	-0.556	-0.863	-0.871	0.409	-0.935
Pct 65 and Over	0.711	0.656	0.808	0.448	0.920	0.835	-0.452	0.910
Population Per Household	-0.896	-0.855	-0.803	-0.799	-0.938	-0.844	0.492	-0.951
Pct 1-2 Person Households	0.868	0.852	0.850	0.866	0.873	0.833	-0.479	0.970
Pct 6+ Person Households	-0.458	-0.653	-0.694	-0.340	-0.436	-0.886	0.023	0.606
Pct Women In Labor Force	0.618	0.784	0.208	0.125	0.025	-0.738	-0.273	0.542
Pct One Unit	-0.933	-0.852	-0.478	-0.780	-0.504	-0.052	0.975	-0.814
Pct Three or More Units	0.974	0.934	0.567	0.781	0.613	0.045	-0.968	0.761
Median Number of Rooms	-0.777	-0.770	-0.696	-0.715	-0.390	-0.072	0.817	-0.612
Pct 2 Rooms or Less	0.935	0.835	0.871	0.740	0.500	0.208	-0.876	0.761
Pct 7 Rooms or More	-0.228	-0.222	-0.227	0.302	0.070	-0.011	-0.005	-0.007
Pct Owner Occupied	-0.796	-0.889	-0.532	-0.828	-0.525	0.209	0.913	-0.710
Pct Renter Occupied	0.796	0.889	0.532	0.828	0.525	-0.209	-0.913	0.710
Pct Built Before 1940	0.655	0.516	0.559	0.421	0.571	0.100	-0.797	0.780
Pct Built 1950-1960	-0.483	-0.539	-0.394	-0.521	-0.632	-0.075	0.749	-0.747
Median School Years	-0.272	-0.234	-0.152	-0.127	-0.042	0.349	0.260	-0.034
Pct Grade School	0.237	0.305	0.201	0.144	0.144	-0.364	-0.308	0.094
Pct College	-0.023	0.026	-0.017	-0.032	-0.011	0.230	0.084	0.121
Pct White Collar	0.036	-0.019	0.027	0.116	0.186	0.638	0.078	0.052
Pct Blue Collar	0.045	0.029	-0.006	-0.109	-0.173	-0.634	-0.099	-0.141
Median Income: Families	-0.365	-0.447	-0.239	-0.231	-0.073	-0.046	0.404	0.085
Pct Incomes Under $4,000	0.465	0.706	0.383	0.305	0.257	-0.079	-0.471	0.151
Pct Incomes $10,000 +	-0.210	-0.300	-0.120	-0.165	0.087	0.069	0.125	0.340
Pct Professional	0.021	0.110	0.159	0.297	0.235	0.378	0.142	0.233
Pct Managerial	-0.146	-0.311	0.034	-0.078	0.084	0.314	-0.249	-0.228
Pct Clerical	0.238	0.400	-0.067	-0.125	0.107	0.737	0.280	0.198
Pct Sales Workers	0.068	-0.336	-0.029	0.150	-0.028	0.579	0.257	-0.027
Pct Craftsmen	-0.503	-0.628	-0.495	-0.395	-0.201	0.037	0.592	-0.304
Pct Operatives	0.008	-0.072	0.030	-0.205	-0.253	-0.416	0.047	-0.058
Pct Service Workers	0.324	0.602	0.415	0.121	0.184	-0.629	-0.507	0.148

TABLE 26--Continued

Variable	Lancaster	Minne-apolis-St. Paul	Providence-Pawtucket	Richmond	San Bernadino-Riverside	St. Peters-burg	St. Peters-burg	Tampa
Factor	2	1	2	4	2	1	3	3
Pct Laborers	0.358	0.184	0.032	0.019	-0.098	-0.674	-0.140	0.002
Pct Unemployed	-0.015	0.332	0.304	0.077	0.005	-0.147	-0.289	-0.021
Median Home Value	-0.326	-0.235	0.120	-0.084	0.053	0.156	-0.096	-0.163
Pct Less than $10,000	0.246	0.221	-0.117	-0.168	0.027	-0.272	0.075	0.242
Pct $20,000 or More	-0.176	-0.217	-0.003	-0.040	0.010	-0.005	-0.099	-0.086
Median Rent	-0.209	-0.567	-0.305	-0.389	-0.265	0.027	0.438	-0.424
Pct Under $40	0.321	0.593	0.477	0.329	0.107	-0.486	-0.311	0.296
Pct $100 or More	-0.187	-0.473	-0.153	-0.307	-0.296	0.007	0.347	-0.322
Pct Sound	-0.726	-0.427	-0.163	-0.198	-0.008	0.448	0.370	-0.295
Pct Deteriorating	0.685	0.419	0.249	0.156	0.080	-0.347	-0.397	0.358
Pct Dilapidated	0.760	0.338	-0.018	0.231	-0.111	-0.628	-0.292	0.098
Pct 1.01 or More	0.041	-0.268	-0.396	0.049	-0.562	-0.845	-0.164	-0.335
Pct Less than 0.50	0.101	0.164	0.196	0.029	0.807	0.740	0.227	0.289
Pct Negro	-0.045	0.151	0.066	0.084	-0.050	-0.771	-0.305	0.035
Pct Other Non-white	0.032	0.610	0.417	0.175	0.019	0.018	0.052	0.127
Pct NBFMP	0.133	0.188	0.030	0.048	0.102	0.799	0.183	0.100
Pct Foreign Born	0.679	0.449	0.413	0.205	0.197	0.877	-0.113	0.057
Pct U.K.	-0.063	0.086	0.130	0.153	0.572	0.850	-0.021	0.281
Pct Ireland	-0.132	—	0.396	0.071	—	0.571	-0.467	0.554
Pct Norway	—	0.198	—	—	—	—	—	—
Pct Sweden	—	-0.009	-0.046	—	0.346	0.505	0.273	-0.154
Pct Germany	0.125	0.248	-0.099	0.105	0.540	0.829	0.091	0.241
Pct Poland	0.065	-0.041	0.095	0.029	0.011	0.390	0.114	0.059
Pct Czechoslovakia	—	—	—	-0.099	—	—	—	—
Pct Austria	0.585	-0.024	—	—	—	—	—	—
Pct Hungary	—	—	—	—	—	—	—	—
Pct U.S.S.R.	-0.054	0.091	0.156	-0.014	0.251	0.275	-0.066	0.019
Pct Italy	0.308	—	-0.065	0.123	0.063	0.427	0.184	0.040
Pct Canada	-0.018	0.307	0.033	0.130	0.270	0.730	0.108	-0.024
Pct Mexico	—	—	—	—	-0.103	—	—	—

Notes As in Table 8.

TABLE 27
FACTORS IN WHICH RACIAL OR ETHNIC STATUS IS ASSOCIATED WITH SOCIOECONOMIC STATUS

Variable	Birmingham	Canton	El Paso	Lan-caster	Provi-dence-Pawtucket	Richmond	San Berna-dino-Riverside	St. Peters-burg	Tampa
Factor	1	3	1	3	3	2	5	1	1
Pct Negro	0.705	0.827	0.061	0.764	0.807	0.845	0.804	0.771	0.870
Pct Incomes Under $4,000	0.731	0.554	0.794	0.419	0.507	0.667	0.274	0.079	0.651
Pct Service Workers	0.760	0.560	0.169	0.528	0.587	0.833	0.783	0.629	0.786
Pct Laborers	0.369	0.802	0.829	0.473	0.212	0.754	0.393	0.674	0.882
Pct Unemployed	0.725	0.693	0.433	0.193	0.543	0.562	0.622	0.147	0.501
Pct Under $40	0.822	0.387	0.820	0.217	0.252	0.420	0.369	0.486	0.483
Pct Sound	-0.856	-0.794	-0.797	-0.213	-0.741	-0.544	-0.066	-0.448	-0.815
Pct Deteriorating	0.666	0.752	0.806	0.243	0.437	0.616	0.096	0.347	0.689
Pct Dilapidated	0.696	0.772	0.635	0.107	0.858	0.293	0.001	0.628	0.790
Pct 1.01 or More	0.666	0.656	0.838	0.572	0.269	0.615	0.185	0.845	0.684
Pct 0.50 or Less	-0.530	-0.450	-0.287	-0.202	0.058	-0.223	0.064	-0.740	-0.262
Median School Years	-0.750	-0.538	-0.889	-0.216	-0.128	-0.476	-0.285	-0.349	-0.731
Pct Grade School	0.790	0.512	0.919	0.336	0.179	0.441	0.302	0.364	0.703
Pct College	-0.485	-0.285	-0.707	0.013	-0.073	-0.170	-0.221	-0.230	-0.428
Pct White Collar	-0.736	-0.545	-0.793	-0.376	-0.168	-0.519	-0.159	-0.638	-0.722
Pct Blue Collar	0.737	0.548	0.763	0.316	0.166	0.526	0.367	0.634	0.715
Median Income: Families	-0.551	-0.351	-0.577	-0.141	-0.291	-0.220	-0.103	0.046	-0.447
Pct Incomes $10,000 +	-0.334	-0.168	-0.407	0.051	-0.143	-0.138	-0.062	-0.069	-0.264
Pct Professional	-0.444	-0.451	-0.839	-0.163	-0.089	-0.227	-0.120	-0.378	-0.436
Pct Managerial	-0.406	-0.210	-0.364	0.030	-0.109	-0.128	-0.180	-0.314	-0.432
Pct Clerical	-0.809	-0.793	-0.875	-0.836	-0.192	-0.741	-0.393	-0.737	-0.859
Pct Sales Workers	-0.638	-0.545	-0.461	-0.465	-0.193	-0.462	-0.093	-0.579	-0.774
Pct Craftsmen	-0.239	-0.204	0.219	-0.189	-0.045	-0.738	-0.166	-0.037	-0.306
Pct Operatives	0.682	0.274	0.817	0.217	-0.011	0.155	-0.011	0.416	0.463
Median Home Value	-0.424	-0.305	-0.549	0.065	-0.241	-0.294	-0.103	-0.156	-0.321
Pct Less $10,000	0.550	0.596	0.597	0.179	0.107	0.419	0.134	0.272	0.411
Pct $20,000 or More	-0.077	-0.059	-0.068	0.255	-0.023	-0.024	0.006	0.005	-0.021
Median Rent	-0.688	-0.409	-0.885	-0.003	-0.103	-0.420	-0.218	-0.027	-0.433
Pct $100 or More	-0.435	-0.270	-0.728	-0.044	-0.004	-0.302	-0.155	-0.007	-0.377

TABLE 27--Continued

Variable	Birmingham	Canton	El Paso	Lan-caster	Provi-dence-Pawtucket	Richmond	San Berna-dino-Riverside	St. Peters-burg	Tampa
Factor	1	3	1	3	3	2	5	1	1
Median Age (Male)	-0.435	-0.278	-0.307	-0.304	0.045	-0.130	-0.054	-0.889	-0.247
Pct Under 15	0.267	0.306	0.291	0.225	-0.046	0.220	0.076	0.871	0.185
Pct 65 and Over	0.064	-0.187	0.326	-0.238	0.171	0.011	-0.001	-0.835	-0.231
Population Per Household	0.298	0.387	0.386	0.349	-0.139	0.274	-0.035	0.844	0.214
Pct 1-2 Person Households	-0.019	-0.240	0.083	-0.179	0.177	-0.012	0.072	-0.833	-0.043
Pct 6+ Person Households	0.509	0.743	0.675	0.610	0.122	0.640	-0.028	0.886	0.575
Pct Women in Labor Force	-0.073	-0.089	0.102	0.004	-0.216	0.038	-0.015	0.738	0.476
Pct One Unit	-0.069	-0.127	-0.413	0.050	-0.130	-0.112	-0.055	0.052	-0.229
Pct Three or More Units	-0.008	0.186	0.396	-0.043	0.138	-0.020	0.181	-0.045	0.163
Median Number of Rooms	-0.588	-0.261	-0.654	0.120	-0.218	-0.102	-0.226	0.072	-0.212
Pct 2 Rooms or Less	0.459	0.258	-0.690	0.010	0.120	0.075	0.272	-0.208	0.152
Pct 7 Rooms or More	-0.295	0.034	-0.203	0.312	-0.076	0.055	-0.138	0.011	-0.122
Pct Owner Occupied	-0.470	-0.314	-0.320	-0.133	-0.276	-0.347	-0.280	-0.209	-0.474
Pct Renter Occupied	0.470	0.314	0.320	0.133	0.276	0.347	0.280	0.209	0.474
Pct Built Before 1940	0.447	0.166	0.591	0.099	0.177	0.461	0.143	-0.100	0.369
Pct Built 1950-1960	-0.466	-0.156	-0.698	-0.066	-0.164	-0.371	-0.080	0.075	-0.346
Pct Other Non-white	-0.113	0.382	-0.757	0.012	0.607	-0.002	0.046	-0.018	-0.090
Pct NBFMP	-0.343	-0.384	0.912	-0.159	-0.351	-0.373	-0.137	-0.799	-0.224
Pct Foreign Born	-0.292	0.203	0.769	-0.057	-0.045	-0.182	-0.116	-0.877	0.021
Pct U.K.	-0.332	-0.598	-0.585	-0.366	-0.246	-0.162	-0.324	-0.850	-0.727
Pct Ireland	-0.312	—	-0.338	-0.078	0.050	-0.438	—	-0.571	-0.464
Pct Norway	—	—	—	—	—	—	—	—	—
Pct Sweden	—	—	—	—	-0.121	—	-0.249	-0.505	-0.370
Pct Germany	-0.402	-0.674	-0.822	-0.032	-0.018	-0.241	-0.167	-0.829	-0.681
Pct Poland	-0.096	-0.016	-0.339	-0.353	0.223	-0.246	-0.191	-0.390	0.385
Pct Czechoslovakia	—	-0.116	—	—	—	-0.569	—	—	—
Pct Austria	-0.141	-0.203	—	0.407	—	—	—	—	—
Pct Hungary	—	0.140	—	—	—	—	—	—	—
Pct U.S.S.R.	0.015	-0.116	-0.052	0.134	0.174	-0.123	-0.155	-0.275	-0.040
Pct Italy	-0.114	0.236	-0.792	-0.167	-0.128	-0.159	-0.082	-0.427	0.117
Pct Canada	-0.335	—	-0.765	0.146	-0.240	-0.099	-0.196	-0.730	-0.612
Pct Mexico	—	—	0.907	—	—	—	0.043	—	—

Notes As in Table 8.

TABLE 28

FACTOR STRUCTURES OF URBANIZED AREAS
IN JOINT POPULATION AND HOUSING ANALYSES

Urbanized Area	A joint socioeconomic status and home value/ rent factor	A racial status factor closely associated with socioeconomic status and housing condition	A racial status factor not closely associated with socioeconomic status and housing condition	A joint family status and home type factor	Separate family status and home type factors
	TYPE OF FACTOR STRUCTURE				
Ann Arbor	1		1	1	
Birmingham	1	1		1	
Canton	1	1		1	
Des Moines	1		1	1	
El Paso	1	1			1
Honolulu	1		1		1
Lancaster	1	1		1	
Minneapolis-St. Paul	1		1	1	
Providence-Pawtucket	1	1		1	
Richmond	1	1		1	
San Bernadino-Riverside	1	1		1	
St. Petersburg	1	1			1
Tampa	1	1		1	

and housing characteristics to see whether the areal associations revealed in the joint population and housing analyses are present in the aggregate population of households in our sample cities. The association of family type and home type will be investigated in detail in Chapter VII so here we concentrate on the association of socioeconomic characteristics and housing value and rent levels,

TABLE 29

CORRELATIONS BETWEEN RACIAL STATUS AND HOUSING CONDITION

Urbanized Area	Per Cent Sound	Per Cent Deterior-ating	Per Cent Dilapi-dated	Standard Error[a]
Correlations with Per Cent Negro				
Ann Arbor	-0.607	0.471	0.659	0.162
Birmingham	-0.712	0.577	0.554	0.105
Canton	-0.733	0.709	0.674	0.139
Des Moines	-0.621	0.632	0.517	0.137
El Paso	-0.156	0.219	0.005	0.152
Honolulu	0.163	-0.338	0.015	0.113
Lancaster	-0.248	0.282	0.125	0.209
Minneapolis-St. Paul	-0.247	0.268	0.142	0.056
Providence-Pawtucket	-0.551	0.302	0.669	0.084
Richmond	-0.664	0.729	0.400	0.112
San Bernadino-Riverside	-0.291	0.297	0.201	0.096
St. Petersburg	-0.732	0.668	0.798	0.112
Tampa	-0.714	0.585	0.723	0.123
Correlations with Per Cent Mexican				
El Paso	-0.848	0.829	0.708	0.152
San Bernadino-Riverside	-0.623	0.546	0.578	0.096

Notes

[a]Standard error of the correlation coefficient. As a rough rule of thumb, if the observed coefficient is 2x the standard error overlaps zero then the coefficient cannot be regarded as statistically significant at the 95 per cent level.

and on the association of racial status and housing condition.

The Association of Household Income and Housing Unit Cost

Ideally, one would want to examine the association between household income and the cost to the household of occupying its home. This is not possible directly because it is difficult to assess the cost of occupying an owned home. A question on the cost of mortgage repayments, maintenance expenses and property taxes was not included in the population and housing census. However, it is possible to construct tables for SMSAs of household income classified by housing value of owner occupied units or monthly rental of renter occupied units. Table 30 gives the distribution of households by housing value and rental classes. The percentages in the tables summ across the rows to yield totals of 100 per cent in each of five income classes. The association between income and price of housing is clear in all SMSAs.

The probability of renting or owning a house varies considerably with income irrespective of the overall mix of rental and owned housing in a housing market. The lower a household's income, the greater chance that it will occupy a rented rather than an owned dwelling. The last two columns of the SMSA sub-tables in Table 30 reveal that there are virtually no exceptions to this generalization. Between 80 and 90 per cent of households with incomes over $10,000 in 1959 owned their homes in the sample cities except in predominantly renter Honolulu where only 68.9 per cent do. In contrast, much lower proportions of the poorest households own their own home, though in many SMSAs (Canton, Des Moines, Lancaster, San Bernadino-Riverside and Tampa-St. Petersburg) a majority of those with incomes less than $3,000 do own their own homes. However, in spatial terms the pattern of housing tenure is associated more closely with the pattern of family status because the relationship between income and tenure is not as strong as that between family type and tenure.

Within each of the major sectors of the housing market, the relationship between income and housing cost is stronger than that between income and tenure. The average pattern of increasing income level associated with increasing rental level or home value is characteristic of all the sample cities. There are considerable

TABLE 30

THE PERCENTAGE DISTRIBUTION OF HOUSING EXPENDITURE BY INCOME GROUP FOR 12 SMSAS, 1960

ANN ARBOR N = 47,272

Household Income Category	Housing Expenditure: Gross Rent Per Month						
	No Cash Rent	Less than $40	$40-$59	$60-$79	$80-$119	$120 or More	Total
Less than $3,000	6.4	6.6	13.1	20.5	39.0	14.5	100.0
$3,000 - $4,999	4.7	2.8	7.2	20.8	52.4	12.1	100.0
$5,000 - $6,999	3.3	1.5	5.8	15.6	53.7	20.1	100.0
$7,000 - $9,999	4.5	0.6	4.2	9.7	49.0	32.0	100.0
$10,000 or More	3.7	0.9	4.6	8.0	36.7	46.1	100.0
Total	4.9	3.3	8.2	17.1	46.6	20.0	100.0

Household Income Category	Housing Expenditure: Value					Tenure	
	Less than $7,500	$7,500-$12,400	$12,500-$19,900	$20,000 or More	Total	Renter	Owner
Less than $3,000	17.2	37.5	33.3	11.9	100.0	57.7	42.3
$3,000 - $4,999	11.8	38.4	40.0	9.8	100.0	52.0	48.0
$5,000 - $6,999	6.3	34.9	48.8	10.0	100.0	36.5	63.5
$7,000 - $9,999	2.7	24.8	53.5	19.0	100.0	29.7	70.3
$10,000 or More	1.5	10.4	37.5	50.4	100.0	13.9	86.1
Total	5.7	25.6	44.2	24.6	100.0	36.0	64.0

BIRMINGHAM N = 181,774

Household Income Category	Housing Expenditure: Gross Rent Per Month						
	No Cash Rent	Less than $40	$40-$59	$60-$79	$80-$119	$120 or More	Total
Less than $3,000	6.5	46.2	32.6	10.9	3.5	0.4	100.0
$3,000 - $4,999	0.4	17.5	39.7	26.1	11.8	1.0	100.0
$5,000 - $6,999	4.4	9.5	27.9	33.3	22.4	2.4	100.0
$7,000 - $9,999	4.6	5.6	17.1	33.0	34.0	5.6	100.0
$10,000 or More	4.1	2.2	10.8	21.3	42.6	18.9	100.0
Total	5.3	28.1	31.8	20.5	12.5	1.9	100.0

Household Income Category	Housing Expenditure: Value					Tenure	
	Less than $7,500	$7,500-$12,400	$12,500-$19,900	$20,000 or More	Total	Renter	Owner
Less than $3,000	66.2	24.5	7.1	2.1	100.0	56.3	43.7
$3,000 - $4,999	49.9	36.5	11.8	1.8	100.0	46.5	53.5
$5,000 - $6,999	30.4	43.7	22.5	3.5	100.0	29.3	70.7
$7,000 - $9,999	17.6	38.6	36.0	8.9	100.0	19.9	80.1
$10,000 or More	8.3	22.4	34.0	35.3	100.0	11.8	88.2
Total	35.6	33.7	21.6	9.2	100.0	38.3	61.7

TABLE 30--Continued

CANTON N = 99,306

Household Income Category	Housing Expenditure: Gross Rent Per Month						
	No Cash Rent	Less than $40	$40-$59	$60-$79	$80-$119	$120 or More	Total
Less than $3,000	8.3	15.3	33.1	29.4	12.4	1.4	100.0
$3,000 - $4,999	5.5	6.0	26.0	37.9	22.5	2.1	100.0
$5,000 - $6,999	5.9	2.9	16.4	36.9	35.7	3.2	100.0
$7,000 - $9,999	4.4	2.5	13.4	29.8	42.8	7.1	100.0
$10,000 or More	5.2	1.2	9.4	20.1	41.9	22.2	100.0
Total	6.3	7.3	23.2	33.0	26.3	3.9	100.00

Household Income Category	Housing Expenditure: Value					Tenure	
	Less than $7,500	$7,500-$12,400	$12,500-$19,900	$20,000 or More	Total	Rent-er	Own-er
Less than $3,000	33.5	39.9	20.8	4.4	100.0	38.5	61.5
$3,000 - $4,999	28.7	40.7	24.8	5.8	100.0	37.2	62.8
$5,000 - $6,999	16.7	38.7	37.2	7.4	100.0	23.7	76.3
$7,000 - $9,999	10.8	32.2	43.0	14.0	100.0	15.5	85.0
$10,000 or More	6.5	21.9	37.0	34.5	100.0	10.7	89.3
Total	18.1	34.8	34.3	12.9	100.0	25.8	74.2

DES MOINES N = 84,352

Household Income Category	Housing Expenditure: Gross Rent Per Month						
	No Cash Rent	Less than $40	$40-$59	$60-$79	$80-$119	$120 or More	Total
Less than $3,000	6.9	16.8	32.9	24.5	15.5	3.4	100.0
$3,000 - $4,999	5.4	6.7	21.2	33.9	27.8	5.1	100.0
$5,000 - $6,999	4.0	3.2	12.6	28.4	39.1	12.8	100.0
$7,000 - $9,999	3.5	2.6	7.1	21.0	42.3	23.4	100.0
$10,000 or More	8.3	2.4	4.4	10.6	34.6	39.8	100.0
Total	5.6	9.0	21.3	26.6	27.6	9.9	

Household Income Category	Housing Expenditure: Value					Tenure	
	Less than $7,500	$7,500-$12,400	$12,500-$19,900	$20,000 or More	Total	Rent-er	Own-er
Less than $3,000	40.3	37.3	18.5	3.8	100.0	49.2	50.8
$3,000 - $4,999	30.8	43.8	21.0	4.5	100.0	41.8	58.2
$5,000 - $6,999	17.3	43.0	35.1	4.6	100.0	25.1	74.9
$7,000 - $9,999	10.0	32.7	46.8	10.5	100.0	15.2	84.8
$10,000 or More	4.5	19.4	48.3	27.7	100.0	11.1	88.9
Total	18.2	35.0	35.1	11.7	100.0	29.3	70.8

TABLE 30--Continued

EL PASO N = 78,270

Household Income Category	Housing Expenditure: Gross Rent Per Month						
	No Cash Rent	Less than $40	$40-$59	$60-$79	$80-$119	$120 or More	Total
Less than $3,000	8.9	46.6	18.9	13.5	10.8	1.4	100.0
$3,000 - $4,999	5.4	18.8	21.9	20.1	30.5	3.4	100.0
$5,000 - $6,999	4.5	8.8	14.6	17.5	44.8	9.9	100.0
$7,000 - $9,999	4.7	6.4	8.3	12.3	49.4	18.9	100.0
$10,000 or More	5.1	3.3	5.2	8.1	38.6	38.7	100.0
Total	6.6	26.7	17.6	15.8	27.1	6.5	100.0

Household Income Category	Housing Expenditure: Value					Tenure	
	Less than $7,500	$7,500-$12,400	$12,500-$19,900	$20,000 or More	Total	Rent-er	Own-er
Less than $3,000	36.5	44.3	15.4	3.9	100.0	65.0	35.0
$3,000 - $4,999	21.4	56.9	19.2	2.5	100.0	49.7	50.3
$5,000 - $6,999	10.1	56.9	29.7	3.3	100.0	36.1	63.9
$7,000 - $9,999	5.9	42.4	44.9	6.9	100.0	24.9	75.1
$10,000 or More	2.3	22.4	44.8	30.5	100.0	14.6	85.4
Total	14.0	45.2	31.6	9.1	100.0	43.6	56.4

HONOLULU N = 117,856

Household Income Category	Housing Expenditure: Gross Rent Per Month						
	No Cash Rent	Less than $40	$40-$59	$60-$79	$80-$119	$120 or More	Total
Less than $3,000	8.6	19.8	18.7	21.9	24.5	6.6	100.0
$3,000 - $4,999	6.1	10.7	16.2	24.5	33.3	9.2	100.0
$5,000 - $6,999	7.0	5.8	15.3	23.5	38.7	10.0	100.0
$7,000 - $9,999	7.0	4.6	13.3	18.3	37.7	19.2	100.0
$10,000 or More	6.7	3.2	8.9	11.6	30.9	38.9	100.0
Total	7.1	9.6	15.2	21.1	33.1	13.9	100.0

Household Income Category	Housing Expenditure: Value					Tenure	
	Less than $7,500	$7,500-$12,400	$12,500-$19,900	$20,000 or More	Total	Rent-er	Own-er
Less than $3,000	10.7	12.1	28.7	48.5	100.0	81.4	18.6
$3,000 - $4,999	7.3	12.8	33.5	46.5	100.0	80.0	20.0
$5,000 - $6,999	3.8	8.0	33.2	55.1	100.0	65.3	34.7
$7,000 - $9,999	2.5	5.6	29.0	62.9	100.0	47.6	52.4
$10,000 or More	1.4	2.7	15.3	80.6	100.0	30.1	68.9
Total	3.3	6.1	24.9	65.7	100.0	59.4	40.6

TABLE 30--Continued

LANCASTER N = 80,487

Household Income Category	Housing Expenditure: Gross Rent Per Month						
	No Cash Rent	Less than $40	$40-$59	$60-$79	$80-$119	$120 or More	Total
Less than $3,000	11.9	17.7	37.6	23.9	7.9	1.0	100.0
$3,000 - $4,999	7.1	6.0	30.9	38.3	16.2	1.5	100.0
$5,000 - $6,999	5.4	2.3	19.6	35.7	30.4	6.5	100.0
$7,000 - $9,999	6.3	3.6	20.4	39.1	27.6	3.0	100.0
$10,000 or More	9.7	3.1	13.6	31.2	30.1	12.3	100.0
Total	8.0	7.6	27.4	34.2	20.0	3.0	100.0

Household Income Category	Housing Expenditure: Value					Tenure	
	Less than $7,500	$7,500-$12,400	$12,500-$19,900	$20,000 or More	Total	Renter	Owner
Less than $3,000	42.9	36.5	16.3	4.4	100.0	40.2	59.8
$3,000 - $4,999	32.5	41.8	22.3	3.5	100.0	43.4	56.6
$5,000 - $6,999	23.3	40.4	30.8	5.6	100.0	31.1	68.9
$7,000 - $9,999	16.7	34.9	38.4	10.0	100.0	23.5	76.5
$10,000 or More	8.1	23.7	32.4	35.7	100.0	13.3	88.7
Total	24.2	36.0	28.9	10.9	100.0	32.3	67.7

MINNEAPOLIS-ST. PAUL N = 440,805

Household Income Category	Housing Expenditure: Gross Rent Per Month						
	No Cash Rent	Less than $40	$40-$59	$60-$79	$80-$119	$120 or More	Total
Less than $3,000	4.9	21.0	24.1	24.2	20.9	4.9	100.0
$3,000 - $4,999	3.5	7.2	17.2	30.7	34.2	7.2	100.0
$5,000 - $6,999	3.8	3.5	10.7	27.7	43.5	10.8	100.0
$7,000 - $9,999	3.5	1.6	7.3	22.2	47.7	17.7	100.0
$10,000 or More	4.1	0.9	4.7	12.8	40.9	36.8	100.0
Total	4.0	9.5	15.8	25.7	34.4	10.5	100.0

Household Income Category	Housing Expenditure: Value					Tenure	
	Less than $7,500	$7,500-$12,400	$12,500-$19,900	$20,000 or More	Total	Renter	Owner
Less than $3,000	15.1	42.9	34.6	7.6	100.0	53.7	46.3
$3,000 - $4,999	9.6	40.0	43.7	6.8	100.0	51.0	49.0
$5,000 - $6,999	4.8	31.0	56.8	7.4	100.0	28.6	71.4
$7,000 - $9,999	2.4	20.6	62.3	14.7	100.0	18.9	80.1
$10,000 or More	1.3	12.0	43.9	42.8	100.0	11.5	88.5
Total	4.9	25.9	51.6	17.6	100.0	31.8	68.2

TABLE 30--Continued

PROVIDENCE-PAWTUCKET N = 247,822

Household Income Category	Housing Expenditure: Gross Rent Per Month						
	No Cash Rent	Less than $40	$40-$59	$60-$79	$80-$119	$120 or More	Total
Less than $3,000	4.3	24.6	39.6	22.3	8.3	0.9	100.0
$3,000 - $4,999	3.4	8.5	36.8	35.4	14.8	1.1	100.0
$5,000 - $6,999	3.2	4.6	32.2	38.5	19.8	1.7	100.0
$7,000 - $9,999	2.8	3.8	25.6	36.1	27.3	4.3	100.0
$10,000 or More	5.3	3.2	15.0	28.2	32.4	15.6	100.0
Total	3.7	12.2	34.5	31.6	16.0	2.2	100.0

Household Income Category	Housing Expenditure: Value					Tenure	
	Less than $7,500	$7,500-$12,400	$12,500-$19,900	$20,000 or More	Total	Renter	Owner
Less than $3,000	23.4	44.5	26.1	6.0	100.0	62.1	37.9
$3,000 - $4,999	17.5	49.1	29.2	4.2	100.0	54.5	45.5
$5,000 - $6,999	9.7	48.3	37.5	4.5	100.0	41.0	59.0
$7,000 - $9,999	6.1	40.1	45.5	8.3	100.0	29.1	70.9
$10,000 or More	3.6	24.0	41.4	31.0	100.0	17.7	82.3
Total	11.1	41.8	37.1	10.1	100.0	44.6	55.4

RICHMOND N = 118,896

Household Income Category	Housing Expenditure: Gross Rent Per Month						
	No Cash Rent	Less than $40	$40-$59	$60-$79	$80-$119	$120 or More	Total
Less than $3,000	5.1	22.8	30.3	24.6	15.2	2.1	100.0
$3,000 - $4,999	4.3	6.0	21.8	32.9	31.6	3.4	100.0
$5,000 - $6,999	2.6	3.0	11.0	28.1	47.9	7.4	100.0
$7,000 - $9,999	2.9	1.4	6.7	21.4	52.0	15.6	100.0
$10,000 or More	4.0	0.0	5.0	14.2	46.1	30.8	100.0
Total	4.1	10.8	20.3	26.6	31.7	6.6	100.0

Household Income Category	Housing Expenditure: Value					Tenure	
	Less than $7,500	$7,500-$12,400	$12,500-$19,900	$20,000 or More	Total	Renter	Owner
Less than $3,000	48.3	32.6	14.0	5.1	100.0	60.6	39.4
$3,000 - $4,999	33.2	44.4	18.8	3.6	100.0	51.5	48.5
$5,000 - $6,999	18.8	45.4	30.9	5.0	100.0	31.2	68.8
$7,000 - $9,999	9.9	38.9	41.0	10.3	100.0	22.0	78.0
$10,000 or More	4.4	19.1	35.6	41.0	100.0	13.9	86.1
Total	19.6	36.2	30.4	13.8	100.0	37.7	62.3

TABLE 30--Continued

SAN BERNADINO-RIVERSIDE-ONTARIO N = 245,284

Housing Income Category	Housing Expenditure: Gross Rent Per Month						
	No Cash Rent	Less than $40	$40-$59	$60-$79	$80-$119	$120 or More	Total
Less than $3,000	10.6	14.2	29.5	27.9	15.3	2.6	100.0
$3,000 - $4,999	7.3	5.2	18.4	33.2	32.6	3.3	100.0
$5,000 - $6,999	5.8	3.8	13.7	29.0	41.9	5.8	100.0
$7,000 - $9,999	4.4	2.5	8.0	22.1	50.0	13.1	100.0
$10,000 or More	5.8	2.6	5.6	15.1	44.5	26.4	100.0
Total	7.6	7.4	19.1	28.1	31.6	6.2	100.0

Housing Income Category	Housing Expenditure: Value					Tenure	
	Less than $7,500	$7,500-$12,400	$12,500-$19,900	$20,000 or More	Total	Renter	Owner
Less than $3,000	29.7	42.0	20.2	8.0	100.0	42.6	57.4
$3,000 - $4,999	18.6	48.3	26.8	6.3	100.0	45.0	55.0
$5,000 - $6,999	11.5	45.6	36.3	6.7	100.0	31.8	68.2
$7,000 - $9,999	5.5	37.3	46.4	10.8	100.0	22.2	77.8
$10,000 or More	2.7	22.6	43.9	30.8	100.0	14.7	85.3
Total	13.4	39.4	35.2	12.1	100.0	33.2	66.8

TAMPA-ST. PETERSBURG N = 264,983

Housing Income Category	Housing Expenditure: Gross Rent Per Month						
	No Cash Rent	Less than $40	$40-$59	$60-$79	$80-$119	$120 or More	Total
Less than $3,000	6.8	19.1	30.3	26.0	14.7	3.1	100.0
$3,000 - $4,999	6.0	6.6	22.7	33.6	26.7	4.5	100.0
$5,000 - $6,999	6.1	3.2	15.2	30.2	35.7	9.6	100.0
$7,000 - $9,999	6.9	2.0	9.8	23.5	38.4	19.5	100.0
$10,000 or More	7.0	1.7	8.0	14.4	32.4	36.5	100.0
Total	6.5	12.1	24.3	28.0	22.7	6.4	100.0

Housing Income Category	Housing Expenditure: Value					Tenure	
	Less Than $7,500	$7,500-$12,400	$12,500-$19,900	$20,000 or More	Total	Renter	Owner
Less than $3,000	35.6	40.8	19.3	4.3	100.0	34.6	65.4
$3,000 - $4,999	26.0	44.3	25.7	4.1	100.0	28.8	71.2
$5,000 - $6,999	18.5	42.2	32.7	6.6	100.0	19.6	80.5
$7,000 - $9,999	12.5	36.4	40.1	11.0	100.0	14.2	85.8
$10,000 or More	5.7	18.9	37.6	37.9	100.0	10.5	89.5
Total	23.4	38.9	28.4	9.3	100.0	26.2	74.8

Notes [a] N refers to the number of housing units in an SMSA.

variations from city to city, however, in the distribution of households within income groups across the housing expenditure spectrum. In Ann Arbor the price levels of housing are high relative to income: some 53.5 per cent of households with less than $3,000 in income who rent a home pay rents of $80 a month or more whereas in Birmingham only 3.9 per cent pay rents of this magnitude. The other cities range between these two extremes of price level. For their higher rents the residents of Ann Arbor get sounder and roomier housing with more basic facilities, running hot water and baths. However, it is cheaper to live in a metropolis like Birmingham if one is poor.

Within the owner occupied sector, the relationship between income and the price of housing occupied is probably even stronger than in the rental market (Table 30). In most SMSAs the largest proportion of wealthy households live in property in the highest value range, and the largest proportion of poor households live in property in the lowest or next to lowest housing value class.

The link between income and housing expenditure is one of the main factors that serves to explain the association between the socioeconomic status of the population and the character of the housing stock. The relationship could be viewed in a different way from that presented in Table 30: we could have computed instead the distribution of incomes of households within any one housing expenditure category.

The distribution of household income within housing expenditure categories is summarized in graphical form in Figures 7 and 8. The median income of households living in housing of a particular rent or value category is plotted against the mid-point of that rent or value category. These graphs show the same relationships as the Table 30 sub-tables but from the housing unit rather than the household point of view. With one or two minor exceptions, the higher the rental or value category is along the money scale, the median income of households occupying that category of housing. The close relationship between housing expenditure and household income revealed in these graphs strongly supports the view that the character of the housing in a residential area "selects" the population mix living in that area. If housing units in different expenditure categories are spatially separated to a high degree in the metropolis, then we should expect, because of the association revealed in the graphs and prior table, to observe a high degree of residential segregation between households in income categories.

The Association of Color and Housing Condition

The "ecological" associations between racial status and housing condition discussed earlier (Table 29) are shown in Table 31 to be characteristic of an aggregate population of households occupying housing units of various conditions. The non-white/white differentials in Table 31, show that in relative terms from 3 to 8 times as many non-white headed households occupy dilapidated homes as do white headed households in those metropolitan areas in which Negroes make up at least 80 per cent of the non-white population, and where there is not a substantial Mexican-American minority. From 2 to 5 times as high a proportion of non-white households occupy deteriorating dwellings as do white households, and only 0.4 to 0.8 as many occupy sound housing units. Further careful analysis would be needed to establish whether these differentials between the races in quality of housing occupied can be ascribed wholly to socioeconomic differences between the races or whether Negro families suffer an extra element of disadvantage in the housing market over and above the disadvantage accumulated in schooling, jobs and income (Duncan, 1969).

In El Paso and San Bernadino-Riverside-Ontario live a substantial proportion of Mexican-Americans. In El Paso the quality of the housing they occupy compares less favorably with that headed by

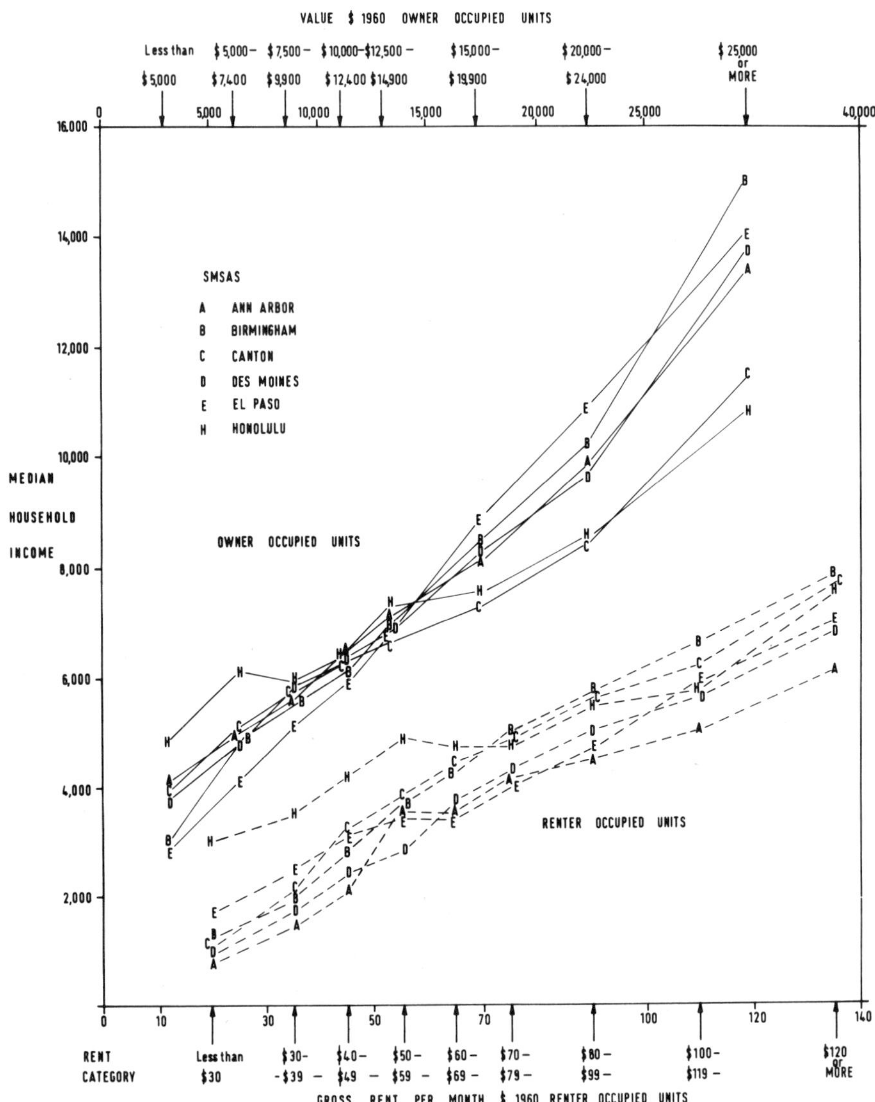

Fig. 7.--Median Incomes of Households Occupying Housing Units of Varying Rent and Varying Value, 6 SMSAs, 1960

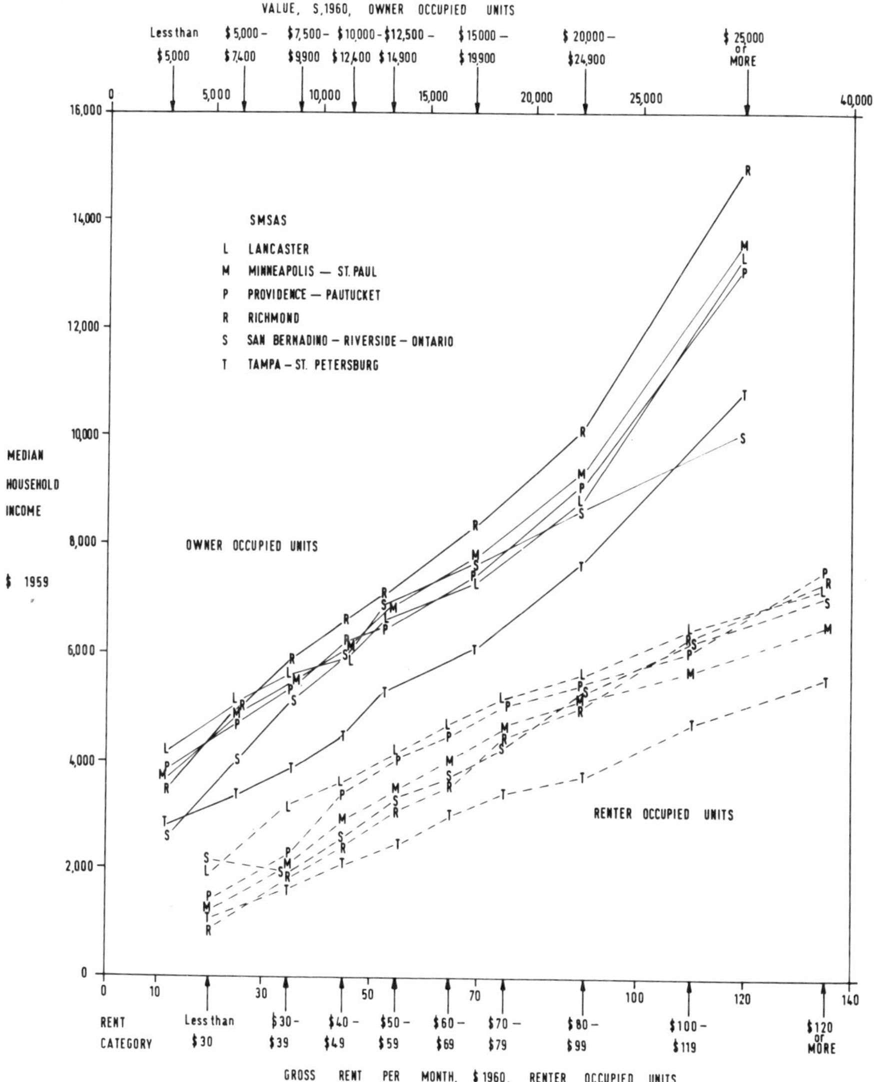

Fig. 8.--Median Incomes of Households Occupying Housing Units of Varying Rent and Varying Value, 6 SMSAs, 1960

TABLE 31

NON-WHITE/WHITE DIFFERENTIALS IN HOUSING CONDITION, 11 SMSAS, 1960

Variable	Ann Arbor	Birmingham	Canton	Des Moines	El Paso	Honolulu
Per Cent, White Households[a]						
Sound	87.96	84.35	83.99	81.31	80.28	86.09
Deteriorating	9.71	11.93	12.91	14.48	13.30	9.28
Dilapidated	2.35	3.72	3.41	4.20	6.42	4.63
	100.00	100.00	100.00	100.00	100.00	100.00
Per Cent, Non-white Households[b]						
Sound	64.83	45.33	35.79	47.32	76.76	71.44
Deteriorating	21.45	32.86	43.35	36.61	16.52	17.83
Dilapidated	13.71	21.81	20.85	16.08	6.72	10.72
	100.00	100.00	100.00	100.00	100.00	100.00
Non-white/white Differentials						
Sound	0.737	0.587	0.426	0.582	0.956	0.830
Deteriorating	2.211	2.754	3.440	2.528	1.242	1.929
Dilapidated	5.833	5.863	6.114	3.828	1.047	2.315

Variable	Minneapolis-St. Paul	Providence-Pawtucket	Richmond	San Bernadino-Riverside	Tampa-St. Petersburg
Per Cent, White Households[a]					
Sound	88.47	87.52	92.29	87.86	89.67
Deteriorating	9.00	10.11	5.90	9.51	7.96
Dilapidated	2.53	2.37	1.81	2.63	2.36
	100.00	100.00	100.00	100.00	100.00
Per Cent, Non-white Households[b]					
Sound	64.92	55.98	63.11	67.17	52.56
Deteriorating	25.97	25.91	25.86	19.86	28.85
Dilapidated	9.21	18.12	11.02	12.98	18.58
	100.00	100.00	100.00	100.00	100.00
Non-white/white Differentials					
Sound	0.734	0.640	0.684	0.765	0.586
Deteriorating	2.874	2.563	4.381	2.089	3.624
Dilapidated	3.640	7.646	6.088	4.928	7.873

Notes

[a]These are occupied housing units with a white head of household plus vacant housing units since they must be calculated as a residual:

Total housing units minus housing units with a non-white head equals white occupied housing units plus vacant units.

[b]The non-white distributions refer to occupied housing units with a non-white head of household.

[c]Non-whites in the case of Honolulu are mainly Orientals.

TABLE 32

NON-WHITE AND WHITE, SPANISH SURNAME/WHITE, NON-SPANISH SURNAME DIFFERNETIALS IN HOUSING CONDITION, 2 SMSAS, 1960

Variable	El Paso	San Bernadino-Riverside-Ontario
Per Cent, White Non-Spanish Surname Households[a]		
Sound	89.44	89.00
Deteriorating	8.44	8.75
Dilapidated	2.11	2.25
	100.00	100.00
Per Cent, Non-white Households		
Sound	76.76	67.17
Deteriorating	16.52	19.86
Dilapidated	6.72	12.98
	100.00	100.00
Per Cent, White, Spanish Surname Households		
Sound	63.16	72.65
Deteriorating	22.37	19.61
Dilapidated	14.47	7.73
	100.00	100.00
Non-white/White, Non-Spanish Differentials		
Sound	0.858	0.755
Deteriorating	1.957	2.270
Dilapidated	3.185	5.769
White, Spanish Surname/White Non-Spanish Surname Differentials		
Sound	0.706	0.816
Deteriorating	2.650	2.241
Dilapidated	6.858	3.436

Notes

[a]These are cooupied housing units with a white head of household with a Non-Spanish surname plus vacant housing units since they must be calculated as a residual form the Tables.

[b]Source for Tables 31 and 32: U.S. Bureau of the Census (1962b).

a white person with a non-Spanish surname ("Anglo" families) than does the quality of housing occupied by households with non-white heads (Table 32). In San Bernadino-Riverside-Ontario Mexican-American households are slightly better off than non-whites.

Conclusions

In this chapter we have examined the factorial dimensions that characterize the housing attributes of residential areas within a sample of 13 urbanized areas. A fairly clear set of factors, of housing type, size and tenure; of home value and rent; of housing condition; and of housing age emerged from the factor analyses. These factors appeared to parallel those of family status, socioeconomic status and race and resources type factors in the population variable factor analyses.

This supposition was confirmed in the joint housing and population factor analysis. The socioeconomic status and home value/rent factor was the most general, characterizing all the urbanized areas studied. The very close links between household income, a diagnostic set of variables in the population variable factor of socioeconomic status (the main factor), and housing value/rent, a diagnostic set of variables in the home value and rent factor were confirmed by an examination of the relevant household contingency tables for the sample SMSAs. Also explored was the close association of housing condition and color which characterized both the "ecological" (factor analyses) and crosstabulation analyses. The disadvantaged position of Negroes in American cities in 1960 was plain to see. Further investigation of this theme of racial disadvantage is reported in Chapter IX.

We now turn from the aspatial analyses of this chapter and the last, and turn our attention to looking at the spatial characteristics of the residential area dimensions that have emerged from the analysis. We do this, with reference to the population characteristics of the residential areas of our sample cities, in Chapters VI, VII and VIII. First, however, we must postpone our spatial analysis for a while to consider how we might construct aggregate indices to measure the position of residential areas on our factorial dimensions that are consistent and comparable across a sample of cities. This we do in Chapter V where factor scores indices derived directly from the analysis are rejected as suffering from too wide a variability in interpretation from city to city, and instead social dimensions are defined that are invariant from one city to another.

CHAPTER V

SOCIAL DIMENSIONS

The Basic Argument

The most obvious way of examining the spatial expression of the patterning of residential areas in America revealed in the factor analyses that are reported in Chapters III and IV would be to plot, on suitable census tract maps of the urbanized areas concerned, the factor scores associated with the most important factors that have been extracted in each analysis. However, as tools with which to examine the spatial manifestation of residential area patterns across a set of cities, factorial dimensions suffer from a number of disadvantages.

The composition of each factor in terms of the loadings of the variables associated strongly with it varies from city to city even for strong and common factors. Consider, for example, the loading of "Median School Years" on the main socioeconomic status factor in the 13 urbanized area analyses (Table 8). The highest loading is 0.963 in Ann Arbor; the 12th highest is 0.785 in Honolulu; but in San Bernadino-Riverside it plummets to 0.492. The loading of "Pct Negro" on this main socioeconomic factor varies from a single positive loading of 0.034 in El Paso to a low of -0.811 in Birmingham. The factors thus differ in their detailed loadings and interpretation, and a map of "socioeconomic status" factor scores for one city would not be strictly comparable to the factor score map for "socioeconomic status" in another.

A second disadvantage of factor scores as indices for evaluating the spatial characteristics of residential dimensions derives from the way in which they are scaled. Factor scores are standardized scores with means of zero, standard deviations of one, and ranges of say +3 to -3 that encompass most of the observations. The standardization is carried out within each factor analysis for each urbanized area factor analysis in our case. They are therefore suitable for examination of the within-urbanized area variation in a dimension, but unsuitable for the examination of between-urbanized area variation. A factor score for a census tract of 2.5 may well reflect a very different median family income level and median school years level in one urbanized area than in another.

This is not to deny the usefulness of the factor analysis carried out in Chapters III and IV. It is essential to know that "socioeconomic status" has very different correlates as a factorial dimension in Southern than in non-Southern cities. But we need a common metrix if we are to evaluate between-city as well as within-city similarities and differences. The same point applies to a consideration of residential patterns at successive points in time, though such an analysis is not pursued here.

Social Dimensions

The comparative and fixed indices that will be used to examine the spatial manifestation of residential patterns we call *Social Dimensions* (to distinguish them from the factorial dimensions of Chapters III and IV). The variables that will enter into these fixed indices are some of those that we have already used in the factor analysis, and, in adopting the combinations of variables that we do, we will be reflecting the covariation of these variables already revealed in the factor analyses. For example, our socioeconomic status index will be made up of measures of education, occupation and income that have been shown to load highly together on the same factor (8 variables in the first 8 rows of Table 8).

In a sense, the creation and use of social dimensions reflects a return to the original methodology of Shevky and Bell (1955) but with certain crucial differences. The social dimensions adopted here are based purely on population information rather than on the mixture of population and housing variables that go to make up the social area indices. They are based on scaling systems that have as their reference points the national distributions of the population on particular attributes. This means that an index defined to range from 0 to 100 will not suddenly produce values of over a hundred when applied to a city different from that on which it was originally based.

A second difference between the social dimensions defined here and the social area indices of Shevky and Bell is in their theoretical underpinning. Whereas Shevky and Bell refer to a broad scheme of societal development and its reflection in urban differentiation, we try, in defining social dimensions, to relate the indices to more particular social processes of learning, working and earning that underly differentiation by socioeconomic status; the life cycle of an individual and of a family that underlies differentiation by family status; and the simple fact of perceived racial classification that underlies differentiation by racial status. The terms we adopt for our social dimensions, very simply, are socioeconomic status, family status and racial status. The statuses refer to the populations of particular areas on scales within defined end points.

The meaning of each of these statuses is considered in more detail in the following pages, measures which have been proposed by previous researchers are described and solutions to the indexing problems posed are outlined.

Socioeconomic Status

In most of the world's societies there is a particular ranking of members of that society. The basis of such hierarchies varies from culture to culture, from country to country, from region to region. In local communities (the rural village, the inner city neighborhood) the basis may be particular leadership traits or peculiar skills that the individual displays. For the purposes of comparative study of larger communities through ascertaining the prestige of individuals or through observing behavior on the local scale, more universal and objective measures that can be replicated across the whole city or across a set of cities are needed.

Although use of more universal measures means adopting a structural definition of social status (what attributes people have) rather than a functional (how do people interact and view each other), these measures do have meaning in the local community in that few such communities in contemporary America are independent of the wider social and economic world.

Berelson and Steiner (1967, Chapter 5) have listed some of the measures that have been used to calibrate social status. Among those listed the following have been used most frequently in the context of American society: ownership of property; income (amount, type and sources); consumption patterns and life styles; occupation or skill and achievement in it; education, learning and wisdom. Most indices of socioeconomic status are made up of one or more of these variables.

Race is another index of social status mentioned in the Berelson and Steiner list. It has functioned as such a differentiator to a greater or lesser degree in various regions at various times in the U.S. It was used by Hoyt as one component of residential area status in his _Structure and Growth of Residential Neighborhoods_. Generally, however, investigators have avoided such prejudiced interpretation of the meaning of race.

Area Based Indices of Socioeconomic Status

One varied group of indices that have been employed apply only to the given residential areas into which the city has been divided up for the purposes of study. These measures are difficult to use with areal units at a different scale or with population groups not areally defined. The "reputational" method has been used by Congalton (1961) in order to assess the social status of the suburbs of Sydney. Some 143 respondents were asked to sort 368 suburbs of Sydney into seven groups according to their perceived social prestige. Highest standing suburbs were scored 1, lowest 7. A median score was interpolated for each suburb and a ranking derived. In order to use this method for comparative purposes, however, the resources of a social survey organization would be needed.

Ranking methods using information concerning the characteristics of residential areas' housing stock and population have been used by De Vise (1967a, 1967b) and by Earickson (1969) for the community areas and suburbs of metropolitan Chicago in a variety of applications. The 250 or so communities of the metropolis were ranked by median income of their families, the average value of their homes and the assessed real estate valuation per resident (or median rent for the city of Chicago community areas). The rankings were summed, applying a weight of two to income and re-ranked according to these composite scores. No explicit rationale was given for the choice of index components, however. Ranking methods have proved useful in individual metropolises for single points in time, but for studying a set of cities their utility is doubtful.

The Shevky Index of Social Rank (described in Chapter I) represents another residentially based socioeconomic status measure in that it includes both population and housing information for areas and cannot be divorced from such areas. The method of scoring is tied to the highest ranked census tract in Los Angeles in 1940, however, and this makes it somewhat unsatisfactory for comparative purposes though it has been used by McElrate (1965). In general, indices of socioeconomic status that combine both population and housing measures are unsuitable if the purpose is to describe the distribution of population within the city and to explain this distribution via models of residential choice and the operation of the housing market.

Population Based Indices of Socioeconomic Status

The most used index of socioeconomic status based purely on population data has been the white collar-blue collar occupational distinction. Lipset and Bendix (1959) used this classification in their comparative survey of social mobility in industrialized nations. Given the differences among occupational classifications in the countries considered, the simple partition of the workforce into manual (lower) and non-manual (higher) portions was appropriate. However, most censuses provide more detailed information on occupations. The problems faced by the user of such data are how the occupations are to be ranked and how the rankings are to be summarized for residential population groups.

The census classification developed by Edwards (1938) has generally been used in the U.S. More recently, Duncan (1961a, 1961b) has developed a continuous scoring scale for occupational categories on the basis of the educational and income levels associated with each occupation and the relation of these levels to the Hatt-North (Hatt and North, 1947) occupational prestige ratings. The educational attainment associated with and the income level achieved by selected occupations were regressed against their scores on the Hatt-North prestige scale. A good fit to this regression enabled Duncan (1961a) to predict the prestige scores of the majority of the occupational categories employed by the U.S. Census but absent from the Hatt-North survey using the education and income levels associated with each occupation together with the regression coefficients from the equation fitted to those occupations, the prestige scores of which were known. The regression equation is

$$X_1 = 0.59X_2 + 0.55X_3 - 6.0$$

where X_1 is the percentage of "excellent" or "good" ratings received by an occupation in the prestige survey, X_2 the proportion of men in the occupation with 1949 incomes of $3,500 or more, and X_3 the proportion of men in the occupation with four years of high school or higher educational attainment. Duncan cautions against using his Socioeconomic Index for Occupations as a more general socioeconomic status index because it involves generalization of individual status through assignment to an occupational class: individual achievement within the occupational category is ignored.

Duncan describes the rationale behind the choice of components for his index as follows (Duncan, 1961a, pp. 116-117):

> We have...the following sequence: a man qualifies himself for occupational life by obtaining an education; as a consequence of pursuing his occupation, he obtains income. Occupation, therefore, is the intervening activity linking income to education. If we characterize an occupation according to the prevailing levels of education and income of its incumbents, we are not only estimating its 'social status' and its 'economic status' we are also describing one of its major 'causes' and one of its major 'effects.'

Following Duncan's argument, Bogue (1969, Chapter 14) suggests that an individual's socioeconomic status might be best measured by an index that combined the education attained and the income gained by the individual. Bogues's Index of Socioeconomic Achievement is constructed as follows (Bogue, 1969, Chapter 14, pp. 439-440):

> (1) calculate the income that would be expected on the basis of educational attainment alone;
> (2) enumerate the actual income that is received;
> (3) average the two to arrive at a combined index;
> (4) if data are collected for several different dates, convert to constant dollars by adjusting for purchasing power;
> (5) convert to an index value by dividing the above by $20,000 and multiplying the result by 100.

The expected income is derived from national census cross-tabulation of income class by educational category for each of eight age groups. An occupational component can be added to the index by calculating the income expected on the basis of the education associated with an occupation and the income directly associated with an occupation. The index is tied to a fixed reference point (100 = an income of U.S. $20,000 in 1959) which would facilitate its use in cross-national research if the exchange rate and living cost problems could be solved. The index can be calculated for individuals, families and larger groups such as residential populations, and for the larger groups the variance of socioeconomic status about the mean can be calculated.

A similarly based but differently constructed Index of Socioeconomic Status has been used extensively in examining the socioeconomic structure of the U.S. population and in the composition of residential population groups. The methodology is explained in detail in U.S. Bureau of the Census (1963b). Comprehensive tabulations of this index and a derived index of status consistency for the U.S. population are contained in U.S. Bureau of the Census (1967). The various tabulations have been analyzed in detail by Nam and Powers (1965) and Powers (1968).

The socioeconomic status index is calculated as follows (Powers, 1968, pp. 445-446):

> (1) The scores for education were obtained by computing a cumulative percentage distribution of the education of chief income recipients in families as of 1959. The score assigned to each category of education was the midpoint of the cumulative percentage interval for the category...
> (2) The scores for family income were obtained in a similar manner.
> (3) The scores for detailed occupations were based on the most recently available data, those for males aged 14 years and over in the experienced civilian labor force as of 1950. The detailed occupations were scored according to the combined average levels of education and income for the given occupation. Thus, the score obtained is an average score for the occupation and it contributes an independent effect to the total socioeconomic score, which also includes the individual's own educational and income levels. Using the number of workers in each occupation, a cumulative percentage distribution was obtained. The score for a given occupation was then determined by taking the

midpoint of the cumulative percentage interval for that occupation.

The procedure involves combining three continuous distributions that are rectangular (the cumulative distributions of education, income, and occupation). The result of this combination is that, because the distributions are closely associated, larger percentages of persons are in the central part of the socioeconomic score distribution and that smaller percentages are at the extremes (Nam and Raveo, 1965, p. 490). When scores for residential area populations are calculated this bunching at the center is even greater. Cross-national or cross-temporal use of this index is possible though again somewhat problematical since the distribution of socioeconomic status in one country or one point in time would have to be calibrated in terms of the scores of the other country or time period.

Properties Desirable for A Comparative Index of Socioeconomic Status

In making a choice among the published indices or in designing one's own, a number of properties should be sought. The index should be based on population information only in order to maintain theoretical clarity. It should be applicable to different sized human groups (the individual, the family, the household, the population of a residential area) in order that different sized cities can be compared and so that aggregate populations can be compared with various disaggregated components. For example, the city's aggregate status could be compared with that of its component residential areas.

The index should be applicable to more than one point in time in order that studies of change be possible. And finally, the chosen index of socioeconomic status should have the same general meaning in the different study areas (e.g. cities) in which it is used. This probably means that use of such an index should be restricted to one society or culture.

Even within the U.S. this assumption may not hold. If we were using Bogue's index, for example, the national education-occupation and education-income relations would not accurately represent the situation in the Southern states. Blau and Duncan state that "... the southern white benefits from a labor market that is adapted to the educational preparation of the labor force it serves, allowing him to obtain jobs from which he might well be barred in the North as a result of his educational shortcomings" (Blau and Duncan, 1967, pp. 217-218).

An Index of Socioeconomic Status for Residential Populations

The index adopted follows fairly closely the methodology used by Nam and Powers (1965), differing from it in the variable categories used, the population base employed and the method for deriving the occupational status component.

The components of the index are education, occupation and income. With Duncan (1969) and Blau and Duncan (1967, Chapter 5) we see education as a partial determinant for occupational and income achievement and with Bogue (1969, p. 434) and Jencks and Riesman (1968) as an indicator of cultural class; we see income as the outcome of employment, a reward graduated according to the skill and effort of the individual filling an occupation and the demand for the work associated with the occupation, and we view occupation as having a social prestige associated with it, part of which can be assessed with reference to education and part with reference to the income associated with the occupation.

A summary distribution for the U.S. of education of persons 25 years and over was converted into percentage form and then cumulated from lowest education category ("No School Years Completed") upward to the highest ("College: 4 Years or More"). The midpoint for each category on the cumulative distribution was then adopted as the score for that category (Table 33). A similar summary distribution for income of families in the U.S. was converted into scores in the same way (Table 34). Calculations of scores for each occupational category used was more complex. The steps were as follows.

(1) Summary cross-tabulations for occupational category by educational category were added together and converted to row-wise percentages form (Table 35).

(2) Scores were calculated for each educational category in this table from the cumulative distribution in the manner described above. These new educational scores were calculated and used instead of the ones in Table 33 because the categories in the two tables were not precisely coincident.

(3) Educational status scores for each occupational category were then calculated by multiplying the educational score for each educational category by the row-wise proportion of that occupational category in the given educational category and then summing these products. This was done for each occupational category.

(4) The same procedure was followed to derive income status scores for each occupational category using the information in Table 36. Again the income scores used were those internal to the table rather than the ones given in Table 34 because of the differences in the two categorizations.

(5) The educational and income scores of an occupational category were then added together and divided by 2 to yield an occupational status score for each category (Table 37).

Comparison of these status scores with those of Duncan, Bogue and Nam and Powers (Table 38) reveals broad similarities but some important differences which are probably not a product of method used as such but rather of the differences in base population and corrections used. Both Duncan and Bogue used age corrections in the course of constructing their indices arguing that education-occupation-income relations change significantly with age of the employed person both for historical and for life cycle reasons. This was not done in the present study as actual rather than potential

TABLE 33

EDUCATION SCORES

Educational Category[a]	Score	Percent in Category	Cumulative Percent
College: 4 Years or More	96.25	7.7	100.1[b]
College: 1 to 3 Years	88.00	8.8	92.4
High School: 4 Years	71.30	24.6	83.6
High School: 1-3 Years	49.40	19.2	59.0
Elementary: 8 Years	31.05	17.5	39.8
Elementary: 5-7 Years	15.35	13.9	22.3
Elementary: 1-4 Years	5.35	6.1	8.4
No School Years Completed	1.15	2.3	2.3

[a]These are the categories for which data on census tract populations is provided by the U.S. Census.

[b]Total doesn't sum to 100.0 due to rounding error.

Source: Calculated from Table 76. — Years of School Completed by Persons 25 Years Old and Over, By Color and Sex, for the United States, Urban and Rural, 1960 and 1950, and for the Conminous U.S., 1940 to 1960. P. 207 of U.S. Bureau of the Census, (1962a).

TABLE 34

INCOME SCORES

Income Categories[a]	Score	Percent in Category	Cumulative Percent
$25,000 and Over	99.45	1.3	100.1[b]
$10,000 - $24,999	91.90	13.8	98.8
$8,000 - $9,999	79.25	11.5	85.0
$6,000 - $7,999	63.85	19.3	73.5
$4,000 - $5,999	42.55	23.3	54.2
$2,000 - $3,999	22.00	17.8	30.9
Under $2,000	6.55	13.1	13.1

[a]The 13 income categories provided for census tracts have been combined to yield 7 here.

[b]The total doesn't sum to 100.0 due to rounding error

Source: Calculated from Table 95. – Income in 1959 Families and Unrelated Individuals, By Color, for the United States, Urban and Rural: 1960. P. 226 of U.S. Bureau of the Census (1962a).

TABLE 35

EDUCATION BY OCCUPATION FOR MALES AND FEMALES IN THE EXPERIENCED LABOR FORCE: U.S., 1960 ROW-WISE PERCENTAGES

Occupation Category	Elementary			High School		College		
	Less Than 5 Years	5 to 7 Years	8 Years	1 to 3 Years	4 Years	1 to 3 Years	4 Years	5 Or More Years
Professional, Technical and Kindred	0.3	0.8	1.9	5.9	16.9	21.5	25.5	27.1
Managers, Officials and Proprietors	2.0	5.7	10.7	17.9	30.8	17.5	11.0	4.5
Clerical and Kindred Workers	0.5	2.5	6.3	19.2	50.5	16.2	3.7	1.1
Sales Workers	1.4	5.6	11.9	25.9	32.1	14.6	6.8	1.8
Craftsmen, Foremen and Kindred Workers	4.1	13.3	19.2	26.5	28.5	6.4	1.5	0.5
Operatives and Kindred Workers	6.5	17.2	21.0	28.6	22.6	3.6	0.4	0.1
Service Workers, Private Household and Other	8.0	17.0	19.7	28.0	20.9	5.4	0.7	0.3
Laborers	14.8	21.4	19.3	25.6	15.3	3.0	0.4	0.2
Totals	5.1	11.2	14.8	22.3	27.3	10.1	5.3	3.8
Cumculative Percentage	5.1	16.3	31.1	53.4	80.7	90.8	96.1	99.9
Score	2.55	10.70	23.70	42.25	67.05	85.75	93.45	98.00

Source: Calculated from Table 28. — Education of the Experienced Labor Force, By Detailed Occupation and Sex, for the United States: 1960. In the U.S. Bureau of the Census (1963d).

TABLE 36

INCOME BY OCCUPATION FOR MALES AND FEMALES IN THE EXPERIENCED LABOR FORCE: U.S., 1960 ROW-WISE PERCENTAGES

Occupation Category	Income Category										
	1.	2.	3.	4.	5.	6.	7.	8.	9.	10.	11.
Professional, Technical and Kindred	7.8	7.2	7.2	10.9	13.1	12.6	10.7	7.9	9.5	8.2	5.1
Managers, Officials and Proprietors	4.5	5.5	6.4	8.8	10.6	12.4	10.4	8.4	10.6	12.2	10.4
Clerical and Kindred Workers	12.3	11.5	16.4	22.0	17.3	11.4	4.6	2.1	1.5	0.7	0.2
Sales Workers	21.5	13.4	12.4	10.1	9.4	9.2	6.8	4.8	5.2	5.3	3.1
Craftsmen, Foremen and Kindred Workers	4.7	5.6	7.9	12.2	16.2	19.1	14.7	9.1	7.3	2.7	0.5
Operatives and Kindred Workers	10.4	12.2	17.2	16.7	16.1	13.7	7.4	3.5	2.0	0.6	0.2
Service Workers, Private Household and Other Workers	37.7	11.8	14.6	10.5	7.2	4.6	2.3	0.9	0.7	0.4	0.1
Laborers	20.9	14.6	16.1	16.6	15.8	9.5	3.7	1.5	0.9	0.4	0.2
Totals	15.1	11.7	12.8	13.9	13.3	11.7	7.5	4.6	4.2	3.1	1.9
Cumulative Percentage	15.1	26.8	39.6	53.5	66.8	78.5	86.0	90.6	94.8	97.9	99.8

Source: Calculated from Table 29. — Earnings of the Experienced Civilian Labor Force By Detailed Occupation and Sex, for the United States: 1960, in U.S. Bureau of the Census (1963d).

<u>Income Categories</u>
1. Under $1,000
2. $1,000 - $1,999
3. $2,000 - $2,999
4. $3,000 - $3,999
5. $4,000 - $4,999
6. $5,000 - $5,999
7. $6,000 - $6,999
8. $7,000 - $7,999
9. $8,000 - $9,999
10. $10,000 - $14,999
11. $15,000 and Over

TABLE 37

OCCUPATION SCORES

Occupation Categories[a]	Education Based Score	Income Based Score	Composite Score[b]	Percentage in Category Male	Percentage in Category Female
Professional, Technical and Kindred	83.19	64.13	73.16	10.3	13.0
Managers, Officials and Proprietors	61.11	70.93	66.02	10.7	13.0
Clerical and Kindred	62.17	45.63	53.90	6.9	29.7
Sales	56.56	48.43	52.50	6.9	8.0
Craftsmen, Foremen and Kindred	43.76	63.44	53.60	19.5	1.2
Operatives and Kindred	37.78	48.28	43.03	19.9	14.5
Private Household } Service, Excluding Provate Household }	38.11	26.58	32.35	0.1	7.9
				6.0	13.4
Laborers, Except Farm and Mine	31.46	39.92	35.69	6.9	0.5

[a]These are the occupational categories reported for census tracts on the 1960 tract tapes. Farmers and farm managers, and Farm laborers and farm foremen were omitted from the analysis as rural occupations. The categories differ from those reported in the census tract volumes (PHC(1) - (180)) in that Farmers and farm managers are not combined with Managers, officials and proprietors, and Farm laborers and farm foremen are not combined with Laborers, except farm and mine.

[b]The composite Occupation Score equals half the sum of the Education Based Score and the Income Based Score.

Sources: Calculated from Table 87 in U.S. Bureau of the Census, 1962a; Tables 28 and 29 of U.S. Bureau of the Census, 1963d.

socioeconomic status was the focius of interest. The other difference is that all the previous work was based on information about males only, whereas in the present study data for males and females are combined since females were also tabulated in the education tables (they were part of the "persons 25 years and over" population base) and contributed to family income. To exclude them from consideration when determining occupational status would not be justified. It would merely reflect a "male chauvinist" attitude on the part of the researcher!

A first Index of Socioeconomic Status is calculated by adding together the residential area scores for the educations, occupations and incomes of the resident population, and dividing this total by three. A second Index of Socioeconomic Status could be calculated, however, using just the tract educational status and income status scores, dividing the sum of these scores by two.

Stated formally, the first Index of Socioeconomic Status is calculated in the following way:

$$S_i^1 = 1/3(\sum_d w_d N_i(d)/\sum_d N_i(d) + \sum_o w_o N_i(o)/\sum_o N_i(o) + \sum_y w_y F_i(y)/\sum_y F_i(y) \quad (6)$$

where S_i^1 is the socioeconomic status score (the first index version) of the population living in zone i, and w_d, w_o, and w_y are the scores of the education categories d, the occupation categories o and the income categories y given in Tables 33, 37 and 34 respectively. $N_i(d)$ refers to the number of persons, 25 years old and over, in education categories d, $N_i(o)$ to the number of persons in the occupational category o and $F_i(y)$ to the number of families in income category y, all in zone i. Similarly, the second Index of Socioeconomic Status, S_i^2 is calculated thus:

$$S_i^2 = 1/2(\sum_d w_d N_i(d)/\sum_d N_i(d) + \sum_y w_y F_i(y)/\sum_y F_i(y)) \quad (7)$$

TABLE 38

A COMPARISON OF OCCUPATION SCORES

Occupation Categories	Duncan		Bogue			Scores U.S. Bureau of Census	This Study		
	1.	2.	3.	4.	5.	6.	7.	8.	9.
Professional, Technical and Kindred	75	79	38	40	39	90	83	64	74
Managers, Officials and Proprietors	57	73	32	42	37	81	61	71	66
Clerical and Kindred Workers	45	69	27	25	26	71 (Clerical and Sales)	62	46	54
Sales Workers	49	70	27	30	29		57	48	53
Craftsmen, Foremen and Kindred Workers	31	64	26	27	27	58	44	63	54
Operatives and Kindred Workers	18	57	23	22	23	45	38	48	43
Service Workers, Excluding Private Household	17	56	23	18	20	34 (Service and Private Household)	38 (Service and Private Household)	27	32
Private Household Workers	8	45	19	9	14				
Laborers	7	44	20	16	18	20	31	40	36
Year for data: Education / Income	1950 / 1949		1960 / 1959			1960 / 1959	1960 / 1959		
Source:	U.S. Census NORC Survey		U.S. Census			U.S. Census	U.S. Census		
Population Base	Employed Males		Employed Males			Employed Males	Employed Males and Females		
Age Correction	Yes		Yes			No	No		
General Method	Regression against prestige scores		Translation of education and income of occupations into income based scores			Scored on a cumulative distribution of ranked occupations	Scored on a cumulative distribution of education and income of occupations		

Indices

1. Duncan's Socioeconomic Index for occupations (Duncan, 1961a, p. 155).
2. Transformation of Socioeconomic Index to National Opinion Research Center occupation prestige scores (Duncan, 1961a, p. 155).
3. Bogue's education based index for occupations (Bogue, 1969, pp. 444-452).
4. Bogue's income based index for occupations (Bogue, 1969, pp. 444-452).
5. Bogue's combined index for occupations (Bogue, 1969, pp. 444-452).
6. Nam and Power's index for occupations (U.S. Bureau of the

TABLE 38--Continued

Indices--Continued

Census, 1967, p. 208).
7. This study's education based index for occupations.
8. This study's income based index for occupations.
9. This study's compositie index for occupations.

TABLE 39

CORRELATION OF THE TWO SOCIOECONOMIC STATUS INDICES

SMSAs	Coefficient of Correlation over Tracts Socioeconomic Status Index One and Socioeconomic Status Index Two
Ann Arbor	0.987
Birmingham	0.998
Canton	0.994
Des Moines	0.988
El Paso	0.996
Honolulu	0.991
Lancaster	0.979
Minneapolis-St. Paul	0.993
Providence- Pawtucket	0.997
Richmond	0.997
San Bernadino-Riverside-Ontario	0.965
Tampa-St. Petersburg	0.986

The two indices are closely related in general as Table 39, reporting the correlations between the first and second versions of the index, reveals. In Chapter VI in which the spatial pattern of socioeconomic status is analyzed, the first index is used predominantly. Use of the second index, though in many ways theoretically preferable (it avoids the assumptions involved in assigning general occupational status scores to the occupations held by a particular residential area population), would not result in radically different patterns.

Family Status or Stage in Life Cycle

The second broad concept to be analyzed is that of the family cycle or life cycle in which the status of the family changes progressively through time. The term family status applies to the stage in family cycle at which a family is located. Measures of population age structure, family size, fertility and household type have long been used as descriptive and predictive variables in demographic research. However, several researchers (Glick and Parke, 1965; Lansing and Kish, 1957, Bogue, 1969) have proposed that it is not the chronological age of an individual that counts in many matters of behavior but rather the relative position he or she occupies in the sequence of family development stages.

Schematically, the family cycle may be viewed as a series of events that separate the significant stages (Table 40). The family cycle may be conceived of entirely as a population process, which seems to be what Glick and Parke intend, or as that coupled with a household formation process, which is what Lansing and Kish intend (Table 40). Historically, in Western Europe and the United States economic development and rising real incomes have meant a finer and finer division of the family cycle in terms of separate households. More and more households are beginning their family cycles as single persons rather than as married couples, often in group quarters while at college but increasingly in private households thereafter, and older couples are more and more financially able to maintain themselves in separate households (Glick, Heer and Beresford, 1968). This articulation of the family cycle in terms of separate residential households suggest the varying composition of families at various stages in the life cycle will be an important dimension differentiating the housing areas of the city in which families live, if housing occupied is related to the needs of the family at the stage in its life cycle which it occupies.

Before considering the various proposals for indexing this

TABLE 40

EVENTS AND STAGES IN THE LIFE CYCLE

A. Glick and Parke: Stages of the Life Cycle[a]

Events	Time Scale	Stages
Birth	0.0, 0.0	
		(Family of origin)
Marriage (First)	23.3, 20.2	
		Family formation
Birth of first child		
		Early childbearing and childrearing
Birth of last child		
		Late childrearing
Marriage of last child	49.2, 47.1	
		"Empty nest"
Death of one spouse	65.7, 63.6	
		Widowhood
Death	66.4, 72.7	

B. Lansing and Kish: Stages in the Life Cycle[b]

Events	Time Scale	Stages
Birth		
		(Family of origin)
Break from family of origin		
		Young Single
Marriage		
		Young married, no children
Birth of first child		
		Young married, youngest child under 6
Youngest child is 6		
		Young married, youngest child 6 or older
Husband aged 45		
		Older married with children
Last child leaves home		
		Older married, no children
Death of one spouse		
		Older single
Death		

TABLE 40--Continued

[a]Source: Glick and Parke, 1965, Glick, Hees and Beresford, 1968. The time scales in the diagrams are not to scale but the median age at which the events listed took place for the United States population in 1960 is given for males and females respectively.

[b]Source: Lansing and Kish, 1957.

---

dimension, we should ask how normal or prevalent is this history of family formation, growth, maturity and dissolution. How important are extended families, broken families and continued bachelor and spinsterhood? Bogue (1969, pp. 369-370) argues that international demographic data on average size of households means that "the nuclear family (husband-wife-children) is the predominant living arrangement almost everywhere in the world." Only one country, he reports, has an average size of family of greater than 6 persons, whereas the extended family may be expected to have a minimum of 7 persons. Both the summarized tract statistics for the sample cities (Table 41) and the summary table for the whole U.S. (Table 42) indicate that extended families are likely to be in a very small minority. Broken families are numerically more significant (Table 42), especially among the non-white, particularly the Negro population, but even so some 94.4 per cent of white families and some 84.4 per cent of Negro families could be unambiguously assigned to a stage in the "normal" life cycle ("married, wife present" plus "widowed" categories). Many of the remaining families could also be considered to be proceeding through the normal life cycle, one that differed from the norm only in having one spouse absent.

Residential Area Based Indices of Family Status

Shevky's Index of Urbanization (which Bell preferred to call the Index of Family Status) was probably the first index that proposed to measure this social dimension. Robson (1969, pp. 54-58)

TABLE 41

STATISTICS FOR POPULATION PER HOUSEHOLD[a]

Urbanized Area	Average	Standard Deviation	Minimum	Maximum
Ann Arbor	3.20	0.62	1.65	4.74
Birmingham	3.47	0.50	1.54	5.00
Canton	3.30	0.38	1.81	4.00
Des Moines	3.09	0.51	1.26	3.94
El Paso	3.89	0.67	2.19	5.11
Honolulu	3.83	0.85	1.16	5.59
Lancaster	3.17	0.35	1.98	3.59
Minneapolis-St. Paul	3.27	0.65	0.03	4.83
Providence-Pawtucket	3.23	0.49	1.24	6.41
Richmond	3.20	0.56	1.16	4.38
San Bernadino-Riverside	3.24	0.55	1.61	4.64
St. Petersburg	2.57	0.43	1.34	3.78
Tampa	3.09	0.44	1.09	3.87

Notes

[a]These are statistics for tract population averages.

TABLE 42

MARITAL STATUS OF FAMILY HEAD BY SEX AND COLOR, FOR THE U.S.: 1960

	White	Non-white
Male Head	92.0	79.1
Single	1.0	0.9
Married, wife present	89.2	74.9
Separated	0.1	0.8
Wife absent, other	0.4	0.6
Widowed	1.0	1.5
Divorced	0.3	0.4
Female Head	8.1	20.8
Single	1.0	2.2
Separated	0.8	6.3
Husband absent, other	0.6	1.5
Widowed	4.2	8.4
Divorced	1.5	2.4
All families	100.0	100.0

Source: Table 12-5 in Bogue, 1969, p. 376.

Original Source: U.S. Bureau of the Census (1963c).

has criticized the index on the grounds that it contained components that do not necessarily vary together ("Fertility" and "Women in the Labor Force"), although for many American cities the two variables were associated. He points out that in the European context social class and the life cycle interact in a complex fashion to determine whether a woman works or not. In addition the index mixes population and housing characterisitcs, a mixture which it is our intention to avoid.

In a paper entitled "Patterns of Family Segregation," Guest (1970) suggested that more than two dimensions were necessary to describe the residential distribution of family types across the American metropolis. He used a classification of families into six types based on the information provided in the census tract statistics: (1) young couples, with husband under 45 but with no children; (2) young families, with husband under 45 with children; (3) old families, with husband over 45 with children; (4) old couples, husband over 45 but with no children; (5) primary individuals, persons living by themselves and (6) single heads, persons living in a family arrangement with relations but no spouse. Proportions in each group were used as variables in a principal components analysis with graphical rotation to a quartimax position. The components that emerged were a <u>Stable Family-Unattached Individuals</u> dimension and an <u>Age</u> dimension. These were similar across 17 metropolitan areas (SMSAs). From these results he argued that no one dimension would fully describe the family residential patterns of the city. This conclusion differs from that arrived at in Chapter III where single dimensions of family status only emerged in all 13 urbanized area analyses. However, only age and household size variables were employed in the analysis rather than a family type classification. So that in using an index based on those variables we are capturing only a part of the variaion in family residential patterns. On the other hand, we will be using an index similarly defined for each city, a considerable strength in comparative analysis.

An Index of Family Status

The methodology followed previously for constructing the Index of Socioeconomic Status is again followed here. The components of the index are age and family size. The relationship in the life cycle between age of household and family size is curvilinear, but if average age of the household is considered it appears that the curvilinearity is not so pronounced, especially when it is realized that the limb of falling family size and rising age takes up considerably more time than the other limb of falling age and increasing family size (Figure 9). Residentially, it turns out that our assumption of co-variation of age and size, made for index construction purposes, is not too bad an assumption for most cities (Table 43).

Age status scores were calculated as follows. A cumulative percentage distribution of age categories for the U.S. in 1960 was computed and scores were derived by taking the mid-point of each category on this cumulative distribution (Table 44). Unfortunately, the age categories available on the census tapes employed in this study were very broad. Hopefully, more detailed distributions can be used in any future studies. Household size scores were computed in the same way by calculating a cumulative distribution and deriving mid-point category scores (Table 45), except that the distribution was cumulated from the largest household categroy down to the smallest.

Family status scores, F_i, were then calculated by adding together the age score and the size score for a census tract's population and dividing by two:

$$F_i = 1/2\left(\sum_a w_a N_i(a)/\sum_a N_i(a) + \sum_s w_s H_i(s)/\sum_s H_i(s)\right) \qquad (8)$$

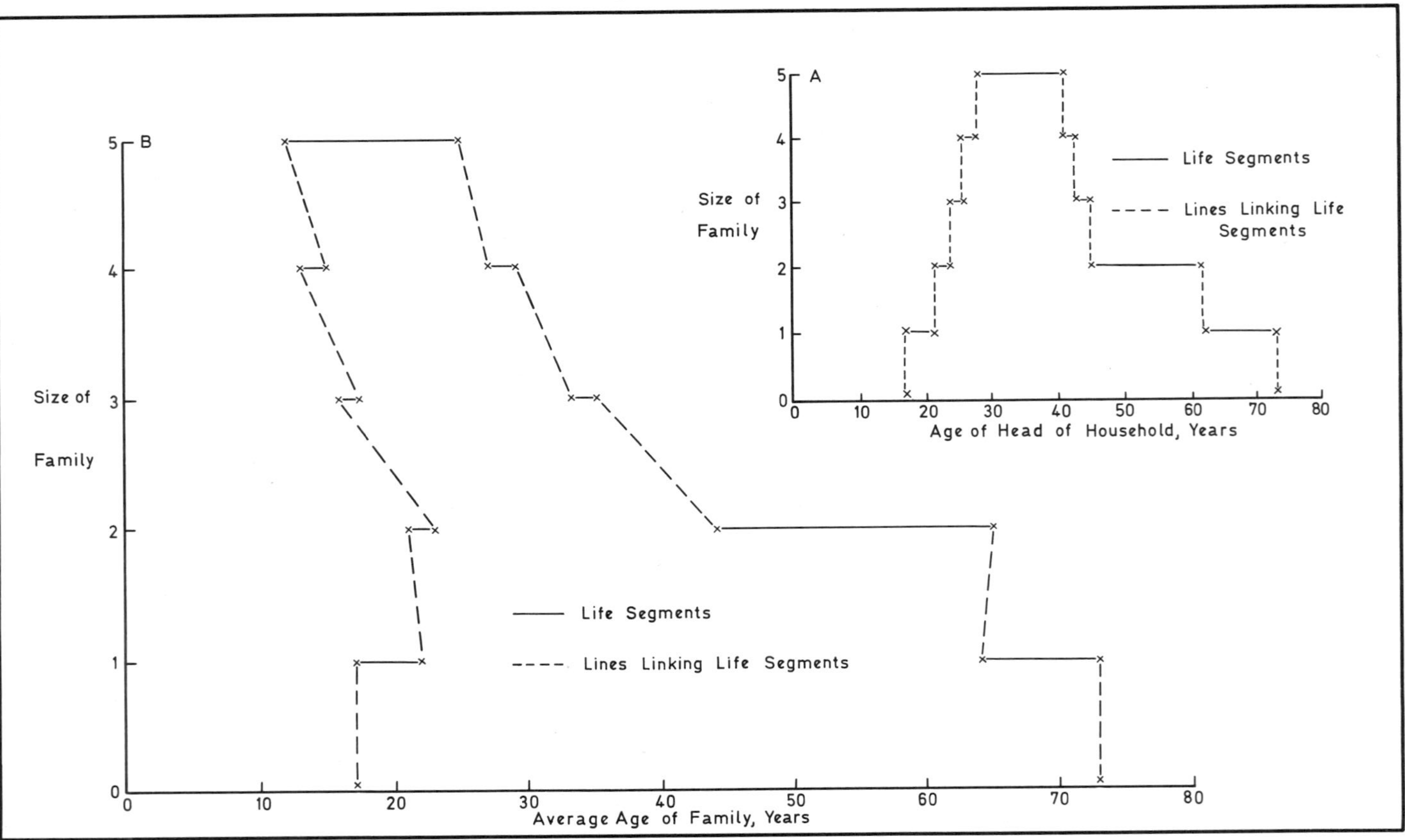

Fig. 9.--The Relationship between Size and Age for a Typical Family

TABLE 43

CORRELATION OF AGE STATUS AND SIZE STATUS FOR 12 SMSAS

SMSAs	Coefficient of Correlation between Age Status and Size Status
Ann Arbor	0.729
Birmingham	0.904
Canton	0.958
Des Moines	0.949
El Paso	0.828
Honolulu	0.682
Lancaster	0.921
Minneapolis-St. Paul	0.939
Providence-Pawtucket	0.806
Richmond	0.735
San Bernadino-Riverside-Ontario	0.763
Tampa-St. Petersburg	0.934

TABLE 44

AGE STRUCTURE SCORES

Age Categories	Percent	Cumulative Percent	Score	Combined Category Score
65 and Over	9.0	100.1[a]	95.60	95.60
60-64	4.0	91.1	89.10	
55-59	4.8	87.1	84.47	
50-54	5.4	82.3	79.60	
45-49	6.1	76.9	73.95	64.75
40-44	6.5	70.8	67.55	
35-39	7.0	64.3	60.80	
30-34	6.7	57.3	53.95	
25-29	6.1	50.6	47.55	
20-24	6.0	44.5	41.50	
15-19	7.4	38.5	34.80	34.80
10-14	9.4	31.1	26.40	21.20
5-9	10.4	21.7	16.50	
Under 5	11.3	11.3	6.65	6.65

Notes

[a]The total does not add to 100.0 due to rounding

Source: Calculated from Table 65. — Age by Color and Sex, for the United States, Urban and Rural: 1960. P.200 of U.S. Bureau of the Census, 1962a.

TABLE 45

HOUSEHOLD SIZE SCORES

Number of Persons in Household	Per Cent of Total Households in the U.S.	Cumulative Per Cent	Score	Combined Category Score
1 person	13.3	99.9[a]	93.25	93.25
2 persons	28.0	86.6	72.60	72.60
3 persons	18.9	58.6	49.15	49.15
4 persons	17.2	39.7	31.10	31.10
5 persons	11.1	22.5	16.95	16.95
6 persons	5.9	11.4	7.95	
7 persons	2.7	5.5	4.15	5.70
8 persons or more	2.8	2.8	1.40	

[a]Total does not equal 100.0 due to rounding error

Source: Calculated from Table J. — Number of Persons and Persons per Room: 1940 to 1960, p.XXIX of U.S. Bureau of the Census, 1963a

where w_a is the score for age category a (Table 44), w_s is the score for size category s (Table 45), $N_i(a)$ is the number of persons aged a in tract i and $H_i(s)$ is the number of households of size s in tract i.

Racial and Ethnic Status

We have indicated in the previous chapter that there is a relationship between membership of a social class and membership of a racial or ethnic group. But this relationship should be left as a matter for empirical investigation rather than something to be included in a socioeconomic status index or racial status index.

As indicators of racial or ethnic group membership simple percentages or derived concentration indices have been widely used and would seem to be the most appropriate measures to use (Bogue, 1967). These are described where they are employed in Chapter VIII.

CHAPTER VI

THE SPATIAL PATTERNS OF SOCIOECONOMIC STATUS

Many observers of the city have noted that there is considerable spatial variation in the social character of its neighborhoods. Each of us probably possesses a crude mental map of the socioeconomic status of the city's residential areas, this status being one of the elements of an area's social character which it was argued in the previous chapter deserved careful measurement by means of an Index of Socioeconomic Status. The index values of the census tracts within the sample cities have been mapped, and the spatial patterns revealed are examined in this chapter.

However, before we embark on that exercise in pattern recognition, we review briefly the propositions about the spatial pattern of socioeconomic status that have emerged from earlier work.

The most prominent spatial model, which dominates both popular and policy discussions about American cities, is that of concentric variation with respect to the center of the city. In popular terms, the concentric variation is simplified into two rings: the poorer and problem-ridden central city, and the richer and problem-free ring of suburbs.

The model has its intellectual origins in the essay by Ernest Burgess (Burgess, 1925) on the effect of city growth on the social organization of the city, and other writers have made similar observations (Banfield, 1970). These may be summarized as follows (Banfield, 1970, p. 23).

(1) _The city's economy and population grow_. The population of the city grows through immigration in response to a growing economy. This population has to be housed, and this means that the physical

extent of the city has to expand correspondingly "in one direction or another — up, down, or from the center outward."

(2) The city expands outwards. The city grows outwards rather than upwards or downwards because this is the cheapest solution in construction and transportation terms. The city population becomes less concentrated in this expansion as urban transportation modes change and become swifter and less expensive.

(3) The city adopts a ring-like structure. The outward expansion of the city is not usually a continuous process, but varies in strength over time. In times of economic prosperity housing is added rapidly on the periphery of the city; downturns in the housing construction cycle mean fewer new homes on the city periphery (Adams, 1970, 37-62). The result of the variation in housing construction is that several distinct rings of housing are formed, differentiated one from another in terms of age. The innermost ring contains the oldest housing, the outermost ring the most recent.

(4) The housing rings will be occupied by different economic groups. Housing of various ages will differ in quality, desirability and price. Aging implies deterioration of the structure, increased maintenance costs and need for considerable expenditure if the highest housing standards are to be maintained. Usually, the oldest housing is in the poorest condition, the newest in the best condition, and this difference will be reflected in the price. The distribution of income will be such that there will be some people who will be able to afford newer housing and the time and money to commute considerable distances to work, and some people whose budgets force them to occupy poorer quality housing and locate near their workplaces. The outer zones of a city will come to be occupied by the "well off" and the inner zones by the "not well off."

(5) The city evolves dynamically through the filtering of housing and the succession of population. Housing will not always be new. Older housing in central locations will be abandoned by the

"well-off" and occupied by the "not well-off," as time passes. This will be possible because the "not well-off" crowd more families or persons into the same space or because the property is subdivided into more housing units of a smaller size. Lower maintenance expenditures and lower levels of service will be tolerated by the "not well-off." The "well-off" will move to newer housing at locations further from the city center. In the post-Second World War period this has meant moving from the central city to the growing suburbs. A process of population succession takes place in any given ring as the housing stock ages and the two groups crudely distinguished here move in and out.

The result of these five processes acting in the city will be a concentric pattern of the socioeconomic status of residential areas within the American city.

Criticisms of the Concentric Ring and Urban Growth Model

A number of criticisms have been levelled at this simple view of the social geography of the city.

The first is that the concentric ring and urban growth model assumes too simple a space for city growth. The uniform circular city will, in reality, be broken up by varied relief and by preferential development along favored transport axes.

A second criticism is that the model assumes that ageing and succession is inevitable and irreversible. However, in nearly all American cities there remains one small area (for example, Boston's Beacon Hill — Firey, 1947), fairly close to the city center in which the housing stock has been maintained and the social composition of the neighborhood preserved. Of course, in non-American cities the central cities have always been held in greater esteem by the elite who have preserved their neighborhoods intact in many cities over long periods of time (Schnore, 1965b).

A third related criticism that might be levelled at the

concentric ring and urban growth model as here described is that the possibility of renewal or re-development has not been allowed for. If the urban renewal program efforts increased the supply of premium housing in the inner city then the decline in the proportion of "well-off" would be reversed.

A fourth criticism of the concentric ring model is that it assigns a minor role to the housing of the "not well-off." However, housing for the "not well-off" section of the population was supplied from the very beginning of the growth of the city (Salins, 1969). The "well-off" population was not large enough at the beginning to fill a whole ring of the city; they had to share areas bordering on the commercial, warehousing and manufacturing central area of the city. Only later in the city's development were the "well-off" numerous enough for it to be possible for the group to fill whole rings of housing in the city.

These observations led workers to formulate alternative spatial models of the social class geography of the city. Foremost among these was the sector and urban growth model of Homer Hoyt (Hoyt, 1939).

The Sector and Urban Growth Model

In this model the nature of the social hierarchy at the time of the city's original development was implicitly recognized: the "well-off" were in a minority and occupied only part of the city. Factors other than those proposed earlier were suggested as important in the location of the "well-off" group.

Hoyt suggested that the most attractive residential locations were pre-empted by entrepreneurs building for the high rent market. These locations were initially characterized by the following features: they were near the office and commercial section of the central business district where the working members of the "well-off" were employed, and they were removed from the side of the city that contained the industries and warehouses (Hoyt, 1939, p.116).

Residential attraction was a function of accessibility to workplace and inaccessibility to noxious facility locations (polluting factories, smelly stockyards). As a bonus this also meant that the "well-off" were residentially separated from the "not well-off" who lived in neighborhoods accessible to their workplaces — the noxious facilities which they could not afford to avoid.

In the sector and urban growth model the same forces of expansion and ageing that were important in the concentric ring and urban growth model play a part. The "well-off" sector extended outward as the "well-off" population grew; the "not well-off" sector extended outwards as well with new housing being supplied on the sector's periphery for the wealthiest of the working class. Some housing is supplied at the periphery even for the very poor in the form of public housing and mobile homes in trailer parks.

In his monograph Hoyt paid most attention to the development and expansion of high status neighborhoods. The paths of expansion of these high status neighborhoods were governed by a number of environmental factors. These were features of the physical environment, features of the man-made environment and features of the social environment. High status residential developments were attracted by pleasant wooded, lakeshore or elevated sites, repelled from the sites of polluting industry and themselves tended to attract similar high status development (Hoyt, 1939, p. 117; Lindberg, 1967 quoted in Pedersen, 1969). Conversely, the less "well-off" were relegated to sites without these amenities.

The sector and urban growth model should, however, be properly viewed as an adaptation of the concentric ring and urban growth model. Hoyt (1939) recognized the importance of economic and demographic growth in shaping the social class geography of the city, and of the processes of ageing of the housing stock and population succession described earlier.

Relaxing the Monocentric Assumption

The two previous models of the distribution of socioeconomic status in the American city contained the implicit assumption that the city was monocentric: that employment was concentrated at one center, and that residential location decisions were made with respect to that center as the destination of work trips. Harris and Ullman (1945) suggested, however, that a city might have several foci or employment centers, and that the resulting urban structure would be multi-nuclear.

The residential location models developed by Lowry (1964), Wilson (1969) and others have expressed this observation in formal mathematical terms. This elementary residential location model has been disaggregated by Wilson to yield a model that locates residentially persons in different wage categories.

The disaggregated residential location model makes explicit some of the verbal statements of the earlier models disscussed, for example, that "the housing rings will be occupied by different economic groups."

An Integrated Model of Social Class Distribution in American Cities

The principal conclusions of our discussion of existing models of the spatial distribution of social classes in cities are here summarized. At this stage, these conclusions are not stated in terms of a formal, mathematical model to be tested, but rather inferences about the spatial patterns of socioeconomic status are drawn from the model which can be compared with observed patterns.

(1) Initially, the small "well-off" class and numerous "not well-off" class are located close to their central workplaces but in separate neighborhoods. The "well-off" occupy the more desirable sites.

(2) As the city's economy grows it expands physically, adding

new housing in the periphery.

(3) This new housing caters for the demands of each of the social classes at the periphery of its area. This converts the initial residential areas into sector-like wedges. There is net out-movement from older housing areas to newer housing areas in each sector on the part of the upwardly mobile in the "not well-off" sector and on the part of the space and family oriented households in the "well-off" sector.

(4) The older housing in inner rings ages and deteriorates (and is ultimately replaced), and comes to be occupied by households poorer than the average in their sector who have in-migrated from outside the city or from outer rings or who have formed new households in the inner city. Some of this population succession may be inter-sectoral in the innermost rings if deterioration goes far enough.

(5) New employment concentrations will spring up at other places in the metropolis as the economy expands and this will alter the simple arrangement of zones and sectors. How much change in the simpler patterns will be effected by the changing distribution of employment is problematical: noxious industry will be confined to particular areas by planning controls or resident pressure. The more affluent residential municipalities will either exclude noxious industry or attract only "clean" economic activities. There may well be a feedback from the residential pattern to the employment pattern that maintains the pre-existing geography of class.

The consequences in terms of the spatial pattern of social class, neglecting the effect of multiple employment locations, are spelled out in Figure 10. This shows the spatial pattern of socioeconomic status that might be expected at a point in time if the processes described above had been in operation for a lengthy period. The model city is divided up into four rings and four sectors, making some 16 zones in all. The socioeconomic status scores for these zones have been arranged so that there is progression from lower to higher status within each sector from inner ring to outer ring, and so that the progressions for each sector are different (Figure 10A). When the socioeconomic status scores for the zones are mapped a mixed concentric ring-axial sector pattern of social class distribution emerges (Figure 10B).

Figures 10C and 10D show what the graphs of socioeconomic status by zone would look like if sectoral pattern were dominant (Figure 10C) or if the concentric pattern were dominant (Figure 10D). We have a spectrum of spatial patterns, then, with the integrated pattern of Figure 10A lying between the extremes of Figures 10C and 10D.

The Empirical Evidence

Several different kinds of evidence have been used in assessing the validity of the models discussed above. The types of evidence that have been used are, briefly, maps of an index of the socioeconomic status of residential areas, summaries of the socioeconomic status of sectors, rings and ring-sector intersections of an urban region, and applications of the analysis of variance as a test of spatial pattern. Here, only the evidence relating specifically to American cities is reviewed. There have been many similar studies of Western non-American cities. A selection of these are reviewed in Timms, 1971, Chapter 5.

Analysis of Map Patterns

Most commonly, the spatial pattern of socioeconomic status (defined in a variety of ways) has been mapped using averages for small areas, usually census tracts or aggregations of census tracts, for central cities or metropolitan areas. This was the technique used by Homer Hoyt in his comparative study of some 142 American cities (Hoyt, 1939). Simplified summaries of the map patterns were produced for a number of those cities. Hoyt's summary maps

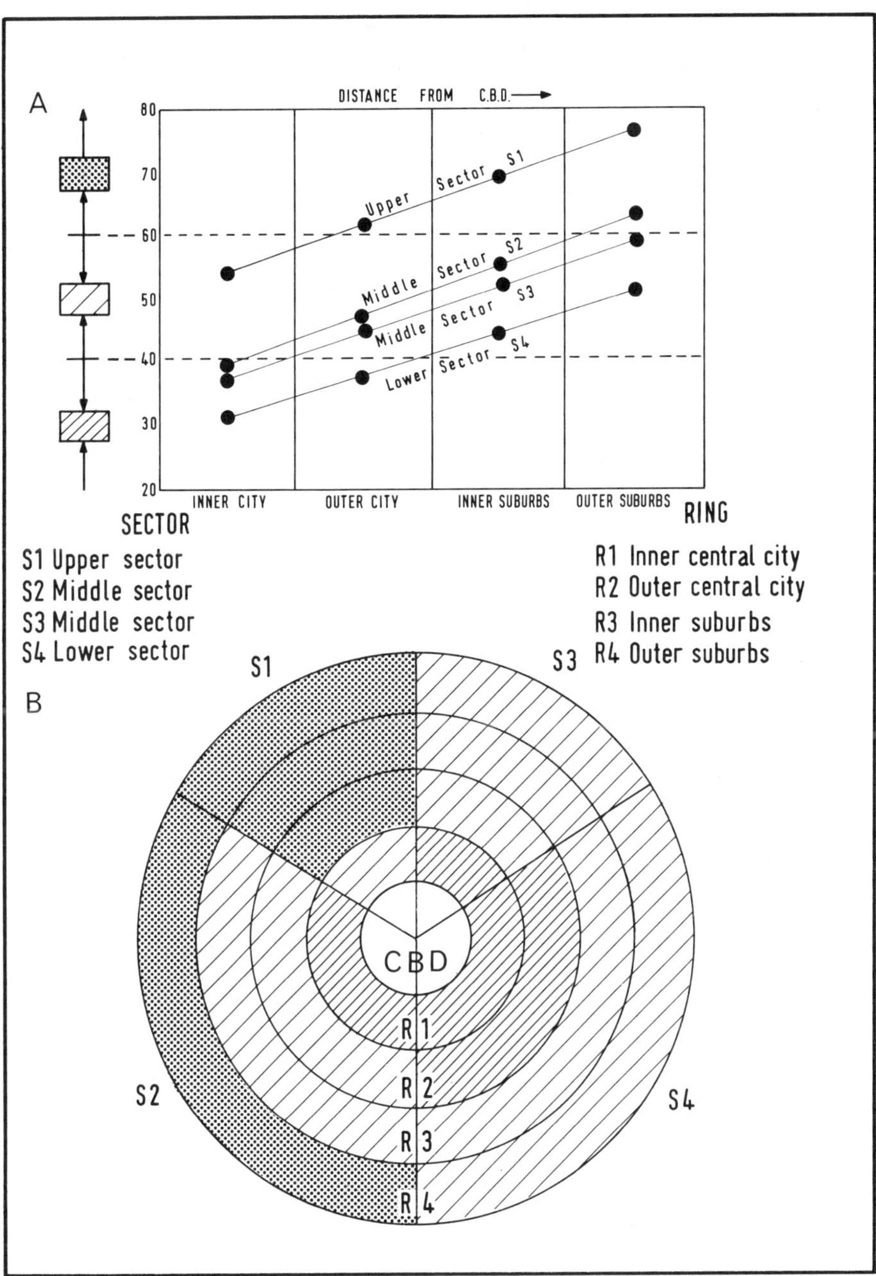

Fig. 10.--An Integrated Ring and Sector Model

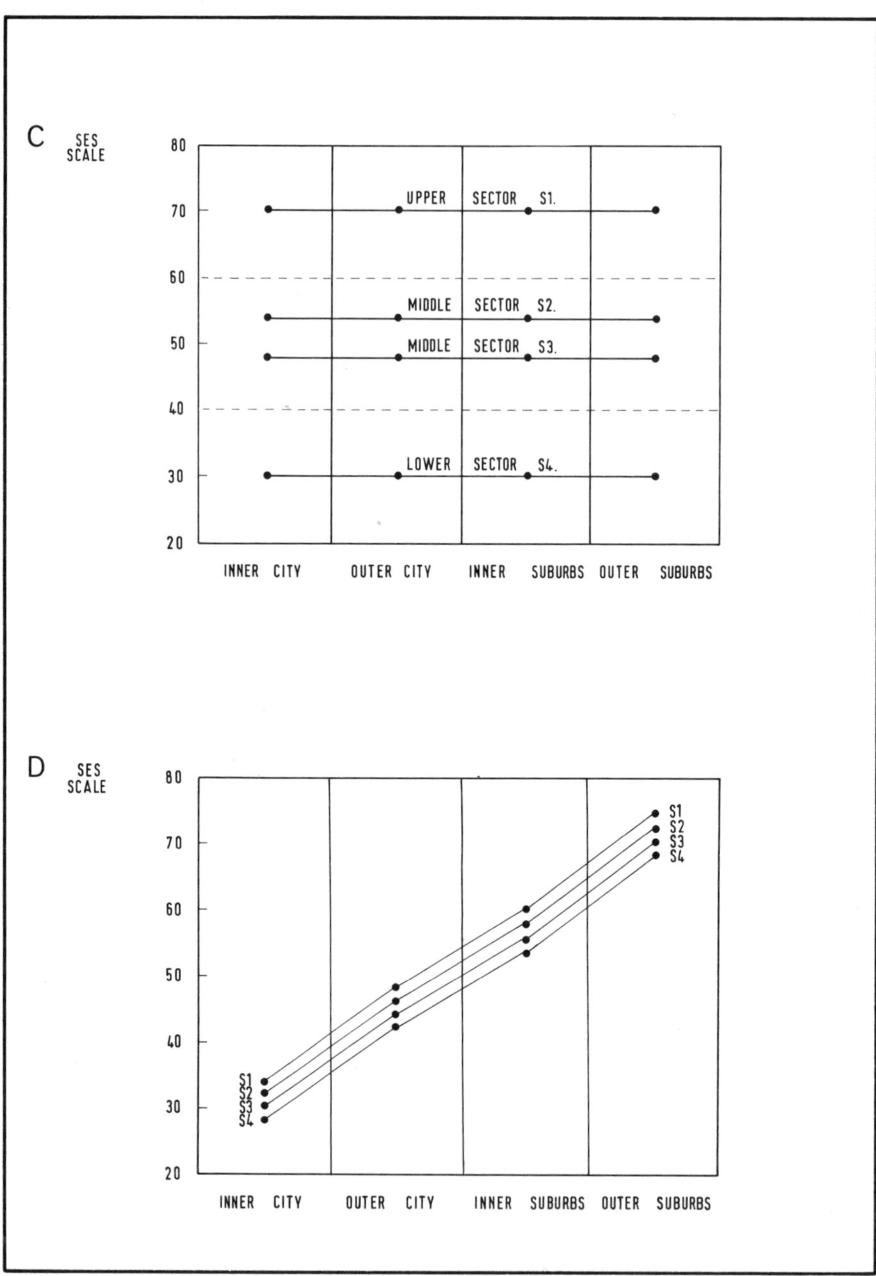

Fig.10.--(Continued)

for Minneapolis and for Richmond are shown in Figure 11 together with a summary of the maps produced in this monograph for those same cities in 1960. These maps show how the location of the highest status areas changes through time. By and large, the highest status areas grow outwards in the same sector as they originated in, although the inner parts of those sectors tend to undergo succession to lower status groups. In Minneapolis in 1960 there is evidence that much larger areas of the newest ring had acquired higher status characteristics than was the case for the ring of immediately prior growth.

Similar map analysis has been carried out more recently by Salins (1969). He studied some 4 medium sized cities (Indianapolis, Buffalo, Spokane, and Kansas City) at 3 points in time (1940, 1950 and 1960). His conclusion was that the social rank pattern was essentially sectoral with the major exception of the lowest status zone which forms a concentrated area at the center of the metropolis. Figure 12 reproduces Salins's idealized social rank pattern. His cities are characterized by one highest status sector flanked by areas fairly high in status. Fairly high status areas form a sector diametrically antipodal to that of the highest ranked families. Between these sectors are the areas of middle to low ranked families which form wedges on both sides of the CBD, (Salins, 1969, p. 242).

In earlier work on metropolitan Chicago (Rees, 1970b, pp. 373-374) the spatial pattern of social rank was found to contain both sectoral and concentric components in about equal measure. The importance of the concentric pattern was ascribed to the almost complete occupance of the inner ring by low status households. This was in part the result of the replacement of white middle class households by lower class black households in the inner parts of formerly middle class sectors. Lower class white households living in the inner city tended to resist the entry of black families into

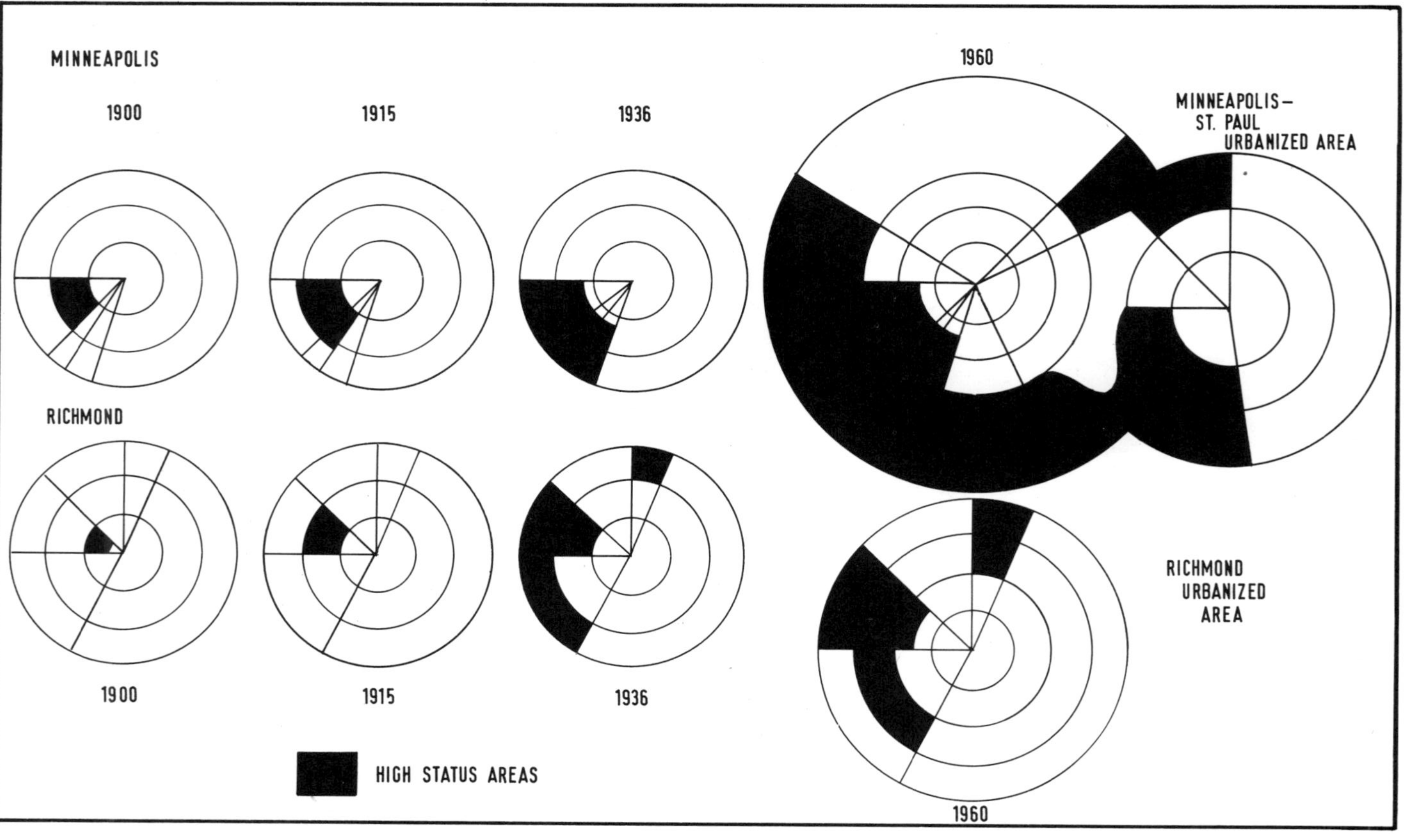

Fig. 11.--Shifts in the Location of High Status Areas in Minneapolis and Richmond (After Hoyt)

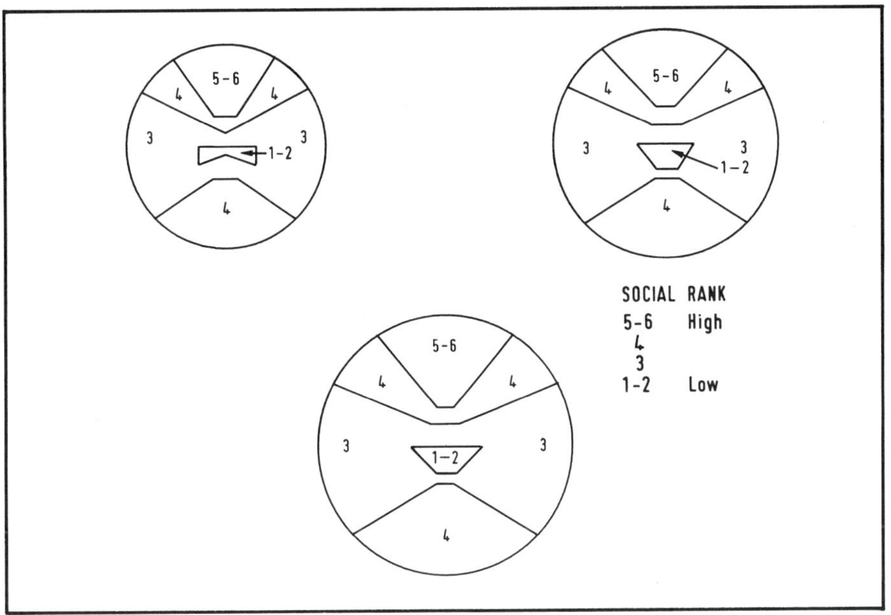

Fig. 12--Idealized Social Rank Patterns (After Salins)

their neighborhoods. The result was largely lower class but racially segregated inner ring.

Ring and Sector Summaries

A second common method of pattern analysis has been the summary of information for small areas in the city in terms of zones which relate to the spatial model being tested. For example, if the concentric ring and growth model were being tested then the zones would be concentric rings centered on the Central Business District. The early empirical work of the Chicago school of urban ecology was of this nature, and much later work has been concerned with such ring variation (Schnore, 1965a).

The basic finding of this work was that socioeconomic status on average increased with increasing distance from the city center until a point in the outer metropolitan ring at which the mix of residential population changed from a dominantly urban based one to a rural population. The average socioeconomic status of households then decreased with increasing distance from the city (Rees, 1970b).

A complication in this work on gradient patterns is the variation in size of the administrative and information unit in relation to the functional urban area (Schnore, 1965a, Chapter 11), but in general the urban ring portion of SMSAs contains the highest ranked population in terms of social status. The central city population falls some way behind but ahead of the rural ring population as Table 46 reveals. The central city average, however, mask a good deal of internal variation.

Use of the Analysis of Variance

In their paper on the spatial patterns of social rank and urbanization Anderson and Egeland (1961) used a two-way analysis of variance to determine whether sectoral or concentric ring variation in these two social area indices was significant or not. Others (Rees, 1970b; Murdie, 1969; Timms, 1970) have later repeated this type of analysis for other cities, and Salins (1969) has used a rather different pattern test. The results for both American and non-American cities are summarized in Table 47.

The North American cities show according to this pattern test a strong sectoral bias. Seven out of nine North American cities in the table show a primarily sectoral pattern and one, Chicago, a mixed sectoral and concentric ring pattern. The British and Australian cities studied by Timms display rather weaker sectoral patterns, though only one, Derby, shows a dominant concentric pattern.

In the case of Chicago the importance of the concentric component was seen as a product of the size, age and heterogeneity of the metropolis in the following way. Massive population succession to lower status immigrant groups took place in the inner parts of sectors which were inhabited by middle class populations further

TABLE 46

MEDIAN SOCIOECONOMIC STATUS SCORES FOR ZONES OF SMSA'S

Zone Averages for All U.S., SMSA's	Socioeconomic Status Score
Central cities	53.6
Urban ring	62.6
Rural ring	50.7
SMSA average	51.7

Source: Ravers (1969).

from the city center because rapid growth of the city's economy encouraged new housing construction on the urban periphery and had the effect of speeding obsolescence and deterioration of the inner ring housing stock as many households preferred to move to newer residences. The dynamic city economy attracted lower status labor to the city and this replaced the departing middle class in inner city neighborhoods. The outward movement of black families was resisted by suburban householders and "succession pressure" was thereby increased on white inner city neighborhoods. Since many of the black families were more concentrated in the lower class than were whites the inner ring of the city became lower status in terms of social class mix as its population mix became blacker.

The larger and older and more racially heterogeneous the city the longer these forces are likely to have been at work. Whether this argument applies to Derby, England is a moot point, however.

A number of methodological problems arise in assessing the analysis of variance results. One of the key assumptions in the normal two-way analysis of variance is that there will be equal numbers of observations in each sub-class of the research design. If sectors and rings are overlaid on a tract map of a city it is unlikely that it will be possible to assign equal numbers of tracts to

TABLE 47

RESULTS OF THE ANALYSIS OF THE SPATIAL VARIANCE OF SOCIOECONOMIC STATUS IN SELECTED CITIES

City	Date	Variable	Variance Ratio F				Summary of Pattern[i]
			Between Sectors	Between Rings	Sectors x Rings	Ratio of Sector F to Rings F	
American cities							
Akron[a]	1950	Social area index-Social Rank	11.64**	1.93	—	6.03	S
Buffalo[b]	1960	Factor-Social Rank	.881[g]	.226[g]	—	3.90[h]	S
Chicago[c]	1960	Factor-Socioeconomic Status	12.47**	10.87**	1.64	1.15	SC
Dayton[a]	1950	Social area index Social Rank	16.97**	2.88	—	5.89	S
Indianapolis[a]	1950	Social area index Social Rank	8.29**	5.77**	—	1.44	Sc
Indianapolis[b]	1960	Factor-Social Rank	.833[g]	.319[g]	—	2.61[h]	Sc
Kansas City[b]	1960	Factor-Social Rank	.824[g]	.257[g]	—	3.20[h]	S
Spokane[b]	1960	Factor-Social Rank	.724[g]	.268[g]	—	2.70[h]	S
Syracuse[a]	1950	Social area index-Social Rank	10.74**	0.54	—	19.89	S
Other Western Cities							
Toronto[d]	1951	Factor-Economic Status	11.86**	0.81	—	14.64	S
Toronto[d]	1961	Factor-Economic Status	27.00**	0.90	3.50**	30.00	S
Luton[e]	1961	Rateable Value	14.70**	5.82	—	2.53	Sc

TABLE 47--Continued

City	Date	Variable	Variance Ratio F				Summary of Pattern[i]
			Between Sectors	Between Rings	Sectors x Rings	Ratio of Sector F to Rings F	
Other Western Cities							
Derby[e]	1961	Rateable Value	5.72*	13.50**	—	0.42	sC
Brisbane[e]	1961	Social area index-Social Rank	9.90**	7.60**	1.80	1.30	Sc
Rome[f]	1951	Social area index-Social Rank	28.59**	28.43**	—	1.00	SC

[a]From Anderson and Egeland (1961).

[b]From Salins (1969).

[c]From Rees (1970b).

[d]From Murdie (1969).

[e]From Timms (1971).

[f]From McElrath (1962).

[g]Salins' indices of sectorality and concentricity.

[h]Ratio of Salins' indices.

[i]S = primarily sectoral; Sc = more sectoral than concentric; SC = both sectoral and concentric
C = primarily concentric; NP = no pattern

each zone (sector-ring intersection). Two operational solutions have been adopted to this problem.

The first solution is to make up the numbers of observations in each sub-class to the maximum observed in any sub-class by inserting imaginary observation values equal to sub-class means (as in Murdie, 1969). Or, alternatively only a minimum but equal number of tracts are assinged to each zone (sector-ring intersection), these being selected randomly, if necessary (as in Anderson and Egeland, 1961; Timms, 1971). Both methods have their drawbacks. The first results in a biased estimate of within zone variance. Within zone variance is underestimated and the probability of making an incorrect decision in rejecting the null hypothesis of equal sector or ring means is larger than the significance test indicates. The second method has the disadvantage of ignoring much of the pattern information available.

Ideally, one should apply a two-way analysis of variance, weighted by the numbers of observations in each sub-class, but time was not availabe to work these methods out properly. The compromise adopted here consists of two separate analyses of variance. A one-way analysis of variance for sectors using the following formulae weighted for observation class numbers (adapted from Hagood and Price, 1952, p. 402):

$$\text{Between class sums of squares} = \sum_j \left[\frac{X_{*j*}}{n_{*j}} \right] - \frac{(X_{***})^2}{n_{**}} \qquad (9)$$

and

$$\text{Total sum of squares} = \sum\sum\sum_{ijk} (X_{ijk})^2 - \frac{(X_{***})^2}{n_{**}} \qquad (10)$$

where X_{ijk} is the value of the variable for the kth tract in the sub-class defined by the intersection of the ith row and jth column; X_{*j*} is $\sum\sum_{ik} X_{ijk}$ or the sum of variable values for class j; X_{***} is $\sum\sum\sum_{ijk} X_{ijk}$ or the sum of all variable values; n_{ij} is the number of observations in sub-class ij; n_{*j} is $\sum_i n_{ij}$ or the number of observations in class j; n_{**} is the total number of observations.

A similar one-way analysis of variance for rings using the same weighted formulae was carried out. These two analyses provide estimates of the significance of sectoral variation and ring variation based on all values without underestimating the within sector or within ring variance.

There is also the additional question of whether the tests of significance associated with the analysis of variance are applicable "in observational situations where the data are observed in the cross-classifications in which they are found rather than in cross-classifications in which they have been randomly placed in experiment" (Hagood and Price, 1952, p. 401). Strictly speaking, the tests are inapplicable, but they are used here as a useful device for describing the magnitude of variation of socioeconomic status with the two spatial classifications.

We now use the three techniques described in this section, ring and sector summaries, the analysis of spatial variance, and the analysis of map patterns, to investigate the spatial pattern of socioeconomic status, as measured by the index developed in Chapter V, in order to assess the evidence for and against the descriptive models outlined earlier in this chapter.

Analysis of the Sample Urbanized Area Patterns

Ring and Sector Summaries

We examine first the ring and sector summaries for our sample of urbanized areas. Each urbanized area was divided into three rings, the inner city, the outer city and the urban fringe, and three equal-sized sectors. The sectors were fitted to the tract map of socioeconomic status so as to maximize the between sector variation and to minimize the within sector variation. Census tracts were assigned to the ring-sector intersections or zones within which the largest part of their area fell. A residual area falling between the boundary of the urbanized area and that of the

SMSA was also defined.

The socioeconomic status scores for each zone was then calculated by averaging the scores of the census tracts making up the zone. Both population weighted and unweighted averages were calculated for the zones of Ann Arbor and since weighting appeared to make very little difference the unweighted averages were calculated for the other SMSAs. Subtables were prepared for ten of the SMSAs showing the socioeconomic status scores of the nine ring-sector zones and for the rest of the SMSA as a whole. These have been assembled in Table 48.

Using this table we can examine a number of the general propositions about the spatial pattern of socioeconomic status put forward in our earlier discussion. The first conclusion we come to when examining Table 48 is that purely concentric variation in socioeconomic status is approached only in the St. Paul part of the Minneapolis-St. Paul SMSA, and that largely sectoral variation is characteristic only of El Paso, where the "sectors" are defined not by geometric orientation to the city center but by the nature of the relief. The lower status areas occupy the lower land of the Rio Grande valley; the higher status areas occupy the hills above. A mixed pattern of concentricity and sectorality is prevalent.

The concentric variation of socioeconomic status pictured in Figure 10D in which the status scores ascend as the traverse from inner city to urban fringe is made is characteristic of Birmingham, Canton, Honolulu, Minneapolis, St. Paul, Providence-Pawtucket and Richmond. In Ann Arbor, Des Moines, El Paso and Lancaster the average socioeconomic status score of the urban fringe tracts is lower than that of the outer city. Here we have a milder version of the rise then fall of socioeconomic status along a traverse outwards from the city center noted for Chicago in Rees (1970b). In all cases, however, the inner city average is lower than the outer city average, and the urbanized area fringe average is higher than the

TABLE 48

SOCIOECONOMIC STATUS SCORES FOR ZONES
IN SELECTED URBANIZED AREAS

ANN ARBOR[a]

Rings	Sectors			Ring Averages
	Western	Northern	Southeastern	
Inner City	55.98	55.82	61.43	59.36
	(55.98)	(56.32)	(61.93)	(59.07)
Outer City	67.56	66.23	72.73	68.70
	(64.17)	(65.90)	(70.08)	(66.72)
Urban Fringe	58.87	63.20	61.07	60.07
	(59.34)	(61.28)	(63.85)	(62.08)
Sector Averages	63.19	62.14	63.67	63.12[b]
	(60.73)	(61.72)	(64.77)	(62.84)[b]
Ypsilanti				53.83[c]
Rural Fringe				50.70
Urbanized Area				59.69
SMSA				57.53

BIRMINGHAM

Rings	Sectors			Ring Averages
	Southeastern	Northeastern	Western	
Inner City	45.46	33.40	37.65	38.84
Outer City	66.68	45.40	44.82	52.30
Urban Fringe	68.45	53.83	43.45	55.28
Sector Averages	60.02	44.21	42.01	45.62
Rest of the SMSA				45.22
Urbanized Area				47.24
SMSA				46.95

CANTON

Rings	Sectors			Ring Averages
	Northwestern	Eastern	Southwestern	
Inner City	53.17	42.67	44.74	46.47
Outer City	59.09	51.71	49.65	53.26
Urban Fringe	62.88	51.11	50.37	56.17
Sector Averages	58.89	47.49	47.83	51.74[d]
Massillon				49.88[e]
Alliance				51.70
Rest of the SMSA				49.81
SMSA				51.21

TABLE 48--Continued

DES MOINES Rings	Sectors Western	Eastern	Southern	Ring Averages
Inner City	51.03	45.73	48.10	48.18
Outer City	67.97	51.12	53.54	56.88
Urban Fringe	62.40	50.32	53.03	55.80
Sector Averages	60.26	49.07	51.96	53.68
Rest of the SMSA				48.84
SMSA				55.47

EL PASO Rings	Sectors Hill	Valley	Ring Averages
Inner City	55.35	33.42	41.25
Outer City	58.72	44.55	53.72
Urban Fringe	61.05	43.60	49.42
Sector Averages	58.35	39.86	48.46[f]
Rest of the SMSA			51.63
SMSA			48.69

HONOLULU Rings	Sectors Western	Northeastern	Southeastern	Ring Averages
Inner City	45.72	54.56	48.35	49.31
Outer City	55.35	60.28	57.36	57.83
City Fringes	54.24	61.18	68.64	58.41
Sector Averages	50.95	58.13	56.52	54.87
Rest of the SMSA				50.21
SMSA				53.48

LANCASTER Rings	Sectors Western	Northern	Eastern	Ring Averages
Inner City	48.52	50.06	45.04	47.15
Outer City	61.89	54.21	50.51	56.16
Urban Fringe	53.95	54.49	48.57	52.74
Sector Averages	54.14	53.61	47.29	51.82
Rest of the SMSA				45.05
SMSA				47.82

TABLE 48--Continued

MINNEAPOLIS

Rings	Sectors			Ring Averages
	Western	Northern	Eastern	
Inner City	51.51	44.91	46.87	48.00
Outer City	59.09	52.25	54.04	54.76
Urban Fringe	64.58	57.65	60.25	61.66
Sector Averages	61.22	53.69	53.86	56.86

ST. PAUL

Rings	Sectors			Ring Averages
	Western	Northern	Eastern	
Inner City	47.08	44.87	47.25	46.48
Outer City	55.81	52.30	55.75	54.90
Urban Fringe	63.05	59.85	55.33	59.91
Sector Averages	55.80	54.57	52.12	54.60
Rest of the SMSA				50.15
SMSA				55.64

PROVIDENCE-PAWTUCKET

Rings	Sectors			Ring Averages
	Western	Eastern	Southern	
Inner City	44.08	52.32	47.85	47.66
Outer City	47.47	47.76	54.55	49.28
Urban Fringe	50.79	51.22	52.46	51.85
Sector Averages	46.93	49.31	52.00	49.78
Rest of the SMSA				45.38
SMSA				48.95

RICHMOND

Rings	Sectors			Ring Averages
	Western	Northern	Southeastern	
Inner City	42.53	40.32	39.00	40.90
Outer City	57.91	56.10	44.82	52.96
Urban Fringe	60.50	57.01	50.04	55.59
Sector Averages	52.01	48.80	44.75	48.76
Rest of the SMSA				46.11
SMSA				48.58

Notes

[a]Where two scores are given in a cell of the table the upper score is the population weighted score; the lower one in parentheses

TABLE 48--Continued

Notes--Continued

is the unweighted score used in the analysis of variance calculations. It is assumed that no significant bias is introduced in the analysis through use of unweighted scores. In subsequent sub-tables of this type just the unweighted scores are reported.

[b]This is the average for the Ann Arbor portion of the Ann Arbor urbanized area.

[c]This is the average for the Ypsilanti portion of the Ann Arbor urbanized area.

[d]This score refers to the Canton portion of the urbanized area.

[e]This score refers to the Massillon portion of the urbanized area.

[f]This is the unweighted score for El Paso urbanized area less tract 17 which contains the CBD.

rural fringe or rest of the SMSA average. That much of the Chicago pattern is applicable to all the cities studied here. The inner city-outer city relationship (the latter having a higher socioeconomic status) holds not only the SMSAs studied but also for all the individual sectors defined within those SMSAs with the one exception of Providence-Pawtucket's Eastern sector.

We cannot make such general statements about which sectors have the highest or lowest scores on the socioeconomic status index because a variety of different factors are at play here. We can, however, examine the extent to which compass orientation plays a part in locating the highest status residents. In a zone of westerly winds one would expect that, since those winds would protect westerly portions of cities from excessive air pollution, the western sectors would be the highest status sectors. A "western" sector can be identified in 10 of the 11 urbanized areas covered in Table 48 (the exception is El Paso) and in 6 of the 10 (Canton, Des Moines, Lancaster, Minneapolis, St. Paul, Richmond) the "western" sector exhibits the highest socioeconomic status of the three sectors. In Birmingham and Honolulu large industrial plants and large military bases respectively occupy the western sector displacing the highest status sector elsewhere. In Providence-Pawtucket the Newport side of Rhode Island Sound has been the prestige place to live. In Ann Arbor, the other urbanized area without a "western" pattern, the location of the University of Michigan to the southeast of the city center means a reorientation of the socioeconomic status pattern in this direction.

The Analysis of Spatial Variance

The relative importances of the sectoral and concentric patterns can be judged, in part, by a series of analyses of variance. This is done by comparison of the F ratios derived from an analysis of sectoral variance and from an analysis of concentric variance. Since the degrees of freedom of the sectoral F and the concentric F are usually equal, this is equivalent to comparing the between sector and between ring variances directly.

Table 49 records the results of the analyses of sectoral and concentric variance for eleven urbanized areas. Each subtable gives the total sums of squared deviations of the census tract socioeconomic status scores from the urbanized area mean for each city. This sum of squared deviations is partitioned, separately, into between and within sectors components and into rings and within rings components. These sums of squared deviations components are normalized by dividing by the degrees of freedom involved and the F ratio of between to within sectors or rings mean sum of squared deviations is computed. If this F ratio exceeds the F_{95} and F_{99} ratios displayed alongside, then the differences between sectors or rings can be regarded as statistically significant at the 95 or 99 per cent confidence level.

The results of Table 49 are consolidated for easy reference in Table 50, and the ratio of sectors F to rings F is there calculated. A ratio of below one indicates that concentric variation is more important than sectoral variation; a ratio of more than one shows that sectoral variation is more important.

The conclusions that we can draw from Table 50 indicate clearly that both spatial patterns are present in the social class geography of American cities. Of the eleven cities, seven exhibit both statistically significant sectoral variation and statistically significant concentric variation. Of the other four, two exhibit some mixture of the two patterns. Only in one city, St. Paul, can the pattern be described as unambiguously concentric, and in the other Twin City, Minneapolis, the pattern is mixed. Only in one city can the pattern be described as exclusively sectoral and in that city such a result reflects the close association of ethnicity and socioeconomic status in El Paso.

It has been suggested (Rees, 1970b) that the larger, older and more heterogeneous a city the more its social status pattern would be concentric, though the sectoral component was expected to remain important. Table 51, which puts together the previous results of Table 47 with those of the present study, reveals that this hypothesis cannot be maintained. Both small and large cities possess patterns that are more concentric than sectoral, though a majority of cities display a pattern more sectoral than concentric. Only a few cities show extreme values of the F ratio, and most show the mixture of spatial patterns suggested in our integrated spatial model. No obvious common denominators among either the "concentric" or "sectoral" cities spring to mind. The balance between the two is probably set by idiosyncratic factors peculiar to each city. We will now examine some of these factors by looking at the map evidence and map correlates for selected cities.

The Map Patterns

The map patterns of socioeconomic status for our twelve sample SMSAs are displayed in Figures 14 through 27. The general key to

TABLE 49

ANALYSIS OF VARIANCE OF SOCIOECONOMIC STATUS IN SELECTED URBANIZED AREAS

Source	Sums of squared deviations	Degrees of Freedom	Mean Sums Squared Deviations	F	F_{95}	F_{99}
ANN ARBOR						
A. Sectors						
Total	1632.740	30	54.425			
Between sectors	99.212	2	49.606	0.91	3.34	5.45
Within sectors	1533.528	28	54.769			
B. Rings						
Total	1632.740	30	54.425			
Between rings	229.848	2	114.924	2.29	3.34	5.45
Within rings	1402.892	28	50.103			
BIRMINGHAM						
A. Sectors						
Total	10577.706	88	120.201			
Between sectors	2105.434	2	1052.717	10.69	3.10	4.87
Within sectors	8472.272	86	98.515			
B. Rings						
Total	10577.706	88	120.201			
Between rings	1458.419	2	729.210	6.87	3.10	4.87
Within rings	9119.287	86	106.038			
CANTON						
A. Sectors						
Total	2409.496	40	60.237			
Between sectors	1207.963	2	603.982	20.48	3.34	5.45
Within sectors	1120.826	38	29.495			

TABLE 49--Continued

Source	Sums of squared deviations	Degrees of Freedom	Mean Sums Squared Deviations	F	F_{95}	F_{99}
CANTON--Continued						
B. Rings						
Total	2409.496	40	60.237			
Between rings	779.387	2	389.694	9.08	3.34	5.45
Within rings	1630.109	38	42.898			
DES MOINES						
A. Sectors						
Total	3997.643	52	75.878			
Between sectors	1344.862	2	672.431	12.67	3.19	5.08
Within sectors	2652.781	50	53.056			
B. Rings						
Total	3997.643	52	76.878			
Between rings	833.139	2	416.510	6.58	3.19	5.08
Within rings	3164.504	50	63.290			
EL PASO						
A. Sectors						
Total	6928.331	42	164.960			
Between sectors	3654.365	1	3654.365	45.76	4.08	7.32
Within sectors	3273.966	41	79.853			
B. Rings						
Total	6928.331	42	164.960			
Between rings	1208.955	2	604.478	4.23	3.23	5.18
Within rings	5719.376	40	124.984			

TABLE 49--Continued

Source	Sums of squared deviations	Degrees of Freedom	Mean Sums Squared Deviations	F	F_{95}	F_{99}
HONOLULU						
A. Sectors						
Total	5661.387	79	71.663			
Between sectors	806.299	2	403.150	6.39	3.13	4.93
Within sectors	4855.088	77	63.053			
B. Rings						
Total	5661.387	79	71.663			
Between rings	1407.103	2	703.552	12.73	3.13	4.93
Within rings	4254.284	77	55.250			
LANCASTER						
A. Sectors						
Total	1085.812	24	45.242			
Between sectors	242.770	2	121.385	3.17	3.44	5.72
Within sectors	843.042	22	38.320			
B. Rings						
Total	1085.812	24	45.242			
Between rings	354.351	2	177.176	5.33	3.44	5.72
Within rings	731.461	22	33.248			
MINNEAPOLIS						
A. Sectors						
Total	12829.79	216	59.40			
Between sectors	2923.88	2	1461.94	31.58	2.99	4.60
Within sectors	9905.91	214	46.29			

TABLE 49--Continued

Source	Sums of squared deviations	Degrees of Freedom	Mean Sums Squared Deviations	F	F_{95}	F_{99}
MINNEAPOLIS--Continued						
B. Rings						
Total	12829.79	216	59.40			
Between rings	6347.04	2	3173.52	104.77	2.99	4.60
Within rings	6482.75	214	30.29			
ST. PAUL						
A. Sectors						
Total	5520.47	104	53.08			
Between sectors	201.67	2	100.84	1.93	3.09	4.84
Within sectors	5318.80	102	52.15			
B. Rings						
Total	5520.47	104	53.08			
Between rings	2883.45	2	1441.73	55.77	3.09	4.84
Within rings	2637.02	102	25.85			
PROVIDENCE-PAWTUCKET						
A. Sectors						
Total	7065.79	141	50.11			
Between sectors	535.44	2	267.72	5.70	3.05	4.75
Within sectors	6530.35	139	40.98			
B. Rings						
Total	7065.79	141	50.11			
Between rings	355.91	2	177.96	3.69	3.05	4.75
Within rings	6709.88	139	48.27			

TABLE 49--Continued

Source	Sums of squared deviations	Degrees of Freedom	Mean Sums Squared Deviations	F	F_{95}	F_{99}
RICHMOND						
A. Sectors						
Total	10620.16	80	132.75			
Between sectors	782.05	2	391.03	3.10	3.13	4.92
Within sectors	9838.11	78	126.13			
B. Rings						
Total	10620.16	80	132.75			
Between rings	3526.75	2	1763.38	19.39	3.13	4.92
Within rings	7093.41	78	90.94			

Notes

F = the F variance ratio; the ratio between within-class variance and between-class variance

F_{95} = the critical F ratio at 95 per cent confidence limits

F_{99} = the critical F ratio at 99 per cent confidence limits

TABLE 50

RESULTS OF THE ANALYSIS OF THE SPATIAL VARIANCE OF SOCIOECONOMIC STATUS FOR THE SAMPLE URBANIZED AREAS

City	Date	Variance Ratio F[a]			Summary of Pattern[b]
		Between Sectors	Between Rings	Ratio of Sectors F to Rings F	
Ann Arbor	1960	0.91	2.29	0.40	sC
Birmingham	1960	10.69**	6.87**	1.56	Sc
Canton	1960	20.48**	9.08**	2.26	Sc
Des Moines	1960	12.67**	6.58**	1.93	Sc
El Paso	1960	45.76**	4.23*	10.82	S
Honolulu	1960	6.39**	12.73**	0.50	sC
Lancaster	1960	3.17	5.33*	0.59	sC
Minneapolis	1960	31.58**	104.77**	0.46	sC
St. Paul	1960	1.93	55.77**	0.07	C
Providence-Pawtucket	1960	5.70**	3.69*	1.54	Sc
Richmond	1960	3.10	19.39**	0.16	sC

Notes

[a]Significance levels: *significant at 5 per cent level; **significant at 1 per cent level.

[b]The letters stand for: S = primarily sectoral; Sc = more sectoral than concentric; SC = both sectoral and concentric; sC = more concentric than sectoral; C = primarily concentric; NP = no pattern.

TABLE 51

SUMMARY OF THE SPATIAL PATTERN RESULTS FOR AMERICAN CITIES

Urbanized Area	Date	Population ('000s)	Ratio of sector F to ring F ratio
Chicago	1960	5,959	1.15
Toronto	1961	1,824	30.00
Toronto	1951		14.64
Buffalo	1960	1,054	3.90[a]
Kansas City	1960	921	3.20[a]
Minneapolis	1960	905	0.46
Providence-Pawtucket	1960	660	1.54

TABLE 51--Continued

Urbanized Area	Date	Population ('000s)	Ratio of sector F to ring F ratio
Indianapolis	1960	639	2.61[a]
Birmingham	1960	521	1.56
Indianapolis	1950	502	1.44
St. Paul	1960	472	0.07
Akron	1950	367	6.03
Honolulu	1960	351	0.50
Dayton	1950	347	5.89
Richmond	1960	333	0.16
El Paso	1960	277	10.82
Syracuse	1950	265	19.89
Des Moines	1960	241	1.93
Spokane	1960	226	2.70[a]
Canton	1960	214	2.26
Ann Arbor	1960	115	0.40
Lancaster	1960	94	0.59

Notes

[a]Ratio of Salins' Index of Sectorality to his Index of Concentricity.

the maps is shown in Figure 13. Tracts have been placed in some eight socioeconomic status score categories ranging from less than 30 to greater than or equal to 70. A score of 70 for a census tract, for example, means that the average status of persons residing in that area lies at the 70 percentile of the national distribution of socioeconomic status: 30 per cent of individuals have greater status and 70 per cent less status in the U.S. population as a whole. Brief commetns are made on each map and then two cities, Birmingham and Des Moines are looked at in more detail.

Figure 14 shows the spatial pattern for Ann Arbor, a college town with a large faculty and student population, with overall a high average status (63 for the urbanized area as a whole). In only

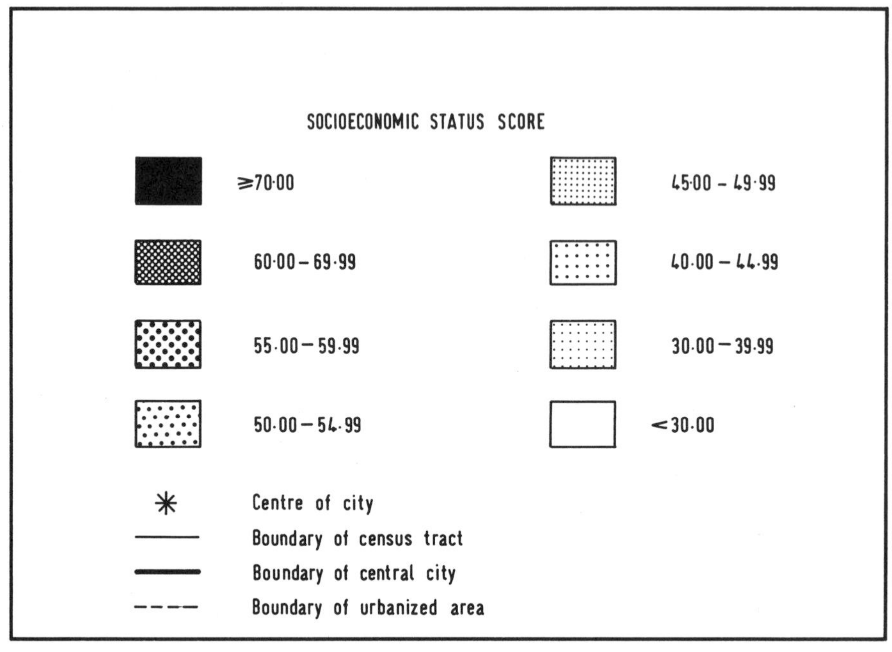

Fig. 13.--The General Key for the Socioeconomic Status Maps

a few rural tracts and those close to the sub-center of Ypsilanti does socioeconomic status fall below the national mean (50). The socioeconomic status map of Birmingham (Figure 15) shows a different pattern of considerable contrasts between residential areas in social class composition. We will look at some of the correlates of this map a little later in the chapter. The Canton map (Figure 16) shows the two center pattern of Ann Arbor with lower status tracts in central Massillon as well as Canton proper. Canton's industrial plants are concentrated in the southern and eastern sectors, and beyond the urbanized area to the southeast lie large strip coal mines, active and abandoned. It is no wonder then that the middle and high status residential areas of the SMSA should be to the north and northwest of the city center. Des Moines' map of socioeconomic status (Figure 17) shows a remarkable similarity to that of Canton with similar orientation of high, middle and lower status neighborhooods. The role of the physical geography of the city shows up in the El Paso map (Figure 18) in the contrast between the Rio Grande valley and the hills behind (pleasanter places to live in the hot summer). This physical division is also coincident with the ethnic division in the city between Mexican Americans and "Anglo" Americans: the former live in the valley, the latter in the hills. The Honolulu map (Figure 19) shows a mixture of spatial and environmental features. The highest status neighborhoods are located in the outer parts of the city in finger like extensions thrusting back into Oahu's main mountain chain and along the Pacific coast around Waikiki Beach and Diamond Head. The central neighborhoods in the docks and military base areas are of much lower status.

Lancaster's map (Figure 20) shows the same mixed sectoral and concentric pattern as Canton and Des Moines but with more contrast between central and peripheral neighborhoods. Minneapolis-St. Paul (Figure 21) shows two repeating patterns rather than one, and a very high status level overall with extensive areas scoring over 60 points on the socioeconomic status scale. Figure 22 shows the socioeconomic status pattern of the two central cities of Providence-Pawtucket and Figure 23 shows the picture for the SMSA as a whole. The high status areas lie to the east of Providence's center and to the south of the central cities along the shoreline. Figure 24 shows the pattern for Richmond, Virginia. A glance forward at the racial status map for this urbanized area (Figure 58) reveals almost complete complimentarity between the two. Figures 25, 26 and 27 show the socioeconomic status patterns of San Bernadino-Riverside and Tampa-St. Petersburg urbanized areas. Both have at least two centers and a rather heterogeneous pattern of high, middle and low status areas. Both SMSAs have lower status rural

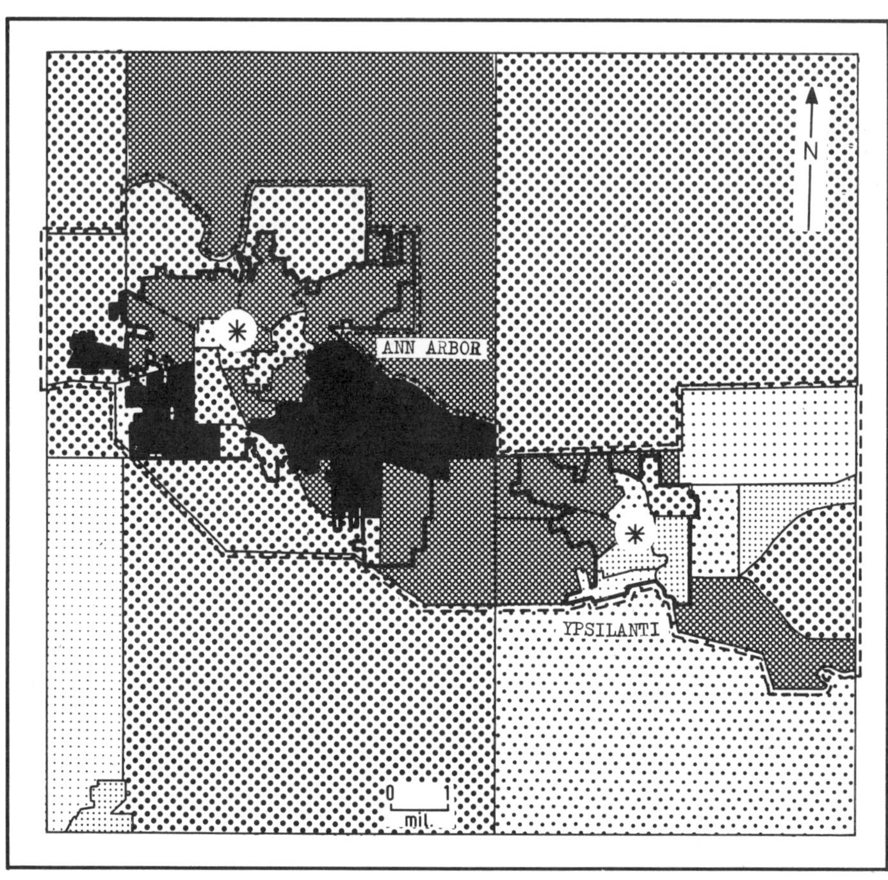

Fig. 14--The Spatial Pattern of Socioeconomic Status, Ann Arbor, 1960

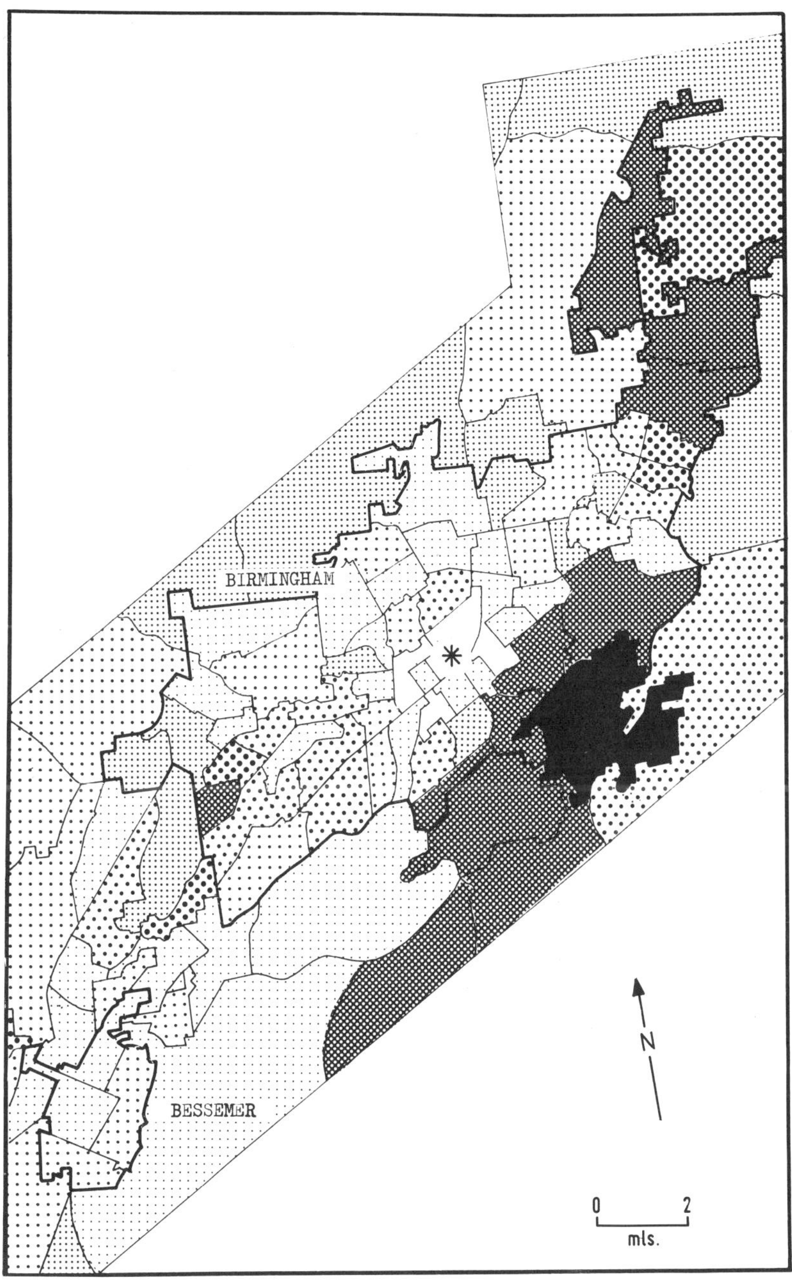

Fig. 15.--The Spatial Pattern of Socioeconomic Status, Birmingham, 1960

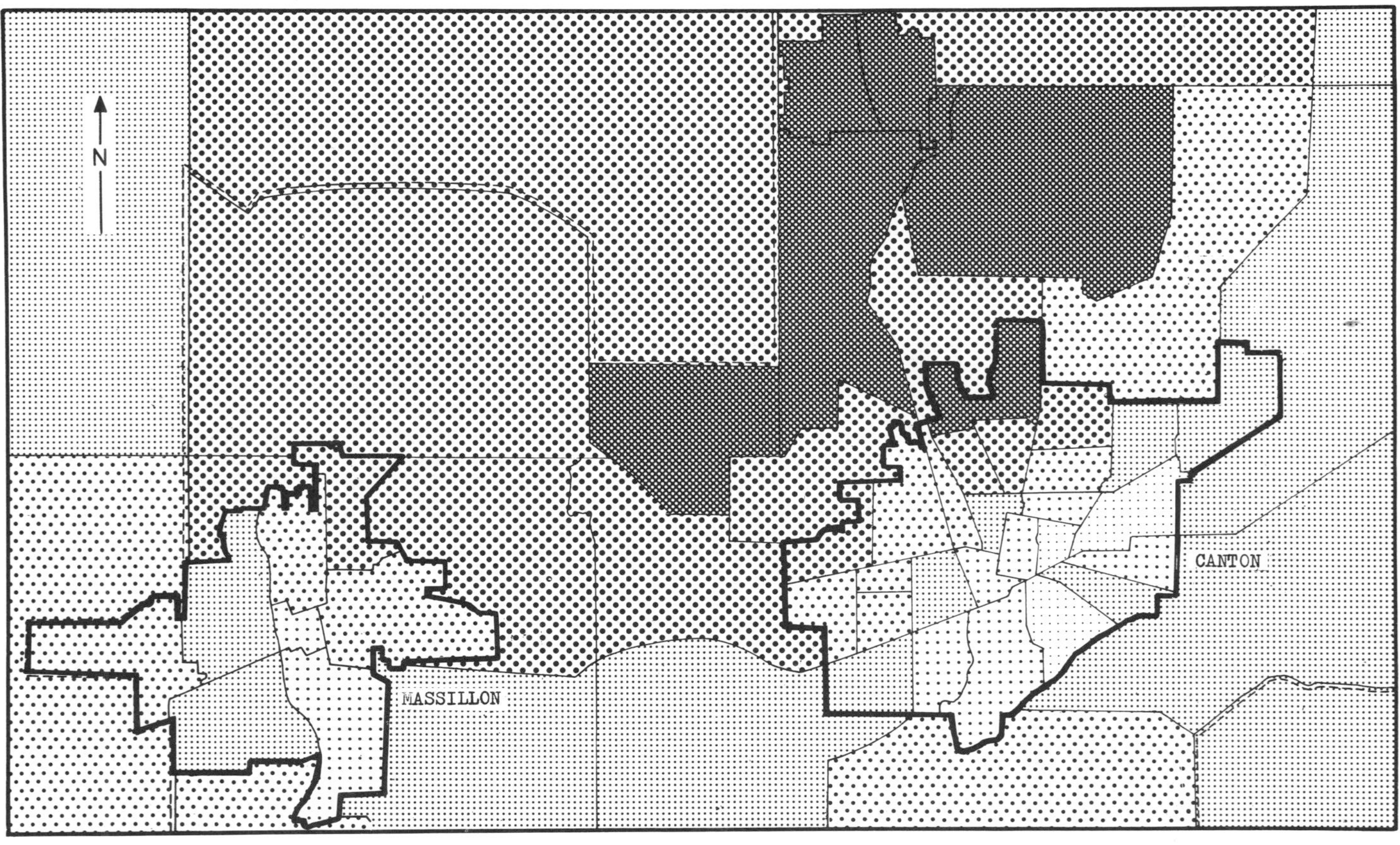

Fig. 16.--The Spatial Pattern of Socioeconomic Status, Canton, 1960

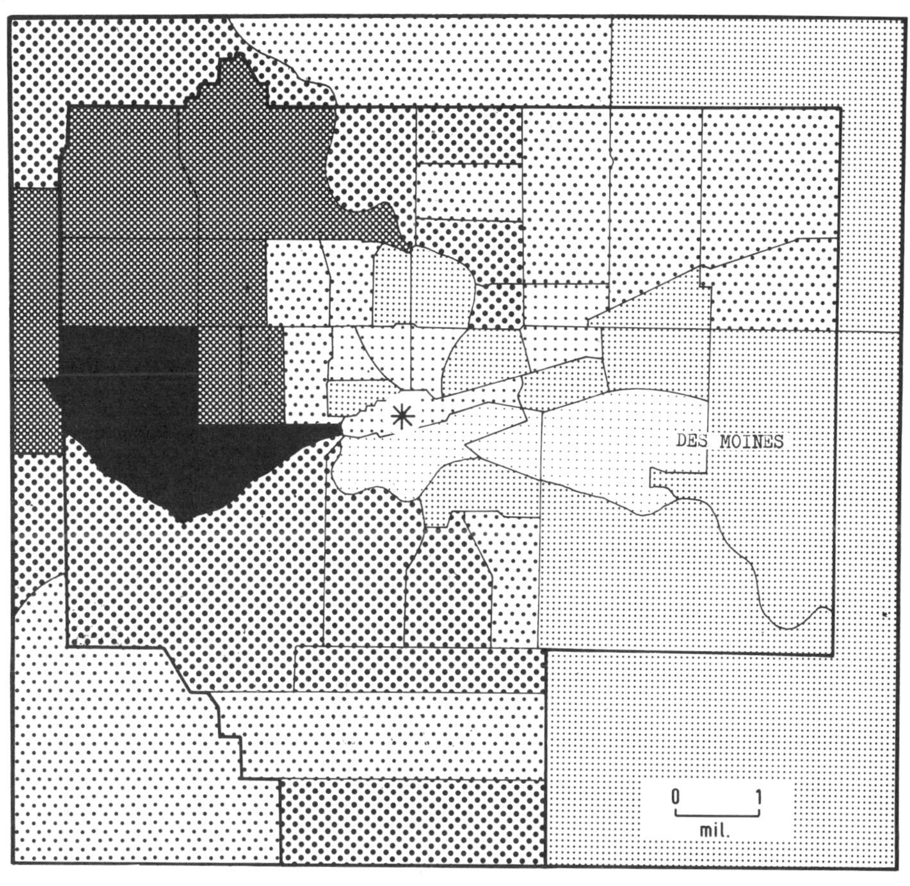

Fig. 17.--The Spatial Pattern of Socioeconomic Status, Des Moines, 1960

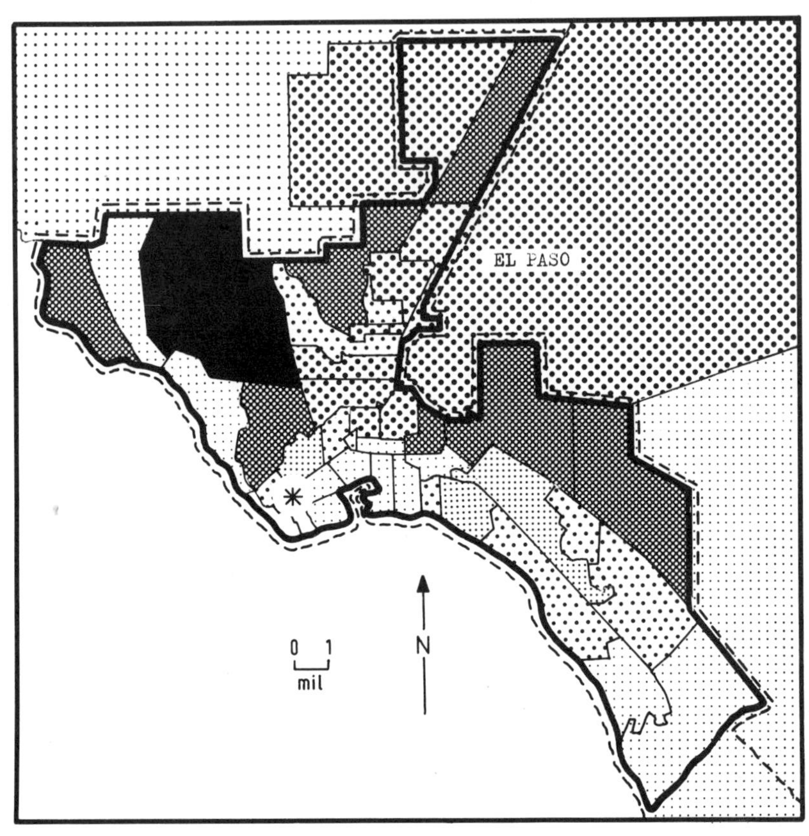

Fig. 18.--The Spatial Pattern of Socioeconomic Status, El Paso, 1960

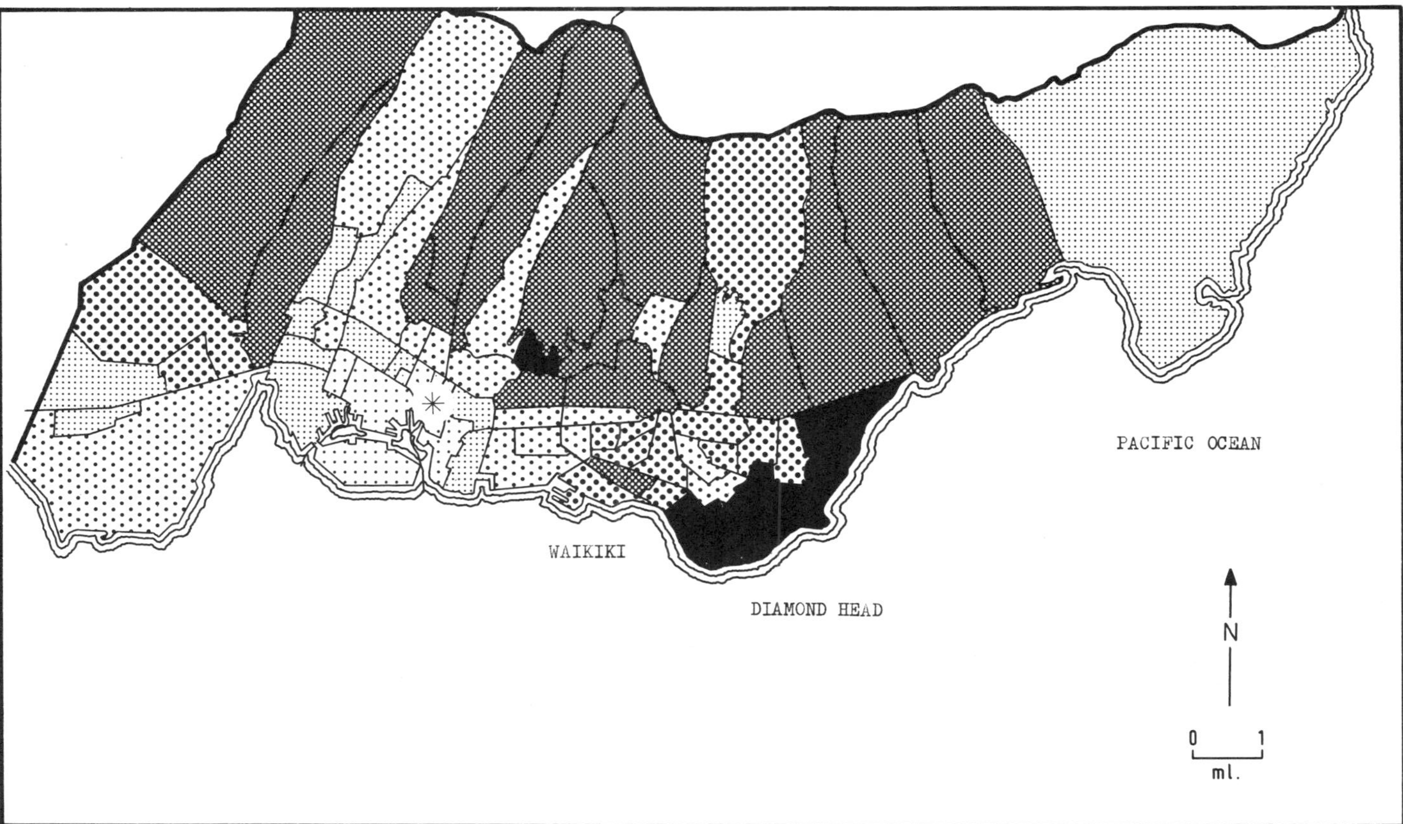

Fig. 19.--The Spatial Pattern of Socioeconomic Status, Honolulu, 1960

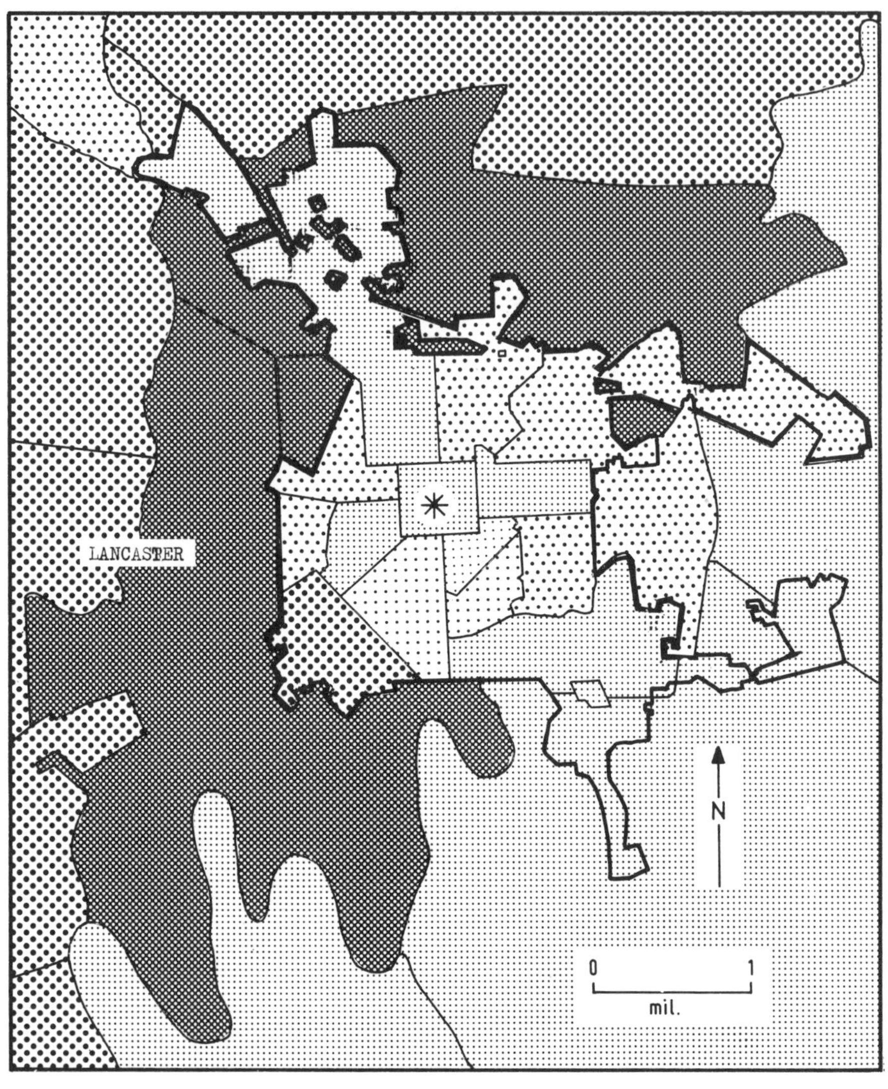

Fig. 20.--The Spatial Pattern of Socioeconomic Status, Lancaster, 1960

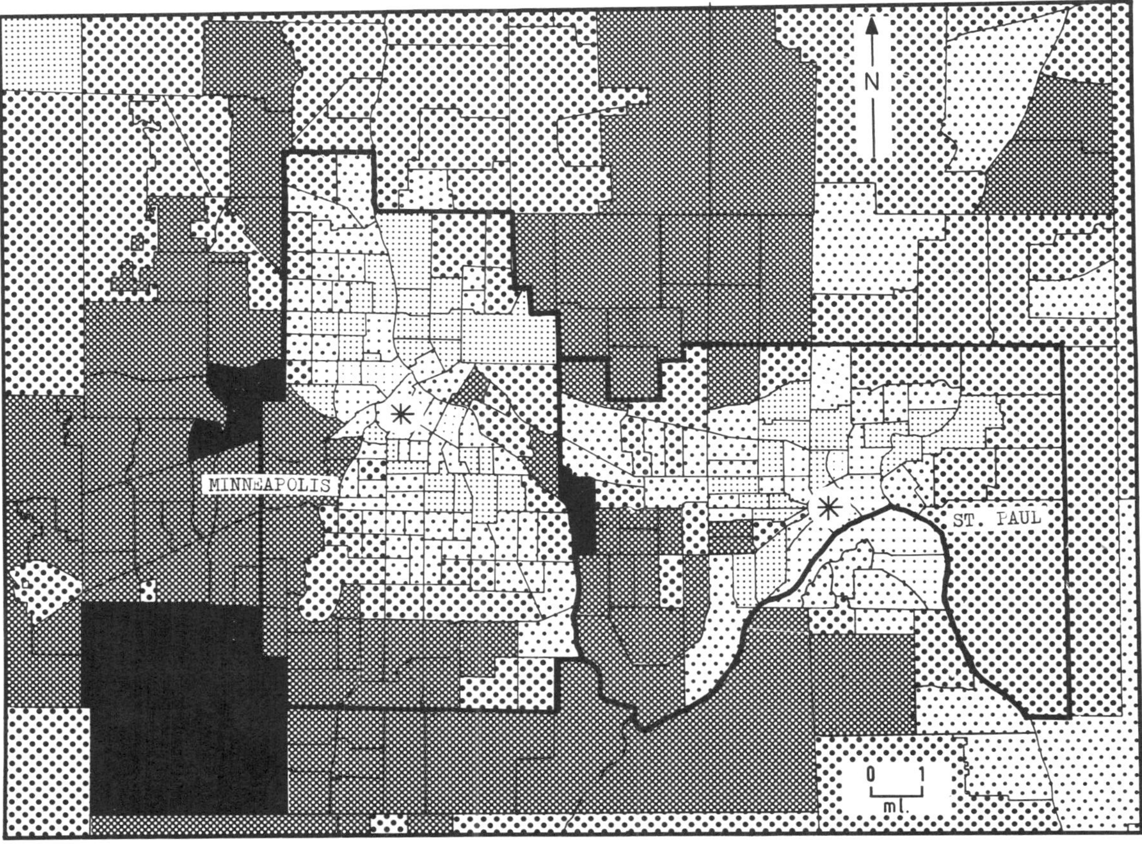

Fig. 21.--The Spatial Pattern of Socioeconomic Status, Minneapolis-St. Paul, 1960

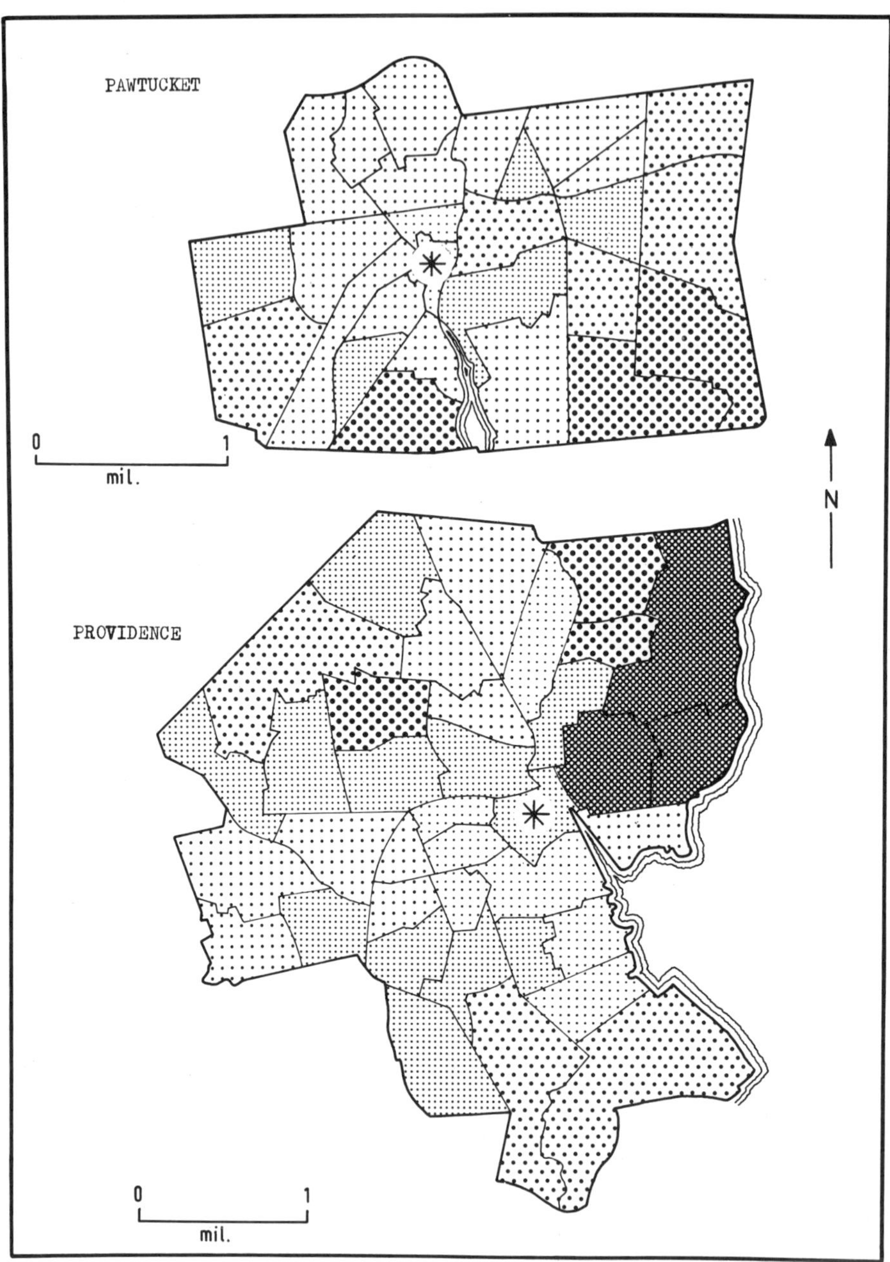

Fig. 22.--The Spatial Pattern of Socioeconomic Status, Providence and Pawtucket Central Cities, 1960

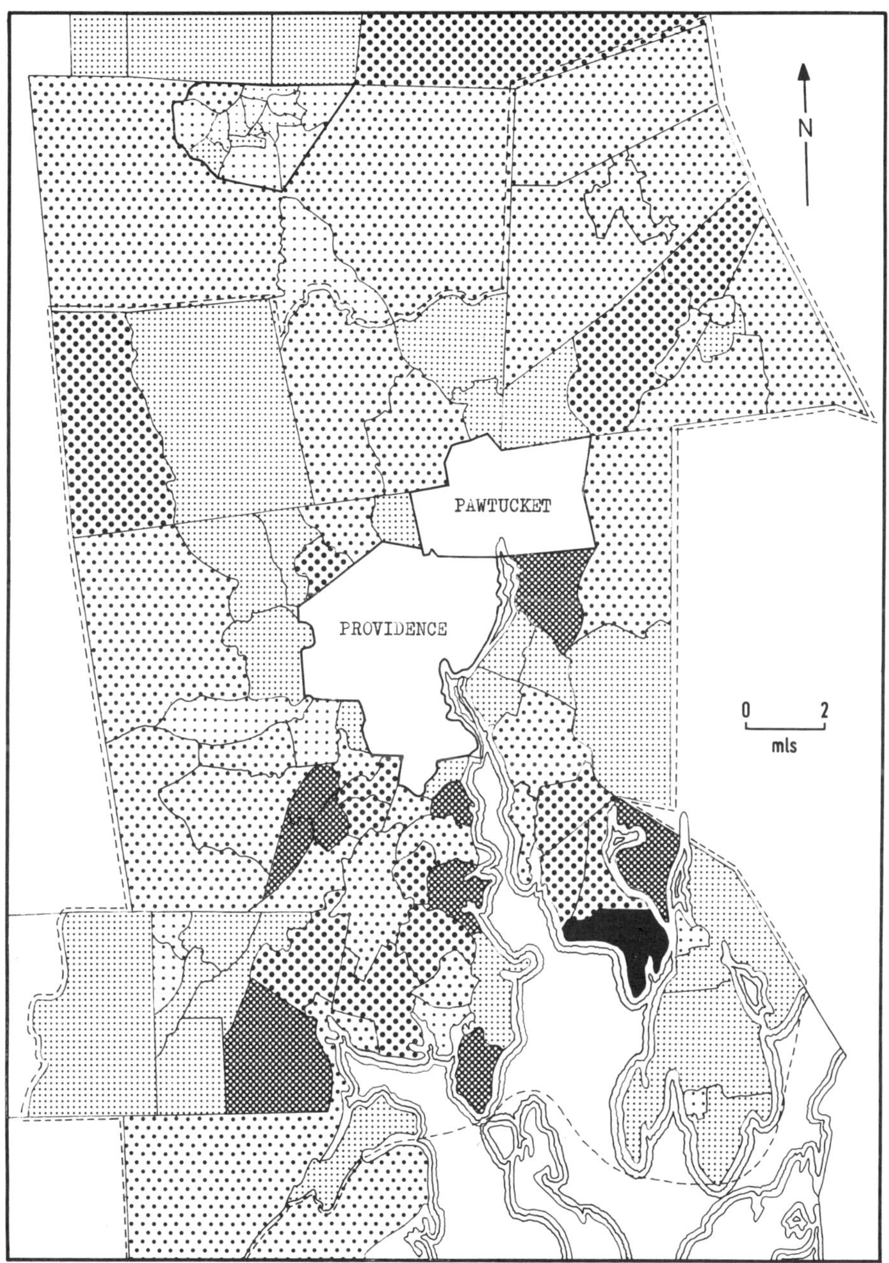

Fig. 23.--The Spatial Pattern of Socioeconomic Status, Providence-Pawtucket SMSA, 1960

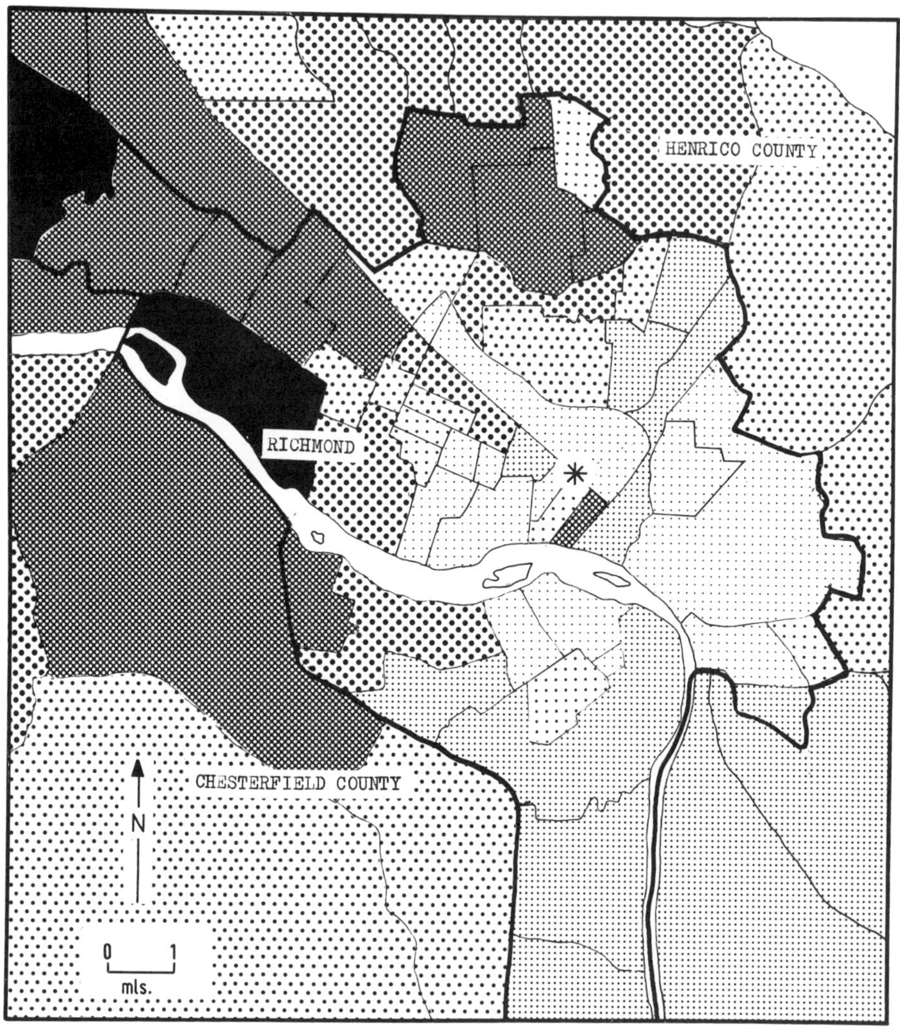

Fig. 24.--The Spatial Pattern of Socioeconomic Status, Richmond, 1960

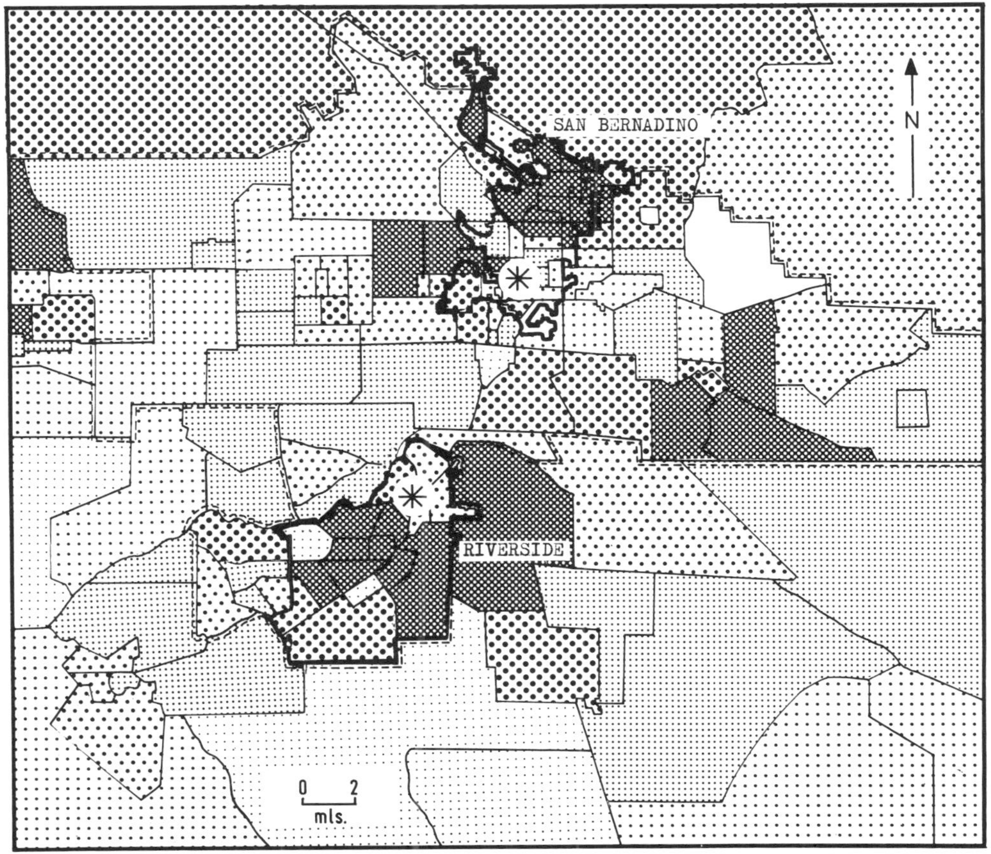

Fig. 25.--The Spatial Pattern of Socioeconomic Status, San Bernadino-Riverside, 1960

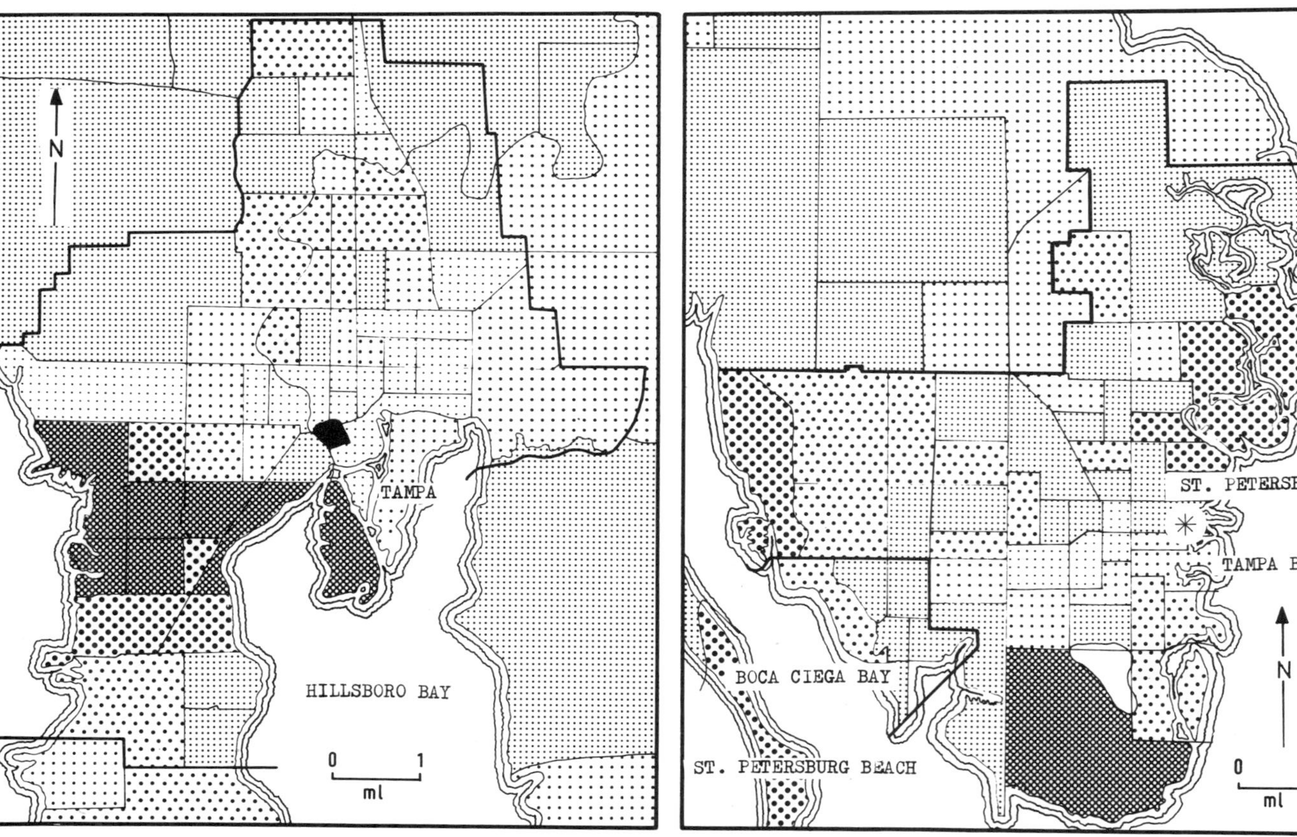

Fig. 26.--The Spatial Pattern of Socioeconomic Status, Tampa and St. Petersburg Central Cities, 1960

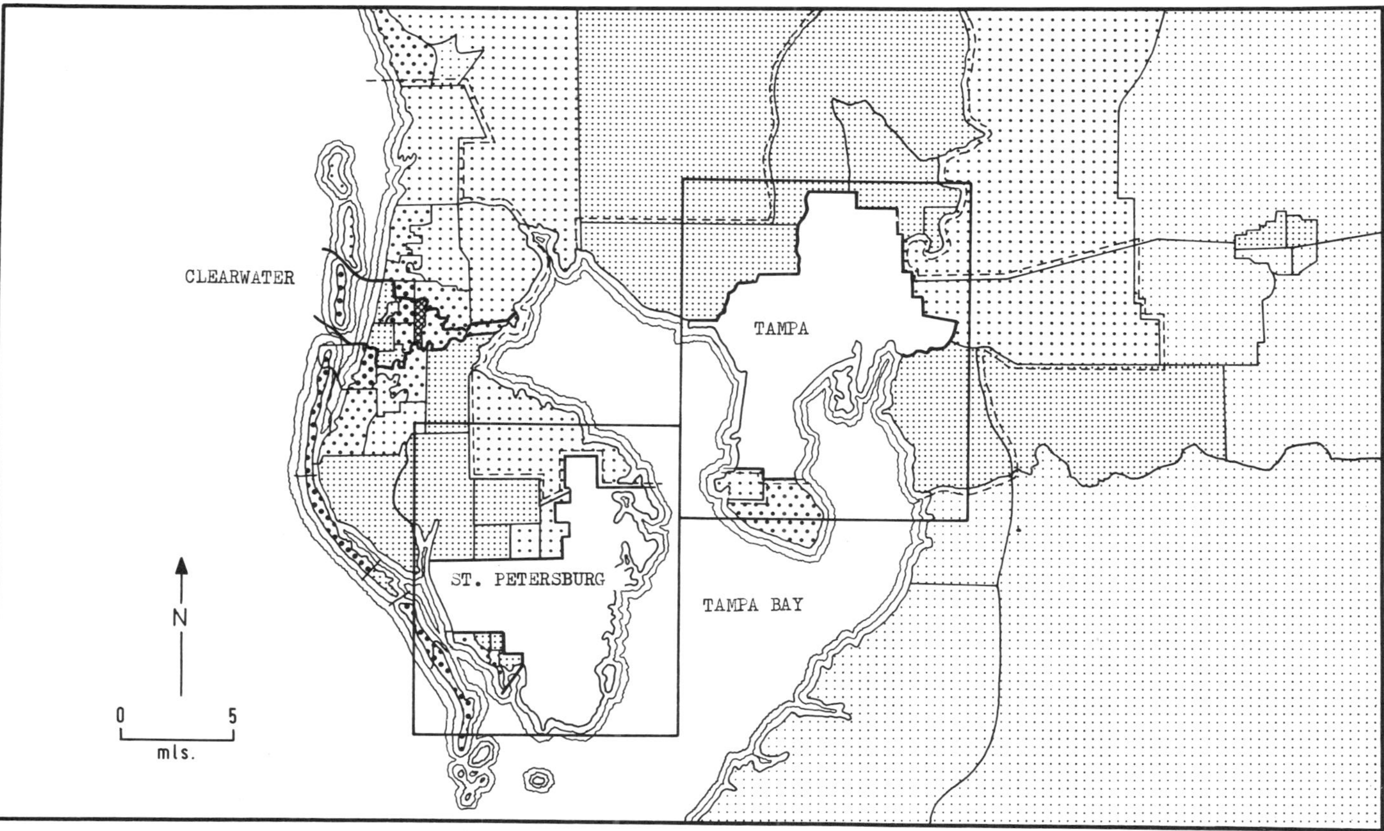

Fig. 27.--The Spatial Pattern of Socioeconomic Status, Tampa-St. Petersburg SMSA, 1960

peripheries and urban cores. They also have more of their high status residential areas within their central cities than the other SMSAs. St. Petersburg's higher status areas cluster on shoreline locations. The middle classes occupy the areas intermediate between the littoral and the central districts, and between the littoral and the periphery of the SMSA.

In general the multi-centered metropolis turns out to be much commoner than urban theory would have us suppose. Of the twelve SMSAs in our sample, six contain two or more major centers around which the residential pattern is "organized." We have acknowledged this in our earlier tests of geometric pattern by including Massillon's inner city tracts with those of Canton and Massillon's outer city tracts in with those of Canton. Minneapolis and St. Paul were treated separately, and no tests were carried out for San Bernadino-Riverside and Tampa-St. Petersburg. Integration of the methodology that explicitly recognizes such "multicentricity" (Wilson, 1969) with the type of pattern study reported here is a fruitful avenue of research to be pursued (Senior, 1973).

The Map Correlates of Socioeconomic Status in Birmingham and Des Moines

We have commented very briefly in the last section on the possible factors that explain some of the idiosyncracies in the maps of socioeconomic status, having prior to that attempted to extract the general patterns. Here we look in detail at a city with a factor structure that revealed close association between socioeconomic status and racial status (Birmingham) and a city in which the association was much looser (Des Moines).

The close association in the case of Birmingham is confirmed if we compare carefully the socioeconomic status map (Figure 15) and the racial status map (Figure 50). The severe degree of socioeconomic disadvantage of Negroes in Birmingham implied in the factor structure is given further support by the map patterns. How, though, do we interpret the spatial distribution of this pattern of disadvantage?

The physical layout of the site of Birmingham (Figure 28) militates against any simple interpretation of the status pattern. Birmingham lies at the southeastern end of the Appalachian ridge and valley country and the urbanized area spreads over several valleys and dividing ridges (Figure 28). In two of the valleys are located the heavy industry for which Birmingham is famed. The residential area adjacent to the large areas of industrial land in the Village Creek and Valley Creek valleys are largely of low status — the homes of the blue collar workers who work in the valley industries. The very lowest status areas, however, are where the concentric ring and growth model places them: around the business district and industrial area at the center of Birmingham.

The highest status areas are located away from the industrial land to the east of the central business district in eastern Birmingham and in the suburbs beyond (Mountain Brook, Homewood and Vestavia Hills), in the hilly country in the northeast part of the urbanized area, and finally in neighborhoods along Flint Ridge between the two industrial concentrations of North Birmingham and Bessemer. The highest status areas are located above the industrial valleys or behind a ridge from them.

Information on the way Birmingham's social status pattern has evolved over the twenty years prior to 1960 is available from an earlier study. (Cohen, 1968). In Figure 29 are plotted tract values of indices which approximate to our socioeconomic status index. They are not precisely comparable being scores of the first principal component of a 1940 and a 1950 factor analysis of socioeconomic data for Birmingham tracts. The variables and loadings which make up these factors are given in Table 52. The factors combine indicators of socioeconomic status (Median Income, Median Years of Education, Median Monthly Rent, Median Value of Housing) and racial

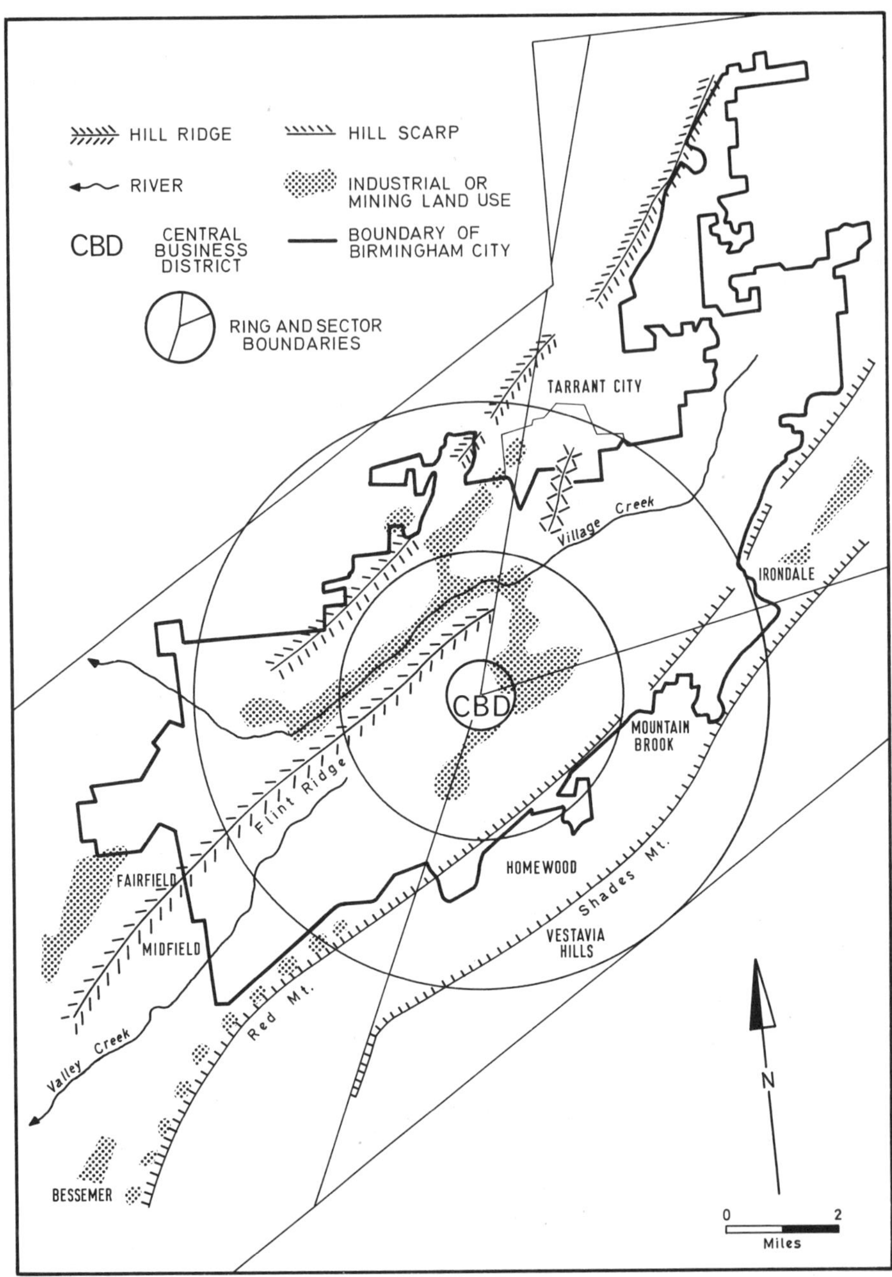

Fig. 28.--Features of the Birmingham Environment

status (Per Cent White, Per Cent Negro): the two statuses are virtually coincident in 1940 and in 1950. This was less true in 1960 though the association was still very strong.

The same features stand out in 1940 and in 1950 as have already been described for the 1960 map. The areas of higher than average socioeconomic status in 1940 persist through to 1960: the western Flint Ridge neighborhoods, the southeastern region between the city center and Red Mountain (excepting the innermost ring of tracts) and the northeastern area of the city. Comparing the 1940 and 1950 maps with the 1960 one gives the impression that the status of Flint Ridge and upper Valley Creek areas has fallen relative to southeastern neighborhoods and the new neighborhoods added on between 1950 and 1960 to the northeast and to the southeast beyond Red Mountain. The process of neighborhood aging, the downgrading of housing stock and the succession to lower status population has taken place on the inner margins of the higher status areas, and on the outer margins new housing development has meant upgrading of the area and occupation by new and higher status families. At least this has occurred to the northeast and southeast of the city center where rural land was available for development but west of the Birmingham portion of Flint Ridge come the industrial towns of Fairfield and Bessemer.

The lower status areas of Birmingham show basically the same distribution in 1960 as they do in 1940, with some additional encroachment into the older, formerly higher status districts. The Village Creek neighborhoods and the residential areas clustered around the center of Birmingham feature in all maps.

This persistence in overall pattern of socioeconomic status over time is characteristic as well of Des Moines. Figure 30 reproduces the residential classification of Des Moines around 1940 derived by Nelson (1949). The environmental correlates of Des Moines' socioeconomic status map are made clear in Figure 30. The city's industries are concentrated around the Central Business

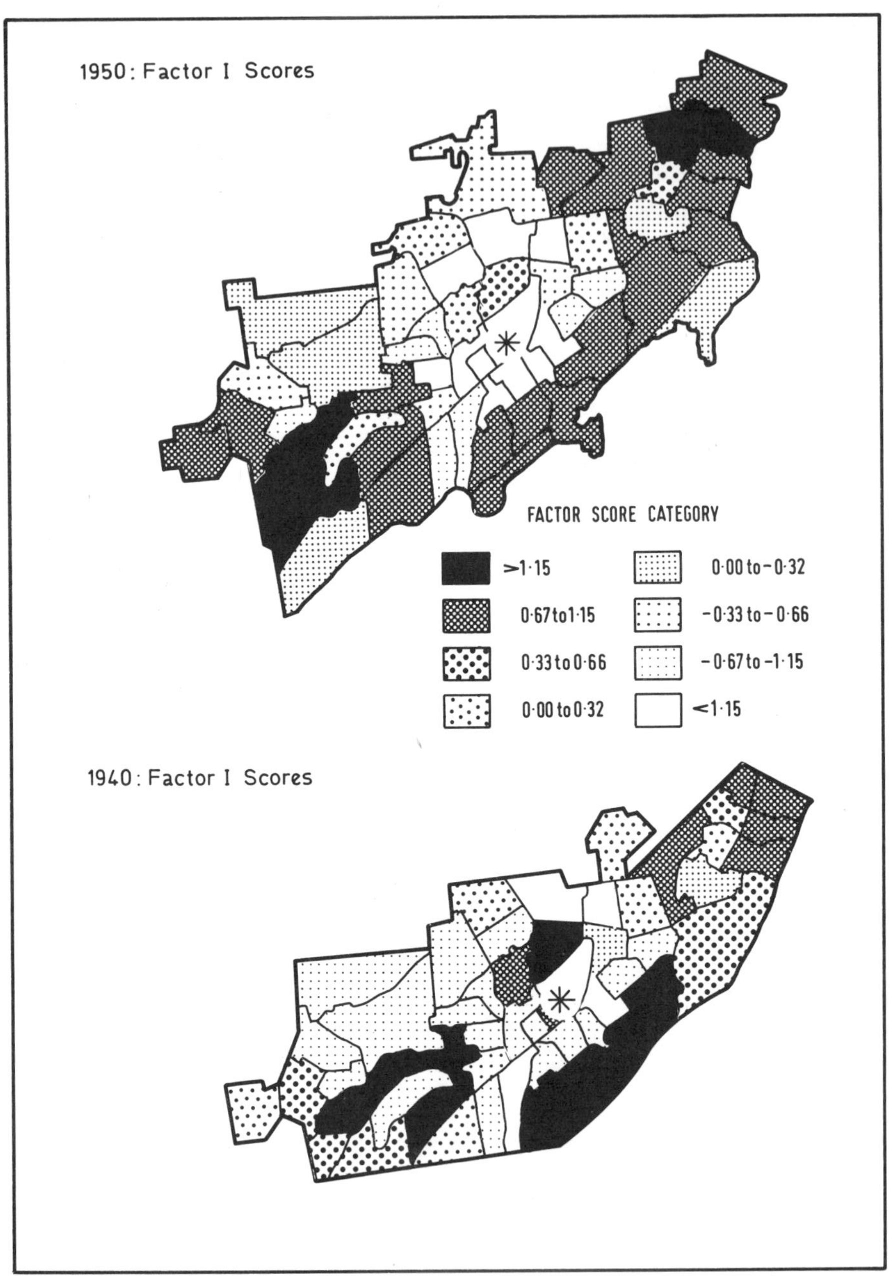

Fig. 29.--The Spatial Pattern of Socioeconomic Status, Birmingham, 1950 and 1940

TABLE 52

FACTOR ANALYTIC RESULTS: BIRMINGHAM, 1950 AND 1940

Variable	Loading	
	Factor 1 1950	Factor 2 1940
Median Income: Families	0.955	–
Per Cent White	0.932	0.902
Per Cent Negro	-0.932	-0.902
Median Years of Education	0.920	0.954
Median Monthly Rent	0.671	0.957
Distance from CBD	0.647	0.279
Median Value of Housing	0.608	0.453
Growth Rate, 1940-50	0.083	
Population Density	-0.319	-0.004

District and north of the Des Moines river east of the center. The Raccoon River valley to the west of the city center is, in contrast, occupied by extensive woods and municipal waterworks. The "elite" western neighborhoods lie away from the factory zone in rolling country overlooking the river woods; the eastern neighborhoods offer easy accessibility to the industrial jobs of the metropolitan area but a poorer residential environment from the amenity point of view.

A comparison of Figures 17 and 30 shows that the change in the social status pattern that took place in the 1940s and 1950s was not dramatic. The southern sector average status has probably risen as it has been developed, but the pattern of the two maps are remarkably similar. As Simmons (1968) has said

> Perhaps the most remarkable aspect of intra-urban migration is the stability of the spatial structure of social characteristics despite high rates of mobility throughout the city.

Residential Segregation of the Social Classes

So far in this chapter we have examined the pattern of socio-economic status in American cities exclusively from the area based point of view. That is, we have focused on the average population

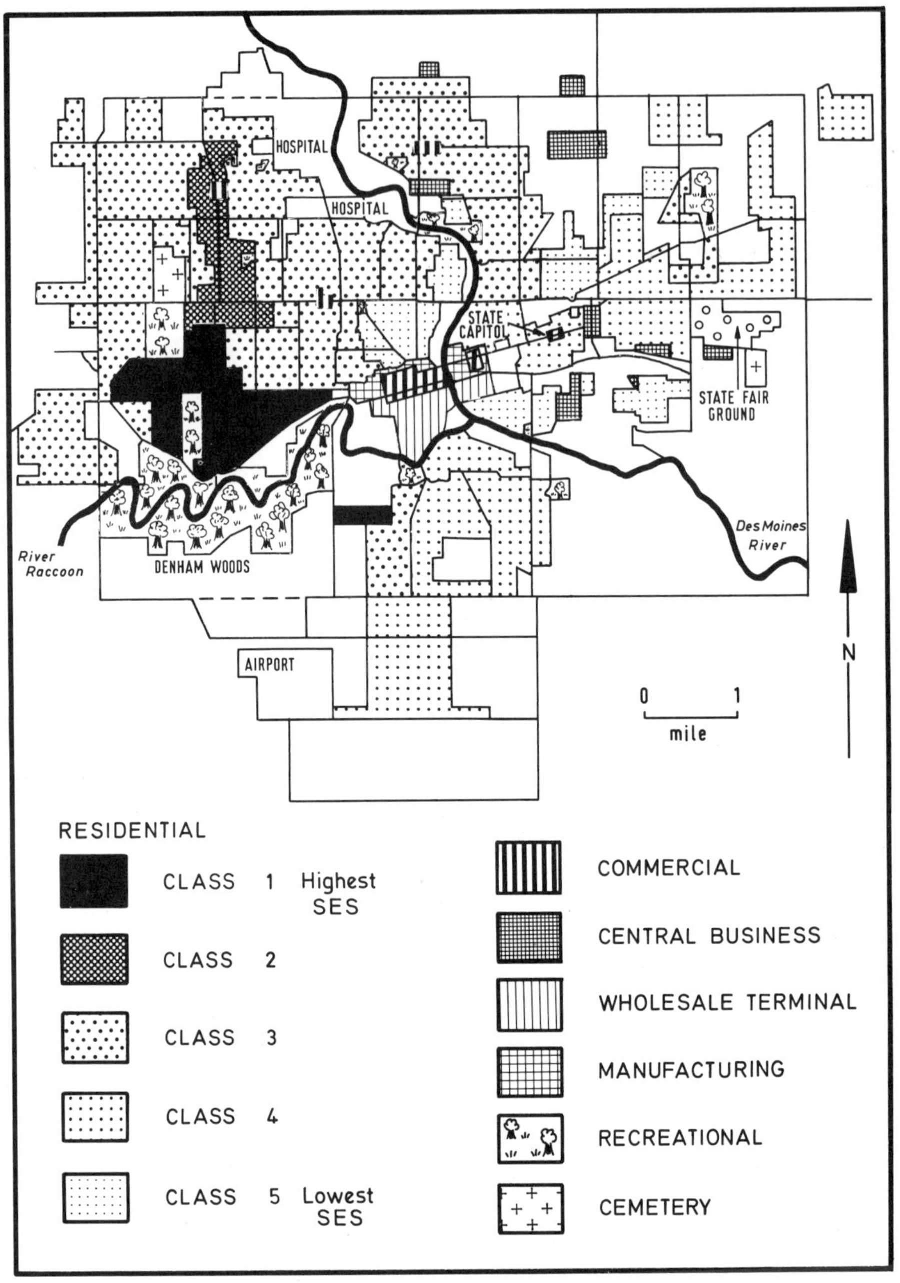

Fig. 30.--The Spatial Pattern of Socioeconomic Status, Des Moines, c. 1940 (After Nelson)

characteristics of residential areas, and in this we are following a long tradition from Burgess (1925) to the present. However, the alternative approach, much employed by sociologists, is to concentrate attention on the social group, rather than on the residential area. The focus is on the average areal characteristics of social groups and, in particular, on the spatial distance between them. Are social groups ordered in the residential space of the city in a way that reflects their social ordering? If so, to what extent are different social groups spatially proximate or spatially segregated?

The methodological approach adopted is the computation of measures of spatial association/disassociation of which the commonest is the index of dissimilarity between the distributions of two social groups (Duncan and Duncan, 1955b; Taeuber and Taeuber, 1965; Bogue, 1967). A detailed discussion of this index is given in Chapter VIII where it is extensively used. Here it will suffice to say that the index varies between 0 and 100, with 0 indicating that there is no dissimilarity in the distributions of the two groups compared and with 100 indicating complete dissimilarity between the two groups in question.

To examine the degree to which groups in the population, differing as to their socioeconomic status (which we can loosely call "social classes"), are residentially segregated, we need to adopt operational definitions of such groups. In their paper on Chicago the Duncans (Duncan and Duncan, 1955a) examined the residential segregation of occupational groups. As we saw in our discussion of indices of socioeconomic status, some occupational groups are rather mixed in their socioeconomic status. One alternative that might be adopted is to use educational groups. Educational groups are sets of persons classified according to their degree of educational attainment. Another possibility is to use the income classes into which families are grouped. Since all these variables

— education, occupation and income — went into the construction of our socioeconomic status index, we examine in turn the residential segregation exhibited by educational groups, by occupations and by income classes.

The Residential Segregation of Educational Groups

The populations resident in census tracts are divided in the published statistics into some eight groups on the basis of years of schooling completed. The inter-group indices of dissimilarity for each urbanized area have been calculated and are reported in Table 53. If educational attainment is a good index of cultural class and neighbor preference, then we should expect that the greater the difference in attainment between groups the greater their separation in space in the urbanized area.

If educational distance between educational groups is a good predictor of the spatial distance between them then the indices of dissimilarity reported in Table 53 should show the relations specified in Table 54. Table 55 confirms that only 4 out of 546 relations between adjacent dissimilarity indices in Table 53 are in directions other than those predicted in Table 54. The four exceptions all involve the "No School Years Completed" category which is small in all the urbanized areas.

The segregation indices for each educational group display the U shaped distribution reported by Duncan and Duncan for occupational groups in Chicago. The index of segregation is the index of dissimilarity calculated when a particular group and the rest of the population are compared. The groups at either end of the educational spectrum are most residentially segregated from the rest of the population. Groups in the middle of the educational range exhibit the lowest indices of residential segregation. Ten out of 13 urbanized areas record minimum segregation indices for the group with "High School: 1 to 3 Years" attainment and in 11 out of 13 urbanized areas the "No School Years Completed" group is the most isolated. The average index of segregation level lies between 22 and 32 for all urbanized areas except St. Petersburg, which has an average of 18.83. This low level of spatial polarization can be interpreted in terms of the area's function as a retirement center: the role of education as a spatial sorting device is less important among retirees, and its predictive power with respect to housing expenditure is much lower. Segregation by educational group is therefore less pronounced in St. Petersburg than in the other urbanized areas.

Residential Segregation of Occupational Groups

The indices of dissimilarity between major occupation groups are reported in Table 56. The ordering of these indices is by no means as regular as it was for the educational attainment groups or as reported by Duncan and Duncan (1955b) for Chicago and by Timms (1971) for Brisbane (their results are reproduced at the end of Table 56). No urbanized area has less then 4 disagreements (Table 57) with the model of Table 54, substituting occupation groups for educational groups.

The discrepancy results not so much from a disagreement over the ranking of the occupation groups[1] as from the differences in composition of those groups. The majority of disagreements with the social distance model involve the professional and managerial groups, and service workers. In almost all of the urbanized areas there are some instances where managers are more segregated from groups lower down the occupational hierarchy than are professionals. The occupational groups in this study comprise both males and females. The professional group contains a relatively high proportion

[1]Duncan's prestige based index of socioeconomic status for occupations is in agreement with this study's composite index for occupations with the one exception that service workers and laborers are differently ranked.

TABLE 53

THE SPATIAL SEPARATION OF SOCIAL CLASSES AS MEASURED FOR EDUCATIONAL ATTAINMENT GROUPS USING THE INDEX OF DISSIMILARITY FOR THE 13 URBANIZED AREAS

ANN ARBOR

Educational Category	Per Cent[a]	S[b]	2.	3.	4.	5.	6.	7.	8.
1. No School Years Completed	0.52	41	25	31	36	35	43	51	61
2. Elementary: 1 to 4 Years	2.25	38		22	31	29	40	50	58
3. Elementary: 5 to 7 Years	7.58	33			14	14	31	44	58
4. Elementary: 8 Years	12.57	25				9	24	36	51
5. High School: 1 to 3 Years	15.20	24					19	33	50
6. High School: 4 Years	21.05	16						22	37
7. College: 1 to 3 Years	13.61	17							23
8. College: 4 Years or More	27.22	41							

BIRMINGHAM

Educational Category	Per Cent[a]	S[b]	2.	3.	4.	5.	6.	7.	8.
1. No School Years Completed	2.89	36	11	20	29	36	50	60	68
2. Elementary: 1 to 4 Years	10.01	35		16	27	33	47	58	65
3. Elementary: 5 to 7 Years	17.05	23			12	19	35	48	58
4. Elementary: 8 Years	11.78	16				11	27	41	52
5. High School: 1 to 3 Years	21.95	11					18	34	47
6. High School: 4 Years	19.77	21						20	34
7. College: 1 to 3 Years	8.24	32							16
8. College: 4 Years or More	8.29	45							

CANTON

Educational Category	Per Cent[a]	S[b]	2.	3.	4.	5.	6.	7.	8.
1. No School Years Completed	1.66	42	25	32	38	39	51	59	65
2. Elementary: 1 to 4 Years	4.04	34		19	27	30	43	53	60
3. Elementary: 5 to 7 Years	12.03	22			12	17	30	42	51
4. Elementary: 8 Years	19.58	13				10	21	34	44
5. High School: 1 to 3 Years	21.12	8					15	30	40
6. High School: 4 Years	29.09	16						17	28
7. College: 1 to 3 Years	6.92	27							14
8. College: 4 Years or More	5.55	37							

DES MOINES

Educational Category	Per Cent[a]	S[b]	2.	3.	4.	5.	6.	7.	8.
L. No School Years Completed	0.63	43	38	37	39	40	46	56	65
2. Elementary: 1 to 4 Years	2.34	34		17	22	24	39	53	64
3. Elementary: 5 to 7 Years	7.40	27			12	14	31	47	60
4. Elementary: 8 Years	15.13	20				6	22	39	53
5. High School: 1 to 3 Years	18.59	17					19	36	50
6. High School: 4 Years	33.70	12						21	36
7. College: 1 to 3 Years	12.25	26							16
8. College: 4 Years or More	9.96	42							

TABLE 53--Continued

EL PASO

Educational Category	Per Cent[a]	S[b]	2.	3.	4.	5.	6.	7.	8.
1. No School Years Completed	4.64	50	13	25	47	56	66	71	72
2. Elementary: 1 to 4 Years	11.78	46		18	40	49	59	65	67
3. Elementary: 5 to 7 Years	13.52	29			22	33	43	50	54
4. Elementary: 8 Years	9.37	15				14	25	34	38
5. High School: 1 to 3 Years	15.38	15					16	24	33
6. High School: 4 Years	25.51	25						12	22
7. College: 1 to 3 Years	10.72	29							14
8. College: 4 Years or More	9.08	35							

HONOLULU

Educational Category	Per Cent[a]	S[b]	2.	3.	4.	5.	6.	7.	8.
1. No School Years Completed	5.01	36	24	25	30	34	40	54	57
2. Elementary: 1 to 4 Years	6.55	28		14	20	25	33	49	52
3. Elementary: 5 to 7 Years	10.20	23			13	19	26	45	47
4. Elementary: 8 Years	10.21	16				14	20	39	42
5. High School: 1 to 3 Years	16.13	13					15	32	37
6. High School: 4 Years	33.15	13						24	28
7. College: 1 to 3 Years	8.22	29							15
8. College: 4 Years or More	10.53	34							

LANCASTER

Educational Category	Per Cent[a]	S[b]	2.	3.	4.	5.	6.	7.	8.
1. No School Years Completed	0.69	42	32	29	42	40	47	58	62
2. Elementary: 1 to 4 Years	3.24	32		21	28	28	40	51	58
3. Elementary: 5 to 7 Years	13.32	22			15	17	29	39	47
4. Elementary: 8 Years	22.12	13				9	18	31	40
5. High School: 1 to 3 Years	20.39	8					14	29	38
6. High School: 4 Years	24.73	13						19	27
7. College: 1 to 3 Years	7.02	25							9
8. College: 4 Years or More	8.49	34							

MINNEAPOLIS-ST. PAUL

Educational Category	Per Cent[a]	S[b]	2.	3.	4.	5.	6.	7.	8.
1. No School Years Completed	0.68	48	36	40	43	46	52	59	64
2. Elementary: 1 to 4 Years	2.16	31		16	21	26	36	46	54
3. Elementary: 5 to 7 Years	7.56	25			12	19	30	40	49
4. Elementary: 8 Years	19.24	20				12	23	34	44
5. High School: 1 to 3 Years	17.12	12					14	28	38
6. High School: 4 Years	30.10	13						18	29
7. College: 1 to 3 Years	12.44	22							15
8. College: 4 Years or More	10.71	34							

PROVIDENCE-PAWTUCKET

Educational Category	Per Cent[a]	S[b]	2.	3.	4.	5.	6.	7.	8.
1. No School Years Completed	3.14	34	21	29	31	32	42	52	55
2. Elementary: 1 to 4 Years	4.29	28		15	23	26	37	48	54
3. Elementary: 5 to 7 Years	15.58	21			14	17	29	40	48
4. Elementary: 8 Years	18.76	11				8	19	32	41

TABLE 53--Continued

PROVIDENCE-PAWTUCKET--Continued

Educational Category	Per Cent[a]	S[b]	2.	3.	4.	5.	6.	7.	8.
5. High School: 1 to 3 Years	22.85	9					15	28	37
6. High School: 4 Years	22.19	15						16	28
7. College: 1 to 3 Years	6.70	26							18
8. College: 4 Years or More	6.49	35							

RICHMOND

Educational Category	Per Cent[a]	S[b]	2.	3.	4.	5.	6.	7.	8.
1. No School Years Completed	1.67	43	16	29	41	42	54	62	66
2. Elementary: 1 to 4 Years	7.33	41		22	35	36	51	61	66
3. Elementary: 5 to 7 Years	17.63	26			16	19	34	48	55
4. Elementary: 8 Years	9.59	16				13	25	38	46
5. High School: 1 to 3 Years	20.57	12					17	33	42
6. High School: 4 Years	22.92	18						19	28
7. College: 1 to 3 Years	10.39	30							13
8. College: 4 Years or More	9.91	39							

SAN BERNADINO-RIVERSIDE

Educational Category	Per Cent[a]	S[b]	2.	3.	4.	5.	6.	7.	8.
1. No School Years Completed	1.48	49	25	36	46	48	55	58	66
2. Elementary: 1 to 4 Years	3.98	37		18	30	33	44	50	60
3. Elementary: 5 to 7 Years	9.27	26			17	20	33	39	51
4. Elementary: 8 Years	14.44	16				11	22	29	42
5. High School: 1 to 3 Years	23.10	13					17	26	39
6. High School: 4 Years	31.59	14						13	26
7. College: 1 to 3 Years	14.61	20							17
8. College: 4 Years	1.52	33							

ST. PETERSBURG

Educational Category	Per Cent[a]	S[b]	2.	3.	4.	5.	6.	7.	8.
1. No School Years Completed	0.81	34	25	27	33	34	39	42	47
2. Elementary: 1 to 4 Years	3.61	30		19	29	29	35	41	46
3. Elementary: 5 to 7 Years	12.06	19			14	15	23	30	36
4. Elementary: 8 Years	19.53	11				8	14	21	28
5. High School: 1 to 3 Years	19.93	7					10	19	25
6. High School: 4 Years	25.18	10						11	17
7. College: 1 to 3 Years	11.13	17							11
8. College: 4 Years	7.76	23							

TAMPA

Educational Category	Per Cent[a]	S[b]	2.	3.	4.	5.	6.	7.	8.
1. No School Years Completed	2.42	43	14	25	42	45	57	65	65
2. Elementary: 1 to 4 Years	7.78	38		19	35	39	50	59	59
3. Elementary: 5 to 7 Years	15.81	25			19	23	37	46	50
4. Elementary: 8 Years	14.85	14				10	24	35	40
5. High School: 1 to 3 Years	20.91	10					16	29	34
6. High School: 4 Years	23.50	21						16	23
7. College: 1 to 3 Years	8.46	29							14
8. College: 4 Years	6.27	33							

Notes

[a]Per Cent = Per Cent of Urbanized Area total in each category.

[b]S = Index of Segregation.

TABLE 54

MODEL ORDERING OF THE DISSIMILARITY INDICES[a]

Educational Categories	1.	2.	3.	4.	5.	6.	7.	8.
1. No School Years Completed	—	D_{12}	$< D_{13}$	$< D_{14}$	$< D_{15}$	$< D_{16}$	$< D_{17}$	$< D_{18}$
2. Elementary: 1 to 4 Years	D_{21}	—	D_{23}	$< D_{24}$	$< D_{25}$	$< D_{26}$	$< D_{27}$	$< D_{28}$
3. Elementary: 5 to 7 Years	D_{31}	$> D_{32}$	—	D_{34}	$< D_{35}$	$< D_{36}$	$< D_{37}$	$< D_{38}$
4. Elementary: 8 Years	D_{41}	$> D_{42}$	$> D_{43}$	—	D_{45}	$< D_{46}$	$< D_{47}$	$< D_{48}$
5. High School: 1 to 3 Years	D_{51}	$> D_{52}$	$> D_{53}$	$> D_{54}$	—	D_{56}	$< D_{57}$	$< D_{58}$
6. High School: 4 Years	D_{61}	$> D_{62}$	$> D_{63}$	$> D_{64}$	$> D_{65}$	—	D_{67}	$< D_{68}$
7. College: 1 to 3 Years	D_{71}	$> D_{72}$	$> D_{73}$	$> D_{74}$	$> D_{75}$	$> D_{76}$	—	D_{78}
8. College: 4 Years	D_{81}	$> D_{82}$	$> D_{83}$	$> D_{84}$	$> D_{85}$	$> D_{86}$	$> D_{86}$	—

Notes

[a]Although $D_{ij} = D_{ji}$, the indices are shown twice in order to display the inequality signs conveniently.

TABLE 55

AGREEMENTS WITH MODEL FOR THE 13 URBANIZED AREAS[a]

Urbanized Area	Agreements
Ann Arbor	41
Birmingham	42
Canton	42
Des Moines	41
El Paso	42
Honolulu	42
Lancaster	40
Minneapolis-St. Paul	42
Providence-Pawtucket	42
Richmond	42
San Bernadino-Riverside	42
St. Petersburg	42
Tampa	42

Notes

[a]The total number of agreements possible is 42. The agreements were calculated using tables of the dissimilarity indices corrected to 2 decimal places to avoid the tie problems of using the integers reported in Table 53.

of women whereas there are few women, relatively speaking, in the managerial category. The women in the professional group undoubtedly occupy lower status and lower income jobs within the group than do the men and their presence pulls the average income of the professional group below that of the managerial. However, ranking the professional group below the managerial would not help improve the number of agreements except in the cases of Minneapolis-St. Paul, Richmond and St. Petersburg.

The service worker group in this study combines the service worker, excluding private household, category with the private household group. The private household category contains a number of live-in servants or workers who have to live close to their domestic place of employment, and this results in a lower level of spatial separation from white collar groups (containing the employers of some of them) than would be expected on the basis of the socioeconomic ranking of the occupation. The service worker anomaly shows up, however, even in the Chicago table where the private household worker category is ignored. The wide distribution of service jobs in neighborhoods of all social ranks and the necessity of lower paid service workers to live near their jobs may explain this deviation from the social distance-spatial separation relationship. This effect does not, however, show up in the southern urbanized areas of Birmingham, Richmond, St. Petersburg and Tampa. In those cities the private household labor force is largely black, and evidently the force of racial segregation prevents black private household workers from living as close to their work as do private household workers in non-Southern cities.

One striking feature of the urbanized area results (Table 56) is the gap between white and blue collar occupations. The transition between clerical workers and craftsmen is always marked by a fairly substantial jump in dissimilarity index value, a jump larger than that between any two other adjacent occupation groups. This

TABLE 56

THE SPATIAL SEPARATION OF SOCIAL CLASSES AS MEASURES FOR OCCUPATIONAL GROUPS USING THE INDEX OF DISSIMILARITY FOR 13 URBANIZED AREAS, CHICAGO AND BRISBANE

ANN ARBOR

Major Occupational Group	Per Cent[a] Male	Female	S[b]	2.	3.	4.	5.	6.	7.	8.
1. Professional, Technical and Kindred Workers	30.5	26.4	31	26	28	23	45	55	35	43
2. Managers, Officials and Proprietors	9.7	2.5	28		19	27	33	46	43	41
3. Sales Workers	6.4	5.3	16			15	25	37	30	31
4. Clerical and Kindred Workers	7.3	30.0	14				28	39	26	34
5. Craftsmen, Foremen and Kindred Workers	14.9	0.9	26					21	36	31
6. Operatives and Kindred Workers	16.4	8.4	39						37	25
7. Service Workers	10.9	26.2	25							25
8. Laborers, except Farm and Mine	4.0	0.3	26							

BIRMINGHAM

Major Occupational Group	Per Cent[a] Male	Female	S[b]	2.	3.	4.	5.	6.	7.	8.
1. Professional, Technical and Kindred Workers	9.7	13.9	31	16	18	24	37	47	51	57
2. Managers, Officials and Proprietors	11.6	4.3	33		14	22	36	50	56	62
3, Sales Workers	9.2	8.2	25			13	27	43	51	57
4. Clerical and Kindred Workers	7.7	31.2	26				22	40	49	56
5. Craftsmen, Foremen and Kindred Workers	20.7	0.9	23					24	39	43
6. Operatives and Kindred Workers	23.1	7.1	25						21	23
7. Service Workers	7.8	34.0	36							15
8. Laborers, except Farm and Mine	11.2	0.4	38							

CANTON

Major Occupational Group	Per Cent[a] Male	Female	S[b]	2.	3.	4.	5.	6.	7.	8.
1. Professional, Technical and Kindred Workers	10.0	14.6	27	14	17	17	28	37	38	49
2. Managers, Officials and Proprietors	9.9	3.5	27		17	21	29	37	40	48
3. Sales Workers	7.3	11.6	16			11	20	26	29	39
4. Clerical and Kindred Workers	7.9	31.7	12				15	22	26	36

TABLE 56--Continued

CANTON--Continued

Major Occupational Group	Per Cent[a] Male	Female	S[b]	2.	3.	4.	5.	6.	7.	8.
5. Craftsmen, Foremen and Kindred Workers	24.2	1.3	12					14	23	27
6. Operatives and Kindred Workers	26.3	12.4	17						17	21
7. Service Workers	5.4	23.9	22							20
8. Laborers, except Farm and Mine	8.9	1.1	29							

DES MOINES

Major Occupational Group	Per Cent[a] Male	Female	S[b]	2.	3.	4.	5.	6.	7.	8.
1. Professional, Technical and Kindred Workers	11.9	13.7	28	12	15	24	37	45	40	45
2. Managers, Officials and Proprietors	14.7	4.2	26		12	25	35	43	40	44
3. Sales Workers	11.4	8.4	18			16	27	36	33	39
4. Clerical and Kindred Workers	10.0	45.1	11				20	27	22	31
5. Craftsmen, Foremen and Kindred Workers	20.8	1.7	17					14	24	21
6. Operatives and Kindred Workers	18.4	7.1	26						21	16
7. Service Workers	7.4	19.5	23							20
8. Laborers, except Farm and Mine	6.5	0.3	27							

EL PASO

Major Occupational Group	Per Cent[a] Male	Female	S[b]	2.	3.	4.	5.	6.	7.	8.
1. Professional, Technical and Kindred Workers	12.5	15.3	29	12	18	16	34	49	40	58
2. Managers, Officials and Proprietors	15.9	5.5	24		18	16	30	44	35	53
3. Sales Workers	8.2	9.5	15			9	23	36	27	45
4. Clerical and Kindred Workers	9.4	32.0	17				21	36	29	48
5. Craftsmen, Foremen and Kindred Workers	21.9	1.0	14					20	18	34
6. Operatives and Kindred Workers	16.0	12.1	28						17	19
7. Service Workers	7.4	24.1	19							24
8. Laborers, except Farm and Mine	8.8	0.5	38							

TABLE 56--Continued

HONOLULU

Major Occupational Group	Per Cent[a] Male	Per Cent[a] Female	S[b]	2.	3.	4.	5.	6.	7.	8.
1. Professional, Technical and Kindred Workers	12.5	17.0	26	15	16	20	34	38	29	44
2. Managers, Officials and Proprietors	12.6	5.2	23		16	21	33	37	28	43
3. Sales Workers	6.5	9.3	14			13	24	28	20	37
4. Clerical and Kindred Workers	9.1	32.2	13				18	24	19	34
5. Craftsmen, Foremen and Kindred Workers	26.5	1.4	16					10	14	23
6. Operatives and Kindred Workers	14.6	12.3	20						15	18
7. Service Workers	8.6	21.9	13							23
8. Laborers, except Farm and Mine	7.1	1.0	19							

LANCASTER

Major Occupational Group	Per Cent[a] Male	Per Cent[a] Female	S[b]	2.	3.	4.	5.	6.	7.	8.
1. Professional, Technical and Kindred Workers	12.5	14.5	26	15	18	20	29	36	35	34
2. Managers, Officials and Proprietors	12.1	2.7	25		19	27	27	34	34	35
3. Sales Workers	9.5	9.3	10			12	15	21	20	24
4. Clerical and Kindred Workers	7.9	27.3	12				14	19	19	22
5. Craftsmen, Foremen and Kindred Workers	21.5	1.8	10					13	16	18
6. Operatives and Kindred Workers	21.0	23.4	17						8	14
7. Service Workers	8.4	20.0	17							15
8. Laborers, except Farm and Mine	7.1	1.0	19							

MINNEAPOLIS-ST. PAUL

Major Occupational Group	Per Cent[a] Male	Per Cent[a] Female	S[b]	2.	3.	4.	5.	6.	7.	8.
1. Professional, Technical and Kindred Workers	15.1	14.6	21	18	17	22	28	35	29	37
2. Managers, Officials and Proprietors	12.8	3.2	27		14	29	31	40	36	41
3. Sales Workers	9.7	8.9	19			21	24	33	29	35
4. Clerical and Kindred Workers	10.3	40.1	12				19	22	17	26
5. Craftsmen, Foremen and Kindred Workers	21.3	1.2	17					16	23	23
6. Operatives and Kindred Workers	17.9	11.7	22						19	16
7. Service Workers	6.7	19.8	18							20
8. Laborers, except Farm and Mine	6.2	0.4	23							

TABLE 56--Continued

PROVIDENCE-PAWTUCKET

Major Occupational Group	Per Cent[a] Male	Per Cent[a] Female	S[b]	2.	3.	4.	5.	6.	7.	8.
1. Professional, Technical and Kindred Workers	9.9	11.3	22	15	16	18	25	35	25	38
2. Managers, Officials and Proprietors	11.1	2.6	24		16	20	26	37	30	39
3. Sales Workers	7.9	6.5	17			13	18	30	23	32
4. Clerical and Kindred Workers	8.6	29.5	10				13	22	16	27
5. Craftsmen, Foremen and Kindred Workers	23.8	2.6	12					16	20	22
6. Operatives and Kindred Workers	26.1	34.3	22						20	18
7. Service Workers	7.5	12.4	15							21
8. Laborers, except Farm and Mine	5.1	0.7	22							

RICHMOND

Major Occupational Group	Per Cent[a] Male	Per Cent[a] Female	S[b]	2.	3.	4.	5.	6.	7.	8.
1. Professional, Technical and Kindred Workers	12.1	14.8	29	17	16	21	36	47	53	58
2. Managers, Officials and Proprietors	13.9	3.0	31		17	24	34	48	59	61
3. Sales Workers	10.7	8.0	22			14	26	41	54	57
4. Clerical and Kindred Workers	10.4	36.4	21				22	35	52	55
5. Craftsmen, Foremen and Kindred Workers	19.2	1.2	25					25	49	50
6. Operatives and Kindred Workers	19.0	12.8	27						30	31
7. Service Workers	8.5	23.5	44							15
8. Laborers, except Farm and Mine	6.3	0.3	42							

SAN BERNADINO-RIVERSIDE

Major Occupational Group	Per Cent[a] Male	Per Cent[a] Female	S[b]	2.	3.	4.	5.	6.	7.	8.
1. Professional, Technical and Kindred Workers	13.8	17.8	24	14	14	16	30	39	28	44
2. Managers, Officials and Proprietors	14.2	5.9	20		11	14	26	35	28	41
3. Sales Workers	7.7	8.5	17			11	23	33	25	39
4. Clerical and Kindred Workers	6.2	35.6	14				21	29	21	35
5. Craftsmen, Foremen and Kindred Workers	26.3	1.0	15					14	18	24
6. Operatives and Kindred Workers	17.0	7.9	23						19	17
7. Service Workers	6.6	23.1	16							23
8. Laborers, except Farm and Mine	8.3	0.4	28							

TABLE 56--Continued

ST. PETERSBURG

Major Occupational Group	Per Cent[a] Male	Female	S[b]	2.	3.	4.	5.	6.	7.	8.
1. Professional, Technical and Kindred Workers	11.6	14.1	17	16	14	12	24	29	31	41
2. Managers, Officials and Proprietors	17.1	6.8	22		15	18	29	34	34	45
3. Sales Workers	11.9	12.0	17			10	23	29	32	43
4. Clerical and Kindred Workers	6.8	28.5	15				20	26	31	40
5. Craftsmen, Foremen and Kindred Workers	23.8	1.4	18					15	31	34
6. Operatives and Kindred Workers	12.5	7.7	18						22	25
7. Service Workers	8.1	29.1	25							18
8. Laborers, except Farm and Mine	8.3	0.4	32							

TAMPA

Major Occupational Group	Per Cent[a] Male	Female	S[b]	2.	3.	4.	5.	6.	7.	8.
1. Professional, Technical and Kindred Workers	8.6	11.0	25	14	14	17	31	40	42	51
2. Managers, Officials and Proprietors	15.3	4.6	26		12	15	29	41	45	52
3. Sales Workers	10.9	11.6	20			10	24	36	41	49
4. Clerical and Kindred Workers	7.1	29.3	21				24	36	41	49
5. Craftsmen, Foremen and Kindred Workers	21.8	1.2	19					21	36	40
6. Operatives and Kindred Workers	18.7	15.9	23						24	27
7. Service Workers	7.3	26.0	32							18
8. Laborers, except Farm and Mine	10.4	0.5	36							

CHICAGO[c]

Major Occupational Group	S[d]	S[e]	1.	2.	3.	4.	5.	6.	7.	8.
1. Professional, Technical and Kindred Workers	30	21	..	13	15	28	35	44	41	54
2. Managers, Officials and Proprietors	29	20	8	..	13	28	33	41	40	52
3. Sales Workers	29	20	11	7	..	27	35	42	38	54
4. Clerical and Kindred Workers	13	9	20	18	17	..	16	21	24	38
5. Craftsmen, Foremen and Kindred Workers	19	14	26	23	25	12	..	17	35	35
6. Operatives and Kindred Workers	22	16	31	29	30	16	14	..	26	25
7. Service Workers	24	20	31	31	30	19	25	19	..	28
8. Laborers, except Farm and Mine	35	29	42	41	42	32	30	21	24	..

TABLE 56--Continued

BRISBANE[f]							
Major Occupational Group	S	2.	3.	4.	5.	6.	7.
1. Professional	16	11	12	17	19	27	32
2. Managerial	14		11	16	18	25	28
3. Sales/Clerical	7			11	13	20	25
4. Skilled Manual	5				8	16	24
5. Semi-skilled Manual	9					14	23
6. Unskilled Manual	17						20
7. Personal Service	26						

BRISBANE [g]					
Major Occupational Group	1.	2.	3.	4.	5.
1. Professional/Managerial	..	35	40	42	46
2. Clerical/Sales	16	..	26	29	32
3. Skilled Manual	20	10	..	22	25
4. Semi-skilled Manual	23	15	7	..	22
5. Unskilled Manual	30	20	15	10	..

Notes

[a]Per Cent of total employed, male and female, in the urbanized area.

[b]The index of residential segregation.

[c]From Duncan and Duncan, 1955b.

[d]The index of segregation calculated using census tracts.

[e]The index of segregation calculated using ring sector zones. The values in the Chicago table above the diagonal refer to census tracts, below the diagonal to ring sector zones.

[f]From Timms (1965).

[g]From Timms (1971). Entries above the diagonal are for 339 census districts, below the diagonal for 28 electoral divisions.

jump seems less marked in the male based tables of Chicago and Brisbane indices, suggesting that the gap observed in the 13 urbanized area results may reflect the spatial polarization of a dominantly female clerical group and a dominantly male craft group. This polarization was occasionally observed in the factor structure of an urbanized area.

The indices of residential segregation display the general U shaped distribution observed for Chicago and Brisbane (Table 56)

TABLE 57

AGREEMENTS WITH MODEL FOR 13 URBANIZED AREAS, CHICAGO AND BRISBANE[a]

Urbanized Area	Agreements	Urbanized Area	Agreements
Ann Arbor	27	San Bernadino-Riverside	35
Birmingham	39	St. Petersburg	34
Canton	39	Tampa	35
Des Moines	33	Chicago: Census Tracts	33/42
El Paso	32	Sector-Ring Zones	38/42
Honolulu	35	Brisbane: 7 Groups	30/30
Lancaster	35	5 Groups	
Minneapolis-St. Paul	29	Collectors' Dist.	12/12
Providence-Pawtucket	30	Electoral Dist.	12/12
Richmond	36		

Notes

[a]The total number of agreements possible for the 13 urbanized areas is 42. The agreements are calculated using tables of the dissimilarity indices corrected to 2 decimal places to avoid the tie problems involved in employing the integers in Table 56.

with similar deviations from a regular pattern as observed above. The professional and managerial groups have roughly comparable indices of segregation and the service worker group has a lower index than the operative group ranked higher in terms of prestige and income.

Residential Segregation of Income Groups

The relationship between social distance and spatial distance proves to be very strong when social distance is measured in terms of family income (Table 58 and 59). The wider the gap separating the incomes of two families the less likely they are to live together in the same neighborhood. The level of inter-group residential segregation is higher for income groups than for occupation groups in all urbanized areas and is higher for income groups than for education groups in 9 out of 13 urbanized areas (Table 60).

TABLE 58

THE SPATIAL SEPARATION OF SOCIAL CLASSES AS MEASURED FOR INCOME GROUPS USING THE INDEX OF DISSIMILARITY FOR 13 URBANIZED AREAS

ANN ARBOR

Income Group	Per Cent[a]	S[b]	2.	3.	4.	5.	6.	7.
1. Less than $2,000	6.2	29	14	22	32	36	45	71
2. $2,000 - $3,999	11.3	26		17	26	32	43	72
3. $4,000 - $5,999	19.7	20			16	24	38	68
4. $6,000 - $7,999	21.9	15				13	29	63
5. $8,000 - $9,999	15.6	16					23	58
6. $10,000 - $24,999	23.5[c]	30						43
7. $25,000 or More	1.9[c]	57						

BIRMINGHAM

Income Group	Per Cent[a]	S[b]	2.	3.	4.	5.	6.	7.
1. Less than $2,000	15.9	34	14	30	43	49	60	84
2. $2,000 - $3,999	20.6	25		20	34	40	54	81
3. $4,000 - $5,999	23.8	16			17	27	43	76
4. $6,000 - $7,999	17.1	20				14	33	70
5. $8,000 - $9,999	9.7	24					23	62
6. $10,000 - $24,999	11.7[c]	41						46
7. $25,000 or More	1.4[c]	70						

CANTON

Income Group	Per Cent[a]	S[b]	2.	3.	4.	5.	6.	7.
1. Less than $2,000	7.3	25	13	21	29	33	39	64
2. $2,000 - $3,999	13.8	23		15	26	30	38	66
3. $4,000 - $5,999	26.3	12			14	20	30	60
4. $6,000 - $7,999	23.7	11				9	19	54
5. $8,000 - $9,999	13.7	14					15	52
6. $10,000 - $24,999	14.4[c]	25						41
7. $25,000 or More	1.0[c]	55						

DES MOINES

Income Group	Per Cent[a]	S[b]	2.	3.	4.	5.	6.	7.
1. Less than $2,000	7.0	35	28	29	37	42	47	61
2. $2,000 - $3,999	12.5	25		18	25	31	40	57
3. $4,000 - $5,999	23.4	17			15	21	32	54
4. $6,000 - $7,999	24.2	14				12	25	51
5. $8,000 - $9,999	15.1	14					17	45
6. $10,000 - $24,999	16.1[c]	26						36
7. $25,000 or More	1.6[c]	46						

EL PASO

Income Group	Per Cent[a]	S[b]	2.	3.	4.	5.	6.	7.
1. Less than $2,000	11.1	35	15	33	47	53	56	72
2. $2,000 - $3,999	23.6	27		23	36	44	46	70
3. $4,000 - $5,999	24.0	13			15	27	37	65
4. $6,000 - $7,999	16.4	20				15	28	59
5. $8,000 - $9,999	12.0	27					18	53

TABLE 58--Continued

EL PASO--Continued

Income Group	Per Cent[a]	S[b]	2.	3.	4.	5.	6.	7.
6. $10,000 - $24,999	11.8[c]	35						41
7. $25,000 or More	1.2[c]	60						

HONOLULU

Income Group	Per Cent[a]	S[b]	2.	3.	4.	5.	6.	7.
1. Less than $2,000	7.2	35	28	29	37	42	47	61
2. $2,000 - $3,999	12.2	25		18	25	31	40	57
3. $4,000 - $5,999	20.3	17			15	21	32	54
4. $6,000 - $7,999	19.1	14				12	25	51
5. $8,000 - $9,999	14.3	14					17	45
6. $10,000 - $24,999	24.8[c]	26						36
7. $25,000 or More	2.1[c]	46						

LANCASTER

Income Group	Per Cent[a]	S[b]	2.	3.	4.	5.	6.	7.
1. Less than $2,000	6.3	23	13	16	25	30	42	59
2. $2,000 - $3,999	14.3	22		15	23	29	39	57
3. $4,000 - $5,999	26.0	13			13	19	33	51
4. $6,000 - $7,999	23.4	8				8	24	44
5. $8,000 - $9,999	14.3	12					18	39
6. $10,000 - $24,999	15.4[c]	29						25
7. $25,000 or More	1.4[c]	43						

MINNEAPOLIS-ST. PAUL[d]

Income Group	Per Cent[a]	S[b]	2.	3.	4.	5.	6.	7.
1. Less than $2,000	5.3	29	15	23	32	35	42	69
2. $2,000 - $3,999	10.2	27		20	30	33	40	68
3. $4,000 - $5,999	22.1	15			14	20	32	66
4. $6,000 - $7,999	26.0	13				11	24	62
5. $8,000 - $9,999	16.2	13					18	57
6. $10,000 - $24,999	18.5[c]	25						44
7. $25,000 or More	1.7[c]	58						

PROVIDENCE-PAWTUCKET

Income Group	Per Cent[a]	S[b]	2.	3.	4.	5.	6.	7.
1. Less than $2,000	8.8	22	13	20	27	31	40	68
2. $2,000 - $3,999	17.7	18		13	21	27	36	66
3. $4,000 - $5,999	28.2	10			12	19	29	63
4. $6,000 - $7,999	21.7	12				11	22	59
5. $8,000 - $9,999	11.2	15					16	56
6. $10,000 - $24,999	10.9[c]	26						45
7. $25,000 or More	1.5[c]	59						

TABLE 58--Continued

RICHMOND

Income Group	Per Cent[a]	S[b]	2.	3.	4.	5.	6.	7.
1. Less than $2,000	9.9	42	18	38	51	55	60	77
2. $2,000 - $3,999	17.1	40		26	40	45	51	72
3. $4,000 - $5,999	22.8	16			18	23	37	65
4. $6,000 - $7,999	20.4	18				9	24	56
5. $8,000 - $9,999	13.1	21					20	52
6. $10,000 - $24,999	15.0[c]	33						37
7. $25,000 or More	1.8[c]	57						

SAN BERNADINO-RIVERSIDE

Income Group	Per Cent[a]	S[b]	2.	3.	4.	5.	6.	7.
1. Less than $2,000	9.9	22	11	18	27	34	43	60
2. $2,000 - $3,999	17.6	25		15	27	35	44	63
3. $4,000 - $5,999	24.0	15			16	26	36	57
4. $6,000 - $7,999	21.0	12				13	24	49
5. $8,000 - $9,999	12.4	18					15	43
6. $10,000 - $24,999	12.1[c]	30						33
7. $25,000 or More	3.0[c]	49						

ST. PETERSBURG

Income Group	Per Cent[a]	S[b]	2.	3.	4.	5.	6.	7.
1. Less than $2,000	16.8	16	11	15	21	28	35	60
2. $2,000 - $3,999	29.3	14		12	18	25	34	61
3. $4,000 - $5,999	22.5	7			10	18	28	56
4. $6,000 - $7,999	14.1	12				12	23	52
5. $8,000 - $9,999	7.4	17					16	45
6. $10,000 - $24,999	8.8[c]	28						36
7. $25,000 or More	1.2[c]	54						

TAMPA

Income Group	Per Cent[a]	S[b]	2.	3.	4.	5.	6.	7.
1. Less than $2,000	15.4	25	12	25	33	40	50	73
2. $2,000 - $3,999	24.8	19		18	26	33	44	72
3. $4,000 - $5,999	25.2	12			12	24	25	68
4. $6,000 - $7,999	16.1	15				15	27	63
5. $8,000 - $9,999	8.6	23					19	57
6. $10,000 - $24,999	8.8[c]	35						43
7. $25,000 or More	1.2	65						

Notes

[a]Per Cent of total families in the urbanized area.

[b]Index of Residential Segregation (index of dissimilarity of group vs the rest of the population).

[c]This is an estimated percentage calculated in the following way:

Urbanized area % in category =

$$\frac{\text{SMSA families in category}}{\text{SMSA families in \$10,000 or More category}} \text{ Urbanized Area in \$10,000 or More category}$$

TABLE 58--Continued

Notes--Continued

[d]The residential segregation index values for Minneapolis-St. Paul are for the SMSA rather than the Urbanized Area.

TABLE 59

AGREEMENTS WITH MODEL FOR 13 URBANIZED AREAS[a]

Urbanized Area	Agreements	Urbanized Area	Agreements
Ann Arbor	29	Minneapolis-St. Paul	30
Birmingham	30	Providence-Pawtucket	30
Canton	30	Richmond	30
Des Moines	30	San Bernadino-Riverside	26
El Paso	30	St. Petersburg	29
Honolulu	30	Tampa	30
Lancaster	30		

Notes

[a]The total number of agreements possible for the 13 urbanized areas is 30.

TABLE 60

AVERAGE LEVELS OF INTERGROUP SOCIAL CLASS SEGREGATION

Urbanized Area	Education Groups	Occupation Groups	Income Groups
Ann Arbor	34.88	32.23	37.35
Birmingham	35.52	36.17	43.79
Canton	33.87	26.35	32.72
Des Moines	35.76	28.02	35.51
El Paso	38.65	29.56	40.57
Honolulu	31.18	24.79	34.43
Lancaster	32.68	21.97	29.61
Minneapolis-St. Paul	33.83	25.68	35.84
Providence-Pawtucket	30.55	23.37	33.08
Richmond	36.74	37.52	41.54
San Bernadino-Riverside	34.66	24.78	32.84

TABLE 60--Continued

Urbanized Area	Education Groups	Occupation Groups	Income Groups
St. Petersburg	25.95	26.46	29.31
Tampa	35.28	31.43	37.36

Income is thus a more marked spatial sorting variable on average than either education or occupation. The amount of money available to a household for expenditure on housing will determine in part where it will live, and income is clearly more closely related to housing expenditure than occupation or education.

The tables of inter-group dissimilarity indices show the richest group, those families with incomes of $25,000 per year or over, to be highly segregated residentially from the rest of the population, even from the $10,000 to $24,999 group. This high degree of spatial separation may in part be simply the product of the small size of the group in relation to the other income groups, but it is unlikely that this is the whole story. Much of this high degree of residential segregation is a result of voluntary location in residentially exclusive enclaves, many of which have zoning ordinances aimed at preventing the construction of homes for any but the wealthy and some of which have police guards posted at their borders instructed to exclude "undesirable" visitors.

The residential segregation indices for the income groups of the 13 urbanized areas show the pronounced U shaped distribution already noted for educational and occupational groups. The middle incomes have the widest spatial spread in the urbanized area and in consequences are the least residentially segregated. Both the rich and the poor are spatially concentrated and more residentially segregated than the middle income groups, though for the poor this concentration is the product of having to find cheap accommodation rather than something of their own choosing.

Conclusions

In this chapter we have discussed the various models that seek to describe the ways in which the socioeconomic status pattern of a city's residential areas has evolved and to describe the nature of that pattern at a point in time in a selection of cities. A compromise view was put forward that saw both the sectoral pattern and the concentric pattern as being important.

Previous analyses of the spatial variance of socioeconomic status had suggested, in contradiction to this compromise view, that the sectoral pattern was dominant, with the exception of a study of Chicago. Analysis of the spatial variance of the index of socioeconomic status defined in this study for the sample urbanized areas suggested that the spatial pattern was almost always mixed, that a concentric pattern was usually present and was occasionally dominant.

Although the detailed map patterns of neighborhoods of different status were quite varied across the sample of cities studied, the consequences of the map patterns in terms of the segregation of the different social classes were quite uniform. The social classes, when defined in terms of education or income, were clearly and markedly separated in residential space. Groups at the extremes of the distributions of education or income were quite isolated. Occupational groups were less spatially segregated but this probably reflected the internal heterogeneity in terms of education and occupation of the major occupations making up the census classification.

The spatial features, which Hoyt had suggested tend to determine the distribution of social status, were seen to be in operation in the sample cities. Higher status areas were located away from the industrial and high pollution districts, and were situated in areas of landscape amenity, and often, at least in Northern cities, on the western, prevailing wind side of the city. In all cities the inner city contained the main concentration of poverty.

The geography of socioeconomic status within America's cities is thus seen to be made up of some elements of surprising variety and some elements of surprising uniformity. Thus, although all the cities exhibited a rising gradient of socioeconomic status from the inner city outwards, the importance of ring variation itself varied greatly from city to city. Despite the multiplicity of factors particular to each city that determined the location of the low, middle and high socioeconomic status neighborhoods, the net result in terms of the pattern of spatial distances separating the various status groups was uniform across all cities.

CHAPTER VII

THE SPATIAL PATTERNS OF FAMILY STATUS

In Chapter III a consistent feature of the factor analyses of the urbanized areas in the sample was a dimension of variation of census tract populations which was labelled Family Status. The concept of the family life cycle was described in more detail in Chapter V and an index that measured the position of a residential area population on a scale of family status was outlined. In this Chapter the spatial patterns revealed by this index are analyzed.

The General Pattern

Figures 32 through 45 display the patterns of family status that characterize the sample urbanized areas. The dominant pattern is clearly one of concentric variation. This pattern is usually so dominant that pattern tests (analyses of spatial variance) were not performed. Tracts that lie close to the center of the urbanized area or to one of the other employment and growth centers of the urban region score highly on the family status index scale. At the very center of the city are usually one or two tracts scoring above 70. This is the rooming house, skid row area of the city characterized by a population largely made up of single males living in rented accommodation. Beyond skid row is a ring of tracts scoring between 55 and 70 on the family status scale. In this ring live the older families, widows and widowers of the metropolis and young single persons and couples, the "young footloose cosmopolites" as Adams in Abler, Adams and Gould (1971) calls them. The outer parts of the central city and the suburban muncipalities are generally occupied by tract populations scoring from 40 to 55 on the family status scale. These are the areas of families raising children:

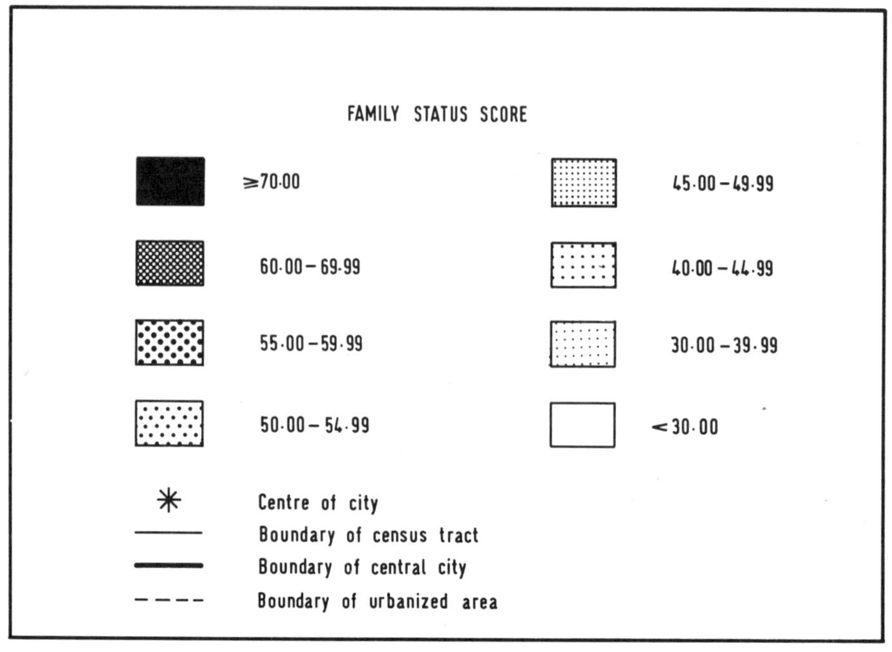

Fig. 31.--The General Key for the Family Status Maps

tracts which score below 50 probably contain the younger families and those scoring above 50 contain the maturer families.

The single score on the family status dimension is, of course, only a summary statistic for a multi-faceted distribution of families and individuals. In order to illustrate the relationship between the index score and the age and household size distributions, data on those distributions has been extracted for some seven tracts in the Des Moines urbanized area (Table 61). The tracts fall in each of the score classes used in the map series except for the lowest which occurs very infrequently. Even the highest scoring tract, tract 34, with the oldest population and smallest household sizes on average, contains some children under five years of age and some households of six or more persons. Conversely, the lowest scoring tract, tract PC-106, contains a small proportion of people

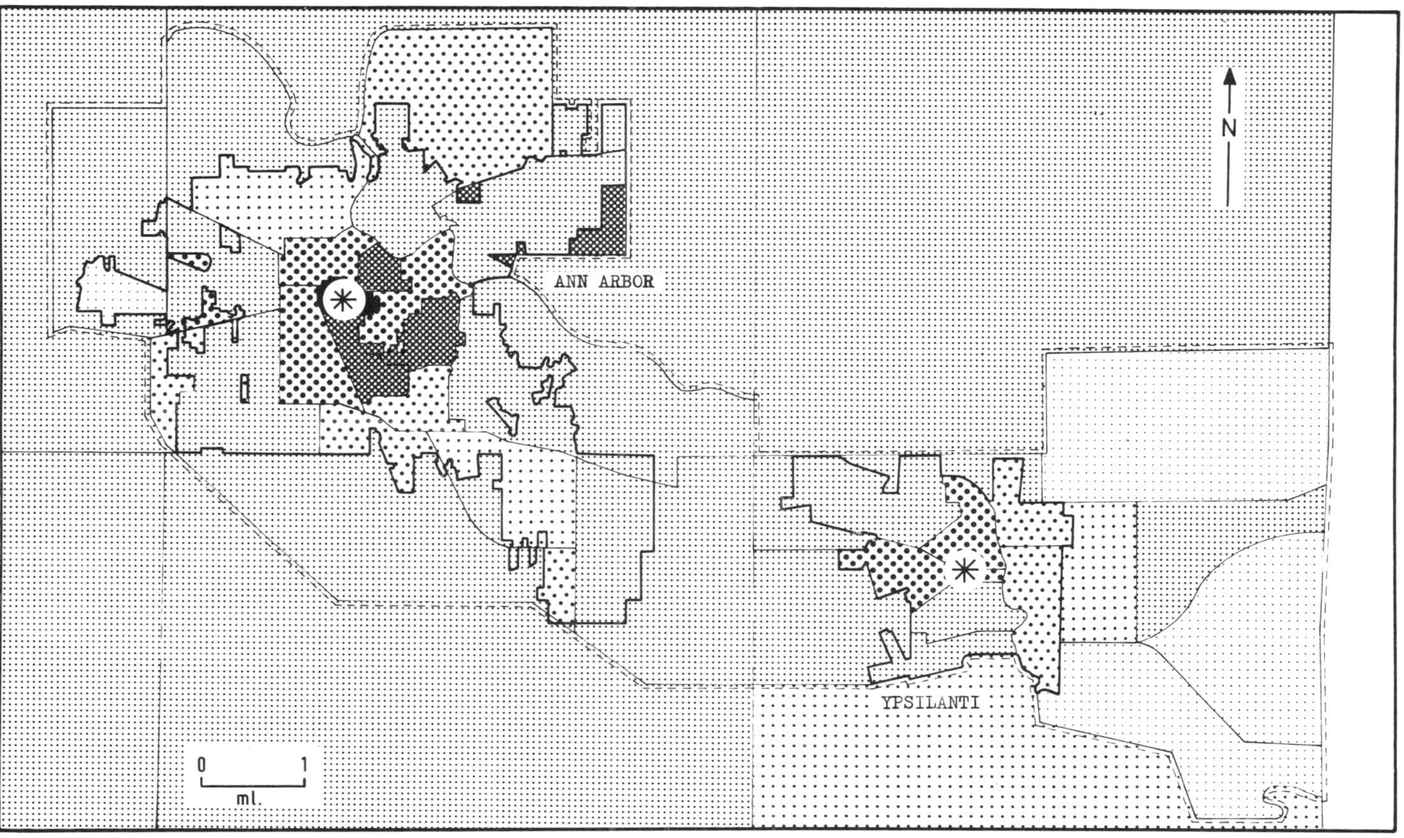

Fig. 32.--The Spatial Pattern of Family Status, Ann Arbor, 1960

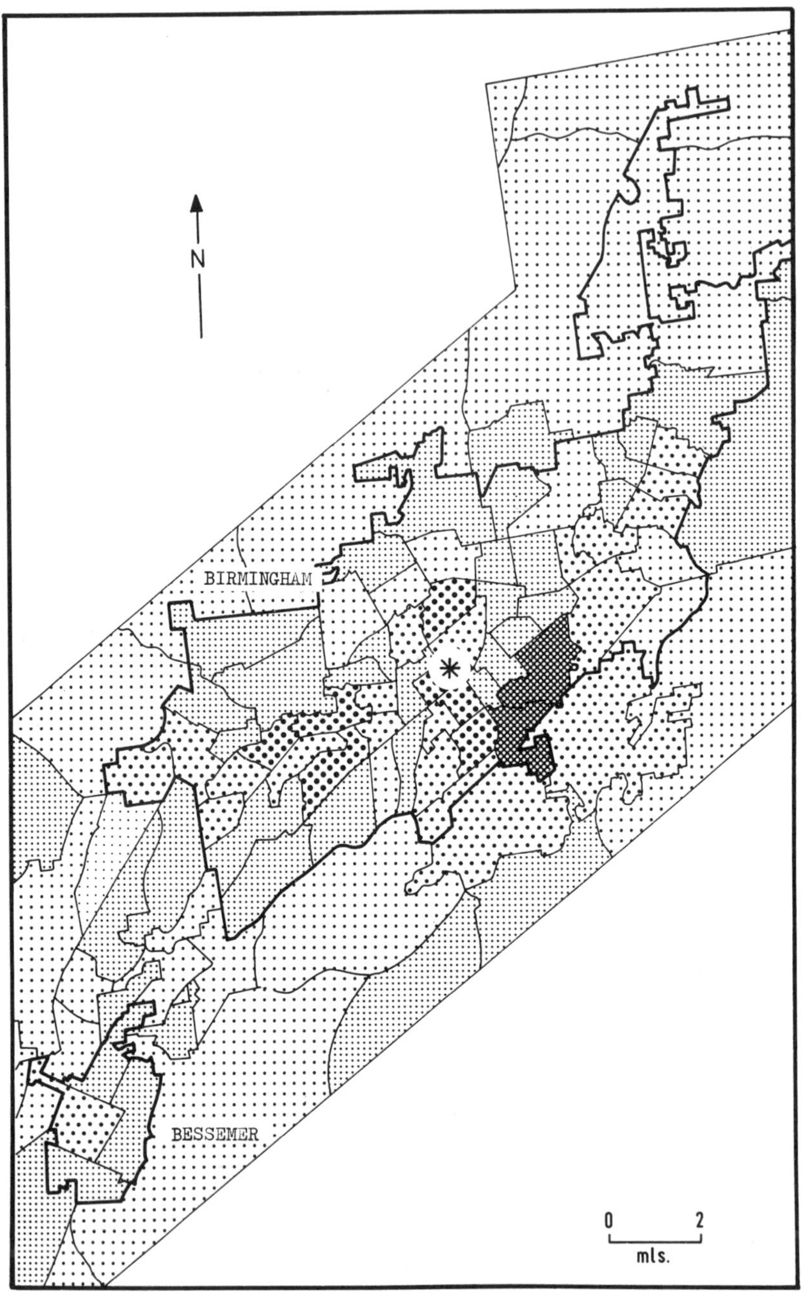

Fig. 33.--The Spatial Pattern of Family Status, Birmingham, 1960

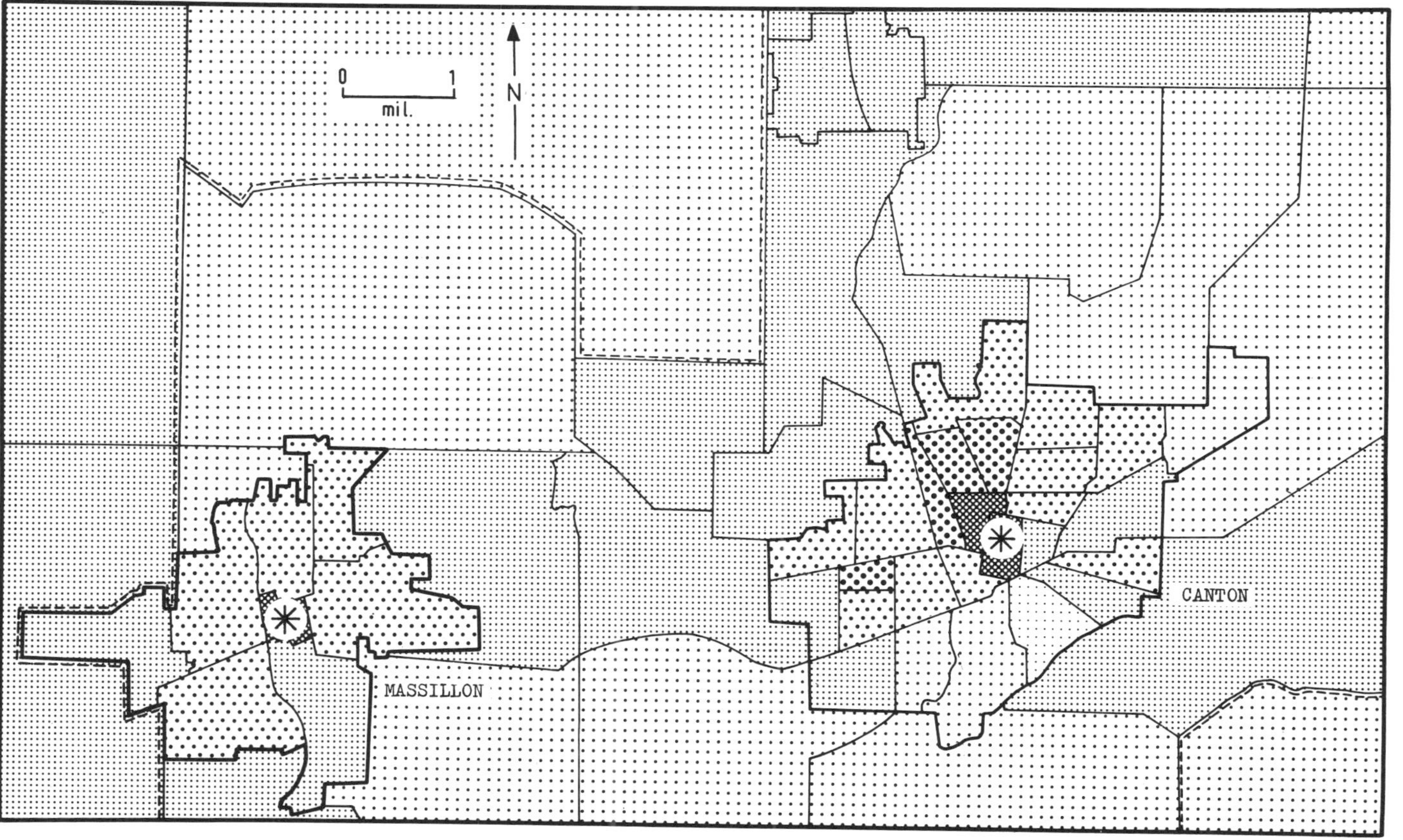

Fig. 34.--The Spatial Pattern of Family Status, Canton, 1960

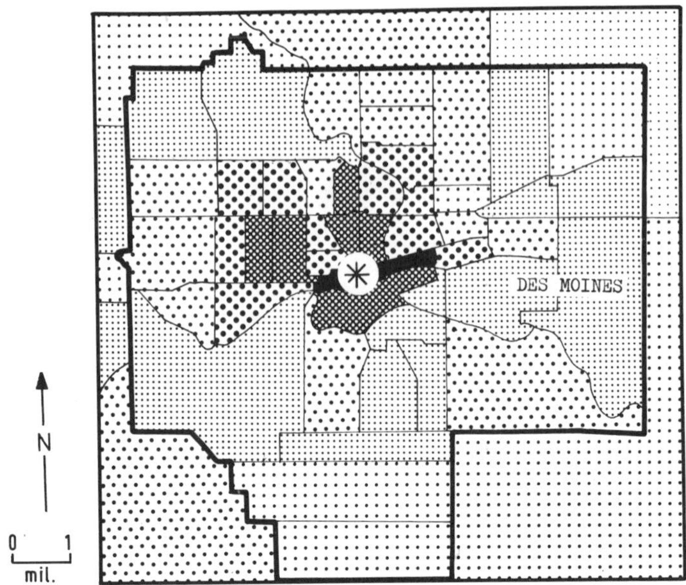

Fig. 35.--The Spatial Pattern of Family Status, Des Moines, 1960

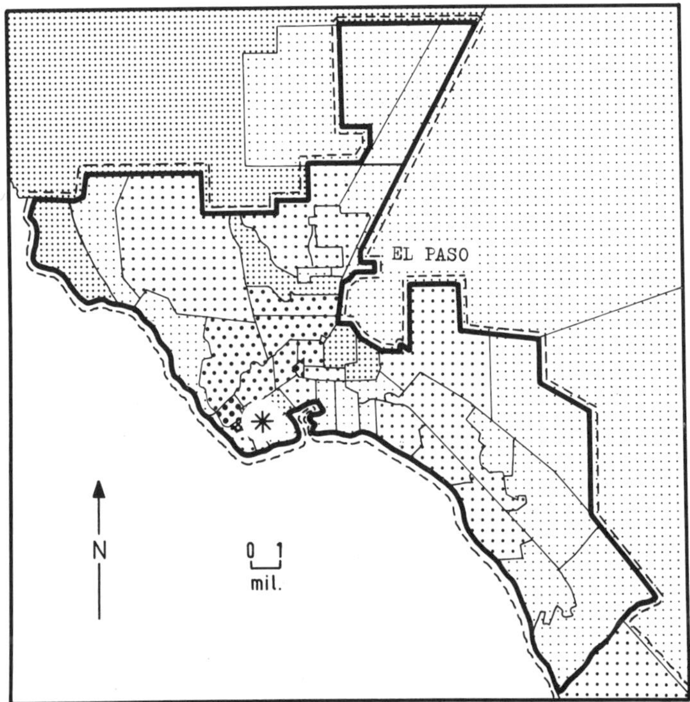

Fig. 36.--The Spatial Pattern of Family Status, El Paso, 1960

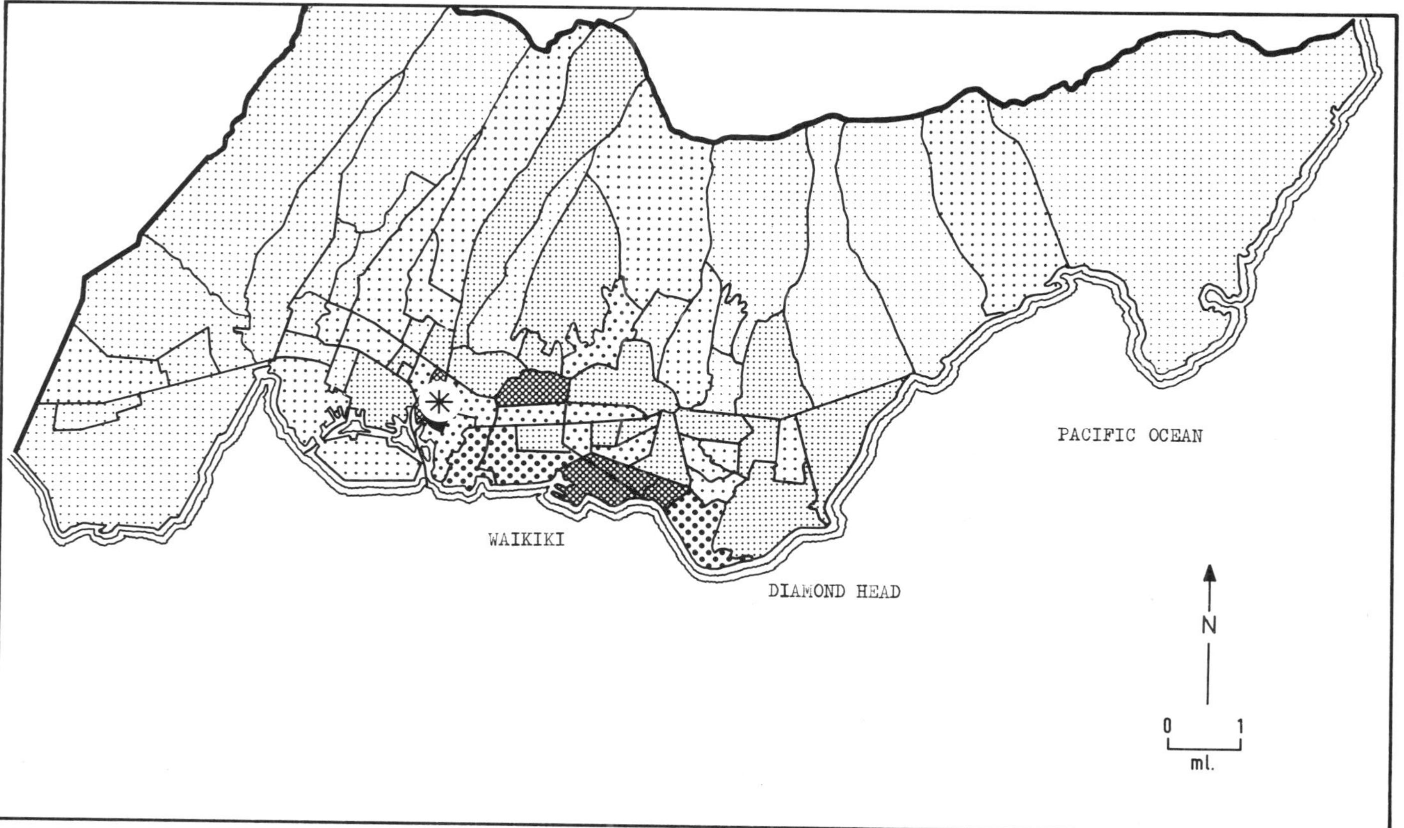

Fig. 37.--The Spatial Pattern of Family Status, Honolulu, 1960

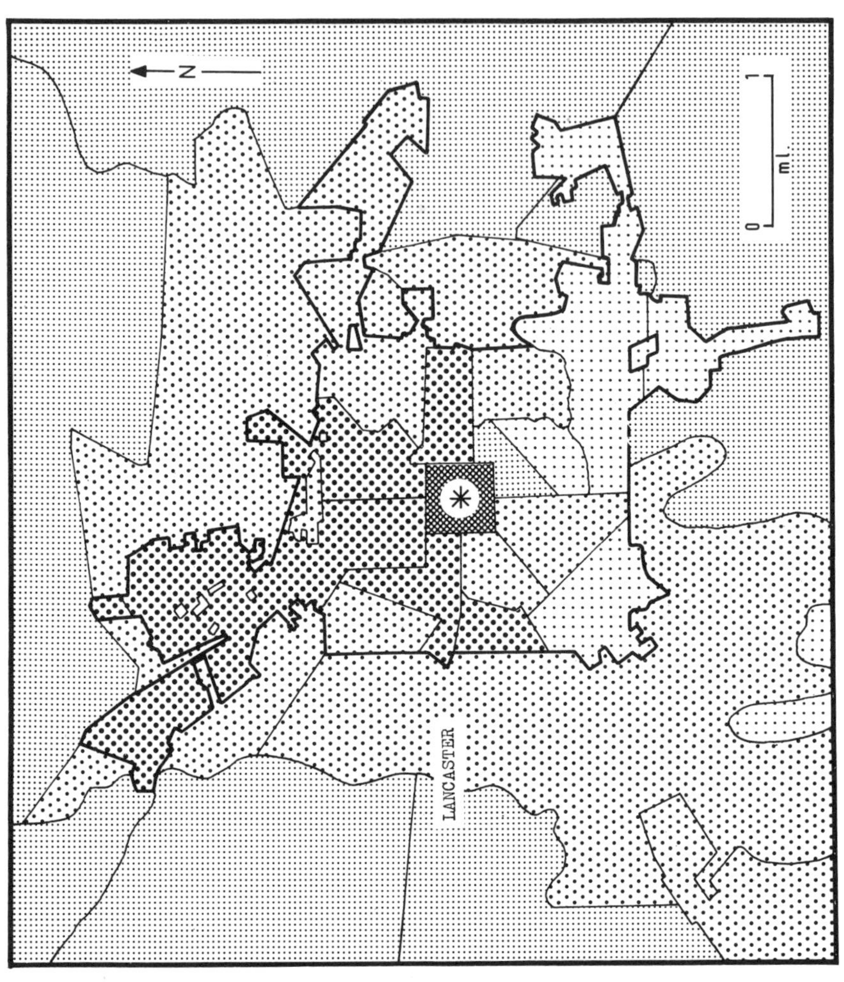

Fig. 38.--The Spatial Pattern of Family Status, Lancaster, 1960

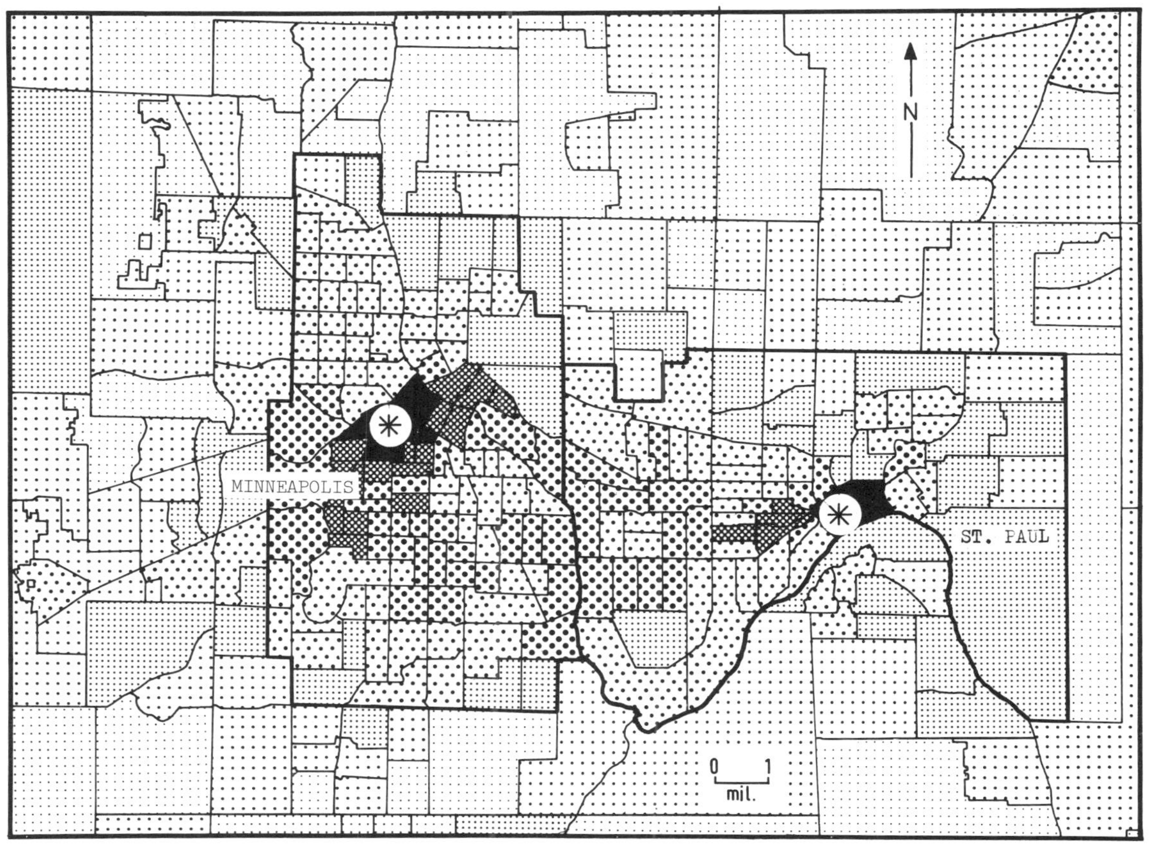

Fig. 39.--The Spatial Pattern of Family Status, Minneapolis-St. Paul, 1960

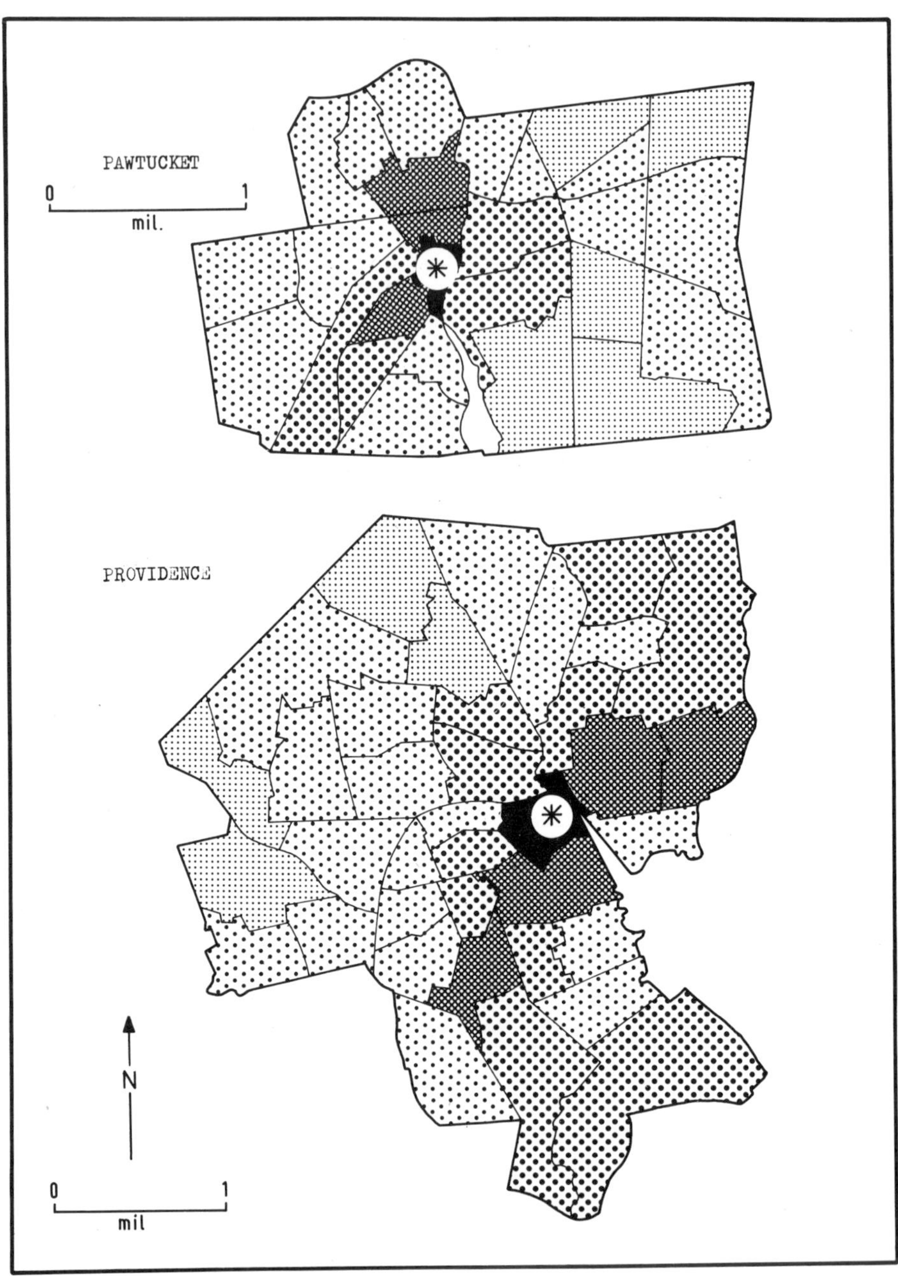

Fig. 40.--The Spatial Pattern of Family Status, Providence and Pawtucket Central Cities, 1960

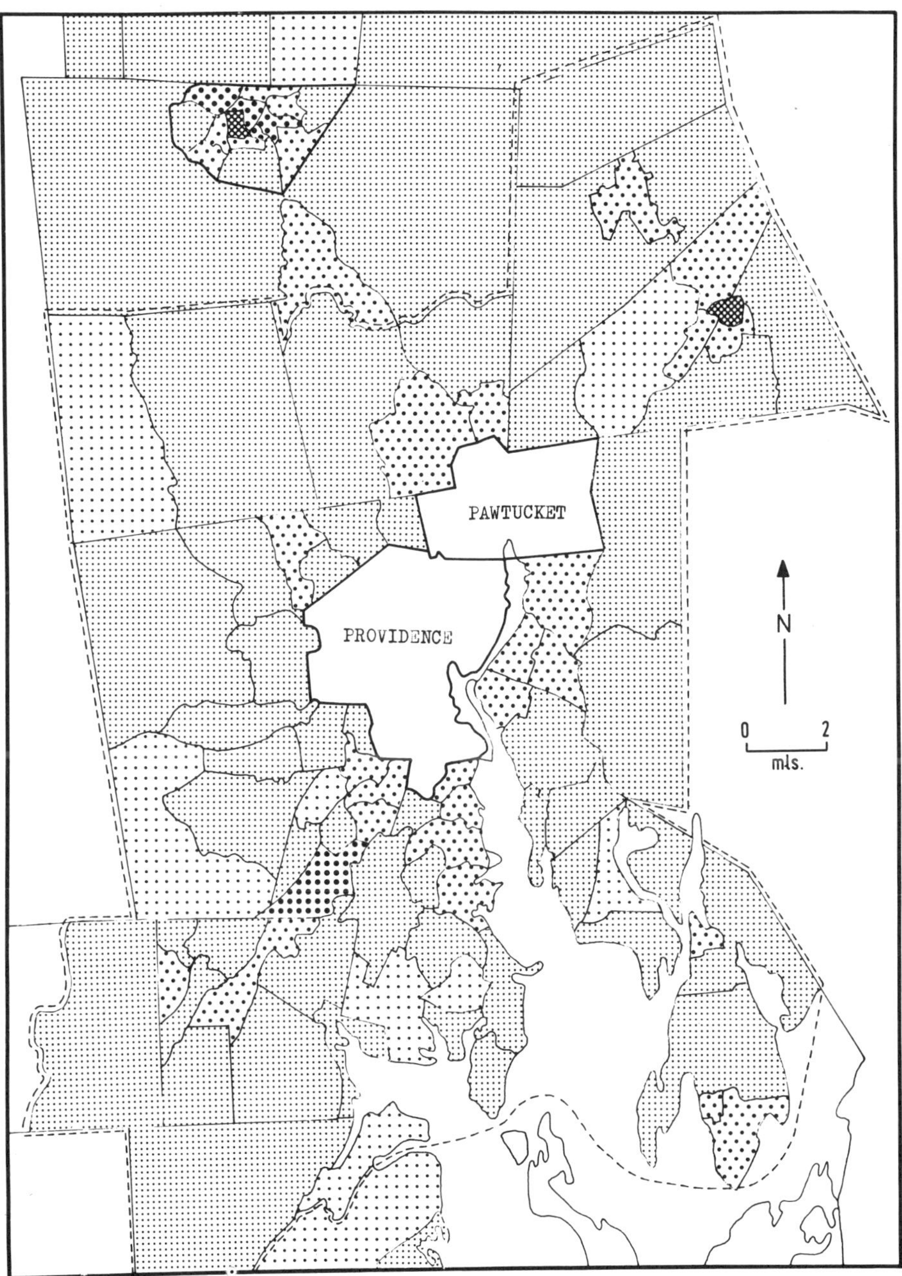

Fig. 41.--The Spatial Pattern of Family Status, Providence-Pawtucket SMSA, 1960

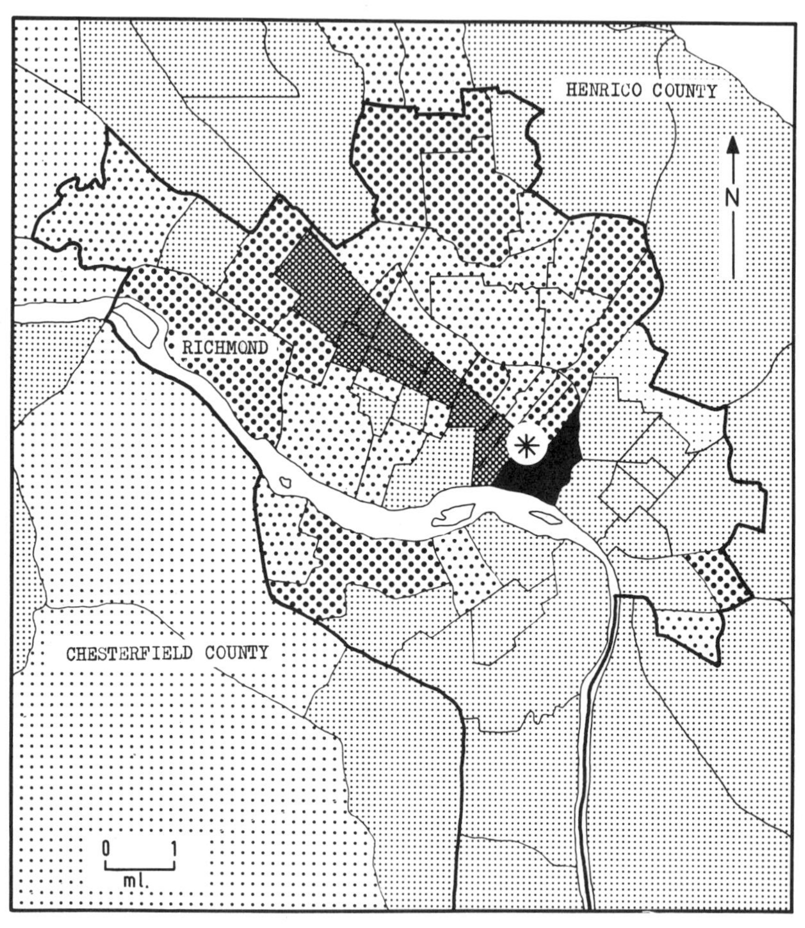

Fig. 42.--The Spatial Pattern of Family Status, Richmond, 1960

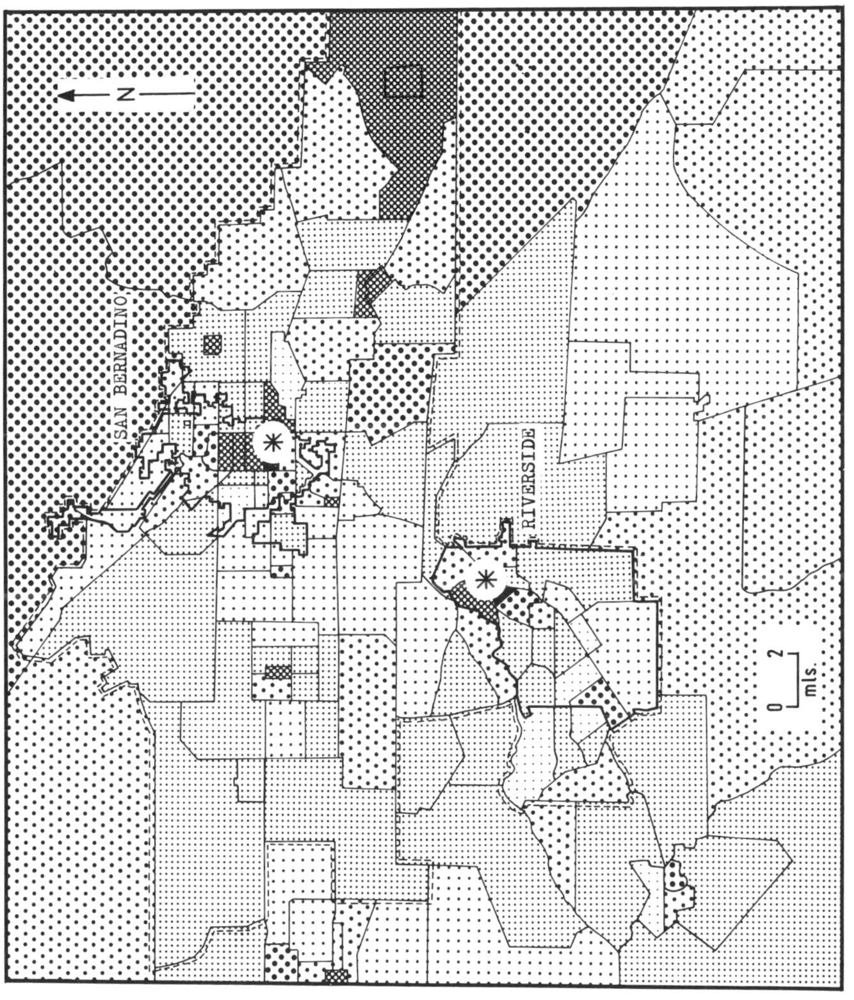

Fig. 43.--The Spatial Pattern of Family Status, San Bernadino-Riverside, 1960

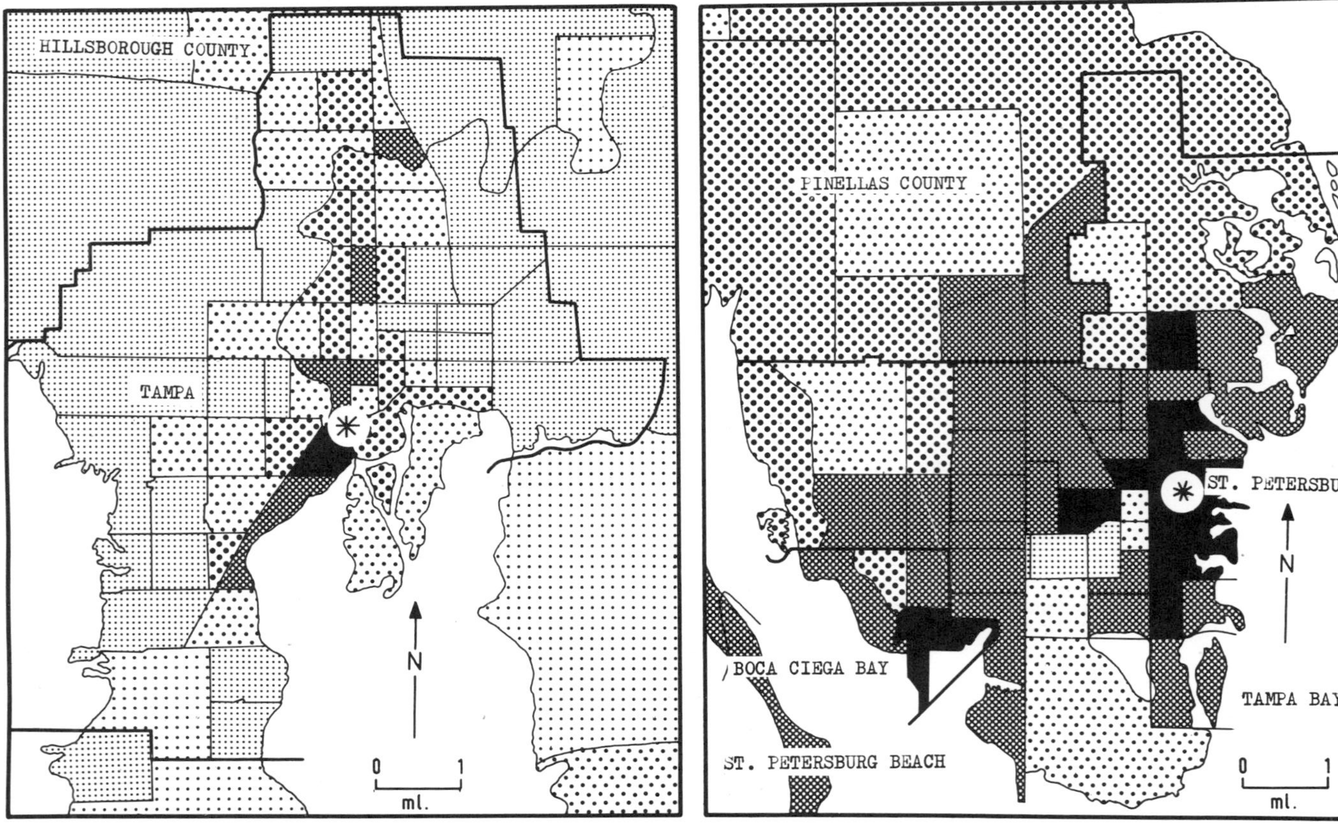

Fig. 44.--The Spatial Pattern of Family Status, Tampa-St. Petersburg Central Cities, 1960

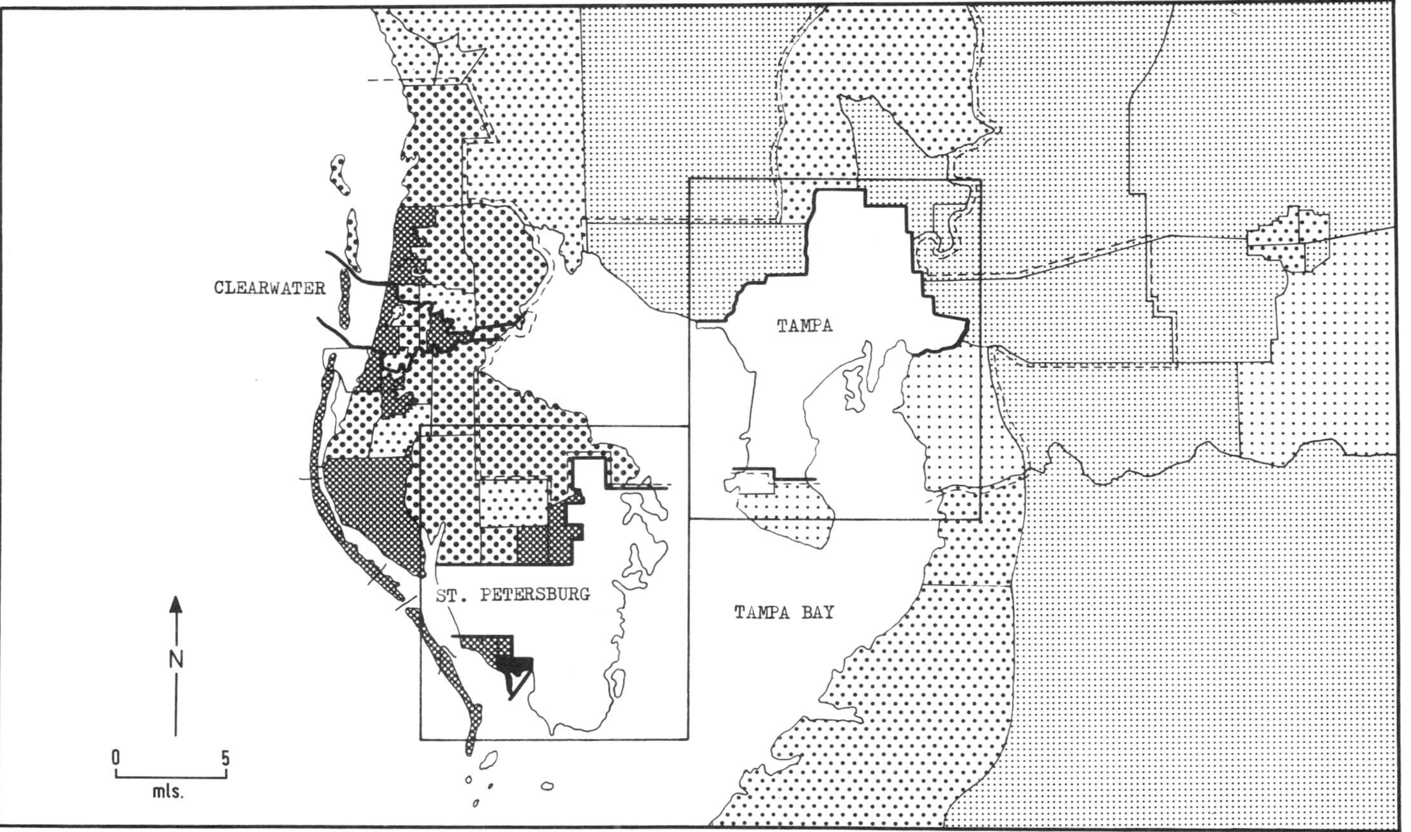

Fig. 45.--The Spatial Pattern of Family Status, Tampa-St. Petersburg SMSA, 1960

aged 65 and Over and a small fraction of 1 person households. The intermixture of age groups in all tracts reflects the basic nature of the family: families necessarily contain persons of very differing ages as a product of the child bearing and raising process. The intermixture of household sizes is, on the other hand, more probably a reflection of the intermixture of housing types offering varying amounts and kinds of shelter attractive to households of different sizes.

The Patterns of Family Status in the Individual Urbanized Areas

Not all of the urbanized areas have as simple a pattern of family status as that described above. The pattern of each study area is briefly described and commented upon.

The pattern revealed for Ann Arbor in Figure 32 is basically concentric but focused on two centers, that of Ann Arbor and that of its neighbor, Ypsilanti. The most familial (lowest scoring) populations reside in the outer areas of Ann Arbor and in the suburban tracts east of Ypsilanti, rather than on the rural periphery of the map.

The pattern for Birmingham (Figure 33) is broadly ring-like in structure, allowing for the idiosyncracies of Birmingham's built up area, constrained as it is by topography. Although the dominant association of the racial variable in Birmingham was shown in Chapter III to be with socioeconomic status, the maps of family status and racial status (Figures 33 and 50, respectively) reveal some association between racial mix and family status in the central area. Some of the central tracts score below 50 on the family status scale and these contain populations 75 per cent of which are Negro. These young families are some of the poorest in the urbanized area, and have not been able, because of their poverty and disadvantage, to exercise the choice for more spacious, suburban living which has been made by better-off families.

The centers of the cities of Canton and Massillon provide twin

TABLE 61

PROFILES OF SELECTED TRACTS, DES MOINES

Characteristic	Tracts						
	34	28	15	41	8	PC-111	PC-106
Family status factor score	3.23	1.17	0.44	-0.05	-0.40	-0.58	-1.81
Family status index score	78.70	62.62	55.53	51.55	47.86	44.69	39.89
Age status score	69.11	59.03	55.05	51.42	48.60	46.30	43.26
Size of household score	88.30	66.21	56.02	51.67	47.13	43.08	36.52
Per cent of persons aged:							
Under 5	1.00	6.45	6.64	9.71	13.61	12.99	16.52
5 to 14	2.16	12.35	18.21	10.06	20.56	24.95	25.72
15 to 19	5.69	6.49	6.38	7.67	4.87	5.13	6.88
20 to 64	66.50	57.35	49.88	54.11	53.91	52.06	46.46
65 and Over	24.66	17.37	16.85	9.46	7.05	4.88	4.43
All ages	100.00	100.00	100.00	100.00	100.00	100.00	100.00
Per cent of households:							
1 person	80.09	29.67	14.86	10.74	7.57	6.47	3.58
2 persons	17.10	38.73	39.01	32.73	27.15	24.34	20.66
3 persons	2.10	14.50	16.07	20.96	21.64	17.93	14.99
4 persons	0.47	7.07	12.08	17.96	23.35	23.63	23.56
5 persons	0.00	4.68	10.34	8.93	11.59	14.58	12.16
6 persons or more	0.23	5.34	7.65	8.68	8.69	13.05	25.06
All households	100.00	100.00	100.00	100.00	100.00	100.00	100.00

Source: Computed from tract information on a U.S. Bureau of the Census SMSA tape for Des Moines SMSA.

foci for the broadly concentric pattern of family status in the Canton urbanized area (Figure 34). However, several of the tracts in southern Canton score lower on the family status scale than a purely concentric model would suggest. This is an area of lower socioeconomic status and Negro concentration. The lowest scoring tract contains the highest proportion of families with low incomes whose poverty prevents them from matching housing needs and housing consumption in the normal life cycle fashion.

The concentric pattern is again dominant in Des Moines (Figure 35), if allowance is made for the fact that the urbanized area grew first and most rapidly in the northwest sector between the Des Moines and Raccoon rivers (Figure 35).

El Paso's family status map (Figure 36) is made up of two components: the "Anglo" portion and the Mexican portion. Within the portion in which the population is predominantly Anglo in composition (see Figure 64) residential populations become younger and larger in household size as distance from the center increases. The population of predominantly Mexican tracts is considerably younger at all distances from the center of the city than the population of Anglo tracts. Within the Mexican section of the city, however, there is still a tendency for centrally located tracts to contain populations higher on the family status scale than tracts located farther out.

The concentric pattern is again evident on the Honolulu map (Figure 37) though the area of highest scores on the family status index (oldest populations, smallest households) extends along the Pacific coast from the docks and Chinatown area to Waikiki beach. The outlying areas of residential settlement in the mountain valleys or in the Pearl Harbor military reservation area all score low on the family status scale. Intermediate areas score in the 40's and lower 50's and have large proportions of maturing families.

Although predominantly concentric in pattern, Lancaster's

family status map (Figure 38) does reveal sectoral components, at least within the central city limits.

The central areas of both of the Twin cities (Minneapolis-St. Paul) house older than average populations living in smaller than average households (Figure 39). Family status scores decrease outward towards the periphery of the urbanized area in a fairly regular fashion. A similar pattern of family status was found by Adams (in Abler, Adams and Gould, 1971, pp. 174-178) for the Minneapolis-St. Paul SMSA, though via a somewhat different approach. Adams used variables which indexed the tract size of groups at various stages in the family cycle in an orhogonal principal components analysis. Some five factors emerged from the analysis which were labelled:

I. Young, Footloose Cosmopolites
II. Blue Collar Working Class Families
III. Rising Young Families
IV. Mature Established Families
V. Aged Declining Families

At first sight Adams' factor analytic results might seem at variance with the single unitary family status factor described in Chapter III for all of the 13 urbanized areas under study. However, this is not necessarily so, for some quite interesting reasons.

The family status indicators used in Chapter III's principal components analyses were carefully selected to be either average values for tract populations (Median Age (Male), Population Per Household) or variables that measured the size of groups at the extremes of the age and household size distributions. This was done in order to preserve the possibility of unidimensional scaling for family status. Once all groups in a distribution are taken into account then it is likely that, even if an ordered scaling of areas in terms of their group composition exists, several separate factors are likely to emerge. This happened for very many of the ethnic and occupational variables in the Chapter III analyses. If the family status scores for census tracts in Minneapolis-St. Paul were to be broken up into age and household size groups, and the percentages of these groups in a tract plotted on a map, that map would in all probability reproduce the distributional patterns revealed in Adams' factors I, III, IV, and V.

The family status pattern of Providence-Pawtucket urbanized area is concentric about the multiple nuclei of the metropolitan region: Providence, Pawtucket, Woonsocket and Attleboro (Figures 40 and 41).

The pattern of family status for Richmond (Figure 42) is basically concentric though not perfectly so. The central areas which have predominantly white populations tend to have higher scores on the family status scale than areas which contain predominantly black populations. Once again the racial dimension is seen to be interacting with one of the two main social dimensions. This particular association, is however, by no means as strong as that between racial and socioeconomic status explored further in Chapter IX.

The map of San Bernadino-Riverside (Figure 43) shows the one feature common to all the family status maps: that of high scores for central area populations. The centers of San Bernadino, Riverside and Ontario show up on the maps as high points. Family status scores within the urbanized area are lower than the levels attained in the central areas, and are lowest in the residential areas that ring the cities of Riverside and Ontario. Beyond the urbanized area in the rural periphery populations are much older and households smaller in size.

Tampa-St. Petersburg's population is, on average, the oldest of any in the U.S., a reflection of its national importance as a retirement center. The map of Tampa (Figure 44) shows the familiar pattern of decreasing family status scores and increasing importance of familism as a life style as one makes the traverse from city center to urbanized area boundary (Figure 45).

The St. Petersburg urbanized area likewise shows a concentration of tract populations scoring above 70 on the family status scale at the center of the city. However, there are large areas of the city of St. Petersburg and of the Gulf Coast of the St. Petersburg urbanized area in general which score between 60 and 70 on the family status scale. These are the neighborhoods with high concentrations of retired persons. Most of the remainder of the urbanized area of St. Petersburg scores above 55 indicating that retired persons have settled throughout the urban region.

Residential Segregation of the Age and Household Size Groups

The emergence of a family status factor and a clear concentric pattern in the family status maps implies that families at different points in the life cycle are residentially segregated from one another. We can examine the extent of residential separation of different family types by computing indices of dissimilarity for the two distributions that tell us something about family types: age of persons and size of households (Tables 62 and 63 repectively).

The principal feature of Tables 62 and 63 is the low level of residential segregation of both age and size groups. Many of the dissimilarity index values for age groups are scarcely greater than would be expected from random assignment of persons of different age groups to the census tracts in the study areas. Taeuber and Taeuber report values of 12 to 15 for the index of dissimilarity using random assignment procedures (Taueber and Taeuber, 1965, pp. 231-235), and a large number of the Table 62 values are of this order of magnitude or lower. In particular, the average intergroup dissimilarity indices for both age and size groups (Table 64) are well below those for socioeconomic status groups (Table 60) or ethnic groups (Table 89).

In the case of age groups, the low levels can be attributed

TABLE 62

THE RESIDENTIAL SEGREGATION OF AGE GROUPS FOR 13 URBANIZED AREAS[a]

ANN ARBOR

Age Group	S	2	3	4	5
1. Under 5	23	11	47	23	41
2. 5 - 14	24		47	24	37
3. 15 -19	37			34	46
4. 20 - 64	12				26
5. 65+	30				

HONOLULU

Age Group	S	2	3	4	5
1. Under 5	13	10	16	15	30
2. 5 - 14	13		13	14	25
3. 15 - 19	9			10	20
4. 20 - 64	10				20
5. 65+	21				

BIRMINGHAM

Age Group	S	2	3	4	5
1. Under 5	9	5	9	11	20
2. 5 - 14	8		7	9	19
3. 15 - 19	7			9	15
4. 20 - 64	7				13
5. 65 +	15				

LANCASTER

Age Group	S	2	3	4	5
1. Under 5	9	6	15	9	18
2. 5 - 14	9		16	8	20
3. 15 - 19	12			13	17
4. 20 - 64	4				12
5. 65+	14				

CANTON

Age Group	S	2	3	4	5
1. Under 5	8	6	10	7	23
2. 5 - 14	8		9	7	23
3. 15 - 19	7			7	17
4. 20 - 64	3				17
5. 65+	19				

MINNEAPOLIS-ST. PAUL

Age Group	S	2	3	4	5
1. Under 5	16	10	21	17	37
2. 5 - 14	15		18	14	36
3. 15 - 19	10			8	22
4. 20 - 64	7				23
5. 65+	27				

DES MOINES

Age Group	S	2	3	4	5
1. Under 5	11	5	16	11	27
2. 5 - 14	11		16	10	27
3. 15 - 19	10			10	17
4. 20 - 64	5				18
5. 65+	21				

PROVIDENCE-PAWTUCKET

Age Group	S	2	3	4	5
1. Under 5	8	6	11	9	18
2. 5 - 14	9		10	9	19
3. 15 - 19	6			6	15
4. 20 - 64	4				12
5. 65+	14				

EL PASO

Age Group	S	2	3	4	5
1. Under 5	11	5	16	13	35
2. 5 - 14	12		14	13	34
3. 15 - 19	10			12	26
4. 20 - 64	9				26
5. 65+	29				

RICHMOND

Age Group	S	2	3	4	5
1. Under 5	16	7	18	17	37
2. 5 - 14	13		14	13	33
3. 15 - 19	8			9	24
4. 20 - 64	7				22
5. 65+	26				

TABLE 62--Continued

SAN BERNADINO-RIVERSIDE					
Age Group	S	2	3	4	5
1. Under 5	14	8	14	15	35
2. 5 - 14	12		10	11	33
3. 15 - 19	7			8	27
4. 20 - 64	6				24
5. 65+	27				

TAMPA					
Age Group	S	2	3	4	5
1. Under 5	12	7	13	13	27
2. 5 - 14	9		9	9	25
3. 15 - 19	7			7	18
4. 20 - 64	5				18
5. 65+	20				

ST. PETERSBURG					
Age Group	S	2	3	4	5
1. Under 5	20	9	16	18	34
2. 5 - 14	14		9	11	28
3. 15 - 19	9			7	22
4. 20 - 64	6				7
5. 65+	22				

Notes

[a]S refers to the Index of Segregation. The other figures are all indices of dissimilarity between pairs of age groups.

TABLE 63

THE RESIDENTIAL SEGREGATION OF HOUSEHOLD SIZE GROUPS FOR 13 URBANIZED AREAS

ANN ARBOR						
Size Group	S	2	3	4	5	6
1. 1 person	39	28	39	50	54	52
2. 2 persons	14		15	27	32	32
3. 3 persons	11			16	24	27
4. 4 persons	22				14	22
5. 5 persons	27					17
6. 6 persons +	28					
BIRMINGHAM						
Size Group	S	2	3	4	5	6
1. 1 person	26	21	27	33	32	34
2. 2 persons	11		10	15	17	28
3. 3 persons	9			10	11	26
4. 4 persons	14				8	27
5. 5 persons	13					24
6. 6 persons +	26					

TABLE 63--Continued

CANTON						
Size Group	S	2	3	4	5	6
1. 1 person	27	22	26	34	33	30
2. 2 persons	9		9	16	16	18
3. 3 persons	6			11	11	14
4. 4 persons	14				10	15
5. 5 persons	12					13
6. 6 persons +	15					
DES MOINES						
Size Group	S	2	3	4	5	6
1. 1 person	36	28	36	44	46	42
2. 2 persons	10		11	20	23	22
3. 3 persons	9			11	14	17
4. 4 persons	17				9	14
5. 5 persons	19					13
6. 6 persons +	19					
EL PASO						
Size Group	S	2	3	4	5	6
1. 1 person	37	32	35	44	45	44
2. 2 persons	20		15	24	28	34
3. 3 persons	9			14	16	25
4. 4 persons	17				10	24
5. 5 persons	18					20
6. 6 persons +	25					
HONOLULU						
Size Group	S	2	3	4	5	6
1. 1 person	41	24	40	46	49	55
2. 2 persons	20		17	25	29	37
3. 3 persons	11			14	18	27
4. 4 persons	14				9	20
5. 5 persons	17					15
6. 6 persons +	28					
LANCASTER						
Size Group	S	2	3	4	5	6
1. 1 person	28	25	29	33	33	33
2. 2 persons	7		9	11	13	18
3. 3 persons	7			8	10	15
4. 4 persons	12				9	15
5. 5 persons	12					16
6. 6 persons +	15					
MINNEAPOLIS-ST. PAUL						
Size Group	S	2	3	4	5	6
1. 1 person	39	31	39	47	49	48

TABLE 63--Continued

MINNEAPOLIS-ST. PAUL--Continued

Size Group	S	2	3	4	5	6
2. 2 persons	15		13	24	28	29
3. 3 persons	8			15	19	21
4. 4 persons	19				10	15
5. 5 persons	21					13
6. 6 persons +	23					

PROVIDENCE-PAWTUCKET

Size Group	S	2	3	4	5	6
1. 1 person	28	23	28	33	34	32
2. 2 persons	8		9	14	15	16
3. 3 persons	8			10	12	13
4. 4 persons	13				9	12
5. 5 persons	14					13
6. 6 persons +	13					

RICHMOND

Size Group	S	2	3	4	5	6
1. 1 person	34	26	36	45	42	41
2. 2 persons	14		14	23	23	28
3. 3 persons	9			12	14	23
4. 4 persons	19				9	27
5. 5 persons	16					22
6. 6 persons +	24					

SAN BERNADINO-RIVERSIDE

Size Group	S	2	3	4	5	6
1. 1 person	29	21	31	37	39	40
2. 2 persons	15		16	22	26	29
3. 3 persons	11			13	16	22
4. 4 persons	17				9	19
5. 5 persons	19					16
6. 6 persons +	23					

ST. PETERSBURG

Size Group	S	2	3	4	5	6
1. 1 person	27	23	29	35	37	39
2. 2 persons	12		12	18	22	29
3. 3 persons	11			10	15	21
4. 4 persons	17				10	18
5. 5 persons	20					17
6. 6 persons +	26					

TABLE 63--Continued

TAMPA						
Size Group	S	2	3	4	5	6
1. 1 person	27	21	28	34	35	34
2. 2 persons	10		11	17	19	25
3. 3 persons	8			10	13	19
4. 4 persons	15				9	19
5. 5 persons	15					17
6. 6 persons +	20					

Notes

[a]S refers to the Index of Segregation which the index of dissimilarity between a group and the rest of the population. The other figures in the table are all indices of dissimilarity between pairs of size groups.

fairly straightforwardly to the nature of family living. Families living in the same housing unit will often contain persons of very disparate ages — parents and children. The most spatially separate group is, in 12 cases out of 13, the oldest group of persons 65 years of age and over.

The most segregated size group is that of single persons in all urbanized areas studied. Although neither retired persons nor single member households are as separated residentially from the rest of the population as the most segregated social classes or ethnic groups, their relative isolation may make their integration into community life and care more difficult. On the other hand, many younger single persons enjoy their spatial separation from family living. The working age group, 20 to 64, is the least spatially separate because of its large size and parental function. The under fives and 5 to 14 age group are fairly coincident, usually having their lowest dissimilarity indices with each other. The 15 to 19 age group is more segregated: the older members of this age group will be forming separate households for the first time usually in a different neighborhood or in a different city from that in

TABLE 64

AVERAGE INTER-GROUP DISSIMILARITY INDICES
FOR AGE GROUPS AND HOUSEHOLD SIZE GROUPS

Urbanized Area	Age Group Average	Household Size Group Average
Ann Arbor	33.55	29.97
Birmingham	11.82	21.56
Canton	12.61	18.61
Des Moines	15.97	23.19
El Paso	19.30	27.38
Honolulu	17.39	28.32
Lancaster	13.28	18.37
Minneapolis-St. Paul	20.78	26.70
Providence-Pawtucket	11.51	18.18
Richmond	19.21	25.74
San Bernadino-Riverside	18.55	23.75
St. Petersburg	16.17	22.46
Tampa	14.63	20.66

which they grew up.

When the dissimilarity indices for size groups are examined, the relationship observed in the social class tables shows up again: the more dissimilar the household socially (in terms of size) the more spatial separation on average between them. Table 65 shows from 15 to 20 agreements out of 20 with the relationship specified generally in Table 54. The U shaped distribution of group _vs_ the rest of the population indices is also characteristic of household size groups.

It would be interesting to be able to trace the historical changes over time in the level and pattern of the spatial separation of age and household size groups but no comparable tables have yet been calculated for earlier years for American cities.

Relationship between Family Characteristics and Housing Characteristics Expectations

TABLE 65

AGREEMENTS WITH MODEL FOR HOUSEHOLD SIZE GROUPS FOR 13 URBANIZED AREAS[a]

Urbanized Area	Agreements
Ann Arbor	19
Birmingham	18
Canton	15
Des Moines	18
El Paso	19
Honolulu	20
Lancaster	16
Minneapolis-St. Paul	19
Providence-Pawtucket	18
Richmond	17
San Bernadino-Riverside	20
St. Petersburg	20
Tampa	18

Notes

[a]The total number of agreements possible for the 13 urbanized areas is 20.

The residential segregation of family types was seen as a function of the segregation within the urban area of types of dwelling considered suitable or attractive by families at various stages in their life cycles. Different family types choose to occupy different kinds of housing accommodation, adapted to their particular needs subject to the constraints that they must be able to afford the needed accommodation, and they must be allowed to occupy it (the income and racial discrimination constraints). We can spell out this hypothesis, first elaborated in connection with Chicago, (Rees, 1970b, pp. 311-313; Able, Adams and Gould, 1971, pp. 173-174) in the form of a table (Table 66). This table shows what kind of housing families at various stages in their life cycle should

TABLE 66

THE RELATIONSHIP BETWEEN FAMILY TYPE CHARACTERISTICS AND HOUSING UNIT CHARACTERISTICS

Family Types Defined By Stage in Life Cycle (After Lansing and Kish)[a]	Family Characteristics[b]			Housing Characteristics[b]			Other Characteristics[b]	
	Age of Head[c]	Size	Marital Status of Head	Size: No. of Rooms	Type: Units in Structure	Tenure	Age	Location
Young single	17-22	1	Single	1-2	3+	Rented	Pre-1940	Inner City
Young, married no children	23-25	2	Married	1-3	1-2, 3+	Rented	Pre-1940	Inner City
Young, married, youngest child under 6	26-34	3-6+	Married	2-5	1-2	Rented, Owned	1950-1960	Suburbs
Young, married, youngest child 6 or over	35-44	3-6+	Married	2-7+	1-2	Owned	1950-1960	Suburbs
Other married with children	45-54	3-6+	Married	2-7+	1-2	Owned	1940-1950	Outer City, Suburbs
Older married, with children	55-64	2	Married	1-3	3+	Owned	Pre-1940	Inner City, Outer City
Older single	65+	1	Single, Widowed, or Divorced	1-2	3+	Owned, Rented	Pre-1940	Inner City, Outer City

Notes

[a]From Lansing and Kish, 1957.

[b]The characteristics are stated in terms of the classification used in the Census tables.

[c]These ages are illustrative of the typical age of the head of the family. However, many heads of families of particular types may lie outside the range given.

occupy if their needs and housing are matched. Average or model relationships only are given in the table and in practice there will be considerable variation around each average relationship.

For example, if a young family with children cannot afford spacious accommodation suited to their needs they will be observed to be living in housing smaller than the average posited in the table. At the early stages in the life cycle small housing units, rented and built some time ago, are occupied. As the family grows it moves to larger accommodation (Rossi, 1955). This the family will seek to own, though most families will be paying off a mortgage for a good part of their lives. These homes will on average be newer than those occupied at earlier stages and will be single family homes rather than apartments. When the children have departed the family may readjust its living space to its reduced needs or it may stay put and use the surplus space for occasional visitors. In both cases older than average housing will tend to be occupied because apartment accommodation in which the family may have relocated is usually older on average than single family dwellings (at least in 1960) or because the housing unit in which a family may choose to remain will have aged with its inhabitants.

The most direct evidence of the propositions stated in Table 66 would be a set of crosstabulations of family types and housing characteristics for the urbanized areas studied. It would be possible using both simple crosstabulations from the Metropolitan Housing volumes of the Census and techniques for reconstructing crosstabulations to build such tables. Such an attempt is, however, left to future work. Here some more readily available evidence of association between particular family and particular housing characteristics is described.

Relationship Revealed By Factor Analysis

As we saw in Chapter IV a family status and home type factor

(Table 26) emerged in the factor analysis of the joint population and housing variable set for 10 out of the 13 urbanized areas. This factor was characterized by high loadings of the age and household size variables, the housing type, room size, tenure and housing age variables. This pattern, which follows directly from the expectations of Table 66, is most clearly visible in the components from the Canton, Des Moines, Lancaster, Minneapolis-St. Paul, San Bernadino-Riverside and Tampa analyses. A less pronounced version of this pattern is characteristic of Ann Arbor, Birmingham, and Richmond, though in the Ann Arbor analysis two of the age variables load most highly on another factor and in the Birmingham analysis the family status indicator loadings are not as high as the housing characteristic ones.

The El Paso factor analysis reveals that the housing size and tenure characteristics are definitely not associated with the stage in family cycle variables nor with those of housing type and age. This may reflect the differences between Mexican Americans and Anglo Americans in the matching of household and housing characteristics. At any given household size the Mexican household will occupy less space than the Anglo household. Because the Mexican American population of El Paso is relatively large this will mean that there will only be a weak association between life cycle characteristics and housing size/tenure types.

In Honolulu, household size and housing structure/size/tenure type are associated on one factor, but the age variables load on another, together with housing age and other selected housing variables in the second set. This deviation from the normal pattern is probably related to the particular racial and immigrant age structure of Honolulu.

The final deviant factor structure is that of St. Petersburg where the family status indicators and Table housing variables load highly on separate factors. This is presumably because many of the older households who have retired to St. Petersburg buy types of housing that in other cities only larger and younger families purchase. There are other older and smaller households in St. Petersburg which occupy smaller and older property. Hence the lack of association between family status characteristics and housing type characteristics.

A Sample Crosstabulation

A crosstabulation which is fairly easily extracted from the Metropolitan Housing tables (U.S. Bureau of the Census, 1963d) is that of tenure *vs* household size. The distribution of households by size in renter and owner occupied housing for the 12 sample SMSAs is detailed in Table 73, and serves to illustrate more directly the link between household and housing characteristics seen in the factors described in the last section. The size distribution of households in rented accommodation is more concentrated in the smaller categories than is owner occupied housing. This is true of all 12 SMSAs, though in Birmingham, Lancaster, Richmond, San Bernadino-Riverside and Tampa-St. Petersburg a higher proportion of households in rented accommodation are households with 6 or more persons than in owner occupied housing. Many of these households may be in rented accommodation because their large size reduces the income available for housing expenditure and owned accommodation of the required size cannot be afforded.

Behind the difference between renter occupied and owner occupied housing in the size distribution of households lies the difference between renter and owner occupied housing in terms of size of housing unit. Owner occupied housing units are on average larger in size than rented units, and more suited to the larger family.

A Simple Model

The relationships between family type or status characteristics and housing unit attributes can be embodied in a simple model

TABLE 67

THE DISTRIBUTION OF HOUSEHOLDS BY SIZE IN RENTER AND OWNER OCCUPIED HOUSING FOR 12 SMSAs, 1960

Tenure	Persons in Households	Ann Arbor	Birmingham	Canton	Des Moines	El Paso	Honolulu
Renter	1	24.92	16.85	18.98	32.74	15.40	14.69
	2	31.61	26.89	25.69	28.05	21.00	19.29
	3 and 4	30.76	31.95	35.69	27.32	34.45	37.85
	5	6.15	9.01	9.36	5.65	11.82	12.55
	6 or More	6.56	15.30	10.27	6.25	17.32	15.62
	Total	100.00	100.00	100.00	100.00	100.00	100.00
Owner	1	7.65	6.91	8.01	8.97	6.65	4.48
	2	26.87	27.89	28.76	30.13	21.23	15.53
	3 and 4	37.88	41.27	38.53	37.85	36.69	35.79
	5	14.51	11.87	12.78	12.27	15.55	17.17
	6 or More	13.09	12.05	11.92	10.68	19.88	27.03
	Total	100.00	100.00	100.00	100.00	100.00	100.00
Index of Dissimilarity		22.01	13.19	10.98	23.72	8.76	16.08

TABLE 67--Continued

Tenure	Persons in Households	Lancaster	Minneapolis-St. Paul	Providence-Pawtucket	Richmond	San Bernadino-Riverside	Tampa-St. Petersburg
Renter	1	15.61	31.18	20.67	17.76	22.93	27.11
	2	25.13	30.06	28.17	29.71	24.91	29.05
	3 and 4	36.43	27.07	35.90	32.11	32.40	27.02
	5	11.23	6.09	8.39	8.95	9.11	7.44
	6 or More	11.60	5.60	6.87	11.47	10.65	9.38
	Total	100.00	100.00	100.00	100.00	100.00	100.00
Owner	1	8.25	7.17	8.12	6.31	11.33	13.02
	2	29.77	26.41	27.77	27.06	32.94	40.33
	3 and 4	39.04	37.04	40.13	44.26	33.55	31.44
	5	11.76	14.35	12.82	12.55	11.88	8.48
	6 or More	11.16	15.02	11.16	9.82	10.30	6.74
	Total	100.00	100.00	100.00	100.00	100.00	100.00
Index of Dissimilarity		7.79	27.66	12.95	15.73	11.95	16.73

Source: Calculated from U.S. Bureau of the Census, 1963d.

that allocates different kinds of families to residential zones on the basis of the kind of housing found there. This model assumes the supply of housing in the various zones as given.

Ideally, the family types should be defined using all the characteristics associated with the life cycle concept discussed in Chapter V and summarized in Table 66. And the housing unit type should be similarly defined using the characteristics found to be associated with family status in the factor analyses described earlier. To do the job properly would necessitate retabulation of the original census forms or household records using such a special purpose classification or use of a set of techniques that estimated the necessary tract joint distributions from the various single variable distributions. These tasks are not attempted here. Instead a simple version of the model is defined and tested:

$$H_i(s) = \sum_{\tau=1}^{2} (U_i(\tau)\ P_*(s|\tau)) \qquad (9)$$

where s refers to the size of household category, τ to the tenure class of the housing unit, $H_i(s)$ to the number of households of size s in zone i, which we are attempting to predict, and $U_i(\tau)$ is the number of occupied housing units of tenure τ in zone i. The conditional probability $P_*(s|\tau)$ is the probability that a household living in a housing unit of tenure v will be of size s. This probability is for the whole of the study area, in this case the SMSA. Thus,

$$P_*(s|\tau) = H_*(s,\tau)/H_*(*,\tau) \qquad (10)$$

where $H_*(s,\tau)$ is the joint distribution of household size and household tenure in the SMSA as a whole and $H_*(\tau)$ is the number of housing units in a tenure category in the SMSA.

The results of the model for Des Moines are shown in Table 68.

TABLE 68

GOODNESS OF FIT OF FAMILY STATUS MODEL FOR DES MOINES

Persons in Households	Index of Dissimilarity between Observed and Expected Distributions of Households of Different Sizes
1	16.68
2	7.50
3 and 4	7.31
5	12.56
6 or more	15.29

Indices of dissimilarity were calculated between the observed distribution of households of each size category and the distribution predicted by the model for the census tracts of the urbanized area. The indices of dissimilarity are remarkably small for such a simple model. Best predicted are households with 2 persons or 3 and 4 persons. The majority of Des Moines' renter and owner occupied households fall in these two categories combined so that this is not surprising. Where the probabilities of a household type differ between renter and owner occupied categories rather more (see Table 67, Des Moines column) observations and model predictions are further apart. Does the goodness of fit of the model vary from census tract to census tract over the urbanized area as well as over household categories?

We plot for each census tract in the Des Moines urbanized area the number of households of one person in size against the observed number of households. We obtain the scattergraph shown in Figure 46. The deviations from a perfect relationship (the predicted number equalling the observed for each census tract) are systematic. Above the mean number of observed and predicted households, which are the same, the model tends to underpredict the number of house-

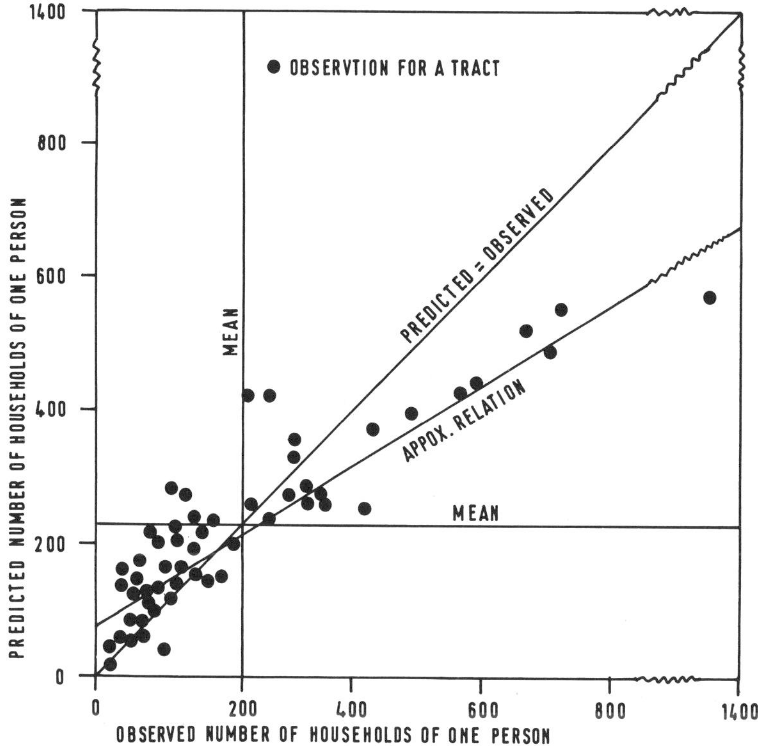

Fig. 46.--Predicted and Observed Numbers of Households of One Person in Des Moines

holds in a tract, and below the mean the model tends to overpredict the number of households. This implies that among the city's rental housing units those that contain one person households tend to be located in those tracts with the highest concentration of rental units. The rental units in tracts which have a majority of owner occupied units are more suited to households of two or more persons.

The deviations from the model are also systematic spatially (Figure 47). The number of one person households in the inner area to the north and west of the Central Business District is consistently underpredicted; the number of such households in the less accessible city tracts and in the suburban tracts bordering on Des

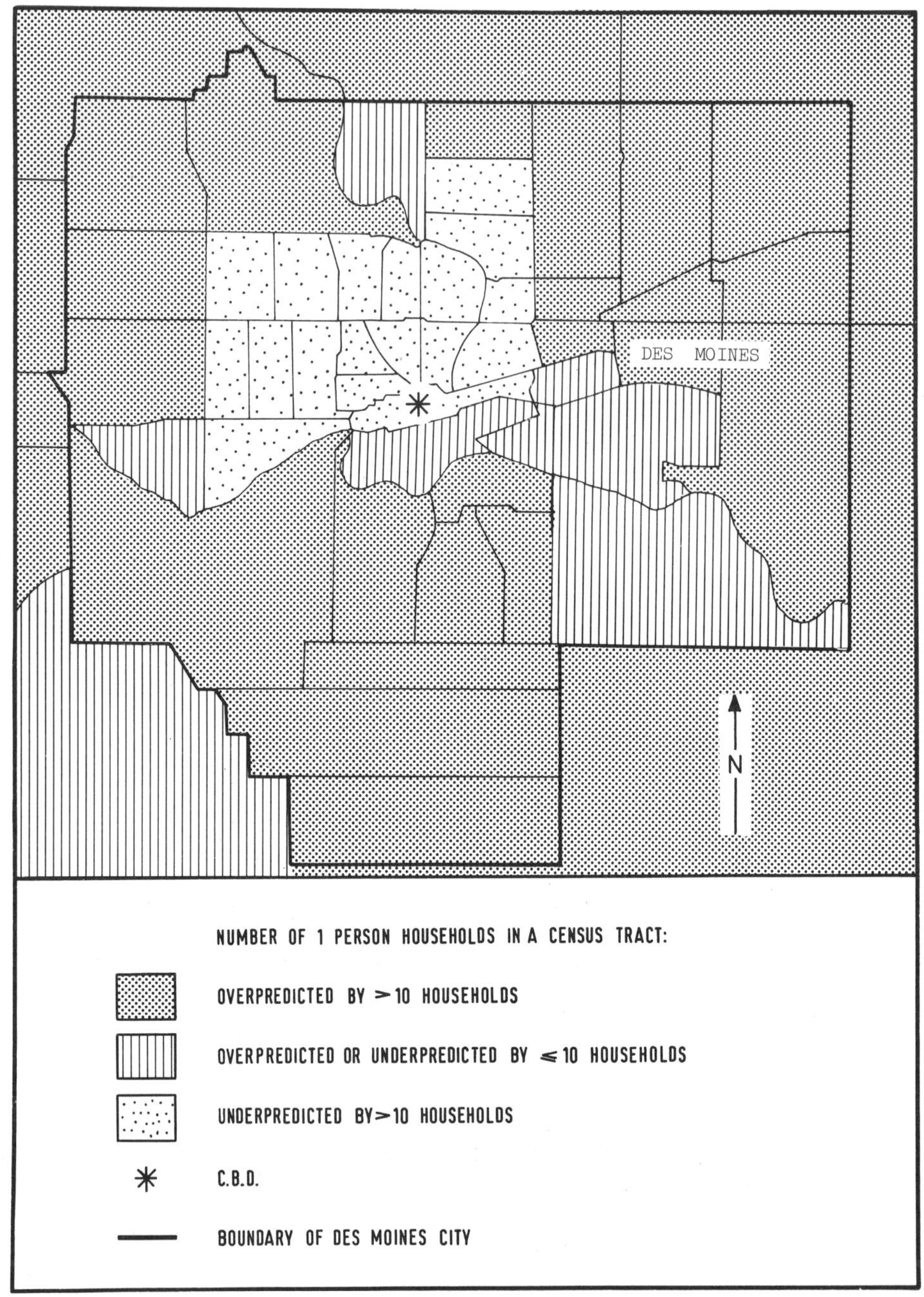

Fig. 47.--Deviations from the Family Status Model for One Person Households, Des Moines

Moines city is consistently overpredicted. The rental units in the outer tracts are generally single family homes or large apartments unsuited to one person households.

Obviously, the efficacy of the model would be greatly improved if the housing stock could be disaggregated by size of unit and type, and if necessary crosstabulations were available at the SMSA scale. However, it is probable that deviations of the sort observed with the simple model would still occur though at a reduced scale. These kinds of deviations are characteristic of models that use probabilities calculated at an aggregate scale to predict probabilities at a more spatially disaggregate scale. Such models will always tend to dampen variation in the way that the family status model does.

Conclusions

We have examined in this chapter the spatial patterns exhibited in our sample of cities by the family status dimension identified in the factor analyses reported in Chapter III and measured, for comparative purposes, by the family status index derived in Chapter V. This examination has shown that families of different types are distributed in a fairly regular pattern within the American city. The inner central city contains the greatest concentrations of older persons and single person households. The outer city and suburbs contain younger families and larger households. The periphery of the metropolis contains a fairly wide mixture of age groups and family sizes.

Exceptions to this general pattern occur if there is a substantial minority population in socioeconomic disadvantage in the city. The minority population may be constrained by poverty and discrimination to the inner city. Within the residential area occupied by the minority group the outer neighborhoods will contain the highest concentrations of young families, but these neighborhoods will be considerably nearer the center of the city than the corresponding "familial" areas occupied predominantly by the majority population.

Where the age structure of an urbanized area's population is particularly old, as in the retirement city of St. Petersburg, we have observed substantial numbers of older and smaller households living in outer city or suburban areas.

The residential segregation of family types was shown to be generally low, despite the distinctive pattern of family status, with the possible exception of single person households.

A simple model relating family type and housing type was proposed as an explanation of the pattern of family status. A variety of evidence was presented that tended to support this model of aggregate residential choice. The major deviation from the model was the non-coincidence of family status and housing type, size and tenure scores in St. Petersburg. However, this was the exception that tended to prove the rule. The residential location decisions that produced such a non-coincidence were those of large numbers of households moving on retirement to sunny Florida, seeking and being able to afford a spacious, owned, single family home.

We turn now to look in detail at the final of the major dimensions that characterize the residential patterning of American cities: that of racial status. In the next chapter, Chapter VIII, the spatial patterns of racial and ethnic groups in our sample of American cities in 1960 are analyzed.

CHAPTER VIII

THE SPATIAL PATTERNS OF RACIAL AND ETHNIC GROUPS

Neighborhoods in American cities differ considerably one from another not only in the social class composition of their populations and in the mix of family and household types but also in the proportions of the various racial and ethnic groups that live there. We look first at the way such groups are defined as an essential preliminary to our discussion. Then we consider the factors that could be said to influence the ways in which racial and ethnic groups are distributed in American cities. The map patterns of the most distinct minority group, Negroes, are then examined. The qualitative picture provided by the maps is sharpened up by a consideration of the quantitative degree of clustering and assimilation present in the map patterns. An interpretation of the results of this examination is put forward, and one of the components of this interpretation is tested out by use of an economic segregation model. The chapter concludes with a discussion of the patterns of residence and segregation of foreign stock groups.

Racial and Ethnic Definitions

On birth, an individual shows, for the first time, racial characteristics (anatomical and physiological features) and is ascribed a birthplace of origin. In the course of his or her upbringing the individual acquires a language, a religion or lack of one, and a culture. Further change in the course of life in these attributes is rarely possible in the case of race, difficult in the case of language and culture and not too difficult in the case of religion though there are strong pressures on the individual to stay faithful. The easiest characteristic to shed is probably regional origin:

migration and an accent change can obliterate most of its effects. These ascriptive characteristics contrast with those associated with social class in which achievement plays an important role in a socially mobile society and with those associated with the life cycle which undergo steady transformation in the course of time.

The significance of individual ascribed characteristics for the social geography of the city varies from society to society and from one time period to the next. Few societies, however, lack groups who are differentiated by one or more ascribed characteristics and who concentrate spatially in the city. In some countries at some times the "rules" governing the spatial distribution of such groups have been quite explicit. The Group Areas Act in South Afica and the laws confining the Jewish population to city ghettoes in Eastern Europe spring immediately to mind as particularly pernicious examples. In American cities the "rules" have never been as explicit, and it is the purpose of this chapter to review some evidence concerning the implicit rules governing racial and ethnic group distribution in U.S. cities.

The definition of race adopted by U.S. Census takers is a mixture of national origin and supposed biological characteristics. In the Census of Population and Housing the head of each household is asked to identify each member of the household and to classify them into one of the following categories: White, Negro, American Indian, Japanese, Chinese, Filipino, Hawaiian, Part-Hawaiian, Aleut Eskimo or other. People of mixed race are not recognized (with the exception of Part-Hawaiians). This definition of race follows social practice: the offspring of mixed marriages between whites and those of other races are generally assigned to the latter group in U.S. society. The information provided in published form for census tracts adopts a threefold division of the population into white, Negro and other races; for city blocks information is available only for housing units occupied by white or non-white heads.

The term "ethnic" has been employed in many different ways. The orignial Greek meaning was "pertaining to a nation" ("ethnos", a nation) and ethnic groups have been defined as consisting of persons with a common national heritage and origin. The term is most often applied to groups living in a country different from that of their origin. The problem with the concept of an ethnic group is that the group is difficult to identify. After the initial generation of immigrants ethnic group classification may or may not have social significance. The person of foreign national descent may have fully assimilated into American culture and may no longer maintain ties with fellow ethnics. On the other hand, there are others who though several generations removed from their original immigrant ancestors have a high level of ethnic consciousness. The Bureau of the Census defines a member of a particular national origin group as a person born in a foreign land or the offspring of parents, one of whom was born in a foreign land. Persons born in Puerto Rico or of Puerto Rican parents and whites with Spanish surnames are additionally recorded in cities where their numbers are thought to be substantial.

Some 19 or so racial and ethnic groups can be identified at the census tract level in most of the metropolitan areas studied here. The percentage breakdown of each metropolitan area's population into this set of groups is set out in Table 69 together with the equivalent breakdown for the U.S. as a whole. Two metropolitan areas, Birmingham and Richmond, have large Negro minorities; one area, Honolulu, has a majority of its population in the other non-white races category, made up mainly of Japanese, Chinese, Filipinos and Pacific Islanders. Two metropolitan areas, El Paso and San Bernadino-Riverside-Ontario, have substantial Mexican American populations: 44 per cent of El Paso's and 12 per cent of San Bernadino's population is described as white with Spanish surname. Another two metropolitan areas, Minneapolis-St. Paul and Providence-Pawtucket, have substantial foreign stock populations (25 per cent and 41 per

TABLE 69

RACIAL AND ETHNIC COMPOSITION OF THE U.S. POPULATION AND 12 METROPOLITAN AREA POPULATIONS: PERCENTAGES

Ethnic Group	U.S.	Ann Arbor	Birmingham	Canton	Des Moines	El Paso	Honolulu
White	88.57	92.40	65.37	94.56	95.90	96.62	35.74
Negro	10.52	6.82	34.58	5.37	3.95	2.73	0.97
Other Races	0.90	0.76	0.04	0.06	0.13	0.62	63.28
NWNP[a]	69.58	74.04	62.37	78.56	84.09	58.57	26.27
NBFMP	13.56	13.21	2.33	11.76	9.47	23.38	31.76
FB	5.43	5.15	0.67	4.24	2.34	14.67	9.45
U.K.	1.60	2.15	0.67	1.75	1.57	0.75	0.78
Eire	0.99	0.33	0.09	0.28	0.53	0.22	0.19
Norway	0.43	0.21	0.02	0.05	0.58	0.06	0.12
Sweden	0.58	0.29	0.06	0.15	1.36	0.13	0.15
Germany	2.41	3.84	0.32	2.39	1.85	1.58	0.74
Poland	1.55	1.06	0.13	0.64	0.30	0.28	0.19
Czechoslovakia	0.51	0.27	0.03	0.75	0.18	0.12	0.07
Austria	0.61	0.43	0.08	0.63	0.20	0.20	0.12
Hungary	0.39	0.44	0.04	0.75	0.06	0.10	0.08
U.S.S.R.	1.28	0.82	0.02	0.47	0.50	0.26	0.19
Italy	2.53	0.57	0.62	3.04	1.39	0.39	0.34
Canada	1.77	4.01	0.12	0.46	0.62	0.69	0.74
Mexico	0.97	0.11	0.01	0.05	0.21	30.41	0.14
All Other and Not Reported	3.35	3.83	0.64	4.61	2.49	2.86	31.74

TABLE 69--Continued

Ethnic Group	Lancaster	Minneapolis-St. Paul	Providence-Pawtucket	Richmond	San Bernadino-Riverside-Ontario	Tampa-St. Petersburg
White	98.66	98.15	98.04	73.60	95.28	88.46
Negro	1.28	1.39	1.76	26.28	3.67	11.46
Other Races	0.05	0.45	0.19	0.11	1.04	0.07
NWNP[a]	92.97	73.16	56.98	68.86	75.01	70.01
NBFMP	4.34	20.22	30.61	3.43	13.77	11.97
FB	1.35	4.77	10.45	1.31	6.50	6.48
U.K.	0.59	1.10	5.55	0.71	1.95	2.90
Eire	0.18	0.66	3.38	0.18	0.40	0.78
Norway	0.02	3.55	0.12	0.05	0.37	0.27
Sweden	0.06	5.12	1.06	0.05	0.63	0.69
Germany	1.86	4.22	0.92	0.73	1.92	2.73
Poland	0.26	1.32	2.01	0.26	0.44	0.51
Czechoslovakia	0.11	0.72	0.07	0.15	0.25	0.29
Austria	0.21	0.79	0.37	0.15	0.34	0.39
Hungary	0.12	0.23	0.07	0.08	0.34	0.29
U.S.S.R.	0.31	1.11	1.69	0.45	0.54	0.41
Italy	0.63	0.51	9.38	0.42	1.12	1.77
Canada	0.34	2.24	10.38	0.38	2.14	2.23
Mexico	0.02	0.18	0.01	0.19	6.24	0.09
All Other and Not Reported	0.99	3.23	6.03	1.11	3.57	5.09

Notes

[a]NWNP — Native whites of native parents. The size of this group in each tract is estimated by substracting the number of foreign born (FB) and native born of foreign or mixed parents (NBFMP) from the number of whites. This procedure underestimates the number of NWNPs by the number of non-whites included in the foreign stock total. In most cities this number is very small and the error introduced tolerable. Numbers of NWNPs were not so calculated for Honolulu census tracts because the number of foreign stock non-whites is substantial in that city.

cent respectively). There are other metropolitan areas with low proportions of minority groups (Lancaster, Des Moines). In other words the sample of cities to be studied includes a great variety of ethnic and racial mixes which should ensure generality for any substantial conclusions we are able to make.

Factors Influencing the Spatial Distribution of Racial and Ethnic Groups

Before an examination is made of the spatial patterns exhibited by various racial and ethnic groups in the sample cities, some hypotheses about the determinants of those patterns are outlined.

Five sets of determinants can be recognized:

(1) the "normal" set of residential choice factors;
(2) preferences for living among people of the same kind;
(3) limitation on the range of choice of certain groups by others;
(4) the assignment rules of public institutions concerned with providing residential space; and
(5) the influence of time on the above determinants

We discuss each set of determinants in turn.

Factors which affect every residential location decision are the income of the household, its size and composition, its preference as to space occupied and accessibility to locations outside of the home (workplace, shops, theaters, parks and so on). The household's income largely determines the resources available for home purchase or rent, and sets limits on the price that can be paid. The household's size and composition influences the amount of take-home income available for housing, but more importantly also strongly affects the size and type of home desired. Preferences for space around the home and workplace location may together determine how far from the city center the household locates. We have examined the outcomes of these residential choice factors in terms of residential area patterns in Chapters VI and VII.

These universal influences will affect the spatial distribution of racial or ethnic groups because such groups will differ in these attributes that determine residential choice. In the past many groups migrating to American cities were poorer than the host population and possessed fewer skills and educational qualifications. As a result of their poverty they were forced to find cheap housing, and this was located dominantly in the central areas of the cities. This meant that their initial spatial distribution was different from that of the host population as a whole, many of whom had moved out to the growing fringe of the city with its more spacious and dearer housing. As immigrant groups moved up the social and economic ladder the differences between them and the host population diminished and the degree of spatial separation could diminish as a result.

However, as will be shown later in the chapter, differences in the incomes earned or money spent on housing by different ethnic groups account for only a portion of the observed differences in spatial distribution amongst the racial and ethnic groups. There are another set of factors related to such differences, in spatial distribution, namely preferences for living among members of one's own group rather than among those of other groups. People with the same language, customs, culture and educational level will be preferred as neighbors. This set of preferences includes preference for a set of community institutions associated with a particular group: the place of religious assembly, the school associated with the language or religion, the ethnic association, the social club catering to the cultural tastes of one particular group. These institutions require a certain minimum threshold population for existence, and these thresholds can best be reached through clustering of the ethnic group.

Neither of the preceding sets of determinants may account for the spatial patterns we observe. In this case, it is probable that a free and equal opportunity market in housing is not in operation. The range of choice of one or more groups is being restricted by the actions of other groups. Many of the vacancies in the housing market may be denied to members of a racial or ethnic group when they apply. Or considerable social pressure may be exerted on a household of one group that moves into a neighborhood dominated by another group. After a number of such learning experiences members of the discriminated-against group may no longer attempt such applications and will voluntarily exclude themselves from such hostile neighborhoods.

The instruments of restriction or exclusion in American cities have been many and various and they have generally been directed against Negro Americans. Legal restrictions such as zoning ordinances or covenants prevented sale of property to Negroes. Threats of violence have often been used to frighten away prospective black purchasers; fire bombings have frequently occurred when a black family has moved into a white neighborhood. More common are techniques such as "sorry, no vacancy" or "I'm afraid it's been sold." These practices have been made illegal under the Civil Rights Legislation, and courts have ruled against landlords or prospective sellers who follow such practices and against whom buyers have brought legal actions. However, considerable time, energy and expertise must be invested in such proceedings and black families searching for a home are understandably reluctant to undertake such investments. A final method of restriction which is used is to deny information on vacancies to black householders. Prospective clients are only shown lists of property in black neighborhoods and not property in white areas. Negro realtors are not admitted to multiple listing schemes. In all these ways the range of housing opportunities available to members of certain minority groups is restricted.

The above discussion has been conducted in the context of the private housing market of large numbers of sellers and buyers, builders, renters, owners, realty companies and so on. However, substantial numbers of people (though more in many European countries than in America) are supplied with housing by publicly owned or privately owned institutions. People who live in public housing, in college dormitories or married student housing, in army barracks or married quarters, in correctional institutions may have the same needs as people who find their housing needs met in the private housing market. But they are also subject to the explicit rules of the institution, which may differ considerably from the implicit "rules" governing the behavior of the private market. The institution, being more in the public eye than the private renter or seller, must be more careful to observe the legal requirements of equal opportunity in housing allocation, for example. Army bases, campus housing and correctional institutions will not generally be racially segregated (all races will have equal opportunity of access to such housing as is offered).

The influence of the public sector will not always be in the direction of less residential segregation of racial groups, however. In Chicago, for example, a great many more white households are eligible on an income basis for public housing than apply to live in such units. Public housing projects are located in predominantly black neighborhoods and poor whites prefer not to live in such areas, even though it might be to their economic advantage to occupy a public housing unit.

Implicit in some of the points made above is the influence of time on the spatial pattern of racial or ethnic groups. The initial settlement location of pioneer members of a group who usually have a number of similar opportunities in different neighborhoods to choose from may have a profound effect on the location of the group population in future years. For instance, the neighborhood of Bridgeport in inner Chicago was originally settled by Irish laborers working on the Illinois and Michigan Canal in 1848. For more than a century since then "Bridgeport has remained Irish, providing muscle for the city's yards, mills and factories, and more than its share of political leadership." (Mayer and Wade, 1969, p. 28) Over time the spatial distribution of an ethnic or racial group will evolve as the characteristics of the group change, as preferences for ethnic community living change and as the reactions of the host population change. The members of the group may move up the economic ladder. and be able to afford a wider range of housing. Second and subsequent generations of immigrants will have learnt the language of the city (or country) and adapted themselves to its culture. Their need for group institutions may decline or certain of them may be shared with other ethnic groups (the Catholic church and parochial school). Their preferences for things "ethnic" may diminish and preferences for things American may increase. Or a new hybrid sub-culture may emerge, a cross between that of the former country and that of America.

A number of alternative spatial futures confront the changing racial or ethnic group. It may diffuse and become assimilated into some wider melting pot; it may relocate *en masse*; it may expand from its original concentration through the process of invasion and succession; or it may do a combination of these things.

Let us examine these general propositions in the light of work that has been done on the spatial patterns of ethnic and racial groups, and in the light of what we can learn from the spatial patterns of racial and ethnic groups in a small sample of metropolitan areas.

The Spatial Patterns of Negroes in American Cities

In Figures 49 through 60 the distribution of Negro populations is plotted for thirteen urbanized areas. The general features displayed by most maps are as follows.

High scoring tracts (areas with high proportions of Negro residents) tend to cluster near the city center. The level which is high will vary from one urban area to another. In Lancaster (Figure 53), for example, no tract contains in 1960 a Negro majority whereas

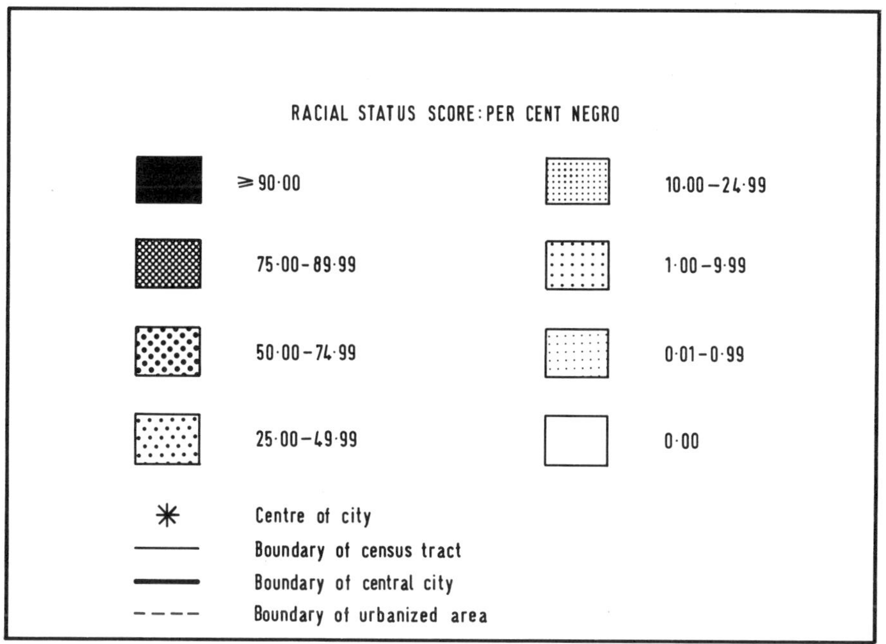

Fig. 48.--The General Key for the Racial Status Maps

in another area, Ann Arbor (Figure 49), one tract's population is 90 per cent Negro.

Tracts in which Negroes are concentrated do not fill up all the available area in the inner city. Large areas of the inner city have a dominantly white population, even in cities like Birmingham (Figure 50) which has a substantial Negro population (35 per cent of the metropolitan area total). In Birmingham there are tracts near the city center with white proportions of over 90 per cent. The euphemistic use of "inner city neighborhood" as a substitute for Negro neighborhood is thus incorrect with reference to the 1960 situation. Although considerable succession has taken place from white to Negro in the inner city in the intervening period the two terms are probably still not equivalent (Berry _et al_, 1976, pp. 47-84).

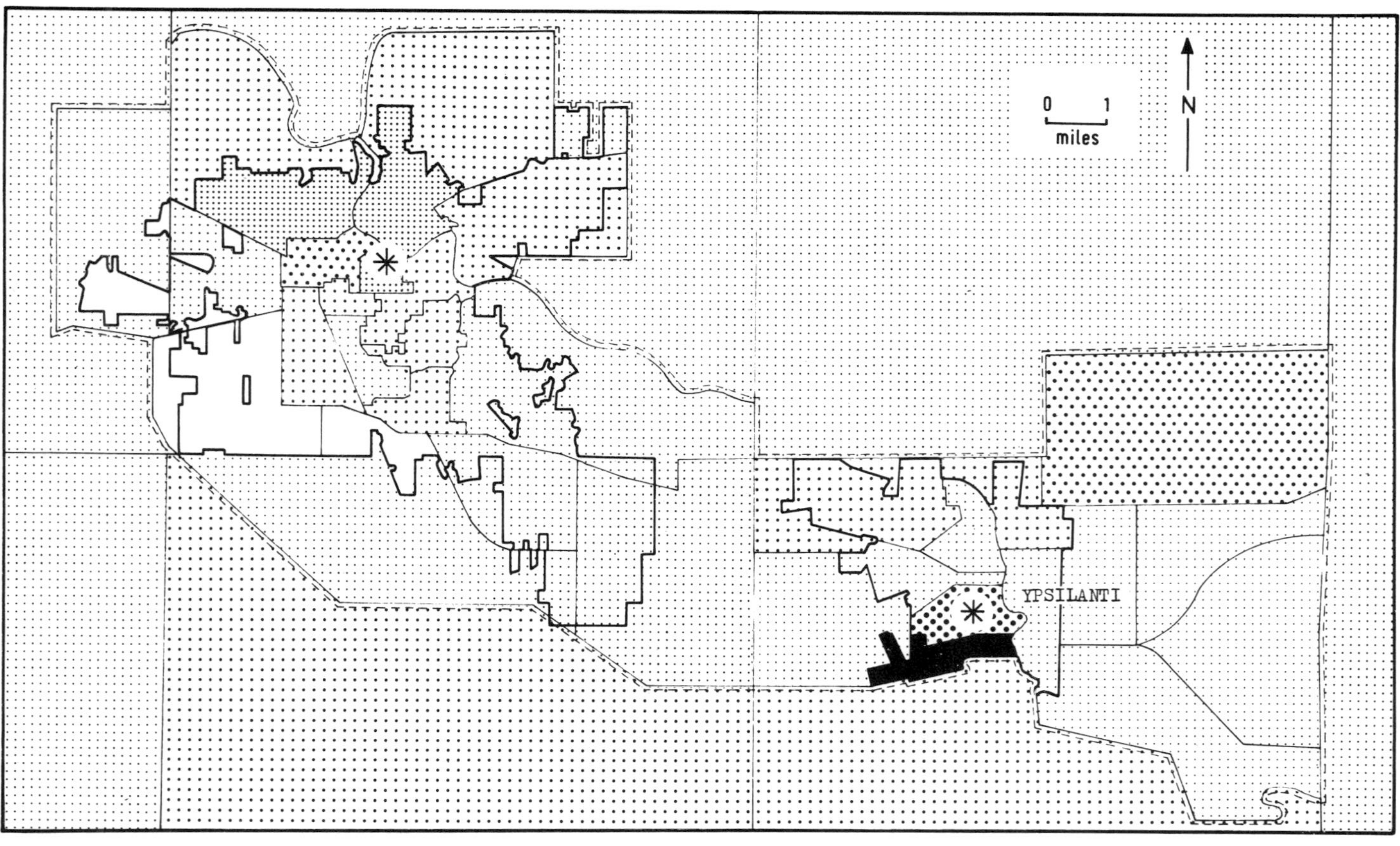

Fig. 49.--The Spatial Pattern of Racial Status, Ann Arbor, 1960

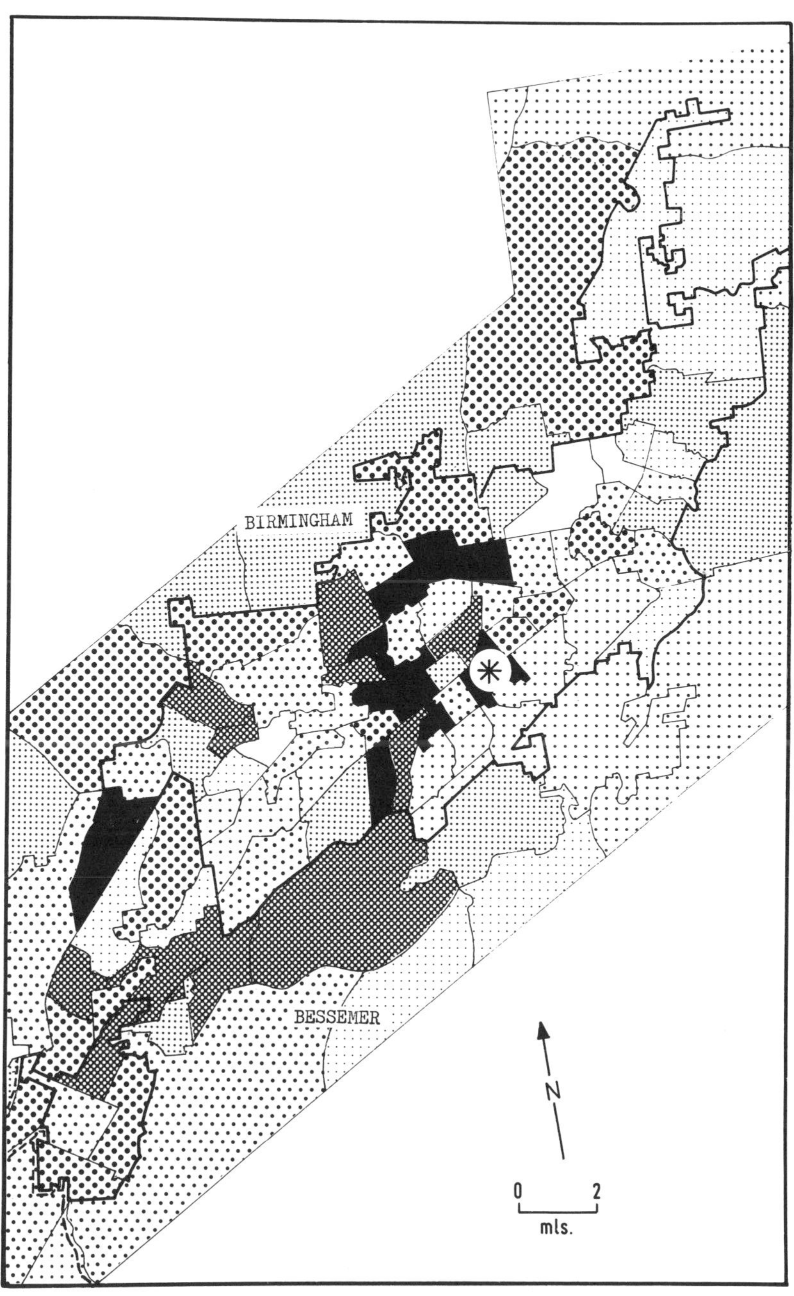

Fig. 50.--The Spatial Pattern of Racial Status, Birmingham, 1960

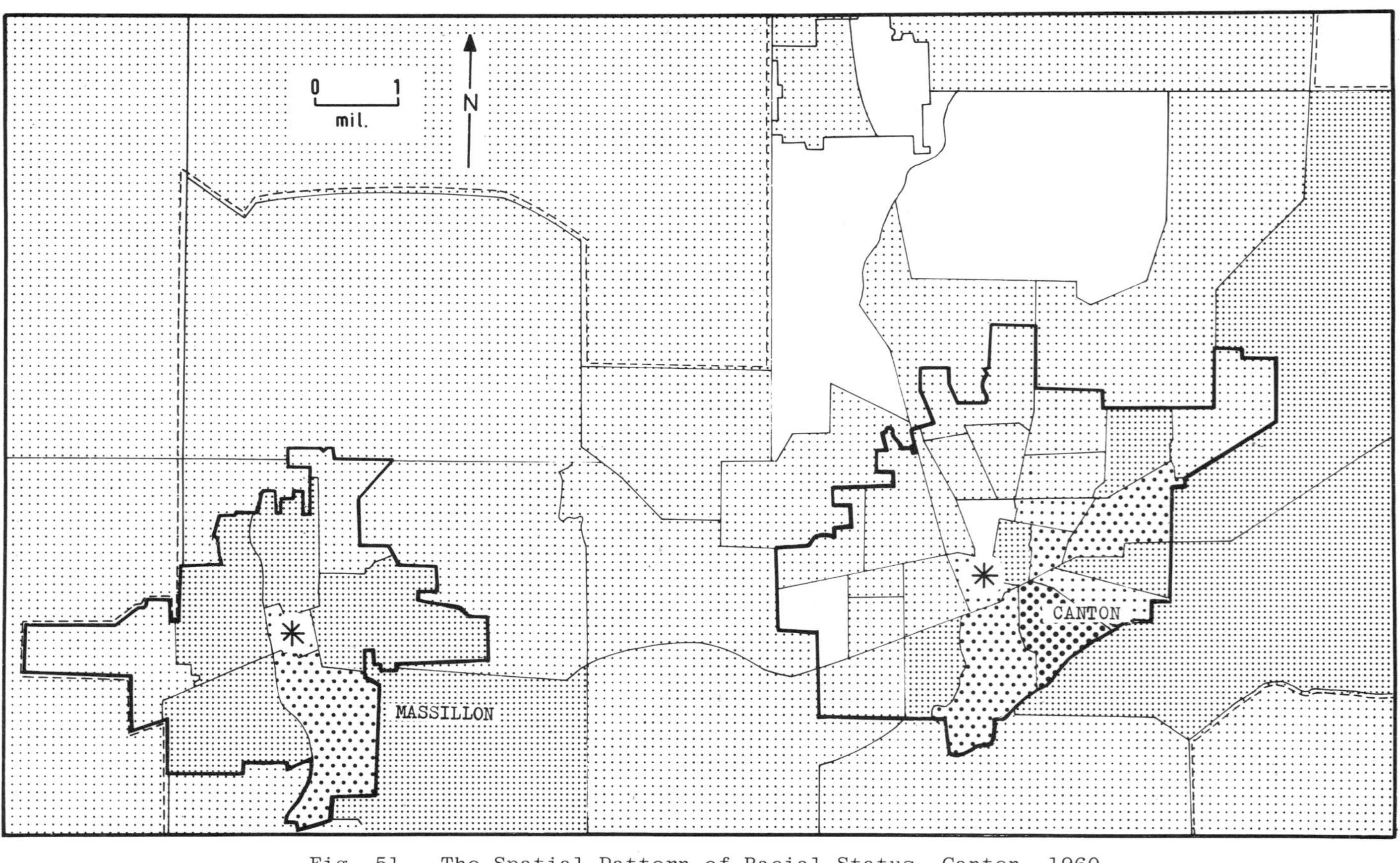

Fig. 51.--The Spatial Pattern of Racial Status, Canton, 1960

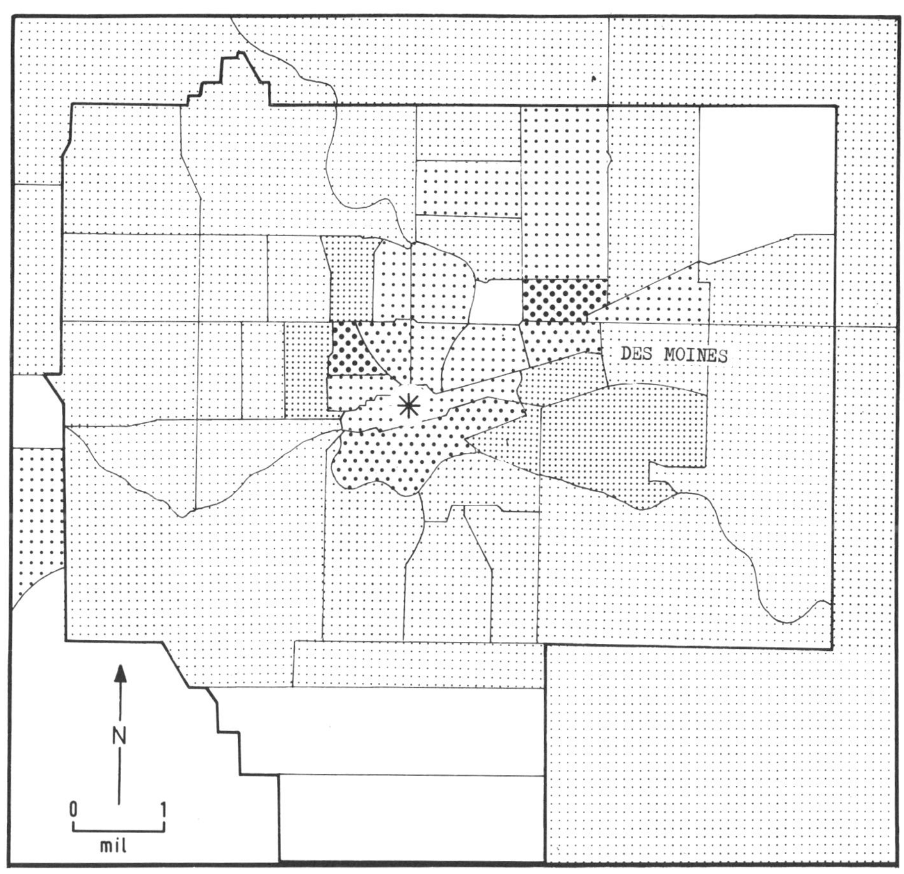

Fig. 52.--The Spatial Pattern of Racial Status, Des Moines, 1960

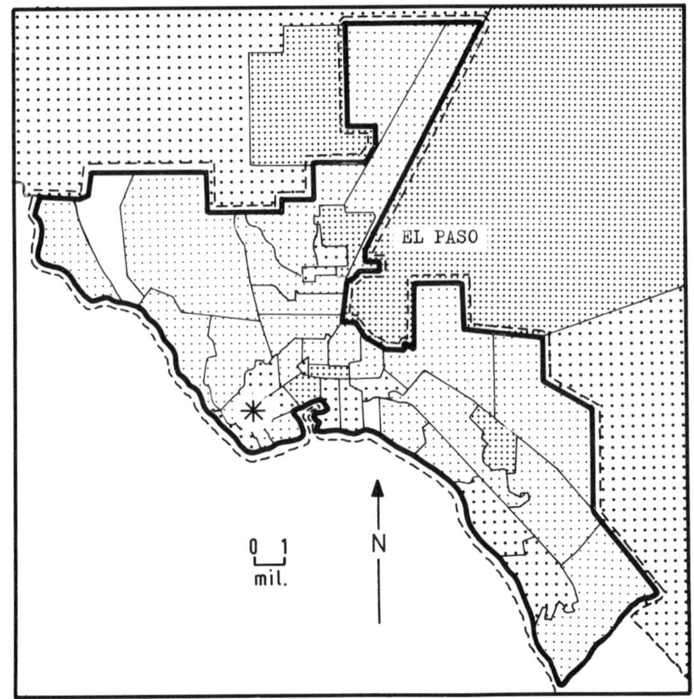

Fig. 53.--The Spatial Pattern of Racial Status, El Paso, 1960

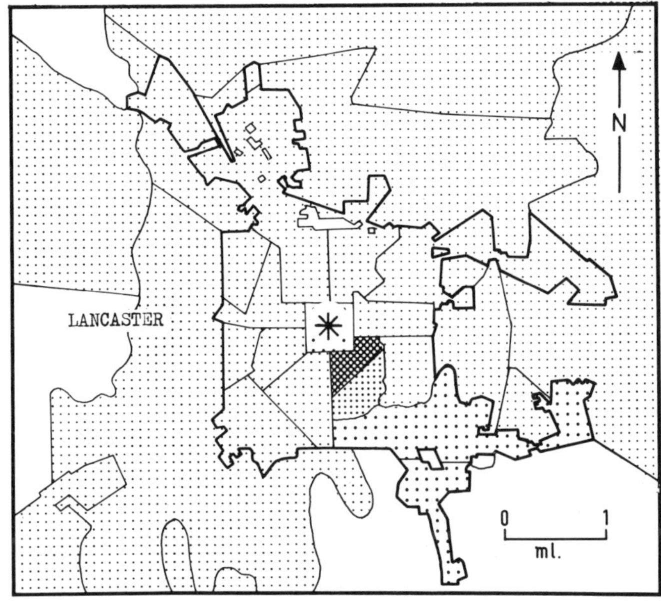

Fig. 54.--The Spatial Pattern of Racial Status, Lancaster, 1960

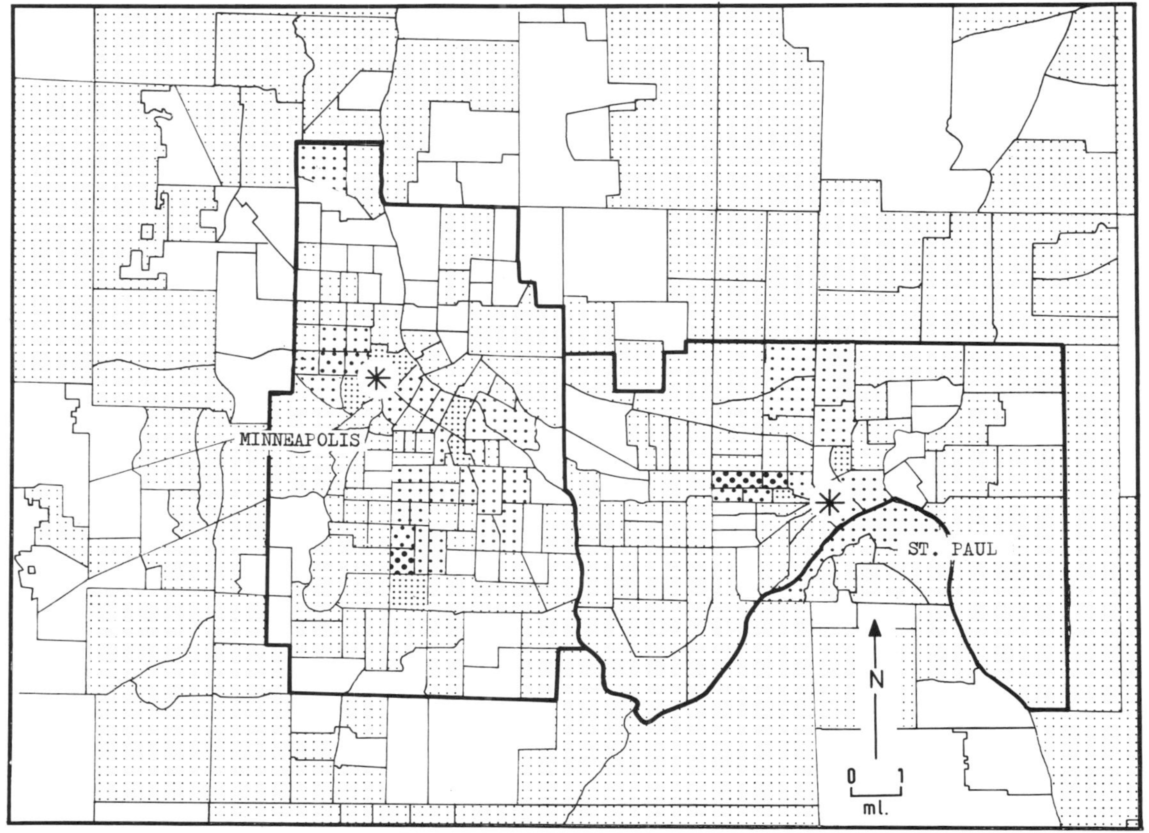

Fig. 55.--The Spatial Pattern of Racial Status, Minneapolis-St. Paul, 1960

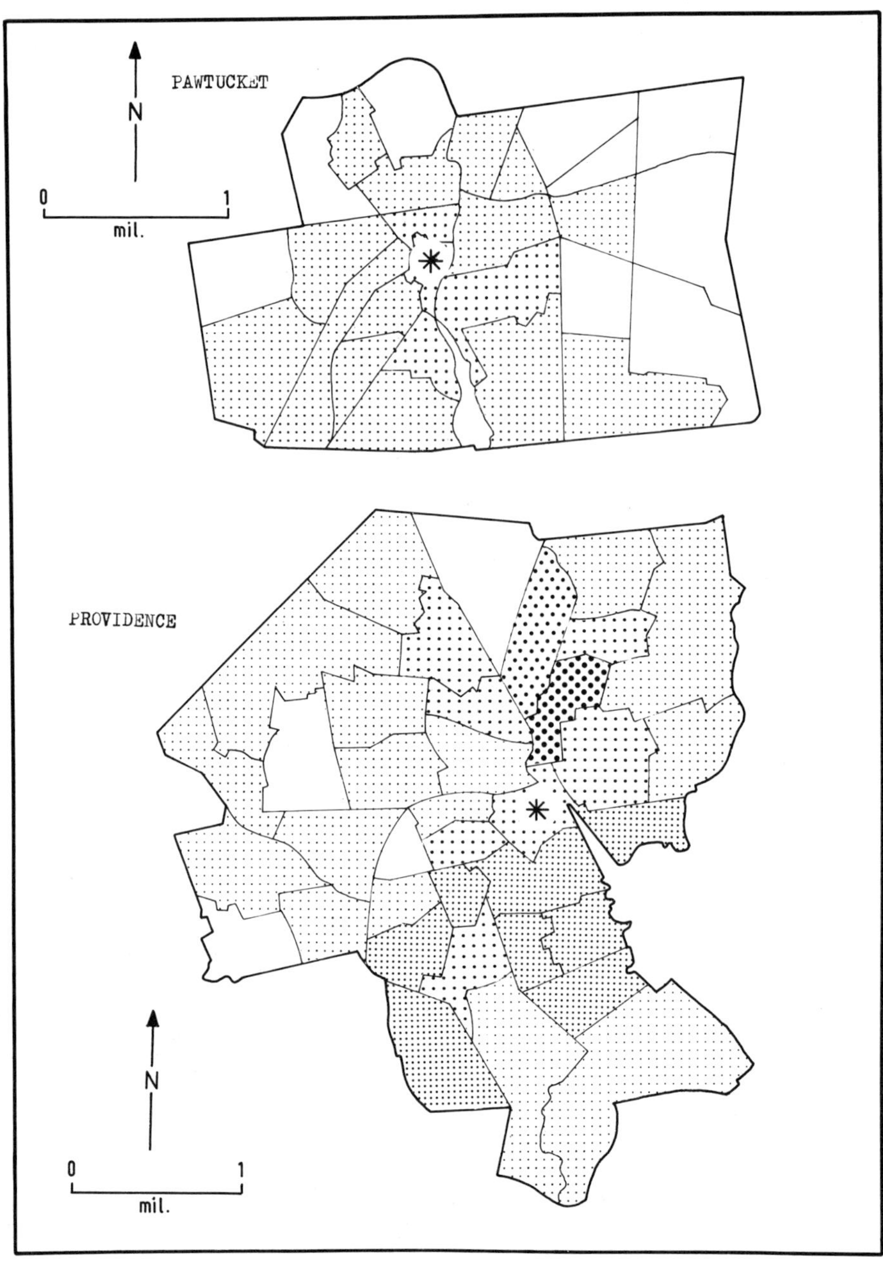

Fig. 56.--The Spatial Pattern of Racial Status, Providence and Pawtucket Central Cities, 1960

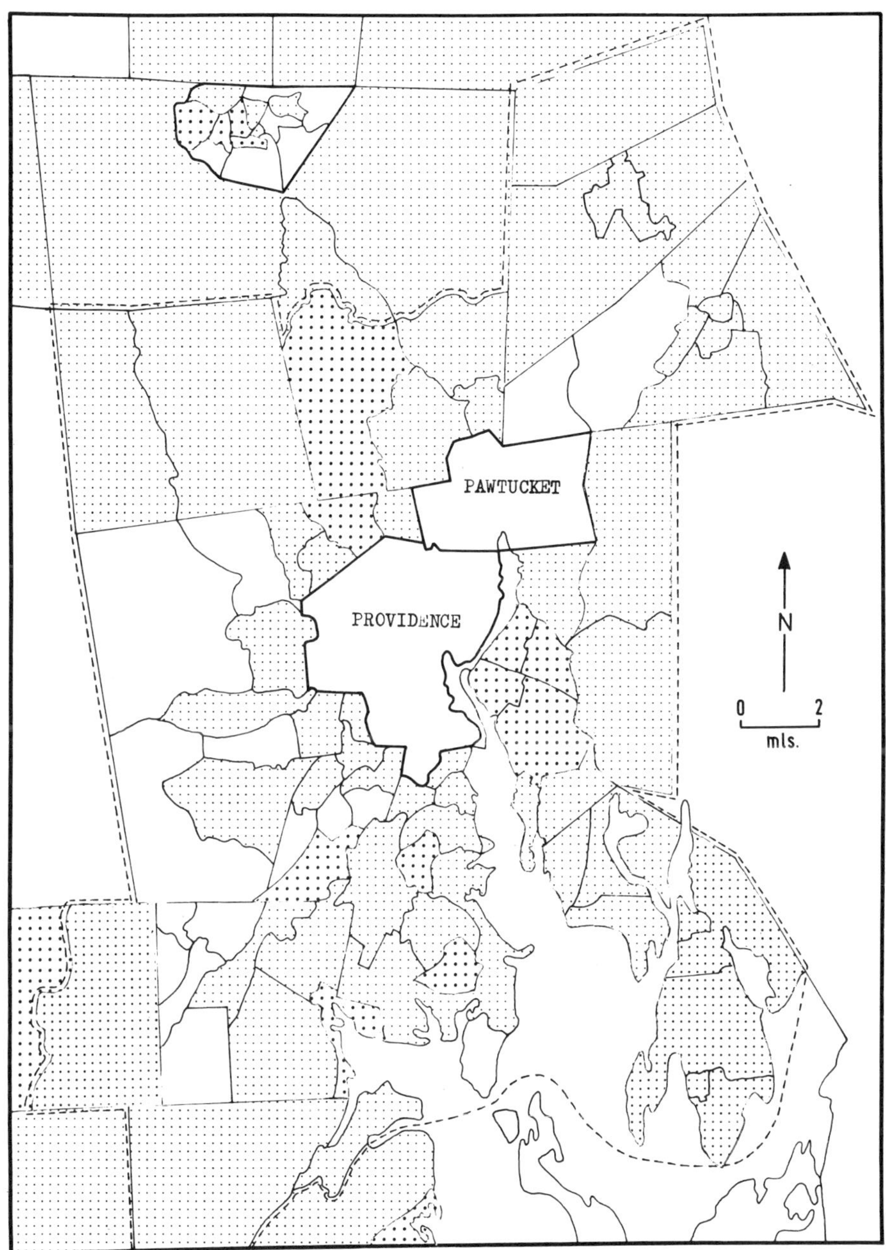

Fig. 57.--The Spatial Pattern of Racial Status, Providence-Pawtucket SMSA, 1960

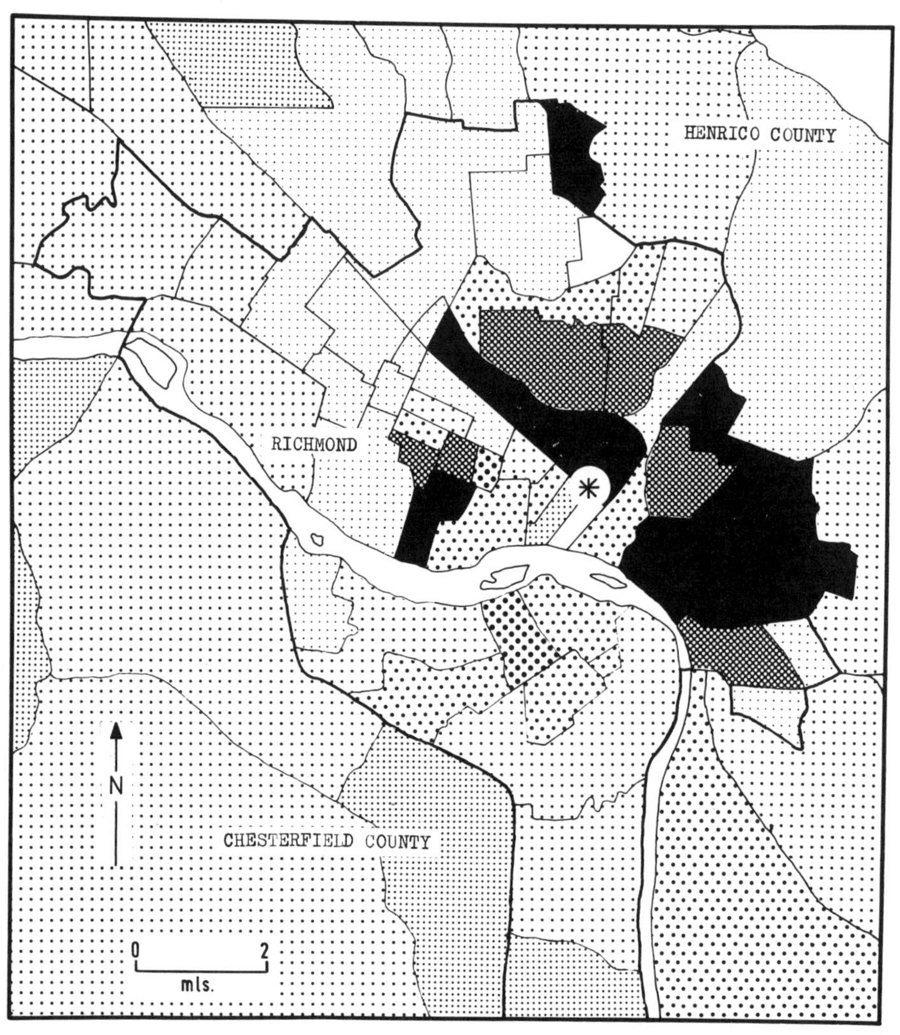

Fig. 58.--The Spatial Pattern of Racial Status, Richmond, 1960

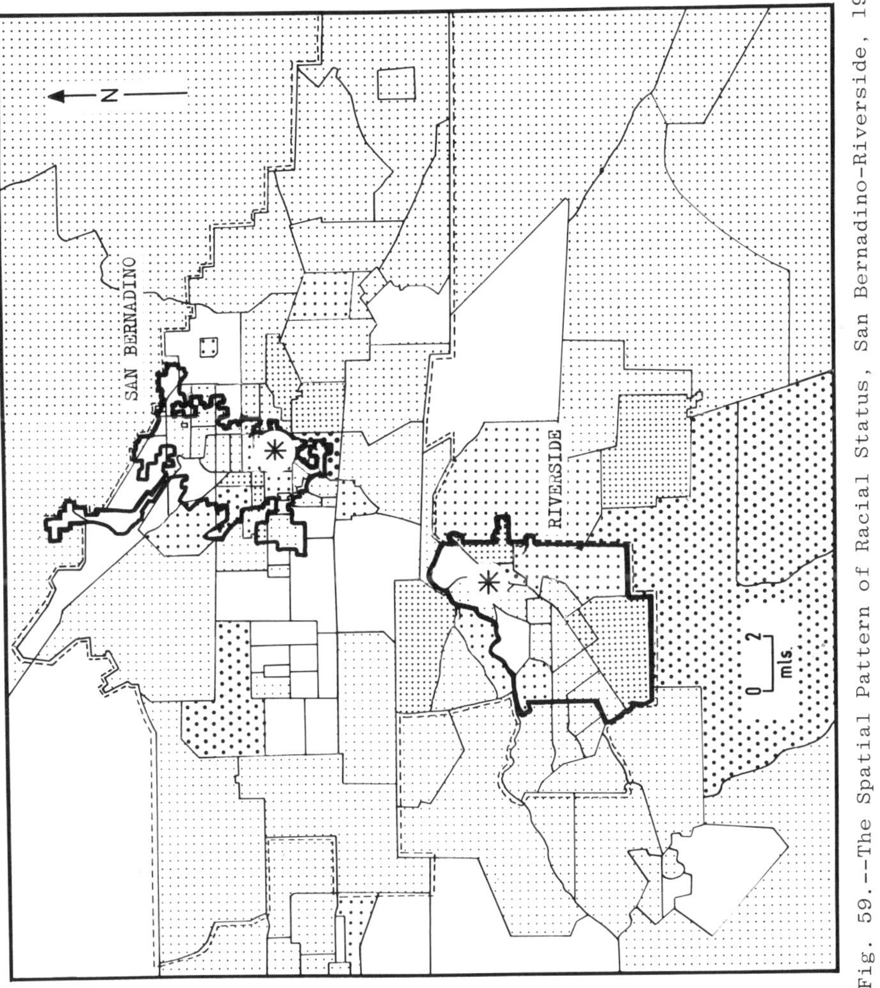

Fig. 59.--The Spatial Pattern of Racial Status, San Bernadino-Riverside, 1960

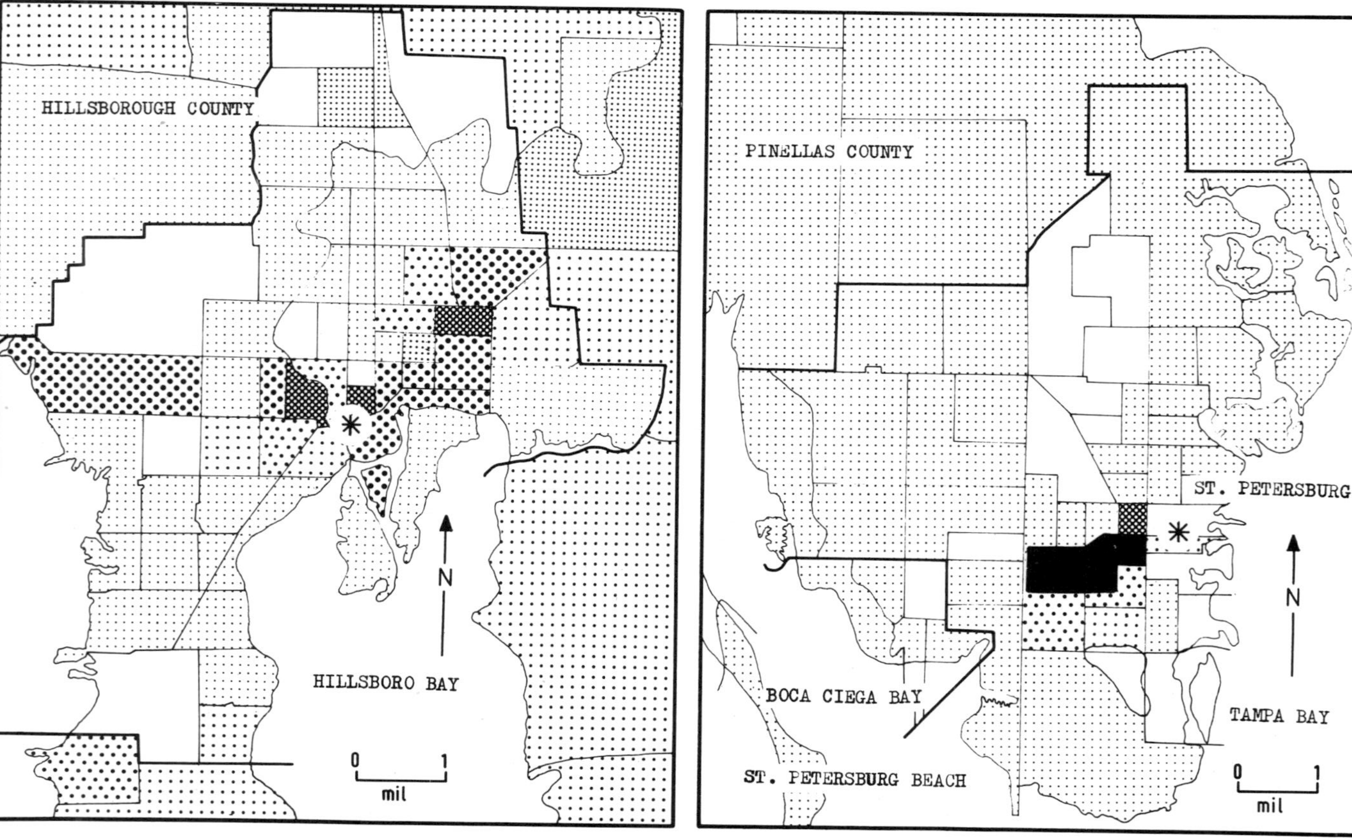

Fig. 60.--The Spatial Pattern of Racial Status, Tampa and St. Petersburg Central Cities, 1960

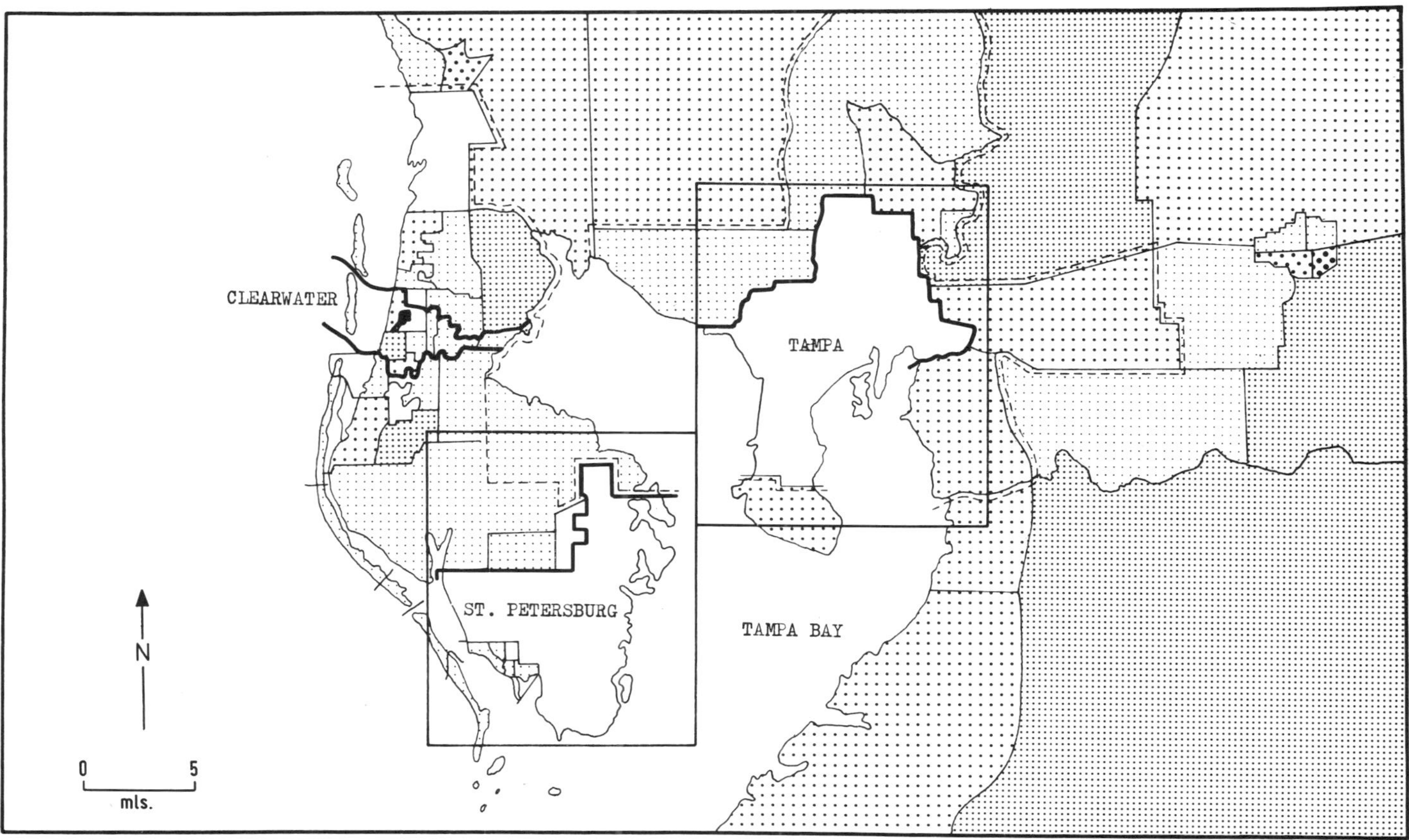

Fig. 61.--The Spatial Pattern of Racial Status, Tampa-St. Petersburg SMSA, 1960

In many cities there is more than one cluster of tracts in which Negroes are concentrated: the inner Ypsilanti and inner Ann Arbor concentrations in the Ann Arbor urban area, (Figure 49); tracts in inner Massillon and inner Canton city in the Canton urban area (Figure 51). The Twin Cities urban area displays three separate clusters (Figure 54): one to the northwest of the Minneapolis city center, another to the south, and a third to the west of the St. Paul commercial core. The inner city neighborhoods near the river and south of the city center also show higher than average numbers of Negro residents. The polycentric pattern of racial minority distribution is repeated in the Tampa Bay urban area (Figures 59 and 60). There are neighborhoods of Negro concentration near the center of St. Petersburg, north and east of downtown Tampa, adjacent to the center of Clearwater and in Plant City on the eastern fringe of the metropolitan area.

The suburban areas of Northern metropolises contain few Negro families. Large numbers of tracts fall in the bottom two categories of the racial status scale (no Negroes, or only 0.01 to 0.99 per cent). In view of the small numbers of Negroes in the total urban populations of several of these Northern metropolises this is not surprising.

The patterns displayed in Southern cities are rather different. Very many more tracts contain concentrations of Negro residents of over 90 per cent than in the non-Southern cities. In this they resemble the larger Northern and Western cities not included in the sample of cities studied: places like New York, Chicago, Los Angeles, Detroit, Cleveland, and Philadelphia in which large sections of the central city are almost exclusively Negro in population composition. Other large sections of these cities and their suburbs are almost exclusively white. Large areas north, west and east of the Richmond central business district are neighborhoods (Figure 57) with over 75 per cent of their populations Negro; in Birmingham large areas are predominantly Negro from Bessemer at the southwestern end of the urban area to suburban areas at the northeastern end (Figure 50). In Richmond and in Tampa-St. Petersburg the tracts lying outside the central city generally have lower than average proportions of Negro families but the proportions are not as low as in the Northern cities in the sample. In the case of Birmingham there are substantial suburban areas which have largely black residential populations.

The western cities in the sample (El Paso, Honolulu, and San Bernadino-Riverside) show a fairly wide scattering of tracts with above average numbers of Negro households. The explanation in some cases is institutional: in El Paso, the extensive tract in the northeastern portion of the map (Figure 52) contains a large U.S. Airforce base at which work and live substantial numbers of Negro Airforce personnel. In Honolulu tracts with above average proportions of Negroes are the ones containing military reservations or military housing.

However, map comparison, such as we have attempted above provides only a qualitative estimate of the spatial patterns of racial and ethnic groups. Quantitative specification of the degree of clustering of racial and ethnic groups is required to make comparisons of both groups and cities more precise. In the next section of this chapter we discuss the problems involved in the measurement of residential clustering and the solutions that have commonly been adopted.

Degrees of Residential Clustering

Design of a suitable index to measure the degree of residential clustering or residential segregation has occupied social scientists for many years. Several excellent discussions of the problems of index design and use are available in the literature. (Duncan and Duncan, 1955b; Taeuber and Taeuber, 1965). Here a much used and simply calculated index is employed, the <u>Index of Dissimilarity</u>. Direct comparison with earlier work on the residential patterns of ethnic groups is possible if this particular index is used. In their review of measures of association for crosstabulations Goodman and Kruskal suggest that the index was first proposed by Corrado Gini, the Italian statistician (Gini, 1914-15 cited in Goodman and Kruskal, 1959). It has since been used by Sargent Florence (1937) and Hoover (1936) in the context of industrial location studies, and by Lieberson (1963), Duncan and Duncan (1955a), Taeuber and Taeuber (1965), Poole and Boal (1973) and many others in the context of ethnic group location and segregation studies.

The index of dissimilarity is calculated in the following way:

$$D_{ab} = (1/2)\ 100 \sum_{i=1}^{n} \left[\frac{N_{ai}}{N_{a*}} - \frac{N_{bi}}{N_{b*}} \right] \qquad (11)$$

where D_{ab} is the index of dissimilarity between the distribution of population group a and the distribution of population group b, N_{ai} indicates the population of group a in area i, N_{bi} indicates population of group b in area i, N_{a*} refers to the total population of group a in the whole urban region, N_{b*} refers to total population of group b in the whole urban region and $|\,|$ signifies the absolute value function such that $|a| = a$ and $|-a| = a$. The areas $i = 1,2,\ldots,n$ are the census tracts into which the urban area is divided.

A particular pair of groups that is frequently compared is any group and the rest of the population. The index of dissimilarity thus calculated is then often referred to as the index of residential segregation. Computationally, it is more convenient to calculate the index of dissimilarity between the group and the total population of the urban area who are members of the group.

Indices of dissimilarity were calculated for each of the cities in the sample for racial groups defined in a variety of ways.

These measures are summarized in Table 70. Indices were calculated on a census tract basis for standard metropolitan statistical areas (SMSAs) and for urbanized areas (UAs). There appears to be little difference between the two sets except in the case of Lancaster where the SMSA is considerably larger than the urbanized area and includes a goodly part of rural Pennsylvania.

These results confirm the map evidence and previous work that Negroes are fairly highly concentrated as a group. The index of dissimilarity has a maximum value of 100 representing complete segregation and a minimum value of 0 representing complete relative coincidence of two distributions. All the values for Negro and non-Negro and Negro and white comparisons exceed 50. They all exceed 64 with the exception of the Honolulu indices.

Indices of dissimilarity between whites and non-whites are included in the table for comparative purposes. The group "non-white," consisting as it does of Negroes and members of other non-white races, is not a very satisfactory one since it lumps together members of very different groups who undoubtedly have very different residential distributions. However, it was the only racial comparison available to the Taeubers at the level of city block, and the one used by them to measure racial residential segregation in some 207 central cities in 1960 (Taeuber and Taeuber, 1965, Chapter 3). The Taeubers argue that the most valid scale at which racial residential segregation in U.S. cities should be measured is that of the city block (Taeuber and Taeuber, 1965, pp. 223-229). However, their argument is, I think, misleading. There is no one valid scale of unit: rather there are a series of possible scale levels at which residential segregation can be measured, and a spectrum of resultant values of the measure used. More preferable than measurement of residential segregation at any single scale level is measurement at a series of scales. Such a series of indices of dissimilarity is reported in Table 71 for Chicago. At the individual level

TABLE 70

DISSIMILARITY INDICES FOR RACIAL GROUPS ON A TRACT BASIS, 1960

SMSAs	Racial Group Comparisons[a]					
	NvsNW	WvsNW	ONWvsN+W	NvsW	NvsONW	WvsONW
Ann Arbor	73	66	55	73	80	56
Birmingham	64	64	56	64	66	58
Canton	75	75	50	75	68	51
Des Moines	77	75	43	77	64	45
El Paso	64	55	38	64	58	38
Honolulu	55	50	51	63	65	50
Lancaster	79	76	50	79	82	50
Minneapolis-St. Paul	84	71	45	84	73	46
Providence-Pawtucket	73	70	51	73	47	52
Richmond	76	76	40	76	60	49
San Bernadino-Riverside-Ontario	72	62	42	72	70	43
Tampa-St. Petersburg	83	83	42	83	77	43
UAs						
Ann Arbor	76	68	49	76	80	49
Birmingham	65	65	55	65	67	55
Canton	75	75	46	75	60	49
Des Moines	77	75	43	77	64	44
El Paso	66	52	36	66	75	36
Honolulu	57	47	47	43	66	47
Lancaster	87	85	37	87	85	37
Minneapolis-St. Paul	84	71	45	84	73	46
Providence-Pawtucket	75	72	50	75	46	51
Richmond	79	79	39	79	60	48
San Bernadino-Riverside	79	71	32	79	69	33
St. Petersburg	89	88	48	89	88	48
Tampa	82	81	35	82	71	39

Notes

[a]The racial groups are as follows:

N - Negro   W - White   ONW - Other Non-white   NN - Non-Negro
NW - Non-white   N+W - Negro and White

segregation is complete because no mixed race category is recognized in the data source, the Census of Population and Housing. If such a category were recognized then the dissimilarity index value at this scale would be a measure of the fecundity of interracial marriages. The household level value (guessed in the diagram) is an estimate of the amount of interracial marriage and the amount of interracial lodging and living together. The block, tract, community area and suburb and city/rest of metropolitan area indices are different scale estimates of residential segregation. About a half of the racial separation observed at the community area and suburb level is accounted for simply by the greater concentration of Negroes in the central city. Dividing the city and rest of the metropolitan area into community areas and suburbs adds another 40 points to the dissimilarity scale. Dividing community areas and suburbs into tracts adds only 9.7 points, and dividing the tracts up into blocks adds only 2.9 further points.

If the units of observation at the various scales are nested (that is, integral numbers of smaller units add up to larger units) then it follows that the level of residential segregation measured at a particular scale is always equal to or greater than that measured using larger units, and less than or equal to that measured with smaller units. We would know, for example, that if we measured residential segregation at the block front level for Chicago that the dissimilarity value would lie somewhere between 92.6 and 99 (given that this latter is a good guess). Bearing these observations in mind, how do the results reported in Table compare with those for the same cities obtained by the Taeubers?

In Figure 61 the results at block and tract level are compared. The value on the vertical axis is that found by the Taeubers at block level for the central city; the horizontal axis records the index of dissimilarity at metropolitan and urbanized area levels for both non-whites <u>vs</u> whites, and Negroes <u>vs</u> whites. The Taeubers'

TABLE 71

A SPECTRUM OF DISSIMILARITY INDEX VALUES FOR CHICAGO SMSA FOR WHITES AND NEGROES

Scale of Unit	Index of Dissimilarity Values	Source
SMSA	0.0	The distributions coincide.
City/Suburbs	39.9	Computed from Census data.
Community Areas & Suburbs	80.0	Computed from data in Kitagawa and Taeuber (1963).
Tracts	89.7	Table 13 in Taeuber and Taeuber (1965).
Blocks	92.6	Table 12 in Taeuber and Taueber (1965).
Households	99.0	Estimated.
Individuals	100.0	Follows from Census definition.

indices are, in almost all cases, despite the difference in study areas, larger than the tract based indices calculated in this study — most of the observations lie to the upper left of the diagonal. However, the metropolitan area and urbanized area results reveal that if comparisons of whites and non-whites are regarded as estimates of Negro-white residential segregation, which appears to be the Taeubers' intention, then the former are undoubtedly underestimates. This is because the other non-white group are less residentially segregated from whites than are Negroes (compare the N _vs_ W column of Table 70 with the W _vs_ ONW column). The only exception is Honolulu, where Negroes are less segregated from whites than are other non-whites, probably because very many of Honolulu's Negro population are connected with the predominantly white military-associated population of Honolulu. Institutionally based integration is the rule rather than private market segregation.

Although choice of unit of observation (blocks or tracts) is

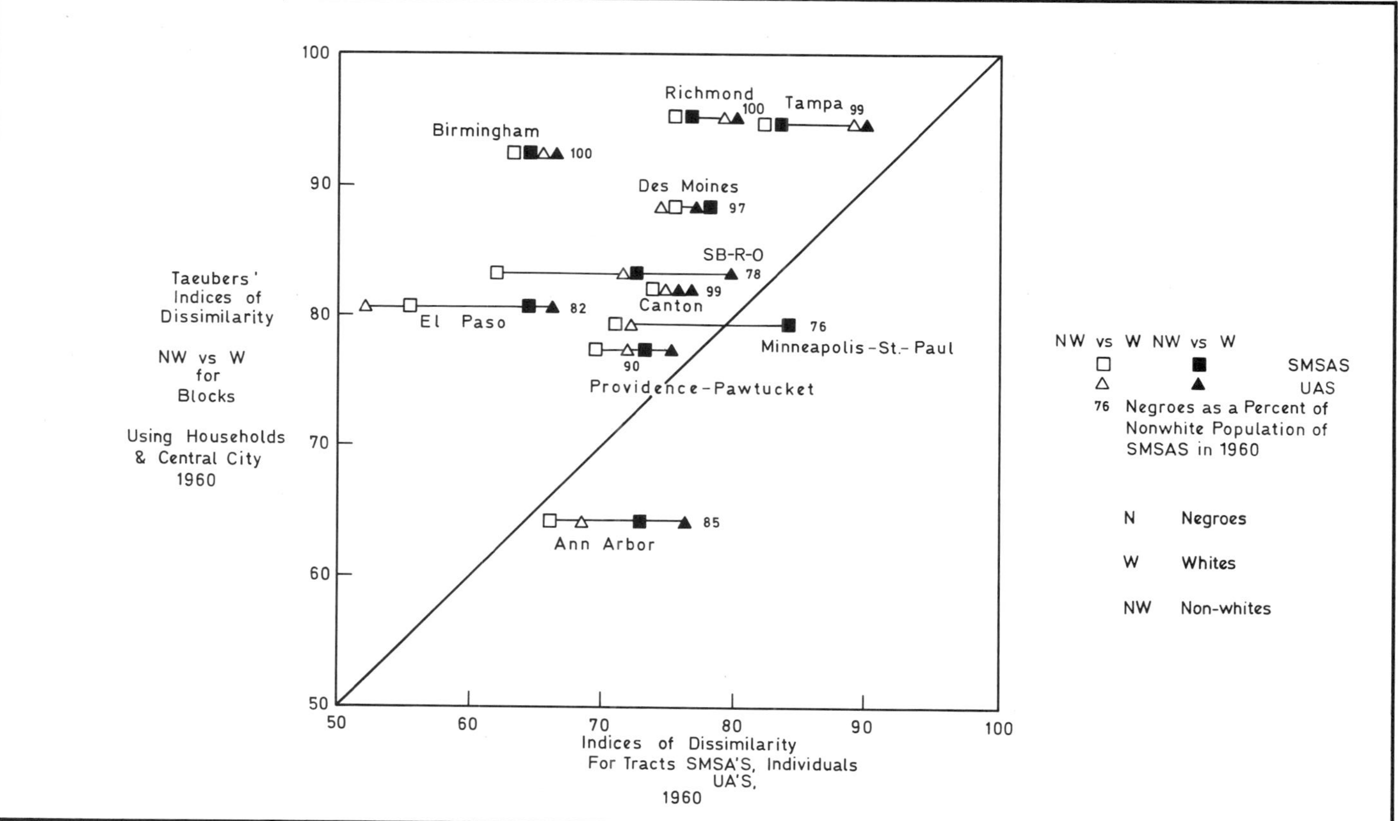

Fig. 62.--Indices of Dissimilarity between the Races at the Tract and Block Level

possible when Negroes and whites are compared, this is not possible when other ethnic groups are considered. The statistics for national groups were published in 1960 on a census tract basis only. We now use our census tract based indices to examine the degree of residential segregation of all the ethnic groups that can be distinguished, and in the next section of the chapter we consider the question of residential assimilation.

Table 70 and Figure 62 reveal that for the sample of urban areas Negroes are highly segregated residentially from the rest of the population and from whites in particular. How do they compare with other ethnic groups in the sample urban areas? From Table 72 it is clear that Negroes are more segregated than any other group in all cities except Birmingham, El Paso and Honolulu. In Birmingham, the Negro group is large and the Russian and Polish foreign stock groups are very small. This probably influences the pattern of dissimilarity indices. In El Paso Negroes are only marginally more segregated than those of Russian foreign stock and in Honolulu only barely more segregated than people of Swedish foreign stock. In both a sizeable proportion of the Negro population is associated with the military and this may account for the relatively lower degree of residential separation. Values of the average level of residential segregation of the ethnic groups over the sample of cities (Table 73) confirm that in 1960 not only were Negroes highly residentially segregated but that they were also on average the most highly segregated group. Gaps of 20 points or more on the dissimilarity scale separate Negroes from the highest of the other ethnic groups.

The association between the distribution of native born whites of native parents and members of other ethnic groups have been used by Lieberson (1963) and Kantrovitz (1969) as indices of residential assimilation. The argument is that the closer the spatial distribution of an immigrant group resembles that of the native population

TABLE 72

RESIDENTIAL SEGREGATION INDICES FOR RACIAL AND ETHNIC GROUPS ON A TRACT BASIS, 1960

Ethnic and Racial Groups	Ann Arbor		Birmingham		Canton		Des Moines		El Paso		Honolulu	
	SMSA	UA	SMSA	UA	SMSA	UA	SMSA	UA	SMSA	UA	SMSA	UA
Negro	73	76	64	65	75	75	77	77	64	66	55	57
Other Non-white	55	49	56	55	50	46	43	43	38	36	51	47
NWNP	28	29	59	59	30	28	24	24	35	37	—	—
NBFMP	15	18	38	38	16	12	13	13	26	25	23	16
FB	26	25	42	42	26	25	19	19	32	31	24	20
U.K.	20	22	35	36	18	19	16	15	32	32	42	46
Ireland	—	—	52	50	—	—	27	27	35	35	47	50
Norway	—	—	—	—	—	—	25	25	—	—	—	—
Sweden	—	—	—	—	—	—	23	23	—	—	52	57
Germany	25	28	42	43	19	18	16	15	36	36	35	35
Poland	30	26	66	65	33	33	—	—	50	51	46	51
Czechoslovakia	—	—	—	—	27	25	—	—	—	—	—	—
Austria	37	38	55	53	26	22	—	—	—	—	—	—
Hungary	41	36	—	—	29	29	—	—	—	—	—	—
U.S.S.R.	42	39	78	78	51	46	43	43	59	63	46	47
Italy	31	25	45	42	30	27	46	45	35	34	45	45
Canada	14	13	56	56	—	—	25	26	32	31	38	40
Mexico	—	—	—	—	—	—	—	—	47	45	—	—

TABLE 72--Continued

Ethnic and Racial Group	Lancaster		Minneapolis-St. Paul		Providence-Pawtucket		Richmond		San Bernadino-Riverside		Tampa-St. Petersburg	Tampa	St. Petersburg
	SMSA	UA	SMSA	UA	SMSA	UA	SMSA	UA	SMSA	UA	SMSA	UA	UA
Negro	79	87	84	84	73	75	76	79	72	79	83	82	89
Other Non-white	50	37	45	45	51	50	40	39	42	32	42	35	48
NWNP	31	21	19	18	17	16	64	66	26	27	37	49	25
NBFMP	28	12	14	13	12	12	29	29	17	14	23	22	14
FB	29	18	24	23	18	17	34	34	25	23	27	27	18
U.K.	28	21	21	21	26	24	30	29	23	21	33	25	15
Ireland	39	26	—	—	27	26	—	—	—	—	38	31	21
Norway	—	—	24	24	—	—	—	—	—	—	—	—	—
Sweden	—	—	23	23	41	40	—	—	29	29	37	29	21
Germany	31	20	19	19	28	26	32	31	21	20	32	24	15
Poland	38	18	38	38	39	40	47	46	31	29	31	31	27
Czechoslovakia	—	—	—	—	—	—	42	41	—	—	—	—	—
Austria	38	31	32	32	—	—	—	—	—	—	—	—	—
Hungary	—	—	—	—	—	—	—	—	—	—	—	—	—
U.S.S.R.	47	34	46	45	51	52	58	56	38	32	40	43	32
Italy	43	23	—	—	52	52	35	36	30	29	33	38	21
Canada	39	38	16	15	37	30	37	36	22	21	30	28	16
Mexico	—	—	—	—	—	—	—	—	53	55	—	—	—

Notes NWNP - Native White of Native Parents; NBFMP - Native Born of Foreign or Mixed Parents; FB - Foreign Born

TABLE 73

AVERAGE RESIDENTIAL SEGREGATION INDICES FOR RACIAL AND ETHNIC GROUPS

Racial or Ethnic Group	Unweighted Average Residential Segregation Index Values		Number of Cities for Which Average is Calculated[a]	
	SMSA	UA	SMSA	UA
Negro	72.77	76.17	12	13
Other Non-white	46.98	43.34	12	13
NWNP	33.39	33.20	11	12
NBFMP	21.07	18.32	12	13
FB	27.04	24.63	12	13
U.K.	26.93	25.10	12	13
Ireland	38.24	33.98	8	9
Norway	24.45	24.18	2	2
Sweden	34.22	31.62	6	7
Germany	27.88	25.35	12	13
Poland	40.41	37.83	11	12
Czechoslovakia	34.54	32.90	2	2
Austria	37.41	35.23	5	5
Hungary	34.70	32.16	2	2
U.S.S.R.	49.97	47.01	12	13
Italy	38.76	34.78	11	12
Canada	31.48	29.22	11	12
Mexico	49.59	50.16	2	2

Notes

[a]Dissimilarity indices were calculated for only 8 of the possible foreign stock groups for each SMSA or UA. The remaining 5 were generally too small for one to be confident that the index was measuring the same thing as in the case of larger groups.

the more assimilated they are. Indices comparing Negro and foreign stock groups with native born whites of native parents for a variety of cities from a variety of sources are collected together in Table 74. The following averages by census year

1910	54.14
1920	60.21
1930	75.78
1950	79.35
1960	77.25

reveal that the residential segregation of Negroes from native whites of native parents increased considerably between 1910 and 1930, and has remained at a fairly high level since then. The drop between 1950 and 1960 may indicate a slight move towards assimilation, though it is more probably due to the different mix of cities and study areas in 1960.

The Economic Segregation Model

Some five factors were earlier suggested as influencing the spatial distribution of a racial or ethnic group. The first set of influences were called the "normal" determinants of residential choice.

The most important of the residential choice determinants in the context of racial residential segregation is undoubtedly income. it has been suggested that the differences between racial groups in income account for the differences in their spatial distributions. As we have noted in an earlier chapter Negroes in most American cities have a less favorable distribution of income than whites. This means that they are likely to live in less valuable owner-occupied housing and lower rental housing units. This inference is confirmed by a set of crosstabulations which can be constructed for Birmingham SMSA (Table 75). This table is a cross-classification of income by housing value by color. Non-whites are shown to be more concentrated in lower rental and lower value housing than whites, and even more concentrated than the differences in incomes between the two groups would lead one to suppose. Within each income class (each column in the table) the proportion of housing units that are occupied by households with non-white heads decreases fairly systematically as the level of rent or value of the home increases. This implies that even when income differences between white and non-white households are controlled non-white households occupy lower rental or valued housing than do whites. This finding

TABLE 74

RESIDENTIAL SEGREGATION OF NEGROES FROM NATIVE BORN WHITES OF NATIVE PARENTS

City	Date	Study Area	Index Value
Ann Arbor[a]	1960	SMSA	73.69
"	1960	UA	76.65
Birmingham[a]	1960	SMSA	64.11
"	1960	UA	64.62
Boston[b]	1910	C	64.1
"	1920	C	65.3
"	1930	C	77.9
"	1950	C	80.1
Buffalo[b]	1910	C	62.6
"	1920	C	71.5
"	1930	C	80.5
"	1950	C	82.5
Canton[a]	1960	SMSA	76.45
"	1960	UA	76.45
Chicago[c]	1910	C	66.8
"	1920	C	75.7
"	1930	C	85.2
"	1930	C	84
"	1950	C	79.7
"	1960	C	82.05
"	1960	SMSA	81.66
Cincinnati[b]	1910	C	47.3
"	1920	C	52.2
"	1930	C	72.8
"	1950	C	80.6
Cleveland[b]	1910	C	60.6
"	1920	C	70.1
"	1930	C	85.0
"	1950	C	86.6
Columbus[b]	1910	C	31.6
"	1920	C	43.8
"	1930	C	62.8
"	1950	C	70.3
Des Moines[a]	1960	SMSA	77.32
"	1960	UA	77.11
El Paso[a]	1960	SMSA	67.18
"	1960	UA	72.52
Jersey City[d]	1960	SMSA	72.1
Lancaster[a]	1960	SMSA	78.60
"	1960	UA	87.10
Minneapolis-St. Paul[a]	1960	SMSA	84.77
"	1960	UA	84.63
Newark[d]	1960	SMSA	75.5
"	1960	C	64.5
New York[d]	1960	CA	80.2
"	1960	SMSA	81.8
"	1960	C	84.4
Patterson-Clifton-Passaic[d]	1960	SMSA	79.1
Philadelphia[b]	1910	C	46.0
"	1920	C	47.9
"	1930	C	63.4
"	1950	C	74.0

TABLE 74--Continued

City	Date	Study Area	Index Value
Pittsburgh[b]	1910	C	44.1
"	1920	C	43.3
"	1930	C	61.4
"	1950	C	68.5
Providence-Pawtucket[a]	1960	SMSA	72.59
"	1960	UA	75.02
Richmond[a]	1960	SMSA	75.99
"	1960	UA	79.09
St. Louis[b]	1910	C	54.3
"	1920	C	65.2
"	1930	C	86.7
"	1950	C	85.8
San Bernadino-Riverside-Ontario[a]	1960	SMSA	73.90
"	1960	UA	80.74
Syracuse[b]	1910	C	64.0
"	1920	C	65.2
"	1930	C	86.7
"	1950	C	85.8
Tampa-St. Petersburg[a]	1960	SMSA	83.59
Tampa[a]	1960	UA	84.12
St. Petersburg[a]	1960	UA	88.84

Notes

[a]Calculated from census tract data in the present study.

[b]Lieberson, 1963, Table 38, p. 122.

[c]Taeuber and Taeuber, 1964, Table 1.

[d]Kantrowitz, 1969, Table 2.

suggests that whites must have more resources available for housing expenditure than non-whites at the same current income level.

These differences between whites and non-whites in incomes and housing expenditures will have an effect on the spatial overlap of the two groups. Non-whites will tend to live in poorer neighborhoods, on average, than whites, and this alone will lead to some spatial separation of the two groups. Several authors have put forward this hypothesis (Lieberson, 1963, pp. 83-91; Taueber and Taeuber, 1965, pp. 69-95; Taeuber, 1968, pp. 5-14; Zelder, 1970, pp. 93-105; Berry, 1970, pp. 93-117) and have tested it by

TABLE 75

PERCENTAGE OF HOUSING UNITS WITH NON-WHITE HOUSEHOLD HEADS IN INCOME/RENT AND INCOME/VALUE CLASSES FOR BIRMINGHAM SMSA, 1960

Rental and Value Classes	Income Class					
	Less than $3,000	$3,000-$4,999	$5,000-$6,999	$7,000-$9,999	$10,000 or More	Total
Less than $40	76.45	71.17	57.27	53.80	47.17	73.99
$40 to $59	64.36	53.53	41.43	43.74	36.82	55.89
$60 to $79	32.51	20.40	13.52	8.64	4.53	19.61
$80 to $119	11.73	4.63	4.72	1.08	2.07	4.51
$120 or More	24.48	14.61	1.92	0.00	0.00	4.93
No Cash Rent	40.40	27.71	13.60	11.16	4.12	31.35
Total, Renters	62.87	40.81	23.19	11.95	7.06	44.93
Less than $7,500	59.11	48.28	30.37	21.51	14.10	45.09
$7,500 to $12,400	31.22	28.70	9.65	8.25	5.04	14.78
$12,500 to $19,900	16.17	15.81	4.86	2.49	1.62	5.18
$20,000 or More	10.60	21.58	5.13	2.60	0.66	2.53
Total, Owners	48.18	34.41	14.44	8.07	3.08	22.37
Total, Housing Units	56.84	37.52	17.30	8.91	3.56	31.37

Source: Calculated from Tables A-2, A-3 and A-13 in U.S. Bureau of the Census (1963d).

calculating the number of non-whites and whites one would expect to live in the various areas of the city if ability to pay for housing was the only residential location criterion. The number of a particular ethnic group expected under the hypothesis to be located in a tract is given by the following:

$$H_i(e) = \sum_v \left[U_i(v)\ P_*(e|v) \right] \tag{12}$$

and $P_*(e|v)$ is given by

$$P_*(e|v) = H_*(e,v)/H_*(e,*) \tag{13}$$

where $H_i(e)$ is the number of households in zone i that are in ethnic group e; $U_i(v)$ is the number of housing units in housing value/rent category v in zone i; $P_*(e|v)$ is the conditional probability for the study area that a household living in a housing unit in rental/value category v will also be in ethnic group e; $H_*(e,v)$ is the number of households in the study area who are in ethnic category e and housing expenditure category v; and $H_*(e,*)$ is the total number of households of ethnic group e in the study area.

Thus, the expected number of an ethnic group e in tract i is equal to the sum, for all the housing value/rental classes, of the proportion of each housing category in the city as a whole occupied by the ethnic group multiplied by the number of people living in housing units of each type in tract i.

The version of this model which uses housing value and rental classes is called the expenditure version. However, incomes have also been used, though the use of these assumes that the same income will buy the same amount of housing for each ethnic group, an assumption we have seen to be invalid in the case of Birmingham. The expected number of an ethnic group in a tract, once calculated, can be compared to (1) the observed number of that group in a tract, or

(2) the expected number of another group in a tract, or (3) the observed number of another group in a tract either tract by tract or for the city as a whole through calculation of a summary index of comparison.

Lieberson's work clearly reveals that the economic segregation model accounts for little of the observed residential segregation of a variety of ethnic groups in Cleveland in 1930 (Lieberson, 1963, Table 23, pp. 88-89). The average level of observed residential segregation of some 17 ethnic groups from native whites of native parents in 45.9 (index of dissimilarity value). The average level of residential segregation using the expected spatial distributions (using housing expenditure by value and rental class as the economic classification) on the other hand was only 12.3. The gap between observed and expected residential segregation was largest for non-whites (61.6) despite the fact that the level of expected residential segregation for this group was also the highest of all the groups (24.0). The difference between expected and observed segregation was also large for Russians (61.4) but the expected segregation level was much lower (4.4).

The Taeubers (Taeuber and Taeuber, 1965, pp. 69-95) confirmed Lieberson's finding that patterns of economic residential segregation do not account for the observed levels of racial residential segregation. They calculated indices of dissimilarity between non-whites and whites on an observed and expected basis for some 15 cities in 1940, 1950 and 1960. Almost all expected indices were less than half the size of the observed, and a majority were under 30 per cent of the observed value. The proportion of the observed accounted for by the economic segregation model declined over the 1940 to 1960 period, as one might have expected given the economic progress of Negroes over those decades and the continued high level of residential segregation. The economic model accounted for more of the observed residential segregation of whites and non-whites in

Southern cities. In a later paper (Taeuber, 1968) Taeuber found that in Cleveland in 1965, for example, the segregation index comparing the expected distributions of Negroes and whites was only 6, whereas the observed index value for actual Negroes and whites was 90.

Results of the Economic Segregation Model for the Sample Urbanized Areas

The two versions of the economic segregation model for ethnic groups were implemented for the white and non-white groups for the thirteen sample urbanized areas. The analysis was restricted to those two groups as the study area crosstabulations of income by color for families and housing expenditure by color by occupied housing units were the only ones easily available. Very good estimates of the necessary crosstabulations could be made for white, Negro and other non-white groups using the color crosstabulations and the separate tabulations for tracts with large numbers of Negroes resident.

The basic models were the housing expenditure model already described and an alternate model which uses the income distribution of families living in a tract rather than the distribution of housing units by value/rent class. The income model is expressed as follows:

$$F_i(e) = \sum_y \left[F_i(y) \cdot P_*(e|y) \right] \qquad (14)$$

where $F_i(e)$ is the number of families of ethnic group e in zone i, $F_i(y)$ is the observed number of families of income class y in zone i; and $P_*(e|y)$ is the probability that a family in income group y belongs to ethnic group e. This probability is for the whole SMSA, and is calculated from the SMSA crosstabulations of color and income:

$$P_*(e|y) = F_*(e,y)/F_*(*,y) \quad (15)$$

The term $F_*(e,y)$ refers to the number of families in ethnic group e in income group y in all the study area census tracts (the whole SMSA in this case); $F_*(*,y)$ is the total number of families in income group y. The expenditure model should, in theory, be a better predictor of white and non-white distribution because it involves the expenditures used in a household's residential location rather than the general resources available for such expenditures (the income model).

The family income and housing expenditure categories used are given in Table 76. Information about the distribution of income and of housing expenditures in the census tracts together with the study area-wide crosstabulations was used to calculate the expected number of white and non-white families and households in the census tracts. The expected and observed numbers of families and households can be compared by calculating the indices of dissimilarity between a variety of pairs of variables. These are set out in Table 77.

In the second column of the first part of the table are compared the white and non-white distributions that would result from the income model. The indices of dissimilarity of these expected distributions range from a low of 2.63 in Honolulu to maximum of 21.30 in Richmond. All are much lower than the residential segregation observed between whites and non-whites, being on average only 15 per cent of the observed segregation. Clearly, as Taeuber (1968) has argued, decreasing the gap between white and non-white incomes will not reduce residential segregation of the two races in American cities by itself.

The variation among cities in the WY vs NY dissimilarity values generally parallels the variation in income differentials between white and non-white in cities. In particular, the two

TABLE 76

INCOME AND HOUSING EXPENDITURES CATEGORIES

Family Income Categories (Income, 1959)	Housing Expenditure Categories
	Value
Under $2,000	Less than $5,000
$2,000 - $3,999	$5,000 - $9,999
$4,000 - $5,999	$10,000 - $14,999
$6,000 - $7,999	$15,000 - $19,999
$8,000 - $9,999	$20,000 - $24,999
$10,000 or more	$25,000 or over
	Rent
	Less than $20
Color Categories	$20 - $39
	$40 - $59
White	$60 - $79
Non-white	$80 - $99
	$100 or over

urbanized areas which revealed particular large disadvantages in Chapter III's factor analyses for black Americans, namely Birmingham and Richmond, record the highest residential dissimilarity values for model expectations in Table 77.

The fourth column of the income model table gives some indication of the shift across the city that would be necessary to equate the observed and expected non-white distributions: on average some 59 per cent. If whites were to move as well into areas of black concentration, this proportion would be reduced. The final column of the income model table indicates the extent of the gap between observed segregation and model segregation. This gap, we have argued, is the product of two sets of forces which Morrill and Donaldson (1972) have labelled external pressures and internal pressures. The external pressures are those exerted by whites outside the black ghetto that force blacks to remain inside the ghetto and extend their residential space by expansion at the ghetto margins only. The internal pressures include the benefits of mutual

TABLE 77

INCOME AND EXPENDITURE MODEL RESULTS FOR THIRTEEN URBANIZED AREAS, 1960

INCOME MODEL	Pairs of groups compared					
	W vs NW	WY vs NY	WY vs W	NY vs NW	(2) as % of (1)	(1) - (2)
Urbanized Area	(1)	(2)	(3)	(4)	(5)	(6)
Ann Arbor	68.13	9.73	12.55	59.89	14.28	58.40
Birmingham	64.82	20.36	15.25	31.54	31.41	44.46
Canton	74.84	9.18	3.48	65.55	12.27	65.66
Des Moines	25.30	11.36	3.60	66.44	15.09	63.94
El Paso	51.96	9.05	5.56	49.95	17.42	42.91
Honolulu	46.77	2.63	31.41	15.28	5.62	44.14
Lancaster	84.57	11.25	3.33	76.39	13.30	73.32
Minneapolis-St. Paul	71.32	9.29	4.18	66.98	13.03	62.03
Providence-Pawtucket	71.85	8.55	2.76	68.16	11.90	63.30
Richmond	78.94	21.30	13.89	46.82	26.98	57.64
San Beradino-Riverside	71.39	10.29	4.88	67.06	14.41	61.10
St. Petersburg	88.48	6.75	5.91	30.82	7.63	81.73
Tampa	81.45	9.68	8.90	66.35	11.88	71.77
Average	71.52	10.72	8.90	58.79	15.02	60.80

TABLE 77--Continued

EXPENDITURE MODEL	Pairs of groups compared					
	W vs NW	WE vs NE	WE vs W	NE vs NW	(2) as % of (1)	(1) - (2)
Urbanized Area	(1)	(2)	(3)	(4)	(5)	(6)
Ann Arbor	68.13	16.35	12.01	59.16	24.00	51.78
Birmingham	64.82	28.32	14.45	27.78	43.69	36.50
Canton	74.84	26.78	5.45	56.17	35.78	43.06
Des Moines	75.30	20.64	7.27	62.11	27.41	54.66
El Paso	51.96	12.03	7.70	50.97	23.15	39.93
Honolulu	46.77	14.14	27.23	16.01	30.23	32.63
Lancaster	84.57	a	a	a	a	a
Minneapolis-St. Paul	71.32	22.89	7.09	62.02	32.09	48.43
Providence-Pawtucket	71.85	22.75	5.27	62.91	31.66	49.10
Richmond	78.94	33.97	14.11	39.54	43.03	44.97
San Bernadino-Riverside	71.39	14.64	7.80	66.17	20.51	56.75
St. Petersburg	88.48	22.47	8.20	72.68	25.40	66.01
Tampa	81.45	25.81	10.50	55.03	31.69	55.64
Average	71.59	21.73	10.59	52.55	30.72	48.71

Key

W - Whites
NW - Non-whites
WY - Whites predicted by income model
a - No expenditure crosstabulation information easily available for Lancaster

NY - Non-whites predicted by income model
WE - Whites predicted by expenditure model
NE - Non-whites predicted by expenditure model

protection, of community institutions, of friends and relatives of the same ethnicity, and of political power through spatial solidarity.

An Interpretation of the Spatial Patterns of Negroes and Whites

It is difficult to measure the relative strengths of such forces directly but if we examine the levels of segregation experienced by other ethnic groups some approximate estimates can be made. The average residential segregation index values over our thirteen urbanized areas are given in Table 73. The index values recorded for other Non-whites (mainly Oriental) and Russians, groups well-known for their community strength and desire to cluster, are 43.34 and 47.01 respectively. If we regard 45 as the likely maximum level of residential segregation of non-Negro ethnic groups in American urbanized areas in 1960 and attribute that level purely to group "background" characteristics and group cohesiveness, then a gap of some 34 points on the index of dissimilarity scale intervenes between that maximum and the observed average residential segregation of Negroes. We can therefore divide the observed segregation into three parts:

10 points due to differences in incomes and therefore ability to purchase housing

35 points due to internal pressures (attractions of a black community)

35 points due to external pressures (discriminating behavior on the part of the white majority).

This "division of the residential segregation cake" may be in error because the color-free residential location model is poorly specified and neglects family status characteristics in particular or because the observed pattern features could be interpreted in a different way. It is offered as a best guess of the likely position in American cities in 1960.

The expenditure model gives higher estimates of the spatial distance between white and non-white expected distributions. This is because non-whites are relatively more disadvantaged vis à vis whites with respect to housing expenditure than they are with respect to income. Table 78 gives the per cents of whites and non-whites in each housing expenditure category for Birmingham SMSA, and the differential between them. The overall index of dissimilarity between white and non-white distributions is 53.94, a higher value than the corresponding ones for the education and income crosstabulations (see Chapter IX).

The average expected level of residential separation of whites and non-whites is nearly 22 points on the dissimilarity index scale for the expenditure model, nearly double that of the income model. The difference between observed and expected dissimilarity indices is still substantial, however, being just under 49. We can correct our earlier estimates of the magnitude of the components of the residential segregation of non-whites to read

20 points due to differences in housing expenditures and ability to purchase housing

25 points due to internal pressures (the attractions of a black community)

35 points due to external forces (discriminatory behavior on the part of the white majority).

The crucial question raised by these estimates is whether there is any possibility of reducing the 35 points due to discrimination in the housing market. Most available evidence in the period between the 1960 census and the present day indicates that there has been little or no reduction in this component despite open housing ordinances, civil rights legislation and federal intervention.

The Spatial Patterns of Foreign Stock Groups

So far the discussion has been largely confined to a consideration of the residential patterns of Negroes and whites. The spatial polarization of black and white Americans has been amply documented.

TABLE 78

THE DISTRIBUTION OF HOUSING EXPENDITURE FOR HOUSEHOLDS HEADED BY WHITES AND NON-WHITES, BIRMINGHAM SMSA, 1960

	Housing Expenditure Category	Per Cent Non-White Households	Per Cent White Households	Differential ($Diff_a$)
Rent	Less than $30	11.67	1.91	6.11
	$30 to $39	14.83	2.35	6.31
	$40 to $49	13.68	3.26	4.20
	$50 to $59	8.96	4.91	1.82
	$60 to $69	3.68	5.43	0.68
	$70 to $79	1.43	4.16	0.34
	$80 to $99	0.57	5.00	0.11
	$110 to $119	0.14	1.86	0.08
	$120 or more	0.12	1.07	0.11
	No Cash Rent	2.10	2.11	1.00
	Subtotal, Renter Units	57.18	32.06	1.78
Value	Less than $5,000	17.47	7.30	2.39
	$5,000 to $7,400	13.24	9.80	1.35
	$7,500 to $9,900	6.23	12.82	0.49
	$10,000 to $12,400	3.30	12.29	0.27
	$12,500 to $14,900	1.29	8.94	0.14
	$15,000 to $19,000	0.85	8.96	0.09
	$20,000 to $24,900	0.26	3.65	0.07
	$25,000 or More	0.19	4.20	0.05
	Subtotal, Owner units	42.82	67.94	0.63
	Total	100.00	100.00	1.00

Source: Calculated from Tables A-2, A-3 and A-13 in U.S. Bureau of the Census (1963d).

The distribution of the various foreign stock groups in U.S. cities is still of interest, however. The foreign stock element, though generally on the decline, was still substantial in 1960. From 3 to 41 per cent of the population of the sample metropolitan areas studied (Table 69) is either foreign born or native born of foreign or mixed parents. If the children of the latter group who still live with them are included then we could probably say that the foreign stock component constitutes from 4 to 50 per cent of the sample metropolises' population. The spatial distributions of the national groups that make up the foreign stock population are still phenomena of considerable interest. The indices of residential segregation for these groups in the twelve SMSAs and thirteen urbanized areas are recorded in Table 72. In all cases second generation immigrants (NBFMP) have lower residential segregation indices than both the foreign born (FB) and native whites of native parents (NWNP).[1]

The transition from higher foreign born residential segregation to the lower NBFMP figure can be interpreted as a part of the process of residential assimilation. The second generation of immigrants is more widely spread than is the first. In subsequent generations (NWNP) there is relative reconcentration in the outer parts of the urbanized areas. This interpretation is confirmed by the distribution of FB, NBFMP, and NWNP in Des Moines SMSA (Figure 63). In all but the two tracts which have large Negro populations NWNP are in the majority, so that relative rather than absolute concentrations of the groups are plotted on the map. Tracts with more than 1.25 times the SMSA per cent of FB (2.34) or NBFMP (9.47) and tracts with more than 1.05 times the per cent of NWNP (84.09) are picked out on the map. The foreign born are concentrated in centrally located tracts (except those with Negro concentrations). The second generation are concentrated in some of the same tracts and others displaced further from the city center to the west. The NBFMP are concentrated in the outer city and in the suburban tracts outside the city itself.

This spatial pattern in which the FB are most centralized and

---

[1]The number of native whites of native parents is calculated by subtracting from the total figures for whites the number of foreign born and the number of native born of foreign or mixed parents. Included in these foreign stock groups, however, is a number of foreign stock non-whites. Thus, the number of NWNP is underestimated by the number of foreign stock non-whites. In most SMSAs this error is acceptably low. In the case of Honolulu, however, the underestimation is too severe for this approximation to the NWNP to be of any use.

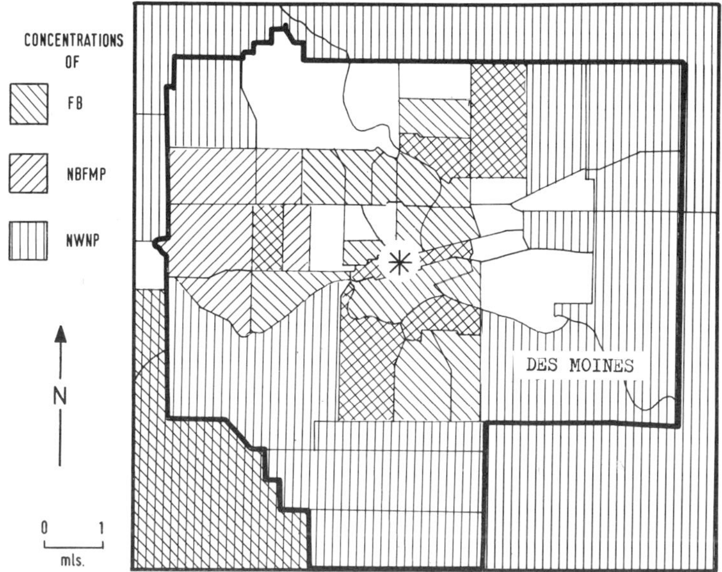

Fig. 63.--The Spatial Distribution of Foreign Stock Groups in Des Moines, 1960

the NWNP the most decentralized with the NBFMP occupying an intermediate position is common to all SMSAs studied. This is apparent from the central city-suburban ratios reported in Table 79. The ratios are calculated by dividing the proportion of an ethnic group living outside the central city by the same proportion for the population as a whole. Ratios of more than one mean that the group in question is more concentrated in the central city than is the total population of the SMSA. Ratios of less than one mean that the group is more concentrated in the suburban portion of the metropolis than is the population as a whole. The average ratio for the SMSAs reported in Table 79 for the FB is 1.23, for the NBFMP is 1.15 and for the NWNP is 0.91. Of the individual groups in the table, Negroes, Other non-whites, Russians and Italians are distinctly more concentrated in the central city than is the total population. A good part of the residential segregation of these groups in the metropolis (Tables 72 and 73) is accounted for by this concentration in some cities whereas relatively little is accounted for in others. Norwegians, Swedes, Czechs and Canadians and the NWNP are distinctly concentrated in the suburban portion of the metropolis. The other groups are moderately concentrated in the central city or cities.

Residential Assimilation

It is possible to follow the process of residential assimilation of an immigrant group rather more closely in the case of Mexican Americans in El Paso and San Bernadino-Riverside (Table 80). There is a substantial decrease in residential segregation as we move through the generations of Mexican Americans. The reconcentration effect noted for the NWNP of Des Moines is again apparent for native non-Spanish surname whites of native parents of El Paso and San Bernadino. A high level of residential segregation persists between Mexican and Anglo Americans in all nativity groups although native born Mexican Americans are less residentially segregated from non-Spanish surname whites than their foreign born co-ethnics. There is a fairly clear distinction in the spatial distributions of Mexican and Anglo Americans in El Paso (Figure 64). The Mexican group is concentrated along the Rio Grande, in the industrial areas of the city and particularly around the city center, fanning out from the main bridge across the river to Mexico. The Anglo group, on the other hand occupies the higher outer tracts of city to the north and east of the center, the more suburban locations.

In examining the relative levels of assimilation of various ethnic groups the most useful measure is the index of dissimilarity between the ethnic group and native whites of native parents as we have indicated earlier in the chapter. These measures for the sample SMSAs are assembled in Tables 81 and 82. The contrast

TABLE 79

SUBURBANIZATION RATIOS FOR RACIAL AND ETHNIC GROUPS

Racial and Ethnic Groups	Ann Arbor	Birmingham	Canton	Des Moines	El Paso	Honolulu	Lancaster	Minneapolis-St. Paul
Negro	0.69	1.15	1.82	1.24	0.79	0.46	3.28	1.80
Other Non-white	2.28	1.00	1.36	1.14	0.86	1.14	1.78	1.64
NWNP	0.95	0.91	0.91	0.98	0.98	—	0.92	0.91
NBFMP	1.23	1.09	1.24	1.04	1.04	1.15	1.67	1.16
FB	1.46	1.15	1.55	1.10	1.06	1.11	1.92	1.37
FS	1.31	1.09	1.30	1.06	1.05	1.14	1.73	1.20
U.K.	1.15	1.06	1.00	1.06	0.95	1.07	1.19	1.10
Ireland (Eire)	1.08	1.11	1.27	1.07	0.99	0.90	1.63	1.39
Norway	1.18	1.31	0.79	1.07	1.00	1.00	0.35	1.23
Sweden	1.21	0.91	0.61	1.08	1.08	1.01	0.41	1.21
Germany	1.21	1.09	1.06	1.05	0.99	0.91	1.95	1.15
Poland	1.10	0.78	1.55	1.11	0.97	0.74	1.47	1.31
Czechoslovakia	1.03	1.06	1.30	0.99	1.06	0.66	1.04	1.22
Austria	1.36	0.83	1.15	1.00	0.99	0.98	1.13	1.26
Hungary	0.85	0.94	0.79	1.05	0.97	0.78	1.88	1.21
U.S.S.R.	1.90	0.69	1.94	1.12	1.04	1.08	1.64	1.35
Italy	1.21	1.39	1.42	1.10	0.91	0.68	2.59	1.30
Canada	1.15	0.96	0.79	1.00	0.93	0.92	0.77	1.05
Mexico	1.21	1.13	1.36	0.90	1.06	0.86	1.29	1.49
Total Population Per Cent in City	39	54	33	78	88	59	22	54

TABLE 79--Continued

Racial and Ethnic Groups	Providence-Pawtucket	Richmond	San Bernadino-Riverside-Ontario	Tampa-St. Petersburg	Chicago	Mean Ratio	No. of Ratios Greater than 1.00
Negro	2.28	1.59	1.53	1.34	1.60	1.50	10
Other Non-white	1.64	1.42	0.49	0.98	1.47	1.33	10
NWNP	0.90	0.78	0.98	0.93	0.79	0.91	0
NBFMP	1.21	0.89	1.07	1.07	1.04	1.15	12
FB	1.04	1.04	0.90	1.06	1.28	1.23	12
FS	1.09	0.93	1.02	1.06	1.11	1.16	12
U.K.	1.08	0.88	1.06	0.96	0.86	1.03	9
Ireland (Eire)	1.47	0.91	1.18	1.02	1.32	1.18	10
Norway	0.70	0.82	0.89	0.93	0.93	0.94	4
Sweden	0.61	0.68	1.21	0.83	0.93	0.91	5
Germany	0.97	0.84	0.98	0.95	0.96	1.09	6
Poland	1.12	1.08	1.12	1.01	1.33	1.13	10
Czechoslovakia	0.83	0.52	1.06	0.93	0.81	0.96	7
Austria	1.21	1.03	1.18	1.05	1.10	1.10	9
Hungary	1.20	0.51	1.14	0.87	1.15	1.03	6
U.S.S.R.	1.78	1.22	1.11	1.08	1.32	1.33	12
Italy	1.37	0.88	0.80	1.28	1.12	1.23	9
Canada	0.69	0.80	1.10	0.92	0.84	0.92	3
Mexico	1.16	1.06	1.01	1.19	1.40	1.16	11
Total Population Per Cent in City	35	54	28	59	57	—	—

TABLE 80

INDICES OF DISSIMILARITY OF SPANISH SURNAME WHITES AND NON-SPANISH SURNAME WHITES IN EL PASO AND SAN BERNADINO-RIVERSIDE URBANIZED AREAS, 1960

El Paso

Mexican American	Anglo American FB	Anglo American NBFMP	Anglo American NBNP	Rest of Population
FB	52.35	56.19	61.98	41.02
NBFMP	48.01	51.20	54.32	34.46
NBNP	49.47	51.27	51.42	30.19
Rest of Population	27.69	27.61	47.79	—

San Bernadino-Riverside

Mexican American	Anglo American FB	Anglo American NBFMP	Anglo American NBNP	Rest of Population
FB	64.52	65.15	66.53	58.59
NBFMP	59.70	60.27	59.52	53.00
NBNP	52.14	52.34	49.82	43.92
Rest of Population	19.89	17.36	32.69	—

Notes

FB - Foreign Born
NBFMP - Native Born of Foreign or Mixed Parents
NBNP - Native Born of Native Parents
Mexican American FB - "White, Spanish Surname: Foreign Born."
Mexican American NBFMP - "Mexico" (Foreign Stock) minus "White, Spanish Surname: Foreign Born."
Mexican American NBNP - "White, Spanish Surname: Foreign Born" plus "White, Spanish Surname: Native" minus "Mexico" (Foreign Stock).
Anglo American FB - "Foreign Born" minus "White, Spanish Surname: Foreign Born."
Anglo American NBFMP - "Native, Foreign or Mixed Parentage" minus "Mexico" plus "White, Spanish Surname: Foreign Born."
Anglo American NBNP - "Total Population" minus "Total Foreign Stock" minus "White, Spanish Surname: Native" plus "White, Spanish Surname: Foreign Born" plus "Mexico."

The terms in quotation marks are those designated in the tract volumes.

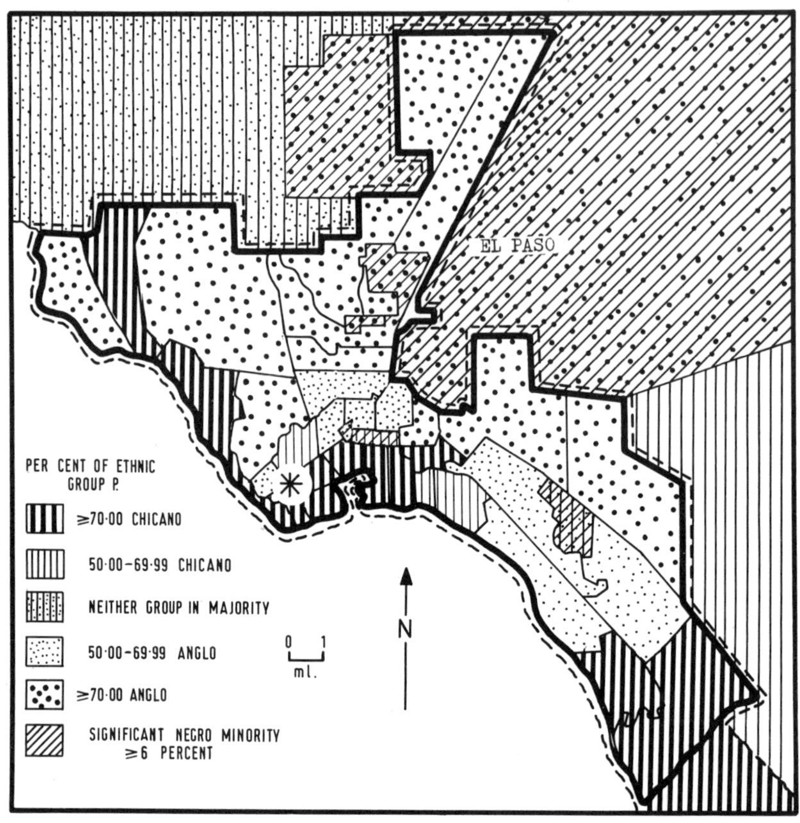

Fig. 64.--The Spatial Pattern of Ethnic Status, El Paso, 1960

between Negroes and other ethnic groups is immediately apparent, and has already been commented on. The "Anglo-Saxon" ethnic groups (British, German and Canadian) appear to be well assimilated, followed by Norwegians, Swedes, Czechs and Irish with slightly lower degrees of residential assimilation. The Southern and East Europeans have higher index values, particularly the Russian group which in almost all cities is composed largely of members of the Jewish faith. Finally, the Mexican group appears to be the most segregated of all the non-Negro groups from the NWNP.

Precise specification of the reasons for these differences in level of residential assimilation is not possible as the necessary information on the characteristics of the groups in the particular metropolitan areas is not available to test the various hypotheses about the ordering of the groups put forward by Lieberson (1963). However, we can make use of some information on the social characteristics of the groups at the national level and compare this with our mean dissimilarity indices.

Economic status plays some part in the differentiation in urban space of the groups, though not a great deal. The scores of a 1962 national sample of male household heads on Duncan's socioeconomic status scale for occupations for the groups are recorded in Table 83. Generally, the higher the occupational status of the group the less residentially segregated it is from native whites of native parents. The ranking correlation coefficient (Spearman's rho) between Table 82's indices of dissimilarity and the estimated occupational status of the ethnic group is -0.54. This is in the direction one would guess but it is only marginally higher than the level, 0.50, at which one is 95 per cent confident in a sampling situation that the value for rho in this particular comparison is different from zero. The association between educational status (years of schooling completed) and the level of residential segregation from NWNP is also -0.54.

A major exception to these relationships is, however, the Russian group. The Russians are the group with the highest educational and occupational status (higher even than the NWNP group) and yet they are the least residentially assimilated of the European ethnic groups. A very strong preference for living in a Jewish community among co-ethnics together with some degree of housing discrimination against Jews in the past undoubtedly account for the residential concentration of the Russian foreign stock group in all the

TABLE 81

INDICES OF DISSIMILARITY OF RACIAL AND ETHNIC GROUPS FROM NATIVE BORN WHITES OF NATIVE PARENTS

Ethnic and Racial Groups	Ann Arbor		Birmingham		Canton		Des Moines		El Paso		Lancaster	
	SMSA	UA	SMSA	UA	SMSA	UA	SMSA	UA	SMSA	UA	SMSA	UA
Negro	74	77	64	65	76	77	77	77	67	73	79	87
Other Non-white	58	51	58	56	51	51	44	44	31	30	51	37
U.K.	20	21	25	24	17	17	15	15	26	26	28	20
Norway	—	—	—	—	—	—	25	25	—	—	—	—
Sweden	—	—	—	—	—	—	22	22	—	—	—	—
Germany	25	29	31	31	19	16	15	15	26	26	33	21
Poland	31	25	60	59	38	34	—	—	44	45	40	16
Czechoslovakia	—	—	—	—	28	25	—	—	—	—	—	—
Austria	38	39	46	43	27	22	—	—	—	—	39	32
Hungary	41	35	—	—	31	31	—	—	—	—	—	—
U.S.S.R.	45	42	74	73	53	48	44	42	57	61	48	35
Italy	32	25	45	42	33	30	45	45	26	23	44	24
Canada	18	17	47	45	—	—	24	24	22	21	39	37
Mexico	—	—	—	—	—	—	—	—	47	46	—	—

TABLE 81--Continued

Ethnic and Racial Groups	Minneapolis-St. Paul		Providence-Pawtucket		Richmond		San Bernadino-Riverside-Ontario		Tampa-St. Petersburg		
										Tampa	St. Petersburg
	SMSA	UA	SMSA	UA	SMSA	UA	SMSA	UA	SMSA	UA	UA
Negro	84	85	73	75	76	79	74	81	84	84	89
Other Non-white	47	47	51	51	49	49	44	34	43	39	48
U.K.	22	22	23	22	21	21	21	20	30	18	13
Ireland			28	27	33	32	—	—	36	27	19
Norway	26	25	—	—	—	—	—	—	—	—	—
Sweden	25	25	39	37	—	—	29	28	35	25	18
Germany	20	20	26	24	22	21	19	18	29	16	13
Poland	40	39	39	40	42	41	31	28	29	25	25
Czechoslovakia	—	—	—	—	35	32	—	—	—	—	—
Austria	33	33	—	—	—	—	—	—	—	—	—
Hungary	—	—	—	—	—	—	—	—	—	—	—
U.S.S.R.	47	46	52	52	55	53	37	31	39	39	31
Italy	—	—	50	50	28	28	29	28	36	45	19
Canada	17	17	34	28	27	26	20	19	27	20	13
Mexico	—	—	—	—	—	—	54	58	—	—	—

TABLE 82

AVERAGE DISSIMILARITY INDICES FOR ETHNIC GROUPS COMPARED WITH NATIVE WHITES OF NATIVE PARENTS

Racial or Ethnic Group	Unweighted Average Residential Segregation Index Values		Number of Cities for Which Average is Calculated	
	SMSA	UA	SMSA	UA
Negro	75.29	78.91	11	12
Other Non-white	48.11	44.78	11	12
U.K.	22.60	19.74	11	12
Ireland	34.74	29.37	7	8
Norway	25.52	24.93	2	2
Sweden	29.79	25.78	5	6
Germany	24.12	20.77	11	12
Poland	39.27	34.37	10	11
Czechoslovakia	31.66	28.30	2	2
Austria	36.74	33.82	5	5
Hungary	35.57	32.93	2	2
U.S.S.R.	50.01	46.13	11	12
Italy	36.80	32.55	10	11
Canada	27.48	24.20	10	11
Mexico	50.48	51.68	2	2

urbanized areas in our sample.

Also recorded in Table 83 is the per cent of foreign stock group estimated to have immigrated into the States since 1940. The association between recent immigration and the degree of residential assimilation is a negative one of -0.55, that is, not in the direction found by Lieberson (1963, p. 152) for some 10 Northern U.S. cities in 1930. Recency of arrival though formerly of some importance appears to play little part in determining the level of residential assimilation of ethnic groups in American cities in 1960. The reason for this reversal in relationship probably lies

TABLE 83

ESTIMATED SOCIAL CHARACTERISTICS OF RACIAL AND ETHNIC GROUPS

Racial or Ethnic Group	Per Cent Immigrated Since 1940[a]	Education Score[b]	Occupation Score[b]	Social Distance[c]		
				Mean Acceptance Score	1926 Rank	1946 Rank
Negro	—	9.04	19.45	—	31	35
Other Non-white	—	11.57	46.57	9.78[d]	30.07[g]	30.14[g]
U.K.	41.1	11.95	49.00	96.33[e]	2.5[h]	4[h]
Ireland	27.3	12.01	44.48	—	5	4
Norway	23.8	11.95	49.00	—	10	7
Sweden	12.9	11.95	49.00	61.00	8	9
Germany	47.0	11.14	43.50	—	7	11
Poland	31.7	11.04	38.65	17.00	17	15
Czechoslovakia	22.3	11.65	42.76	—	20	13
Austria	13.5	11.65	42.76	—	—	—
Hungary	—	11.65	42.76	18.00	—	—
U.S.S.R.	10.3	13.12	52.22	15.00[f]	14	14
Italy	19.5	11.05	37.42	25.33	15	19
Canada	—	11.85	44.34	—	3	2
Mexico	—	8.92	28.60	9.00	27	26

Notes

[a]Estimated percentage of foreign born white population who have immigrated since 1940, by country of birth, for the coterminous U.S., 1960. Source: Taeuber and Taeuber, 1967, Table 3, p. 805.

[b]Derived from Duncan and Duncan, 1968, Table 1, p. 358. Where individual countries are not identified as such in the Duncans' table they have been assigned the mean for the country group to which they belong. The original data on which the Duncans' table is based was a nationwide survey of occupational mobility carried out in 1962 by the Current Population Survey of the U.S. Bureau of the Census (see Blau and Duncan, 1967).

TABLE 83--Continued

Notes--Continued

[c]Source for mean acceptance score: Bogardus (1928) quoted in Banton (1967), Table 3, p.323. The 1926 and 1946 ranks are from Bogardus (1947), p. 58.

[d]The values for Japanese, Chinese and Filipino were averaged.

[e]The value for the English.

[f]The value for Jews, German.

[g]The values for Indian (American), Japanese, Chinese, Filipino, Indians (East) and Japanese Americans were averaged.

[h]The values for English and Scots were averaged.

---

in the 1924 Immigration Act. This established national quotas based on the ethnic composition of the population at the time. These quotas favored immigration form North West Europe. Immigrants from these countries became a relatively more important component of the migration stream to the U.S. They continued to find assimilation fairly easy, being generally a fairly educated or job-skilled migrant stream. This continuing post-Second World War immigration from Britain, Ireland and Germany meant that these groups came to have higher proportions of recent arrivals (Table 83) than less favored groups formerly labelled "new" immigrants.

The suggestion was made by Duncan and Lieberson (1959, pp. 372-373) that the level of residential assimilation of an ethnic group was related to the degree of acceptance of that group by native Americans. If true, this would imply that the more socially acceptable an ethnic group was the more likely it was that the NWNP group would feel comfortable living in close proximity to the ethnic group. Conversely, the more socially accepted ethnic groups would find it easier to find housing vacancies in NWNP dominated neighborhoods; often they would already be connected into the native white communication network. The less socially accepted an ethnic group was the more valued would be relations with the group and the more desirable would living among co-ethnics be.

The social acceptability in America of a variety of nationalities and native minority groups has been measured on several occasions by Emory S. Bogardus. Representative samples of Americans were contacted and were asked to reply in the following terms:

> According to my first feeling reaction, I would willingly admit members of each race (as a class and not the best I have known, nor the worst) to the classifications which I have marked. (Bogardus, 1928, quoted in Banton, 1967, p. 315).

The classifications used by Bogardus in 1926 were:

1. Would accept as relative by marriage
2. Would accept as member of same club
3. Would accept as neighbor
4. Would accept as workmate
5. Would accept as fellow citizen
6. Would accept as visitor to country
7. Would exclude from country.

Bogardus conducted surveys in 1926, 1946 and 1956, and found a remarkable stability in the "social distance" which Americans perceived between themselves and the foreign groups in the survey. His results for 1926 and 1946 are reported in Table 83 for the groups for which we were able to measure residential assimilation. The mean acceptance score was calculated only for the first three items of the Bogardus scale, those which it was felt were most relevant to the question of residential assimilation. The rankings for 1926 and 1946 were for all items in the scale and were taken from Bogardus's 1947 paper. The association between the index of dissimilarity (vs NWNP) of Table 82 and the mean acceptance score for 1926 was extremely close: the ranking correlation coefficient between the two was 0.98 (Spearman's rho). The coefficient for the 1926 rankings and the indices of dissimilarity was 0.83 and for the 1946 rankings 0.85. The preference hypothesis put forward earlier in the chapter is thus strongly supported.

Inter-ethnic Segregation Patterns

One implication of this finding is that ethnic groups should not be conceived of as assimilating into a unified American culture, but rather into at least three separate sub-cultures. This notion has been referred to as the triple melting pot hypothesis in which European ethnic groups are said to merge over time into three general groupings based on religion: Protestant, Catholic and Jewish. We have already seen that the ethnic group that can be fairly unambiguously identified as mainly Jewish — the Russians — is in each of the cities studied fairly highly residentially segregated both from the rest of the population (Table 72) and from native whites of native birth (Table 81). Russians prove to be moderately segregated from most of the other ethnic groups in the sample urbanized areas (Table 84). The only indices of dissimilarity involving Russians out of a total of 130 that fall below 30 are one with Poles of 24 in Ann Arbor and comparisons with Germans, Irish and Poles in St. Petersburg. In other words a residentially distinct Jewish community is characteristic not only of the larger American metropolises (New York, Chicago, Los Angeles, Boston, Philadelphia, Miami, Cleveland) but also of much smaller cities represented by the sample studied here.

A persistent clustering of ethnic groups shows up in Table 84 in most of the urbanized areas. Native whites of native parents, foreign stock of British origin, of German origin, of Canadian origin together with Swedish and Norwegian Americans in the urbanized areas where their residential pattern has been examined all tend to cluster together. Table 84 reveals this pattern clearly in Ann Arbor, Des Moines, El Paso, Minneapolis-St. Paul, Providence-Pawtucket, Richmond, San Bernadino-Riverside and Tampa. In all these cities the indices of dissimilarity within the grouping are all less than 30 whereas most of those ethnic groups outside the cluster are above 30. Though the general level of inter-ethnic segregation is

TABLE 84

INTER-ETHNIC INDICES OF DISSIMILARITY
FOR 13 URBANIZED AREAS

ANN ARBOR

Ethnic Group	2.	3.	4.	5.	6.	7.	8.	9.	10.	11.
1. NWNP	17	29	21	25	42	25	35	39	77	51
2. Canada		28	20	21	33	27	34	35	72	43
3. Germany			26	31	36	33	43	39	75	53
4. U.K.				26	34	30	36	37	78	49
5. Poland					24	29	36	36	77	38
6. U.S.S.R.						40	50	30	76	30
7. Italy							37	44	77	48
8. Hungary								46	81	49
9. Austria									81	80
10. Negro										80
11. Other Non-white										

BIRMINGHAM

Ethnic Group	2.	3.	4.	5.	6.	7.	8.	9.	10.	11.
1. NWNP	24	42	31	73	59	45	42	43	65	56
2. U.K.		45	33	70	56	45	42	41	71	60
3. Italy			50	81	68	61	54	55	65	59
4. Germany				61	50	35	39	45	77	58
5. U.S.S.R.					34	54	58	54	91	73
6. Poland						42	48	46	88	69
7. Canada							42	47	84	65
8. Ireland								53	76	51
9. Austria									82	64
10. Negro										67
11. Other Non-white										

CANTON

Ethnic Group	2.	3.	4.	5.	6.	7.	8.	9.	10.	11.
1. NWNP	17	29	21	25	42	25	35	39	77	51
2. Italy		28	20	21	33	27	34	35	72	43
3. Germany			26	31	36	33	43	38	75	53
4. U.K.				26	34	30	36	37	78	49
5. Czechoslovakia					24	29	36	36	77	38
6. Hungary						40	50	31	76	30
7. Poland							37	44	77	48
8. Austria								46	81	49
9. U.S.S.R.									81	44
10. Negro										80
11. Other Non-white										

TABLE 84--Continued

DES MOINES

Ethnic Group	2.	3.	4.	5.	6.	7.	8.	9.	10.	11.
1. NWNP	15	15	45	23	26	25	27	43	77	43
2. Germany		13	49	25	24	20	24	35	76	64
3. U.K.			48	19	26	20	28	38	78	44
4. Italy				53	54	52	55	66	85	64
5. Sweden					35	21	37	45	81	51
6. Canada						34	30	33	82	50
7. Norway							28	44	78	46
8. Ireland								43	73	44
9. U.S.S.R.									83	61
10. Negro										64
11. Other Non-white										

EL PASO

Ethnic Group	2.	3.	4.	5.	6.	7.	8.	9.	10.	11.
1. NWNP	46	26	26	21	23	45	61	32	73	30
2. Mexico		62	57	58	60	70	75	56	60	55
3. Germany			22	20	22	43	61	30	83	26
4. U.K.				21	29	44	58	29	80	35
5. Canada					21	37	55	33	80	30
6. Italy						38	63	32	74	26
7. Poland							33	50	83	43
8. U.S.S.R.								59	91	68
9. Ireland									80	41
10. Negro										30
11. Other Non-white										

HONOLULU

Ethnic Group	2.	3.	4.	5.	6.	7.	8.	9.	10.
1. Other Non-white	55	44	52	57	62	62	55	67	66
2. U.K.		32	32	45	41	51	39	33	64
3. Germany			26	41	37	42	47	40	55
4. Canada				40	37	40	38	37	56
5. Italy					47	39	53	52	46
6. Ireland						52	40	41	61
7. Poland							53	49	48
8. U.S.S.R.								44	66
9. Sweden									65
10. Negro									

LANCASTER

Ethnic Group	2.	3.	4.	5.	6.	7.	8.	9.	10.	11.
1. NWNP	21	24	20	37	35	16	32	26	87	37
2. Germany		34	30	43	38	26	34	29	87	46
3. Italy			31	49	47	33	43	37	83	49
4. U.K.				37	36	24	33	23	92	40
5. Canada					39	45	45	40	91	51

TABLE 84--*Continued*

LANCASTER--*Continued*

Ethnic Group	2.	3.	4.	5.	6.	7.	8.	9.	10.	11.
6. U.S.S.R.						35	40	33	83	49
7. Poland							32	32	91	39
8. Austria								36	87	46
9. Ireland									89	45
10. Negro										85
11. Other Non-white										

MINNEAPOLIS-ST. PAUL

Ethnic Group	2.	3.	4.	5.	6.	7.	8.	9.	10.	11.
1. NWNP	25	20	25	17	39	47	22	33	85	47
2. Sweden		27	13	25	43	51	28	40	83	48
3. Germany			29	22	37	46	25	26	83	48
4. Norway				25	47	51	28	42	81	45
5. Canada					40	43	22	36	84	47
6. Poland						46	45	38	85	57
7. U.S.S.R.							45	50	85	51
8. U.K.								36	84	51
9. Austria									86	56
10. Negro										73
11. Other Non-white										

PROVIDENCE-PAWTUCKET

Ethnic Group	2.	3.	4.	5.	6.	7.	8.	9.	10.	11.
1. NWNP	28	50	22	27	40	52	37	24	75	51
2. Canada		60	29	39	33	61	50	37	81	60
3. Italy			58	54	63	67	65	54	82	67
4. U.K.				31	40	54	40	29	80	58
5. Ireland					44	39	43	32	70	50
6. Poland						59	60	44	81	64
7. U.S.S.R.							53	46	73	59
8. Sweden								36	76	60
9. Germany									77	55
10. Negro										46
11. Other Non-white										

RICHMOND

Ethnic Group	2.	3.	4.	5.	6.	7.	8.	9.	10.	11.
1. NWNP	21	21	53	28	26	41	32	32	79	49
2. Germany		21	46	31	25	36	31	32	83	50
3. U.K.			52	28	29	42	32	37	81	52
4. U.S.S.R.				49	50	31	53	58	89	60
5. Italy					32	43	38	38	82	54
6. Canada						45	30	38	84	54
7. Poland							48	43	86	61
8. Ireland								44	83	56
9. Czechoslovakia									87	56

TABLE 84--Continued

RICHMOND--Continued

Ethnic Group	2.	3.	4.	5.	6.	7.	8.	9.	10.	11.
10. Negro										60
11. Other Non-white										

SAN BERNADINO-RIVERSIDE

Ethnic Group	2.	3.	4.	5.	6.	7.	8.	9.	10.	11.
1. NWNP	58	19	20	18	28	28	31	28	81	34
2. Mexico		63	63	64	64	65	68	66	55	54
3. Canada			19	22	31	26	31	30	84	38
4. U.K.				17	31	25	30	29	83	41
5. Germany					31	26	30	30	83	39
6. Italy						35	36	31	84	50
7. Sweden							35	33	84	42
8. U.S.S.R.								34	87	47
9. Poland									85	44
10. Negro										69
11. Other Non-white										

ST. PETERSBURG

Ethnic Group	2.	3.	4.	5.	6.	7.	8.	9.	10.	11.
1. NWNP	13	13	13	19	19	18	25	31	89	48
2. U.K.		10	12	19	17	20	24	30	89	51
3. Germany			13	18	16	17	21	29	90	48
4. Canada				19	19	19	23	31	91	49
5. Italy					20	23	23	31	88	49
6. Ireland						25	24	27	90	48
7. Sweden							28	37	90	53
8. Poland								27	91	48
9. U.S.S.R.									92	55
10. Negro										88
11. Other Non-white										

TAMPA

Ethnic Group	2.	3.	4.	5.	6.	7.	8.	9.	10.	11.
1. NWNP	18	16	20	45	27	25	25	39	84	39
2. U.K.		15	19	50	23	27	24	36	87	40
3. Germany			16	51	24	25	26	39	86	42
4. Canada				53	30	27	27	40	87	43
5. Italy					53	51	49	56	68	56
6. Ireland						31	31	44	86	47
7. Sweden							28	36	84	48
8. Poland								36	85	47
9. U.S.S.R.									88	56
10. Negro										71
11. Other Non-white										

high in Birmingham, the NWNP-British-German-Canadian grouping is still the most marked. In Canton the Italian, Czech and Polish groups are as equally associated with the NWNP majority as the German and British groups. In Honolulu European ethnic groups had high dissimilarity indices among themselves though these were lower than those between the majority other non-white group and the white ethnic groups.[1] In Lancaster British, Germans and Irish form a cluster, but the NWNP group shows strong associations with Italians and Poles as well as the "Anglo-Saxon" grouping. Canadians are not strongly associated with the "Anglo-Saxon" group. In St. Petersburg all inter-ethnic indices of dissimilarity involving white groups are low in comparison to the other cities studied. St. Petersburg is the most important retirement center in the eastern U.S. and most of the foreign stock recorded in the city will have migrated there from other metropolises. On this "second" settlement it is probable that ethnic ties are no longer as important as they were for the retirees: they are well established in American society, have made enough money to retire to Florida and do not need the succor of their original ethnic community. Nevertheless the British, German and Canadian groups still exhibit the lowest inter-ethnic indices of dissimilarity and form a distinct cluster.

Overall, in some eight cases out of thirteen, an ethnic cluster involving British, German and Canadian groups (and Swedish and Norwegian where these were analyzed) is clearly present and closely associated with third and later generation Americans. In a couple of other cases the cluster, though less pronounced, is still present and still the most prominent in Table 84, and in a further two

---

[1]Unfortunately, data on Oriental groups at the tract level was not available at the time of analysis. In 1960 the Census reported the composition of Honolulu's urbanized area population to be as follows: white 31 per cent, Chinese 9.1 per cent, Japanese 34.8 per cent, Filipino 8.3, Negro 0.7; of the remainder most were Hawaiian or Part-Hawaiian (16.1 per cent).

urbanized areas the cluster is present but not dominantly associated with the third and later generation group. Thus, there is considerable evidence for the existence of a residential patterning of American cities in which the white Anglo-Saxon Protestant groups coallesce and are spatially separated from other population groups.

The residential reality of the third residential melting pot, proposed, the Catholic, is difficult to assess. No common cluster of ethnic groups stands out in each city that would merit the label Catholic residential group, and we have no information on the distribution of the Catholic population to help us. In three urbanized areas the Italian foreign stock group stands out uniquely in the same way as the Russian group does: in Des Moines, in Providence-Pawtucket and in Tampa. If the indexes between pairs of groups whose members are mostly Catholic are examined few are as low as those in the white Anglo-Saxon Protestant grouping. For example, if we consider pairs of comparisons among Italians, Poles, Irish and Czechs, in only 7 comparisons out of 30 does the index of dissimilarity fall below 30. Three of these cases are in St. Petersburg where all inter-ethnic indices of dissimilarity fall below 30; another three are in Canton where Italians, Poles and Czechs together with the British stock group form a distinct cluster. In general, apart from these exceptions noted above, ethnic groups from Europe's "periphery" (Poles, Czechs, Austrians, Hungarians, Italians, Irish) are characterized by moderate sized indices of dissimilarity with each other and with the other European groups. This implies that each has its own special spatial distribution in the city but one that is not overly concentrated. These "peripheral" European groups share with the more "central" groups (that also include Canadians) a high degree of residential separation from Negro Americans.

Of the remaining ethnic groups Mexicans figure prominently only in El Paso and San Bernadino-Riverside as one might have expected given the distribution of these cities near the U.S. border with

Mexico. In El Paso and San Bernadino-Riverside Mexican Americans are residentially segregated from other groups in the city to a high degree though not as highly as Negro Americans.

The final group included in the tables is that of other non-whites, the composition of which in terms of its component groups undoubtedly varies considerably from city to city. In some urbanized areas Oriental groups (Chinese, Japanese, Filipino) figure prominently; in others American Indians may be the most important element. The value of the indices for this mixed group recorded in Table 84 is therefore somewhat dubious. In general other non-whites exhibit indices of dissimilarity when compared with other groups in the table in the 35 to 45 range. Their average index of residential segregation for the 13 urbanized areas was 43.34, well below that of Negroes and slightly below that for the Mexican and Russian groups. Their average index of dissimilarity when compared with NWNP was 44.78 and was again slightly below the equivalent figures for Russians and Mexicans.

How do these results compare with those for other U.S. cities? Kantrowitz (1969) has calculated indices of dissimilarity for some 13 ethnic groups for the New York-New Jersey Standard Consolidated Area and the New York SMSA for 1960. These are reproduced here in Table 85. The Russians, Austrians, Hungarians and Poles form one distinct cluster: in New York City the Russians are heavily Jewish, the Austrians, Poles and Hungarians largely Jewish. A second cluster links the British, Germans, Irish and Swedes. This "Anglo-Saxon" cluster is probably associated with the NWNP and Canadians though Kantrowitz does not report on these two groups. Italians are highly segregated from all other groups (a pattern we found in Des Moines, Providence-Pawtucket and Tampa), and also surprisingly so are the Norwegians (who were closely associated with the Swedes in Minneapolis-St. Paul and Des Moines in our study). The Norwegians' lowest index of dissimilarity is 45.4 with Swedes in contrast

TABLE 85

INTER-ETHNIC DISSIMILARITY INDICES FOR SELECTED ETHNICITIES IN NEW YORK, 1960

Ethnic Groups	1.	2.	3.	4.	5.	6.	7.	8.	9.	10.	11.	12.	13.
1. U.K.	...	31	50	32	26	45	42	41	43	52	43	80	81
2. Eire	28	...	56	42	34	50	48	46	47	55	46	79	77
3. Norway	51	59	...	45	52	66	64	65	66	71	59	88	88
4. Sweden	32	41	46	...	37	57	52	53	54	61	52	83	85
5. Germany	26	33	56	38	...	46	41	39	41	51	43	80	81
6. Poland	45	52	58	58	47	...	40	23	34	28	51	79	77
7. Czechoslovakia	40	45	66	51	40	42	...	41	34	53	51	82	81
8. Austria	40	47	68	54	40	20	40	...	30	21	50	80	77
9. Hungary	39	44	68	53	39	31	34	25	...	40	54	80	79
10. U.S.S.R.	50	57	73	62	52	20	49	19	33	...	59	81	78
11. Italy	45	48	60	52	46	53	52	53	54	61	...	79	78
12. Negro	80	80	88	84	81	80	82	82	80	82	80	...	66
13. Puerto Rican	80	77	88	84	80	76	79	77	76	78	78	64	....

Source: Kantrowitz, 1969, Table 6, p. 693.

The figures above the diagonal are for the New York-Northeasten New Jersey Standard Consolidated Area; those below are for the New York SMSA.

to 21 in Des Moines and 13 in Minneapolis-St. Paul. Could there be something about New York that makes even fellow Scandinavians antipathetic? In general, however, New York exhibits the same sort of ethnic associations as our wider sample of cities, albeit at a higher average level of residential segregation.

Inevitably, the ethnic segregation patterns of the "Second City" (Chicago) have been extensively studied. The work of Duncan and Lieberson (1959) revealed that the patterns of ethnic segregation had remained remarkably stable over the two decades between 1930 and 1950 (Table 86). The inter-annual correlation between corresponding indices in 1930 and 1950 is 0.93. Levels of segregation did decline somewhat, but not to a remarkable degree. By 1960 the levels of interethnic segregation had declined further, with some notable exceptions. The residential segregation of Negroes with all other groups fluctuated around the already high levels recorded in 1930 in the subsequent decades. The level of residential assimilation (as measured by the NWNP comparisons) increased over the 1930 to 1960 period for Americans of Polish, Czech and Italian descent. For groups already fairly well assimilated in 1930 (Swedes, Germans, British) the level of residential assimilation tended to fluctuate around the 1930 figure, though the Irish experienced slippage in residential assimilation over the three decades. The level of Russian assimilation declined somewhat between 1930 and 1950 but had increased again by 1960. Since groups that had been equally clustered in 1930 as the Russians continued to experience a fall in their index of dissimilarity with native whites of native parents, this suggests a maintenance of a strong group and community preference among Americans of Russian origin, which we have earlier suggested is related to their largely Jewish identity.

Previous work on Chicago (Rees, 1970b, pp. 339-344) confirmed the existence in 1960 of an "Anglo-Saxon" cluster of ethnic groups comprising native whites of native parents, British-Americans,

TABLE 86

INDICES OF DISSIMILARITY AMONG RESIDENTIAL DISTRIBUTIONS OF SELECTED ETHNIC GROUPS IN CHICAGO, 1930 AND 1950

Ethnic Groups in 1930	1.	2.	3.	4.	5.	6.	7.	8.	9.	10.	11.	12.
1. NWNP	...	13	26	28	28	63	61	33	56	64	54	—
2. England and Wales	9	...	25	31	35	65	60	34	50	63	53	84
3. Irish Free State	22	20	...	42	44	68	64	44	60	62	57	84
4. Sweden	24	24	36	...	35	74	69	45	66	73	67	90
5. Germany	20	27	34	25	...	58	59	22	56	66	57	89
6. Poland	64	69	69	71	58	...	47	49	57	51	59	93
7. Czechoslovakia	59	62	61	66	56	50	...	49	63	50	64	93
8. Austria	29	35	38	37	20	50	47	...	48	57	52	88
9. U.S.S.R.	47	47	50	55	48	64	62	42	...	69	57	90
10. Lithuania	61	63	60	68	61	52	46	52	66	...	66	91
11. Italy	51	54	55	63	54	61	64	51	56	66	...	79
12. Negro	—	84	85	90	88	94	93	90	90	91	80	...
Ethnic Groups in 1950	**1.**	**2.**	**3.**	**4.**	**5.**	**6.**	**7.**	**8.**	**9.**	**10.**	**11.**	**12.**
1. NW	...	19	32	33	27	45	49	18	44	52	41	—
2. England and Wales			29	30	30	58	56	26	38	57	46	78
3. Ireland (Eire)				40	44	67	63	38	54	60	52	81
4. Sweden					32	68	66	39	54	66	61	86
5. Germany						56	47	21	47	54	54	85
6. Poland							44	47	58	51	53	91
7. Czechoslovakia								48	61	51	56	89
8. Austria									46	54	46	83
9. U.S.S.R.										68	58	87
10. Lithuania											62	85
11. Italy												70
12. Negro												

Notes Source: Duncan and Lieberson, 1959, Table 1, 2, and 3.

[b]In the first half of the table are the indices for 1930, Foreign Born White above the diagonal, Native White of Foreign and Mixed Parents below the diagonal. In the second half of the table are the indices for 1950 FBWs only. The area of study is the city of Chicago and the areal units used are the Community Areas of the city which are made up of integral numbers of census tracts.

TABLE 87

INDICES OF DISSIMILARITY AMONG SELECTED ETHNIC GROUPS IN CHICAGO, 1960

Ethnic Groups	1.	2.	3.	4.	5.	6.	7.	8.	9.	10.	11.	12.	13.	14.
1. NWNP	...	37	20	30	44	33	38	31	20	19	10	82	55	33
2. Poland	41	...	40	44	54	58	37	55	49	48	40	93	75	48
3. Germany	20	41	...	40	42	38	43	26	22	22	21	88	55	30
4. Italy	32	40	37	...	58	46	46	49	40	40	35	81	65	38
5. U.S.S.R.	48	52	47	56	...	53	60	43	39	39	44	90	60	49
6. Ireland (Eire)	36	50	37	42	51	...	50	34	24	27	38	84	65	38
7. Czechoslovakia	43	43	40	46	65	52	...	51	44	44	36	89	72	41
8. Sweden	27	52	21	45	48	37	46	...	21	20	32	85	56	38
9. U.K.	18	49	18	39	46	30	41	17	...	8	22	83	57	27
10. Canada	17	48	19	40	46	32	43	18	8	...	20	81	53	26
11. Foreign Stock[a]	21	38	27	34	43	34	47	33	27	27	...	85	58	33
12. Negro[b]	82	89	85	81	86	82	89	84	82	81	82	...	75	83
13. Other Non-white[b]													...	51
14. Rest of Population	32	44	26	35	48	35	46	32	24	24	29	80		...

Source: Calculated from census data in Kitagawa and Taeuber (1963).

The figures above the diagonal are for the City of Chicago using data for the 75 community areas of of the City. The Community Areas consist of whole numbers of census tracts. The figures below the diagonal are for the Chicago SMSA using data for the 75 Community Areas, the large suburbs of the metropolis and a large residual zone comprising the rest of the metropolis.

[a]Each foreign stock group is compared to the rest of the foreign stock. Negroes are compared with all the foreign stock group.

TABLE 87--Continued

Notes--Continued

[b]For the SMSA analysis the group non-whites was used rather than the two groups Negro and Other Non-white, as the latter were not easily available.

[c]The index of residential segregation was calculated for each foreign stock group and the rest of the population.

TABLE 88

MEAN INDICES OF DISSIMILARITY FOR CLUSTERS OF FOREIGN STOCK GROUPS, CHICAGO, 1930, 1950 AND 1960

	1930 FBW City	1930 NWFMP City	1950 FBW City	1960 FS City	1960 FS SMSA
Between members of group 1	35.8	29.7	32.9	24.2	23.7
Between members of group 2	58.2	58.7	56.0	49.8	50.3
Between members of group 1 and those of group 2	60.0	57.3	54.6	45.7	45.2

Notes

Group 1 in 1930 and 1950 consisted of Foreign Born Whites or Native Whites of Foreign or Mixed Parents from England and Wales, Eire, Sweden, Germany and Austria.

Group 2 in 1930 and 1950 consisted of FBW and NWFMP from Poland, Czechoslovakia, U.S.S.R., Lithuania and Italy.

Group 1 in 1960 consisted of Foreign Stock from U.K., Canada, Eire, Germany and Sweden.

Group 2 in 1960 consisted of Foreign Stock from Poland, Czechoslovakia, U.S.S.R., and Italy.

Source for table: averages calculated from Tables 86 and 87.

Canadian-Americans, Irish-Americans, Swedish-Americans and German Americans. Russians had their own special spatial distribution and were so closely associated with the Jewish population variable that

TABLE 89

AVERAGE INTER-ETHNIC DISSIMILARITY INDICES FOR SELECTED U.S. URBANIZED AREAS, 1960

Urbanized Area	Index	City, SMSA or SCA	Index
Ann Arbor	32.59	New York-Northeastern New Jersey SCA	46.40
Birmingham	49.05	New York SMSA	46.23
Canton	32.60	Chicago FBW 1930	54.2
Des Moines	33.76	Chicago NWFMP 1930	51.5
El Paso	42.16	Chicago FBW 1950	50.1
Honolulu	41.76	Chicago FS City 1960	38.4
Lancaster	33.83	Chicago FS SMSA 1960	32.0
Minneapolis-St. Paul	34.18		
Providence-Pawtucket	44.42		
Richmond	37.10		
San Bernadino-Riverside	35.87		
St. Petersburg	21.41		
Tampa	32.45		

Sources:

Calculated from Tables 84, 85, 86 and 87. Foreign stock groups only are included in the inter-ethnic average.

the two groups were regarded as largely overlapping in membership. Poles, Czechs and Italians were shown to be associated with the Catholic population variable, and weakly with each other. Tables 86 and 87 reveal these earlier conclusions to be substantially correct: an "Anglo-Saxon" clustering of groups that includes the NWNP, British, Canadian, Germans, Swedish, Irish and Austrians shows up in 1930, 1950 and 1960. Mean indices of dissimilarity within the cluster and between members and groups outside the cluster show this clearly (Table 88). The other ethnic groups not in the "Anglo-Saxon" cluster do not appear to associate together, and, in fact, on average have lower indices of dissimilarity with members of the "Anglo-Saxon" cluster than with the remaining ethnic groups. Each of these groups (Poles, Czechs, Lithuanians, Italians) had its own individual distribution in the city, which was characterized by:

> a multiplicity of ethnic colonies scattered among the residential areas occupied by the native population rather than...a single 'ghetto' for all foreign or Catholic groups (Duncan and Lieberson, 1959).

Overall levels of interethnic segregation varied considerably from city to city (Table 89). Interethnic segregation in New York, as reported by Kantrowitz (1969), appears high compared with the urban areas studied except for Birmingham and Providence-Pawtucket. The Middle Western cities have moderate levels of interethnic residential segregation (32-35), the Southwestern cities have slightly higher levels, probably as a result of the indices involving Mexican Americans. The average segregation level for European and Canadian foreign stock groups only is 37 for El Paso and only 28 for San Bernadino-Riverside. The lowest average interethnic dissimilarity index value is found in St. Petersburg. Many of the index values in the interethnic table for St. Petersburg must be in the random allocation range. For most of the foreign stock inhabitants of St. Petersburg the area is probably one of retirement. The indices of dissimilarity suggest that for people who decide to retire ethnic ties have weakened, and are not of very great importance in deciding a retirement residential location within the St. Petersburg urbanized area. St. Petersburg thus represents the American melting pot at work. However, it is still an exclusively white melting pot.

Tampa shares some of its Gulf coast neighbor's characteristics as a retirement center: however, the relatively high residential segregation of Italians raises the average index level somewhat above that of St. Petersburg. San Bernadino-Riverside may also have "second settlement" characteristics with its low average value of 28 for inter-ethnic indices involving only European and Canadian foreign stock groups. Negroes and Mexican Americans are excluded from the melting pot, however.

Conclusions

In concluding this chapter it would be useful to draw together comments that can be made about the determinants of the spatial patterns of racial and ethnic groups in American cities.

If the only factors influencing those patterns were the "normal" set of residential location determinants (resources for housing expenditure, preferences as to size and type of home, distance of home from work) then we would expect to account for the differences between spatial distributions of various groups using differences in the characteristics of those groups that affected the "normal" residential choice determinants. However, a comparison of white and non-white distributions revealed that relatively little of the residential segregation observed could be ascribed to white-non-white differences in incomes or in housing expenditure. Although no direct information was available for the sample set of cities on the socioeconomic differences among European ethnic groups these are unlikely to be as large as white-non-white differences except in the case of Mexican Americans or Puerto Ricans, and thus even less of the inter-ethnic residential segregation observed could be ascribed to these "normal" residential choice factors.

This is not to deny that the economic status of a group does not determine the kind of housing occupied. But the type of housing commensurate with the economic position of the group is available in many more neighborhoods in the metropolis than are ever occupied by an ethnic group.

Racial and ethnic group preference for living among co-ethnics was suggested as an alternative explanation for the spatial patterns observed. But these preferences were difficult to distinguish from preferences not to live in the same area as members of other racial or ethnic groups. It was suggested that the differences in residential segregation level between the most segregated of the non-Negro ethnic groups and that of Negroes themselves represented a minimum estimate of the amount of extra segregation imposed on Negroes by the exclusion practices of other groups. The average size of this difference was some 24 points on the 100 point scale of the residential segregation index. One metropolitan area, Birmingham, did not lend itself to this interpretation as Russians and Poles had higher residential segregation indices. Jews probably predominate in both ethnic groups in Birmingham and may also suffer exclusion from native southern white residential areas. The spatial separation revealed to exist between native whites of native parents and the various ethnic groups paralleled remarkably the scale of "racial" distance derived by Bogardus in his survey of attitudes to foreign groups. This lent strength to the preference argument.

The influence of public bodies or institutions on the racial and ethnic patterns was fairly small because little of the housing stock in any of the cities was in public or institutional hands. In Honolulu, however, there are extensive areas of military housing occupied on a racially integrated basis, and this may explain the lower level of residential separation of Negroes from white ethnic groups in Honolulu than in cities on the mainland. Tracts largely occupied by a military base or mental hospital occur in most metropolitan areas, and these show a mixed racial and ethnic composition. Their contribution to the overall spatial pattern was small.

Explicit comment on trends through time in the spatial patterning of racial and ethnic groups in the sample metropolises was not possible. However, comparison of the mean indices of dissimilarity of white ethnic groups and native whites of native parents for the metropolitan areas included in this study with very similar measures reported by Lieberson (1963) (Table 90) suggests that levels of

TABLE 90

UNWEIGHTED MEAN INDICES OF RESIDENTIAL DISSIMILARITY BETWEEN FOREIGN STOCK GROUPS AND NATIVE WHITES OF NATIVE PARENTS

Results of Present Study

	SMSA 1960 FS vs NWNP	UA 1960 Fs vs NWNP	City 1960 FS vs NWNP
Ann Arbor	31.17	29.15	
Birmingham	46.87	44.73	
Canton	30.84	27.83	
Des Moines	27.40	26.95	
El Paso	34.83	35.00	
Lancaster	38.78	26.52	
Minneapolis-St. Paul	28.83	28.33	
Providence-Pawtucket	36.45	35.09	
Richmond	32.78	31.63	
San Bernadino-Riverside-Ontario	29.91	28.55	
Tampa-St. Petersburg	32.53		
St. Petersburg		18.81	
Tampa		26.97	
Chicago	31.33		31.33

Lieberson's Results (Lieberson, 1963, Table 4, p. 46)

	City 1930 FBW vs NWNP and NWFMP vs NWNP averaged	City 1950 FBW vs NW
Boston	40.6	37.5
Buffalo	41.3	38.3
Chicago	40.5	35.9
Cincinnati	40.1	39.9
Cleveland	47.6	40.1
Columbus	43.6	38.3
Philadelphia	45.2	40.8
Pittsburgh	43.9	38.4
St. Louis	40.0	37.6
Syracuse	46.2	39.3
Chicago[a]	40.6	36.0

Notes [a]Duncan and Lieberson, 1959, Tables 1, 2, and 3.

residential segregation among foreign stock groups are continuing to decline and that such groups are continuing to disperse in metropolitan areas. Our previous observations on this decline in Chicago confirm this conclusion. One factor aiding such a process is that recent arrivals in most groups have been higher in social and economic status than prior immigrants with the exception of Mexican Americans and Puerto Ricans. However, no such trend of dispersion was observed for Negro Americans.

The principal patterns of inter-ethnic residential segregation were three.

A clustering of white Protestant groups usually including native whites of native parents occurred in most cities. This group tended to be more concentrated in the suburban areas of the metropolis than the general population.

There was a concentration of Jewish population in a small number of neighborhoods of high socioeconomic status. This concentration was usually identified by the pattern of Russian foreign stock segregation, though undoubtedly the Jewish community of each city contained members of German, Polish and Austrian origin as well.

The remaining ethnic groups had their own particular distributions in each city. These spatial distributions were in general separate and distinct from those of other ethnic groups, except in a few cities where they were a particularly dominant group from which it was probable that a good proportion of the native stock was derived. In that case, the ethnic group might be fairly closely associated with the native white of native parentage population (as the Italians were in Canton).

We have now completed our survey of the spatial patterns in 1960 in American cities of the main dimensions of residential area differentiation identified in Chapter III. In general, each dimension (socioeconomic status, family status and racial status) has been examined independently though we have commented from time to time on the connections between the main dimensions. We now bring these comments together in a discussion of the interrelationships between the dimensions in the next chapter.

CHAPTER IX

RELATIONSHIPS BETWEEN THE DIMENSIONS

In this chapter we draw together some threads that have appeared from time to time in earlier chapters. We examine first the association between racial status and socioeocnomic status that has been apparent since Chapter III and attempt some rather more precise statements about the degree of association in each city. We then look at the degree of association between family status and socioeconomic status, and carry out a formal statistical test of their independence.

The Association between Racial Status and Socioeconomic Status

Conclusions from the Factor Analyses

In analyzing the factorial dimensions of the population variable set in Chapter III, we noted that in some cases, as in Birmingham or El Paso, the major socioeconomic status factor included a high loading of the variable "Pct Negro" or "Pct Mexican," and that in other cases, the racial status factor included several moderate loadings of socioeconomic status variables. These findings clearly indicate a substantial degree of association between the concepts "socioeconomic status" and "racial/ethnic status" and that this degree of association tended to vary from city to city.

Table 91 extracts some of the evidence for these observations from Chapter III. In column (5) of the table an assessment of the degree of association is made by assigning ranks to the urbanized areas. Rank I indicates that racial status and socioeconomic status are highly associated; rank II that the association is moderately high; rank III that the link is still present to a degree; and rank IV that the association is fairly weak, though still characteristic

TABLE 91

A RANKING OF THE FACTOR ANALYSES

Urbanized Area	(1)	(2)	(3)	(4)	(5)	(6)
Ann Arbor	-0.439		Yes	Yes	III	
Birmingham	-0.811		Yes	No	I	
Canton	-0.383		Yes	Yes	III	
Des Moines	-0.388		No	No	IV	
El Paso	0.034	-0.895	Yes	No	IV	I
Honolulu	-0.096		Yes	Yes	III	
Lancaster	-0.571		No	No	III-IV	
Minneapolis-St. Paul	-0.291		No	No	IV	
Providence-Pawtucket	-0.164		Yes	Yes	III	
Richmond	-0.376		Yes	Yes	II	
San Bernadino-Riverside	-0.115	-0.235	Yes	Yes	III	II
St. Petersburg	-0.467		Yes	Yes	II	
Tampa	-0.486		Yes	Yes	II	

Notes

Columns:

(1) Loading of Per Cent Negro on Factor 1.
(2) Loading of Per Cent Mexican on Factor 1.
(3) A Factor Listed in Table 11.
(4) "Race and Resources" type factor.
(5) Ranking in terms of association between socioeconomic status and racial status.
(6) Ranking in terms of association between socioeconomic status and Mexican American status.

of the city's social geography. In order to measure the degree of association more precisely we turn to the aggregate crosstabulations by color of the socioeconomic characteristics of SMSA populations in 1960.

The Crosstabulations of Education, Occupation and Income by Color: An Example

Tables which show the educational, occupational and income distributions of whites and non-whites (and in the case of El Paso and San Bernadino-Riverside-Ontario, of whites with Spanish surnames) can be constructed for the sample SMSAs and UAs from information given in the SMSA tract volumes and the State volumes of the Census of Population and Housing. They cannot be constructed for the Negro populations of the sample study areas except by application of special estimation procedures. However, Negroes make up a substantial majority (over 75 per cent) of the non-white population in all the cities studied except Honolulu and comprise over 90 per cent of the non-white populations of Birmingham, Canton, Des Moines, Lancaster, Providence-Pawtucket, Richmond and Tampa-St. Petersburg SMSAs. The crosstabulations will reflect, in a general way, the status of black Americans vis à vis white Americans. If the population of other non-white races in the particular SMSA or UA is largely of oriental origin, the distributions will probably be biased upwardly; if American Indians figure importantly they are less likely to be. In other words, the differentials revealed between white and non-white populations in the tables are unlikely to be over-estimates of the differentials between whites and blacks.

The educational and income tables for Canton, Ohio (Table 92) show features typical of most of the urbanized areas, save Honolulu. In terms of educational and income distributions the white part of the population is more favorably distributed than the non-white, though it must be stressed that a substantial number of non-white families are firmly ensconced in the middle class.

Measures of Association in Crosstabulations: Methods

To measure more precisely the differences between white and non-white socioeconomic distributions (so as to be able to compare distributions in different cities) a number of summary indices of association for cross-classifications were computed for each table as a whole, and these were supplemented with a set of measures specific to each row class in the tables. This set of measures make clear the direction of association evident in the tables.

The first measure of association used is the Index of

TABLE 92

THE EDUCATIONAL AND INCOME DISTRIBUTIONS FOR WHITES AND NON-WHITES IN CANTON URBANIZED AREA, 1960 AND FOR THE U.S. URBAN POPULATION

Years of School Completed	Per Cent of Total in Group			
	White		Non-white	
	Canton	U.S.	Canton	U.S.
None	1.56	2.0	3.15	4.2
Elementary: 1 to 4	3.55	4.0	12.12	14.4
Elementary: 5 to 7	11.22	11.2	25.28	21.7
Elementary 8	19.78	16.6	16.41	13.6
High School: 4	30.04	26.8	13.68	16.8
College: 1 to 3	7.12	10.2	3.59	5.2
College: 4 or More	5.79	9.4	1.66	4.1
Total, Persons 25 Years or More	100.00	100.0	100.00	100.0

Income Category	Per Cent of Total in Group			
	White		Non-white	
	Canton	U.S.	Canton	U.S.
Under $1,000	2.57	3.0	9.29	10.4
$1,000 - $1,999	3.92	4.7	11.79	14.0
$2,000 - $2,999	5.69	6.1	10.59	15.2
$3,000 - $3,999	7.38	7.8	15.01	14.7
$4,000 - $4,999	11.53	10.3	17.22	13.0
$5,000 - $5,999	14.51	12.9	13.19	10.2
$6,000 - $6,999	13.51	12.0	7.67	6.9
$7,000 - $7,999	10.77	10.1	5.07	4.7
$8,000 - $8,	8.10	8.0	3.15	3.4
$9,000 - $9,999	5.98	6.0	3.38	2.4
$10,000 or Over	16.05	19.2	3.64	5.2
Total, Families	100.00	100.0	100.00	100.0

Source: Calculated from data in U.S. Bureau of the Census (1962a) and (1962b).

Dissimilarity, much used in the measurement of the spatial association between two ethnic groups but in fact suitable for use in measuring association in any n x 2 table, where n is the number of rows. This index has a maximum value of 100 indicating no association between the columns of an $n \times 2$ table and a minimum value of 0 indicating complete association between the two columns, in our case the white and non-white populations of the urbanized areas.

The second measure employed is derived from one suggested by Goodman and Kruskal (1954). This measure called Tau B, has the advantage over many of the other measures described in Goodman and Kruskal's paper in that it utilizes a relatively large amount of the information given in the table. What the index does is to measure the relative decrease in the proportion of incorrect predictions as one goes from using simply p_{*1}, the probability of column class 1, and p_{*2}, the probability of column class 2 as the basis for guessing in which column class a randomly chosen individual would fall, to using probability p_{a1}/p_{a*} (the conditional probability of column class 1 given row class a) to guess column class 1, p_{a2}/p_{a*} to guess column class 2 and so on. This relative decrease is given by:

$$\text{Tau B} = \sum_{a=1}^{n} \sum_{b=1}^{m} p_{ab}^{2}/p_{a*} - \sum_{b=1}^{m} p_{*b}^{2}/(1 - \sum_{b=1}^{m} p_{*b}^{2}) \qquad (16)$$

where p_{ab} is probability of a person falling in row a and column b, which is given by the total in cell ab of the table divided by the grand total; p_{a*} is $\sum_{b=1}^{m} p_{ab}$, which equals the probability of a person falling in row a of the table, which is given by the row a total divided by the grand total. There are $a = 1,\ldots,n$ rows, and p_{*b} is $\sum_{a=1}^{n} p_{ab}$, which equals the probability of a person falling in column b of the table, which is given by the column b total divided by the grand total. There are $b = 1,\ldots,m$ columns.
In this case m (the number of columns in the table) is equal to two. The Tau B index can be readily re-expressed in the chi-square-like form

$$\text{Tau B} = \sum_{a=1}^{n} \sum_{b=1}^{m} ((p_{ab} - p_{a*}p_{*b})^2/p_{a*})/(1 - \sum_{b=1}^{m} p_{*b}^2) \quad (17)$$

Tau B takes values between zero and one; it is 0 if and only if there is independence, and 1 if and only if knowledge of row membership completely determines column membership.

An analogous Tau A index can be calculated simply be substituting a for b and b for a in the Tau B formulae. The question asked in this case would be different. It would be: what is the relative decrease in incorrect predictions as we go from knowing the probability of being in a row to knowing the probability of being in a row given the column? How much better, in other words, can we predict a man's occupation in a given urbanized area with a certain occupational distribution if we also know his color? Of course, the answer to this question could also be given by transposing the table and calculating Tau B.

One problem with these summary association measures is that the direction of association is not indicated. In many crosstabulations the classes are not in any particular ordering or ranking, but in the case of the education and income distributions the rows are clearly ranked in terms of more or less years of schooling or more or less dollars of income. The ranking of occupations is a little more ambiguous, but certainly professionals and managers can be ranked above clerical, sales and craft workers, who can be ranked above operatives, who can be ranked above service workers and laborers, who can be ranked above private household workers. Within each group mentioned the ranking varies according to the basis adopted (education needed, income received, prestige accorded, or whether males or females or both are considered). To establish the direction of the association the following measure of white-non-white differential was calculated for each row class in the tables:

$$\text{Diff}_a = (N_{a2}/N_{*2})/(N_{a1}/N_{*1}) \quad (18)$$

where N_{a2} is the number of non-whites in row class a, N_{*2} is the number of non-whites (persons or families) in all the row classes, N_{a1} is the number of whites of row class a, and N_{*1} is the number of whites in all the row classes.

Measures of Association in Crosstabulations: Results

The index of dissimilarity, Tau A and Tau B values for the 13 urbanized areas for the three socioeconomic distributions by color are recorded in Table 93, and Table 94 contains the equivalent values for non-whites, whites of non-Spanish surname, and whites of Spanish surnames for El Paso and San Bernadino-Riverside. The values of the non-white/white differentials in socioeconomic category membership are shown in Tables 95 and 96. In practically all cases the crosstabulations reveal that the non-white group is disadvantageously distributed vis à vis the white population. This is most clearly apparent if the educational and income differentials for a selected few cities are plotted graphically (Figure 64). In general the lines plotted on the graphs slope from left to right; they are above unity to the left and below unity to the right. This means a greater proportion of non-whites than whites are concentrated at the lower ends of the educational and income (and occupational) spectra. The plot for the U.S. urban population as a whole is included on the graph as a point of reference together with three of the thirteen urbanized areas: Birmingham, Des Moines, and Minneapolis-St. Paul. Birmingham and Minneapolis-St. Paul lie at the opposite ends of the spectrum from the point of view of non-white/white differentials: in Birmingham from 3 to 8 times more blacks are found in the two lowest education and income categories as would be the case if they had the same educational and income distributions as whites. Similarly, only a third to a tenth as many blacks are found in the upper two categories of the distributions as would be the case if they had the same educational and income distributions as whites. The corresponding range of ratios for Minneapolis-St. Paul is from 2 to 4 times as many non-whites as whites at the lower end and from two thirds to a third as many non-whites at the higher end except in the last category in the educational distribution where non-whites achieve near equality with whites. The plot for Des Moines lies in between the two extremes and near the U.S. average.

What is strikingly clear from the graphs and from Tables 93, 94 and 95 is the consistency and strength of Negro disadvantage vis à vis whites, particularly when their position is compared with that of other minorities. Mexican Americans in El Paso and San Bernadino-Riverside-Ontario start off at an even greater educational disadvantage than Negroes (Table 94) but by the time this educational disadvantage is translated into monetary remuneration differentials have been substantially reduced to levels about the U.S. urban average for non-white/white differentials in the case of El Paso and substantially below this average in the case of San Bernadino-Riverside-Ontario. The same lack of a carry-through of educational disadvantage occurs in Honolulu for a non-white population of mainly Oriental origin. In fact, when the white and non-white income distributions are examined the disadvantage is with the white population, particularly at the lower end of the income distribution (Table 95).

When non-white/white differentials for education and income are examined they display fairly (though not absolutely) monotonic functions. The occupational differentials are both more pronounced and less regular from city to city. The non-white/white differentials lead to a ranking of male and female occupations rather different from that suggested in Chapter V. The lowest ranked occupations for both males and females are private household workers, laborers, service workers and operatives, in that order. In the first three non-whites are heavily concentrated in almost all urbanized areas in the

TABLE 93

MEASURES OF ASSOCIATION FOR EDUCATION, OCCUPATION AND INCOME CROSSTABULATIONS FOR THE SAMPLE URBANIZED AREAS, 1960

Urbanized Area	Education Crosstabulations		
	D	Tau A	Tau B
Ann Arbor	27.44	0.0490	0.0052
Birmingham	35.41	0.1797	0.0226
Canton	27.39	0.0279	0.0040
Des Moines	23.98	0.0160	0.0018
El Paso	14.52	0.0028	0.0004
Honolulu	21.41	0.0861	0.0088
Lancaster	31.98	0.0240	0.0019
Minneapolis-St. Paul	15.68	0.0030	0.0004
Providence-Pawtucket	13.21	0.0015	0.0002
Richmond	31.86	0.1352	0.0169
San Bernadino-Riverside	15.26	0.0064	0.0010
St. Petersburg	40.28	0.0938	0.0085
Tampa	34.16	0.0972	0.0118
Urbanized Area	Income Crosstabulations		
	D	Tau A	Tau B
Ann Arbor	26.72	0.0308	0.0043
Birmingham	47.23	0.2457	0.0249
Canton	32.82	0.0333	0.0028
Des Moines	35.87	0.0297	0.0024
El Paso	27.72	0.0086	0.0010
Honolulu	11.01	0.0244	0.0016
Lancaster	36.63	0.0103	0.0015
Minneapolis-St. Paul	29.66	0.0103	0.0009
Providence-Pawtucket	31.95	0.0114	0.0009
Richmond	47.21	0.2202	0.0212
San Bernadino-Riverside	31.02	0.0196	0.0020
St. Petersburg	27.07	0.0233	0.0024
Tampa	34.04	0.0625	0.0064
Urbanized Area	Male Occupation Crosstabulations		
	D	Tau A	Tau B
Ann Arbor	30.45	0.0415	0.0051
Birmingham	57.15	0.3336	0.0474
Canton	37.22	0.0591	0.0066
Des Moines	38.09	0.0449	0.0039
El Paso	33.91	0.0281	0.0025
Honolulu	24.48	0.0526	0.0082
Lancaster	43.59	0.0330	0.0031
Minneapolis-St. Paul	32.73	0.0211	0.0019
Providence-Pawtucket	25.47	0.0084	0.0008
Richmond	53.94	0.2877	0.0333
San Bernadino-Riverside	31.72	0.0208	0.0023
St. Petersburg	55.48	0.1751	0.0199
Tampa	50.47	0.2043	0.0262

TABLE 93--Continued

Urbanized Area	Female Occupation Crosstabulations		
	D	Tau A	Tau B
Ann Arbor	47.52	0.1244	0.0230
Birmingham	67.86	0.5281	0.1323
Canton	49.30	0.1346	0.0161
Des Moines	44.04	0.0543	0.0090
El Paso	52.33	0.0352	0.0068
Honolulu	19.01	0.0455	0.0075
Lancaster	50.67	0.0638	0.0078
Minneapolis-St. Paul	33.77	0.0102	0.0021
Providence-Pawtucket	34.28	0.0371	0.0023
Richmond	61.28	0.4494	0.0927
San Bernadino-Riverside	38.87	0.0639	0.0086
St. Petersburg	61.66	0.3763	0.0586
Tampa	63.20	0.4361	0.0717

TABLE 94

MEASURES OF ASSOCIATION FOR EDUCATION AND INCOME CROSSTABULATIONS FOR EL PASO AND SAN BERNADINO-RIVERSIDE, 1960

Measure	El Paso SMSA	San Bernadino-Riverside-Ontario SMSA	El Paso SMSA	San Bernadino-Riverside-Ontario SMSA
	Educational Crosstabulations		Income Crosstabulations	
Index of Dissimilarity				
NW vs WS	41.56	20.84	13.45	16.41
NW vs WNS	17.30	21.50	38.44	31.23
WS vs WNS	54.30	38.49	32.04	20.23
Tau Indices				
Tau A: NW, W	0.0039	0.0086	0.0091	0.0185
Tau A: NW, WS, WNS	0.3201	0.1042	0.1176	0.0231
Tau B: NW, W	0.0006	0.0011	0.0011	0.0017
Tau B: NW, WS, WNS	0.0525	0.0112	0.0147	0.0040

Notes

NW Non-white
WS White: Spanish Surname
WNS White: Non-Spanish Surname

sample. The differential values hover around 1.0 for the operative category: slightly lower than one for female operatives, slightly greater than one for male occupations. Craft, professional, managerial and sales occupations are ranked in that order in terms of non-white/white differentials for the U.S. urban population as a whole for both males and females. The shifted position of professional occupations undoubtedly reflects the operation of objective and universal criteria of selection which make it easier for non-whites to gain entry to the professions than to business jobs (managerial and sales), particularly those "up front" (sales jobs). Clerical occupations occupy different positions along the differential scale in the male than in the female category, though the reason for this is not entirely clear.

A Comparative Assessment of the Association between Racial and Socioeconomic Status

It has been pointed out that the urbanized areas in the sample studied differ considerably in the strength of non-white/white differentials in socioeconomic status. The indices recorded in Table 93 enable us to be a little more precise about the position of the various urban areas on a scale of comparative disadvantage for non-whites. The ranking of the urbanized areas (averaging over the 12 measures recorded in Table 93) is as follows:

1. Birmingham
2. Richmond
3. Tampa
4. St. Petersburg
5. Canton
6. Ann Arbor
7. Des Moines
8. Lancaster
9. Honolulu
10. San Bernadino-Riverside
11. El Paso
12. Minneapolis-St. Paul
13. Providence-Pawtucket

The southern cities in the sample (Birmingham, Richmond, Tampa and St. Petersburg) are clearly distinguished from the other cities by the degree of association revealed in Table 93 between color and social status. Southern cities clearly offered in 1960 their Negro citizens less opportunity vis à vis their white citizens than did other parts of the nation, and this difference was reflected in the

TABLE 95

NON-WHITE/WHITE DIFFERENTIALS IN SOCIOECONOMIC CATEGORY MEMBERSHIP IN 13 URBANIZED AREAS, 1960

Social Category	Ann Arbor	Birmingham	Canton	Des Moines
Educational Categories				
No Schooling	2.9	7.9	2.0	3.9
Elementary: 1 to 4 Years	5.9	6.3	3.4	3.9
Elementary: 5 to 7 Years	2.6	1.9	2.3	2.0
Elementary: 8 Years	1.1	1.0	0.8	1.1
High School: 1 to 3 Years	1.5	0.8	1.2	1.4
High School: 4 Years	0.6	0.5	0.5	0.6
College: 1 to 3 Years	0.5	0.3	0.5	0.6
College: 4 Years or More	0.5	0.3	0.3	0.4
Occupations (Male)				
Professional, technical and kindred workers	0.5	0.2	0.3	0.5
Managers, officials and proprietors, exc. farm	0.2	0.1	0.2	0.1
Clerical and kindred workers	0.6	0.3	0.5	0.8
Sales Workers	0.2	0.1	0.1	0.2
Craftsmen, foremen and kindred workers	1.0	0.4	0.6	0.6
Operatives and kindred workers	1.5	2.1	1.1	1.1
Private household workers	6.2	25.0	7.8	15.2
Service workers exc. private household	2.3	3.7	1.8	4.9
Laborers	3.9	10.5	4.9	3.3
Occupations (Female)				
Professional, technical and kindred workers	0.5	0.6	0.4	0.5
Managers, officials and proprietors, exc. farm	0.1	0.2	0.4	0.1
Clerical and kindred workers	0.3	0.1	0.2	0.4
Sales workers	0.0	0.1	0.3	0.3
Craftsmen, foremen and kindred workers	0.5	0.3	0.2	0.6
Operatives and kindred workers	1.0	1.5	0.8	0.9
Private household workers	5.3	36.2	8.7	5.5
Service workers, exc. private household	2.6	3.2	1.9	2.8
Laborers	2.0	8.5	4.2	1.6
Income Classes				
Under $1,000	2.7	5.7	3.6	3.4
$1,000 to $1,999	2.2	4.0	3.0	3.7
$2,000 to $2,999	2.1	2.6	1.9	2.4
$3,000 to $3,999	1.8	2.1	2.0	2.0
$4,000 to $4,999	1.7	1.2	1.5	1.5
$5,000 to $5,999	1.3	0.6	0.9	0.8
$6,000 to $6,999	0.9	0.4	0.6	0.6
$7,000 to $7,999	1.0	1.3	0.5	0.6
$8,000 to $8,999	0.6	0.2	0.4	0.4
$9,000 to $9,999	0.5	0.2	0.6	0.4
$10,000 or More	0.3	0.1	0.2	0.2

TABLE 95--Continued

Socioeconomic Category	El Paso	Hono-lulu	Lancas-ter	Minnea-polis-St. Paul
Educational Category				
No Schooling	2.4	7.3	5.2	1.9
Elementary: 1 to 4 Years	2.7	2.6	6.1	2.7
Elementary: 5 to 7 Years	2.2	2.0	1.9	1.7
Elementary: 8 Years	1.2	1.5	0.7	0.8
High School: 1 to 3 Years	1.3	1.1	1.1	1.4
High School: 4 Years	0.9	1.0	0.4	0.7
College: 1 to 3 Years	0.6	0.3	0.4	0.7
College: 4 Years or More	0.4	0.4	0.3	1.0
Occupations (Male)				
Professional, technical and kindred workers	0.6	0.5	0.4	0.9
Managers, officials and proprietors, exc. farm	0.4	0.5	0.1	0.4
Clerical and kindred workers	0.4	1.3	0.3	0.9
Sales workers	0.1	0.7	0.3	0.1
Craftsmen, foremen and kindred workers	0.7	1.4	0.4	0.4
Operatives and kindred workers	1.0	1.4	1.3	1.0
Private household workers	13.3	0.6	12.9	4.3
Service workers, exc. private household	5.7	1.5	2.8	5.3
Laborer	1.2	2.1	4.4	1.9
Occupations (Female)				
Professional, technical and kindred workers	0.6	0.5	0.1	0.7
Managers, officials and proprietors, exc. farm	0.4	0.7	1.1	0.4
Clerical and kindred workers	0.2	1.0	0.0	0.5
Sales workers	0.1	0.8	0.2	0.3
Craftsmen, foremen and kindred workers	0.0	1.7	0.0	0.5
Operatives and kindred workers	0.6	3.5	1.3	1.6
Private household workers	2.7	0.7	7.0	2.9
Service workers, exc. private household	3.6	1.5	1.9	2.2
Laborer	0.0	9.2	1.0	2.6
Income Classes				
Under $1,000	1.8	0.5	4.2	3.8
$1,000 to $1,999	2.4	0.8	3.4	2.8
$2,000 to $2,999	2.4	0.7	2.7	2.2
$3,000 to $3,999	2.1	0.8	2.0	2.5
$4,000 to $4,999	1.9	0.8	1.3	1.6
$5,000 to $5,999	1.0	1.0	0.9	0.9
$6,000 to $6,999	0.4	1.3	0.5	0.7
$7,000 to $7,999	0.2	1.3	0.5	0.7
$8,000 to $8,999	0.4	1.4	0.4	0.6
$9,000 to $9,999	0.4	1.3	0.3	0.6
$10,000 or More	0.1	1.0	0.1	0.3

TABLE 95--Continued

Socioeconomic Category	Providence-Pawtucket	Richmond	San Bernadino-Riverside[a]
Educational Category			
No Schooling	1.8	5.7	3.7
Elementary: 1 to 4 Years	1.4	5.4	3.8
Elementary: 5 to 7 Years	1.1	1.9	2.0
Elementary: 8 Years	0.9	1.0	1.0
High School: 1 to 3 Years	1.3	0.9	1.2
High School: 4 Years	0.8	0.5	0.6
College: 1 to 3 Years	0.5	0.3	0.7
College: 4 Years or More	0.6	0.3	0.4
Occupation (Male)			
Professional, technical and kindred workers	0.8	0.2	0.6
Managers, officials and proprietors, exc. farm	0.4	0.1	0.2
Clerical and kindred workers	1.1	0.8	1.1
Sales workers	0.1	0.2	0.1
Craftsmen, foremen and kindred workers	0.6	0.4	0.7
Operatives and kindred workers	1.1	2.1	1.4
Private household workers	2.4	17.0	0.0
Service workers, exc. private household	2.6	5.4	3.2
Laborer	3.2	10.8	2.5
Occupation (Female)			
Professional, technical and kindred workers	0.7	0.7	0.9
Managers, officials and proprietors, exc. farm	0.3	0.2	0.2
Clerical and kindred workers	0.4	0.1	0.3
Sales workers	0.3	0.1	0.2
Craftsmen, foremen and kindred workers	1.0	0.4	0.8
Operatives and kindred workers	0.8	1.1	0.7
Private household workers	10.3	27.4	5.8
Service workers, exc. private household	2.0	5.5	1.4
Laborer	2.2	6.8	0.8
Income Classes			
Under $1,000	3.4	5.2	3.0
$1,000 to $1,999	2.6	5.2	2.2
$2,000 to $2,999	2.4	4.0	1.8
$3,000 to $3,999	1.5	2.5	1.8
$4,000 to $4,999	1.1	1.3	1.5
$5,000 to $5,999	0.6	0.8	1.0
$6,000 to $6,999	0.6	0.4	0.6
$7,000 to $7,999	0.5	0.3	0.6
$8,000 to $8,999	0.6	0.3	0.4
$9,000 to $9,999	0.3	0.2	0.2
Over $10,000	0.2	0.1	0.2

TABLE 95--Continued

Socioeconomic Category	St. Petersburg	Tampa	U.S. Urban Average
Educational Categories			
No Schooling	6.9	3.8	2.1
Elementary: 1 to 4 Years	7.8	4.5	3.6
Elementary: 5 to 7 Years	2.8	1.8	1.9
Elementary: 8 Years	0.7	0.7	0.8
High School: 1 to 3 Years	0.9	0.9	1.1
High School: 4 Years	0.4	0.4	0.6
College: 1 to 3 Years	0.2	0.3	0.5
College: 4 Years or More	0.3	0.4	0.4
Occupations (Male)			
Professional, technical and kindred workers	0.2	0.4	0.3
Managers, officials and proprietors, exc. farm	0.2	0.1	0.2
Clerical and kindred workers	0.1	0.3	0.7
Sales workers	0.0	0.1	0.2
Craftsmen, foremen, and kindred workers	0.6	0.5	0.5
Operatives and kindred workers	2.1	1.4	1.3
Private household workers	8.1	15.8	8.0
Service workers, exc. private household	2.7	2.3	2.8
Laborer	6.9	7.1	3.7
Occupations (Female)			
Professional, technical and kindred workers	0.4	0.4	0.6
Managers, officials and proprietors, exc. farm	0.1	0.1	0.3
Clerical and kindred workers	0.1	0.1	0.3
Sales workers	0.1	0.1	0.2
Craftsmen, foremen, and kindred workers	0.4	0.7	0.6
Operatives and kindred workers	0.7	1.1	1.0
Private household workers	16.9	15.2	8.7
Service workers, exc. private household	1.7	1.6	1.9
Laborer	3.6	1.9	2.3
Income Classes			
Under $1,000	2.2	2.3	3.5
$1,000 to $1,999	1.3	2.3	3.0
$2,000 to $2,999	1.5	1.9	2.5
$3,000 to $3,999	1.6	1.6	1.9
$4,000 to $4,999	1.1	0.9	1.3
$5,000 to $5,999	0.6	0.5	0.8
$6,000 to $6,999	0.5	0.5	0.6
$7,000 to $7,999	0.3	0.3	0.5
$8,000 to $8,999	0.3	0.3	0.4
$9,000 to $9,999	0.2	0.3	0.4
$10,000 or More	0.2	0.2	0.3

Notes [a]Non-white per cent is divided by white, non-Spanish surname parent.

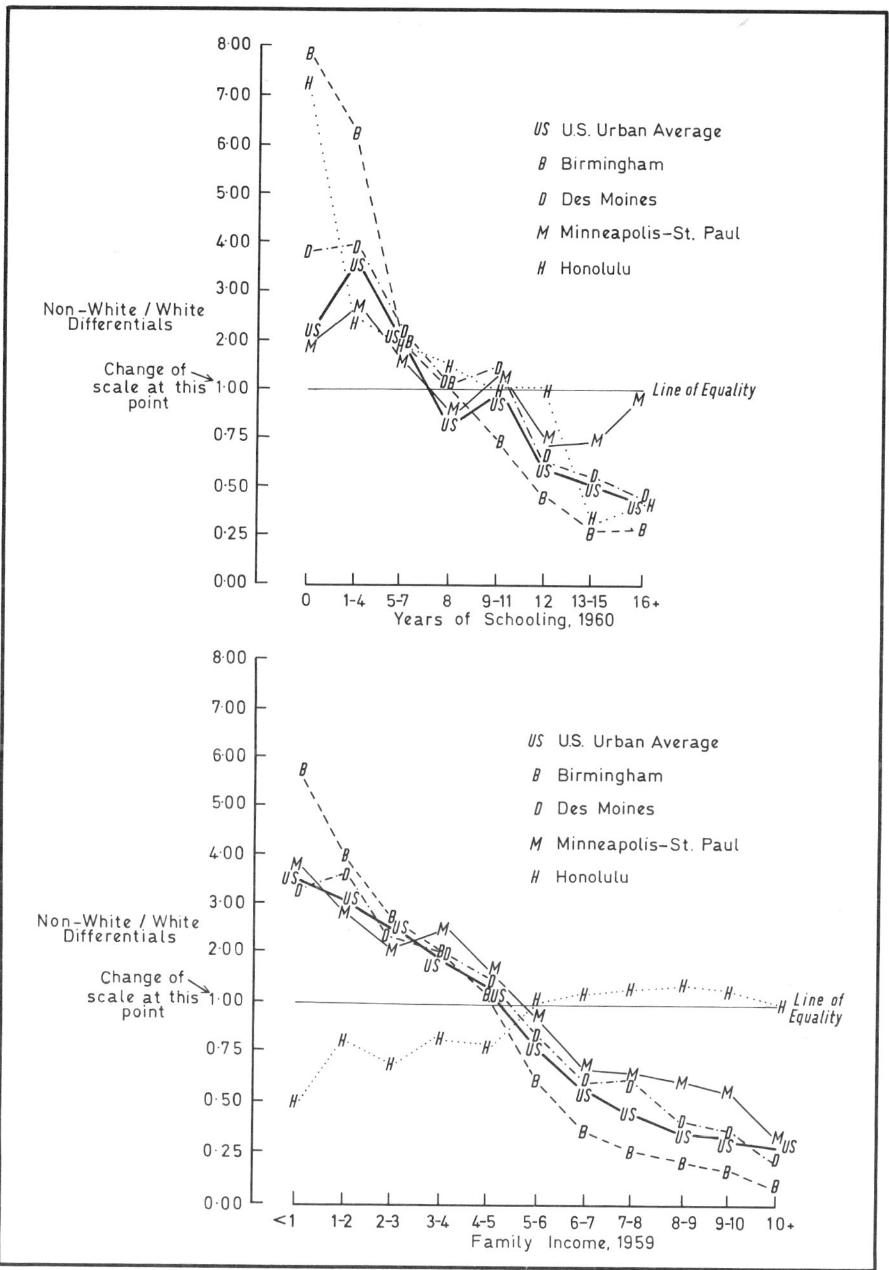

Fig. 65.--Non-white/White Differentials in Education and Income for Selected Urbanized Areas

TABLE 96

EDUCATIONAL AND INCOME DIFFERENTIALS FOR WHITES OF SPANISH SURNAME, WHITES OF NON-SPANISH SURNAME AND NON-WHITES IN EL PASO AND SAN BERNADINO-RIVERSIDE, 1960

Socioeconomic Category	El Paso SMSA		San Bernadino-Riverside-Ontario SMSA	
	WS/WNS	NW/WS	WS/WNS	NW/WS
Educational Categories				
No Schooling	14.7	0.2	14.1	0.3
Elementary: 1 to 4 Years	12.7	0.2	6.9	0.6
Elementary: 5 to 7 Years	4.2	0.5	2.6	0.8
Elementary: 8 Years	1.2	1.0	1.0	1.0
High School: 1 to 3 Years	0.7	1.9	0.9	1.3
High School: 4 Years	0.4	2.6	0.4	1.5
College: 1 to 3 Years	0.2	3.6	0.3	2.6
College: 4 Years or More	0.1	3.2	0.2	2.0
Income Classes				
Under $1,000	2.6	0.7	1.3	2.3
$1,000 to $1,999	2.7	0.9	1.1	2.0
$2,000 to $2,999	2.6	0.9	1.3	1.3
$3,000 to $3,999	1.8	1.2	1.6	1.1
$4,000 to $4,999	1.2	1.6	1.6	1.0
$5,000 to $5,999	0.9	1.2	1.4	0.7
$6,000 to $6,999	0.7	0.6	0.9	0.7
$7,000 to $7,999	0.6	0.3	0.7	0.8
$8,000 to $8,999	0.4	1.0	0.6	0.7
$9,000 to $9,999	0.3	1.2	0.6	0.4
$10,000 or More	0.2	0.6	0.3	0.5

Notes

Source: Tables P-1 and P-5 in U.S. Bureau of the Census (1962b), PHC (1) - 43, and PHC (1) - 135.

WS - White, Spanish Surname
WNS - White, non-Spanish Surname
NW - Non-white

migration of black Americans from the rural South to cities in the non-South. The ranking within the southern group is largely the same on all the Table 93 measures with Birmingham showing the highest associations, often by a substanial margin, followed by Richmond which is some way above Tampa and St. Petersburg. St. Petersburg shows less association between color and family income than the educational and occupational measures would suggest. This is undoubtedly a reflection of the lower incomes of white "retirees," the black population being largely a younger, working population.

Following the southern cities in rank order are a group of functionally varied Northern cities (Canton, Ann Arbor, Des Moines, Lancaster) which show moderate associations between color and social status. It is perhaps a little surprising to find the supposedly "liberal" college town of Ann Arbor with its long established black community among this group. The climate of racial discrimination which partially accounts for the substantial non-white/white differentials observed here is obviously not absent from the groves of academe, as of 1960.

The third group of cities, lower still on the scale of non-white/white differentials, consists of the three "Western" cities in the sample: Honolulu, San Bernadino-Riverside and El Paso. Their position together in the rank order at this level is a reflection of their peculiar ethnic mixes and may be fortuitous. The figures for Honolulu in Table 95 (some of them plotted in Figure 65) reveal that the Tau A and Tau B indices may be misleading in that they indicate no direction in the association: in the case of family incomes non-whites are slightly more favorably distributed than whites, and in the cases of education and occupation the differentials, though favoring whites, look somewhat different from those of other cities. This is reflected in the discrepancy between the ranking of Honolulu on the indices of dissimilarity and the tau indices, the former indicating a much lower ranking than the latter, though in general they are in fairly broad agreement. So that Hononlulu, with its very different non-white racial composition, should be viewed rather separately from the other cities: undoubtedly people of non-white race in Honolulu have open to them much better opportunities than blacks in mainland cities.

The situation in El Paso and San Bernadino-Riverside is rather different. The presence of a Mexican American minority makes straightforward comparison of non-whites and whites more difficult. In Table 95 non-whites are compared with whites with non-Spanish surnames (the "Anglos"), and in Table 96 whites with Spanish surnames are compared with whites of non-Spanish surnames and with non-whites. Both minority groups are disadvantaged vis à vis Anglos in El Paso and San Bernadino-Riverside, and Mexican Americans are more disadvantaged than non-whites with respect to educational attainment (Tables 95 and 96). However, Mexican Americans have a more favorable income distribution than non-whites (Table 96). The level of Tau A for the educational crosstabulations involving all three groups for El Paso is, in fact, higher than that for non-whites and whites in Birmingham, and that for San Bernadino-Riverside-Ontario higher than the Tau A values of Tampa and St. Petersburg. The index values for the income crosstabulations involving all three groups are fairly high for El Paso, fairly low for San Bernadino-Riverside. In terms of the association of ethnic status and social status the rank ordering for cities where we have the information for groups other than Negroes has to be

1. El Paso (on a par with the Southern cities)
2. San Bernadino-Riverside (on a par with the larger northern cities)
3. Honolulu (in a class by itself).

Finally, there are two cities which rank consistently low on the measures of association, Minneapolis-St. Paul and Providence-Pawtucket. These two "twin" urban areas contain fairly low proportions of non-whites, and lie relatively far from the areas of greatest Negro concentration in the southern U.S.. One might speculate that these two factors are related to the access of opportunities allowed blacks in urban labor markets in the United States. However, this can only be put forward as a hypothesis at this stage which might bear further examination.

The associations between racial status and socioeconomic status revealed by the aggregate crosstabulations confirm, by and large, the assessments made earlier on the basis of the factor analyses. Racial and socioeconomic status were clearly seen to be closely connected in the southern cities in the factor analyses, and Birmingham was correctly picked out as being the urbanized area which approached the "caste" model of sociology (one in which classes and racial groups are co-extensive and in which the color line coincides with the class boundary) most closely. The judgmental rankings on the basis of the factor analyses were relatively inefficient in distinguishing the two groups of northern cities that emerged in the crosstabulations analysis although the loadings of Per Cent Negro on Factor 1 (Table 91) in the Providence-Pawtucket and Minneapolis-St. Paul analyses (-0.164 and -0.291 respectively) were definitely lower than those of the other northern cities. The association between Mexican American ethnic status and socioeconomic status showed up strongly in the El Paso factor analysis and moderately in the San Bernadino-Riverside analysis — the relative strength of these associations were confirmed in the crosstabulation analyses. We turn now to an examination of the association between socioeconomic status and family status.

The Association between Family Status and Socioeconomic Status

Implicit in our discussion of residential patterns from Chapter III onwards was the notion that the two principal patterns of socioeconomic status and family status were independent. The principal component analyses of Chapter III revealed for each urbanized area studied orthogonal components which could readily be labelled socioeconomic status and family status. The joint population and housing analyses described in that chapter have, by and large, confirmed the earlier finding. The independence of the two dominant patterns in American cities has been confirmed in other studies but has been shown to be uncharacteristic of other countries to a greater or lesser degree (Abu-Lughod, 1969).

Johnston's Argument

However, Johnston (1971a, 1971b) has challenged the validity of the finding that socioeconomic status and family status are independent dimensions even in developed Western countries. Johnston does not dispute that low correlations are found between socioeconomic status indicators and family status indicators and that these result in orthogonal dimensions of socioeconomic status and family status. He argues rather that these low correlations mask triangular distributions of tracts in a space formed by socioeconomic status on one axis and family status on the other. One quadrant of this space will tend to be empty of tract observations.

A test of Johnston's arguments is fairly easily carried out for the cities in our sample, but we should be clear first what we should expect of such tests. Johnston's argument that socioeconomic status and family status are related should be accompanied by an argument about how these two patterns are related. The case example which Johnston presents is that of Melbourne and derives from work by Lancaster Jones (1969). Johnston presents the following table which records the number of census collector's districts that fall in each portion of social space as defined here

Socioeconomic Status	Family Status		
	Very low	Average	Very high
Very high	54	82	14
Average	0	256	3
Very low		5	55

Low status areas cluster in the very high family status category. There are two possible explanations for this clustering. The first is that fertility is strongly associated with social class: the lower the social class of a family the more children it is likely to contain. The second is that better off families can afford to occupy separate dwellings in separate areas at different stages of their life cycle. The city will not contain, for example, a separate residential district for working class young singles: singles will be mainly middle class, at least from an income point of view. If these arguments apply to American cities we should expect triangular distributions of tracts in social space rather like that of Melbourne.

The Distribution of Census Tracts in Social Space

For a comparative test of Johnston's arguments for our cities we employ our Index of Socioeconomic Status and Index of Family Status defined in Chapter V. These two indices can be used to form the vertical and horizontal axes of a graph, and the values on the indices for each census tract within an SMSA can be plotted in the "social space" so formed. A distribution typical of the Northern cities in the sample is that of Minneapolis-St. Paul SMSA shown in Figure 66. This distribution is similar to that of Chicago plotted in an earlier study (Rees, 1970b), in the clear separation of central city tracts into the left hand half of the graph, of suburban tracts into the upper right quadrant, and of rural tracts within the SMSA into the lower right quadrant. A somewhat different distribution is that for Birmingham (Figure 67) in which the different portions of the metropolis (central city, urban fringe, rural fringe) are less clearly differentiated in social space. Most of the tracts in the left hand half of the graph are central city tracts; most of the suburban tracts lie in the right hand half of the graph, but there is no differentiation of urban and rural fringe by socioeconomic status as there was in Minneapolis-St. Paul.

The spread of census tracts in social space in each of the 12 SMSAs studied is given in Figures 68 and 69. Some of the SMSAs occupy relatively little of the social space (Canton, Lancaster), others a great deal (Honolulu, Minneapolis-St. Paul, Tampa-St. Petersburg). The size of the portion of social space occupied by any

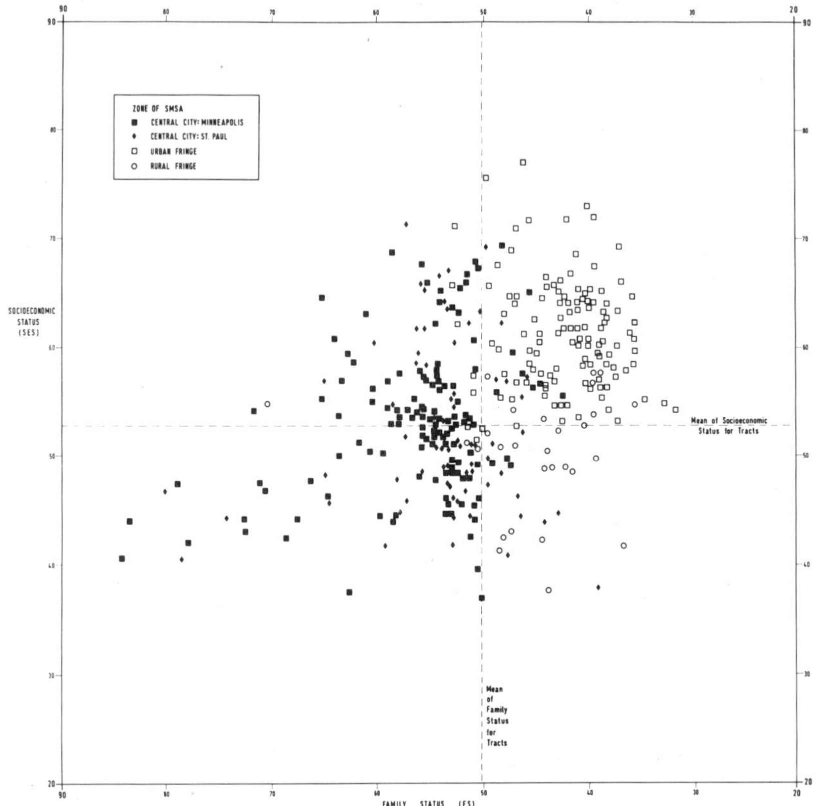

Fig. 66.--The Distribution of Census Tracts in Social Space, Minneapolis-St. Paul SMSA, 1960

one SMSA's tracts is probably related to its size. The larger the SMSA the more differentiated will tract sized areas be. In Figures 66 and 67 and in similar graphs for the other SMSAs (not reproduced here) there appears to be no systematic clustering of tracts in three out of four quadrants.

This impression is supported by the correlation observed between socioeconomic status and family status (Table 97). Six of these correlations are negative, which is presumably the direction of association suggested by the Melbourne table and six are positive. Only three are large in the sense of being more than twice the

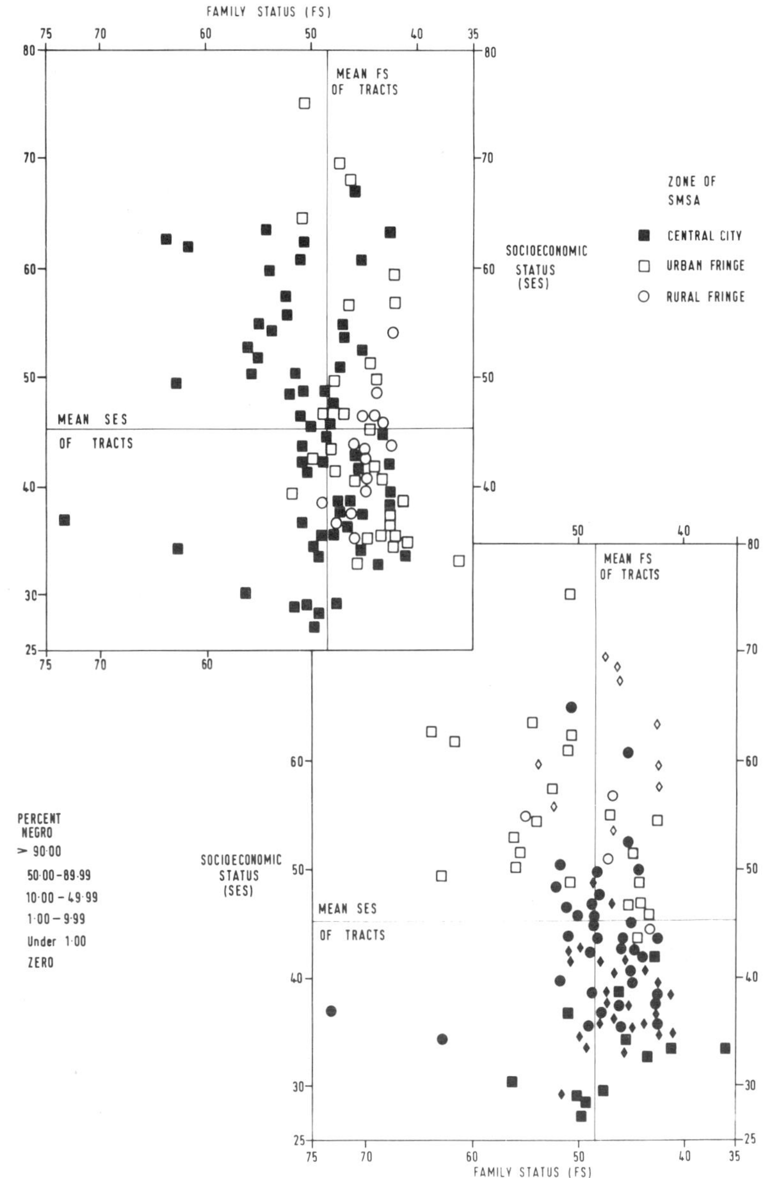

Fig. 67.--Distribution of tracts in social space, Birmingham SMSA, 1960

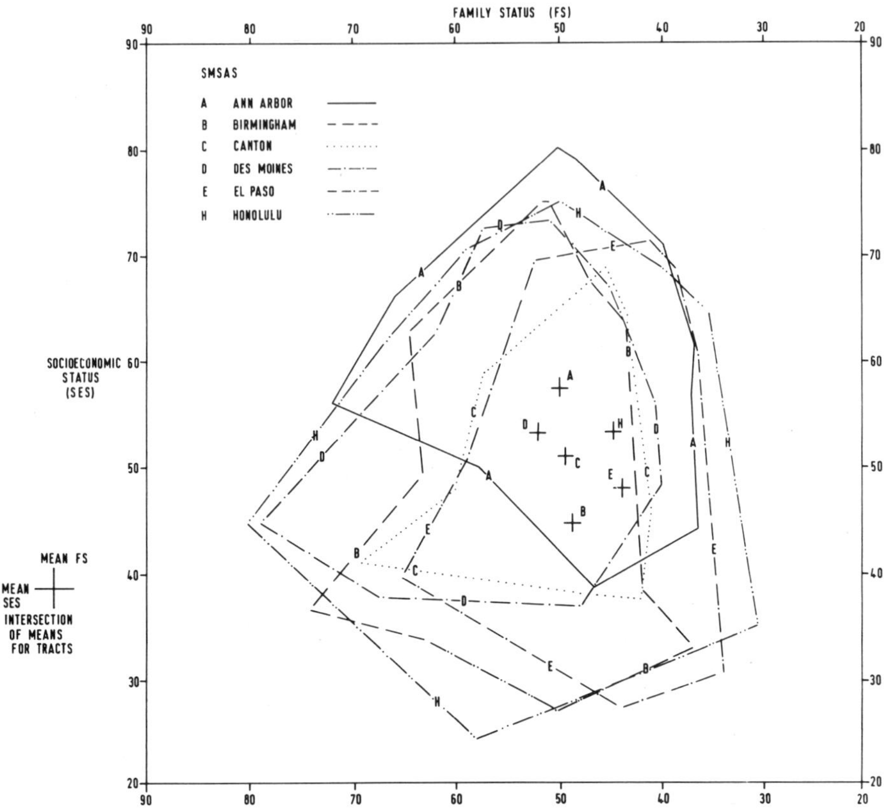

Fig. 68.--The Spread of Census Tracts over Social Space for 6 SMSA's, 1960

standard error of Pearson's r for the particular SMSA.

A Test of the Independence of Family Status and Socioeconomic Status

We can reduce the social space graphs for our 12 SMSAs to simple two by two tabulations by dividing the family status and socioeconomic status scales into two classes: scores of 50 and above, and scores below 50. The numbers of census tracts falling in each cell of the table were counted. These tables were then used to test the hypothesis that socioeconomic status and family

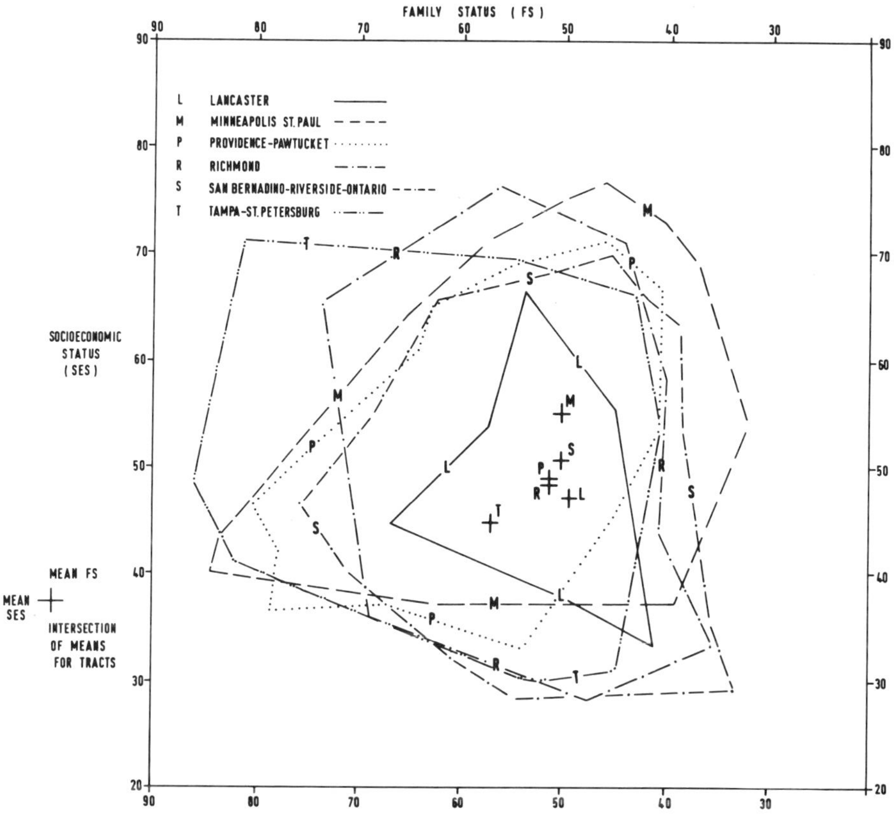

Fig. 69.--The Spread of Census Tracts over Social Space for 6 SMSAs, 1960

status were independent by means of the Chi-square test (Hoel, 1966, p. 240).

The results of this test for all the urbanized areas in the sample studied are given in Table 98. Only three of the tests result in rejection of the hypothesis; in nine cases we have insufficient grounds to reject. There is no systematic pattern of differences between observed number of tracts in a cell and expected number. Six urbanized areas follow one pattern of deviance, seven urbanized areas follow the other. Even amongst the three urbanized areas for which the evidence suggests we should reject the hypothesis of independence of socioeconomic status and family status, the

TABLE 97

ASSOCIATIONS BETWEEN THE SOCIAL DIMENSIONS

SMSA	Socio-economic Status vs Family Status	Socio-economic Status vs Racial Status	Family Status vs Racial Status	Standard Error of the Correlation Coefficient
Ann Arbor	0.074	-0.394	-0.041	0.129
Birmingham	0.176	-0.751	-0.231	0.098
Canton	-0.112	-0.586	-0.122	0.117
Des Moines	-0.178	-0.522	0.201	0.131
El Paso	0.208	-0.181	-0.100	0.146
Honolulu	-0.215	-0.024	-0.088	0.094
Lancaster	0.466	-0.252	-0.029	0.129
Minneapolis-St. Paul	-0.384	-0.282	0.114	0.054
Providence-Pawtucket	-0.343	-0.270	0.213	0.075
Richmond	0.206	-0.767	-0.212	0.108
San Bernadino-Riverside-Ontario	-0.044	-0.340	-0.005	0.071
Tampa-St. Petersburg	0.223	-0.641	-0.308	0.077

Notes

[a]The figures are Pearson's product moment coefficients of correlation.

pattern of deviance is not uniform. In the case of Minneapolis-St. Paul (Figure 66) and Providence-Pawtucket the top left and bottom right quadrants are lacking in observations; in the case of Birmingham it is the top right and bottom left quadrants that are lacking in observations to match the hypothesis of independence. When we examine the four by four table of socioeconomic status and family status for all tracts in the study areas considered together (Table 99), we notice no major gaps or heavily underrepresented cells, nor systematic deficiencies in one particular quadrant.

TABLE 98

RESULTS OF A TEST OF THE INDEPENDENCE OF SOCIOECONOMIC STATUS AND FAMILY STATUS FOR 13 URBANIZED AREAS, 1960

Urbanized Area	Observed Value for χ^2	Decision on H_0 at $P = 0.005$[a]	No. of Tracts	Pattern of Deviation of Observed from Expected[b] SES ≥ 50 FS ≥ 50	SES ≥ 50 FS < 50	SES < 50 FS ≥ 50	SES < 50 FS < 50
Ann Arbor	0.952	Accept	40	+	–	–	+
Birmingham	8.443	Reject	91	+	–	–	+
Canton	0.141	Accept	53	–	+	+	–
Des Moines	0.560	Accept	54	–	+	+	–
El Paso	0.446	Accept	44	+	–	–	+
Honolulu	2.793	Accept	80	–	+	+	–
Lancaster	0.490	Accept	24	+	–	–	+
Minneapolis-St. Paul	30.935	Reject	322	–	+	+	–
Providence-Pawtucket	10.911	Reject	144	–	+	+	–
Richmond	0.990	Accept	81	+	–	–	+
San Bernadino-Riverside	0.109	Accept	109	–	+	+	–
St. Petersburg	2.252	Accept	81	+	–	–	+
Tampa	0.800	Accept	67	+	–	–	+

Notes

[a]The critical value for ^{2} at $P = 0.005$ is 7.879.

[b] + means observed greater than expected; - means observed less than expected

TABLE 99

THE DISTRIBUTION OF CENSUS TRACTS IN SOCIAL SPACE IN 13 URBANIZED AREAS, OBSERVED, EXPECTED AND DIFFERENCES

OBSERVED

Socioeconomic Status Score	Family Status Score				
	≥ 60	50-60	40-50	< 40	Totals
≥ 60	21	74	123	30	248
50-60	49	187	172	43	451
40-50	73	156	125	12	366
< 40	13	32	66	14	125
Totals	156	449	486	99	1190

EXPECTED

Socioeconomic Status Score	Family Status Score				
	≥ 60	50-60	40-50	< 40	Totals
≥ 60	32.51	93.57	101.28	20.63	248
50-60	59.12	170.17	184.19	37.52	451
40-50	47.98	138.10	149.48	30.45	366
< 40	16.39	47.16	51.05	10.40	125
Totals	156	449	486	99	1190

DIFFERENCES

Socioeconomic Status Score	Family Status Score				
	≥ 60	50-60	40-50	< 40	Totals
≥ 60	-11.51	-9.57	21.72	9.37	0
50-60	-10.12	16.83	-12.19	5.48	0
40-50	25.02	17.90	-24.48	-18.45	0
< 40	-3.39	-15.16	14.95	3.60	0
Totals	0	0	0	0	0

Conclusions

It seems that there is not sufficient evidence to reject the proposition that in American cities the two population dimensions of socioeconomic status and family status are independent. There are sufficient small residential areas in most American cities to offer persons of all classes a choice of living in a neighborhood that suits the familial or non-familial situation they find themselves in. Blue collar families as well as white collar families can live in family neighborhoods of single family dwellings; single persons in lower status occupations can reside in apartment districts at suitable rent levels as well as persons in higher paying occupations. It is clearly a major achievement of the American urban system that this range of choice is available to most people.

Set against this achievement is the failure of American urban society to provide equality of opportunity for all racial groups. The tracts in which Negro families constitute 50 per cent of the population or more cluster in the lower portion of the social space graphs. The range of choice of residential area for Negro families is thus very much more restricted than the range available to white families.

CHAPTER X

CONCLUSIONS

In this final chapter we draw together our observations on the residential patterns of American cities in 1960, and attempt to summarize the answers to the questions about residential patterning posed in Chapter I. Our conclusions will be couched in general terms; the exceptions to these generalizations are spelled out in the relevant chapters.

The factor analyses of the same set of population variables in some thirteen urbanized areas revealed a number of dimensions that described the basic socio-geographic patterning of the residential areas of American cities. All of the urbanized areas exhibited a factor on which most of the socioeconomic status indicators loaded highly. In certain cases, other types of variables also loaded highly on this factor, notably in Birmingham ("Pct Negro") and in El Paso ("Pct Mexico"), indicating that in these urbanized areas the socioeconomic status dimension was closely related with racial or ethnic status. In eight of the thirteen urbanized areas a factor was present which was labelled a "Race and Resources" factor (after Rees, 1970b). This factor was made up of moderate to high loadings of some socioeconomic status indicators, particularly those picking out the most disadvantaged sections of the population, together with a high loading of the "Pct Negro" variable. Of the five urbanized area analyses in which such a factor was not identified, two, Birmingham and El Paso, had secondary socioeconomic status factors, the main racial or ethnic status indicator loading on the major socioeconomic status factor. The other urbanized areas not recording a "Race and Resources" type factor were

Des Moines, Lancaster and Minneapolis-St. Paul, where the Negro communities were too small in population size and areal extent for such ecological relationships to show up.

All thirteen of the urbanized areas exhibited a family status factor with a common pattern of loadings, and all showed one or more particular factors that involved one or two high loadings of ethnic group or occupational class loadings. The structures that emerged from the factor analyses of Chapter III thus display both a high degree of variety in the specification of socioeconomic status and racial status dimensions and a high degree of uniformity in the specification of a family status dimension.

In Chapter IV the dimensions of variation that characterized the housing geography of our sample of cities were explored through a factor analysis of housing characteristics taken alone and of population and housing characteristics taken together. The factors that emerged mirrored, in general, those of the population variable analysis of the previous chapter. A home value and rent factor was associated with the socioeconomic status dimension; a housing type, size and tenure factor was associated with the family status dimension; and housing condition variables loaded highly on "factors in which racial or ethnic status is associated with socioeconomic status." The picture of residential patterns put forward in Figure 4 in Chapter 1 received considerable empirical support.

The factor analyses carried out in Chapters III and IV were essentially aspatial in character but it was obviously important to examine the spatial patterns of the most important dimensions emerging from the analysis. It was argued in Chapter V that this required the definition of indices of socioeconomic status, family status and racial status. Factor scores based on Chapter III or IV factor analyses were rejected as unsuitable indices as they varied in definition from city to city. Instead, after an extensive review of the relevant literature, indices were adopted that employed the variables shown to be key indicators of the important factorial dimensions, but in an invariant fashion. The map patterns of the indices were examined in detail in the ensuing chapters.

The view of the spatial patterns associated with the social dimensions that was prevailing (Anderson and Egeland, 1961; Murdie, 1969) was that socioeconomic status was primarily sectoral in pattern, that family status was primarily concentric in pattern and that racial or ethnic groups were clustered in the city in one or more concentrations. The latter two propositions were confirmed, although the "clustering model" applied most aptly to the Northern cities in the sample. In the Southern and Western cities Negro neighborhoods were more widely spread about the urbanized area. The sectoral model of the spatial pattern of socioeconomic status was not, however, confirmed. Virtually all the cities in the sample showed substantial elements of both "sectorality" and "concentricity" in the spatial pattern of socioeconomic status.

The relative strengths of the main dimensions of variation were measured by an analysis of the residential segregation of socioeconomic groups (educational categories, occupation groups and income classes), family status groups (age groups, household size groups) and ethnic groups (races, country of origin groups). The most highly segregated group was that of Negro Americans, and the most potent sorting principle was that of race. Several foreign stock groups followed in level of spatial segregation, but Jewish Americans, Mexican Americans or Italian Americans were by no means as segregated on average as were black Americans. Many other ethnic groups were well integrated in a residential sense (British Americans, Canadian Americans and German Americans).

Social class followed race and ethnicity as a population sorting principle, and was one that showed remarkable uniformity across the diverse studies. The very rich turned out to be as residentially segregated from the rest of the population as Jews, Chicanos or

Italian Americans were. The middle income groups, forming the majority of the population, were least spatially separate; the poor lay somewhere between the middle classes and the rich in degree of segregation in the residential city. When social class is defined in occupational terms there appears to be less spatial segregation than if education or income are used as the bases of measurement. Residential neighborhoods are more mixed in terms of occupational class of their inhabitants than in terms of their income or educational class.

Residential areas are most mixed in their family type composition. Only the elderly and single person households record degrees of spatial segreagion that can be unambiguously declared to be greater than the degree of spatial segregation that might be measured for a group of individuals selected at random.

One important issue raised in Chapter I concerned the independence of the residential patterns observed. In a technical sense the factorial dimensions identified in Chapters III and IV are independent since a principal components model of factor analysis was used with rotation of components according to the normal varimax criterion. However, an examination of the distribution of the variance of variables grouped into socioeconomic status, family status and racial and ethnic status sets revealed that there was association between the conceptual dimensions , socioeconomic status and racial status. In Chapter IX this finding, based on the analysis of the characteristics of residential areas, was extended into a more precise analysis of the degree of association of color and socioeconomic indicators in the aggregate city populations. The varying degree of socioeconomic disadvantage suffered by Negroes in comparison with whites was documented. Southern cities were shown to exhibit this disadvantage to the greatest degree. Mexican Americans in Western cities also suffered disadvantage with respect to Non-Spanish surname whites in terms of educational, occupational and income attainment; the disadvantage in income terms, however, was much less than that for education, implying that the effects of deprived background were mitigated in the labor and wages market. This was not the case for Negro Americans. Oriental Americans (Non-whites in Honolulu) suffered moderate educational disadvantage vis à vis whites but were able to more than cancel this out in terms of income, their income distribution being more favorable than that of whites.

The independence of socioeconomic status and family status was also tested and confirmed, by and large, in Chapter IX. Thus, there exist in American cities, at all levels of income, bar the very poorest, a range of choice of neighborhoods in terms of housing and family type mix.

This study has been concerned with the identification of the main geographic patterns that characterize the residential areas of American cities. From time to time explanations for these patterns have been sought. The population patterns were seen through the factor analyses of Chapter IV, to be associated with and in part a product of the housing patterns. The exceptions to this association such as the non-congruity of family status and housing type in St. Petersburg, serve to "prove the rule." Examination of the crosstabulations of housing value/rent and family income confirmed the connection for the socioeconomic status pattern, and examination of the crosstabulations of color and housing conditions confirmed the extension of socioeconomic disadvantage into the housing market.

Although the map patterns in each city were in many senses unique in their explanation, certain map correlates contributed to an explanation in many cities. The westerly orientation of the sector scoring highest on the socioeconomic status scale, as in Canton, Des Moines and Minneapolis, was present in the "Plains" cities where topography or coastline did not interfere, as in Birmingham or St. Petersburg. Residential property attains its highest values, clearly, in the most environmentally desirable neighborhoods, as Hoyt had shown many years ago.

The "housing" explanation, however, proved to be inadequate when reasons were sought for the patterns of racial and ethnic segregation revealed in Chapter VIII. Relatively little of the inter-ethnic group segregation could be ascribed to differences in the socioeconomic or family status composition of the ethnic groups. The clustering of ethnic groups observed had a lot to do with the history of immigrant settlement, and a preference for living among people of the same ethnicity. It was suggested, however, that these factors were insufficient explanation for the very high degree of residential segregation of Negro Americans from non-Negroes, and that significant racial discrimination was occurring in the housing markets of American cities in 1960. In the years since 1960 there has been little or no shift in this pattern of racial residential segregation despite a substantial reduction in Negro disadvantage vis à vis whites in educational attainment and in the job market. Racial polarization continues to characterize the American city.

How general are these conclusions, based, as they are, on a study of some twelve metropolitan areas at one point in time? The SMSAs were chosen, as was indicated in Chapter II, to be as representative a set of 12 as could be selected. Almost all city types defined by Berry and Neils (1969) are represented in the sample. Only the largest cities and mining towns are absent. On that basis we can be fairly confident that the variety of patterns and relationships exhibited in our sample reflects most of the variety in residential patterning in American cities as a whole. Where possible the results of this study have been compared with those of others (particularly in Chapters VI and VIII). The influence of the aggregate characteristics of the SMSAs on the residential patterns within the SMSA has been noted from time to time. The SMSA's overall ethnic composition clearly influences the number of ethnic clusters that are apparent. The main contrasts among the cities are in the degree to which a ring or sector pattern applied in the socioeconomic status map and in the degree to which the residential patterns reflected socioeconomic disadvantage for non-whites. But the remarkable similarity in factor structures, in family status patterns, and in the ordering of the residential segregation of the three sets of social groups tesitifies to the existence of a general American city type, remarkably homogeneoous in its residential patterning.

REFERENCES

Abler, Ronald, John Adams and Peter Gould
1971 Spatial organization. Englewood Cliffs, N.J.: Prentice Hall.

Abu-Lughod, Janet
1966 The Ecology of Cairo, Egypt: a comparative study using factor analysis. Unpublished Ph.D. dissertation, University of Massachusetts, Amherst.

1968 A critical test for the theory of social area analysis: the factorial ecology of Cairo, Egypt. Unpublished paper, Department of Sociology, Northwestern University.

1969 Testing the theory of social area analysis: the ecology of Cairo, Egypt. American Sociological Review, 34:198-212.

Adams, John B.
1970 Residential structure of Midwestern cities. Annals of the Association of American Geographers, 60:37-62.

Anderson, Theodore R. and L. L. Bean
1961 The Shevky-Bell social areas: confirmation of results and reinterpretation. Social Forces, 40:119-224.

Anderson, Theodore R. and Janice A. Egeland
1961 Spatial aspects of social area analysis. American Sociological Review, 26:392-398.

Association of American Geographers
1976a Contemporary metropolitan America: twenty geographical vignettes. Comparative Metropolitan Analysis Project, 1. Cambridge, Mass.: Ballinger.

1976b Urban policy making and metropolitan dynamics: a comparative geographical analysis. Comparative Metropolitan Project, 2. Cambridge, Mass.: Ballinger.

1976c A comparative atlas of America's great cities: twenty metropolitan regions. Comparative Metropolitan Analysis Project, 3. Minneapolis: University of Minnesota Press.

Banfield, Edward C.
1970 The unheavenly city. Boston: Little, Brown.

Banton, Michael
1967 Race relations. London: Tavistock Publications.

Batty, Michael
1972 Dynamic simulation of an urban system. Patterns and Processes in Urban and Regional Systems, A. G. Wilson, ed. London: Pion

Bell, Wendell
1952 A comparative study in the methodology of urban analysis. Unpublished Ph.D. dissertation, University of California at Los Angeles.

1955 Economic, family and ethnic status: an empirical test. American Sociological Review, 20:45-52.

1958 The utility of the Shevky typology for the design of urban sub-area field studies. Journal of Social Psychology, 47:71-83.

Berelson, Bernard and George A. Steiner
1967 Human behavior. Shorter Edition. New York: Harcourt, Brace and World.

Berry, Brian J. L.
1965 Internal structure of the city. Law and Contemporary Problems, 30(1):111-119.

1970 Monitoring trends, forecasting change and evaluating goal-achievement in the urban environment: the ghetto expansion vs. desgregation issue in Chicago as a case study. Regional Forecasting, Michael Chisholm, Allan E. Frey and Peter Haggett, eds. Proceedings of the Twenty-second Symposium of the Colston Research Society, University of Bristol, April 6th to 10th, 1970. London: Butterworth.

1971 Introduction: the logic and limitations of comparative factorial ecology. Economic Geography, 47(2):209-223.

Berry, Brian J. L. et al.
1976 Chicago: transformations of an urban system. Cambridge, Mass.: Ballinger.

Berry, Brian J. L., Peter Goheen and S. Goldstein
1968 Metropolitan area definition: a re-evaluation of concept and statistical practice. Washington, D.C.: Bureau of the Census, Working Paper 28.

Berry, Brian J. L. and Robert A. Murdie
1965 Socioeconomic correlates of housing condition. Toronto: Metropolitan Planning Board.

Berry, Brian J. L. and Elaine M. Neils
1969 Location, size and shape of cities as influenced by environmental factors: the urban environment writ large. The Quality of Urban Environment, Harvey S. Perloff, ed. Baltimore: The Johns Hopkins Press for Resources for the Future.

Berry, Brian J. L. and Philip H. Rees
1969 The factorial ecology of Calcutta. American Journal of Sociology, 74:445-491.

Berry, Brian J. L. and Howard Spodek
1970 Comparative ecologies of large Indian cities. Economic Geography, 47(2):266-285.

Berry, Brian J. L. and Robert J. Tennant
1965 Socioeconomic classification of municipalities in the northeastern Illinois metropolitan area. Commericial Structure. Chicago: Northeastern Illinois Metropolitan Planning Commission.

Beshers, J.
1957 Census tract data and social structure: a methodological analysis. Unpublished Ph.D. dissertation, University of North Carolina.

Blau, Peter M. and Otis Dudley Duncan
1967 The American occupational structure. New York: John Wiley.

Bogardus, Emory S.
1928 Immigration and race attitudes. Boston: Heath.

1947 Changes in racial distances. International Journal of Opinion and Attitudes, 1.

Bogue, Donald J.
1967 Segregation: a model for multiple criteria measurement and multiple variable explanation. Unpublished paper, Department of Sociology, University of Chicago.

1969 The principles of demography. New York: John Wiley

Borchert, John
1961 The twin cities urbanized area: past, present and future. Geographical Review, 51:47-70.

Bourne, Larry S. and Gerald M. Barber
1971 Ecological patterns of small urban centers in Canada. Economic Geography, 47(2):258-265.

Brown, Lawrence A. and Frank E. Horton
1970 Social area change: an empirical analysis. Urban Studies, 7(3):271-288.

Brown, Lawrence A. and Eric G. Moore
1970 The intra-urban migration process: a perspective. Geografiska Annaler, 52, Series B (1):1-13.

Burgess, Ernest W.
1925 The growth of the city: an introduction to a research project. The City, Robert E. Park and Robert D. McKenzie, eds. Chicago: University of Chicago Press, 47-62.

1929 Urban Areas. Chicago: An Experiment in Social Science Research, T. V. Smith and L. D. White, eds. Chicago: University of Chicago Press.

Burns, Leland and Alvin J. Harman
1968 The complex metropolis: part six of a profile of Los Angeles metropolis, its people and homes. Los Angeles: Graduate School of Business, University of California at Los Angeles.

Carey, G. W.
1966 The regional interpretation of population and housing patterns in Manhattan through factor analysis. Geographical Review, 56:551-569.

Carey, G. W., L. Macomber and M. Greenburg
1968 Educational and demographic factors in the urban geography of Washington, D.C. Geographical Review, 58:515-537.

Casetti, Emilio
1969 Alternate urban population density models: an analytical comparison of their validity ranges. Studies in Regional Science, Allen J. Scott, ed. London: Pion.

Cattell, Raymond B.
1966 Handbook of multivariate experimental psychology. Chicago: Rand McNally.

Chicago Renewal Program
1963 An atlas of Chicago's people, jobs and homes. Chicago: Community Renewal Program.

Cliffe-Phillips, Geoffrey, John Mercer and Yue Man Yeung
1968 The urban ecology of Montreal. Unpublished paper, Department of Geography, University of Chicago.

Clignet, Remi and Joyce Sween
1969 Accra and Abidjan: a comparative examination of the theory of increase in scale. Urban Affairs Quarterly, 4:297-324.

Cohen, Yehoshua
1968 A factorial ecology of Birmingham, Alabama. Unpublished paper, Department of Geography, University of Chicago.

Congalton, Athol A.
1961 Status ranking of Sydney suburbs. Studies in Sociology, (1). Kensington: University of South Wales.

Cox, Kevin R.
1968 Suburbia and voting behavior in the London metropolitan area. Annals of the Association of American Geographers, 58:111-127.

Cripps, E. L. and E. A. Cater
1972 The empirical development of a disaggregated residential location model: some preliminary results. Patterns and Processes in Urban and Regional Systems, A. G. Wilson, ed. London: Pion.

De Vise, Pierre
1967a Chicago at mid-century: social status and ecology. Chicago Regional Hospital Study, Working Paper No. 2.7. Chicago: Metropolitan Hospital Planning Council of Chicago.

1967b Chicago's widening color gap. Inter-University Social Research Committee, Report No. 2. Chicago: Inter-University Social Research Committee.

Dickinson, Robert E.
1964 City and region. London: Routledge and Kegan Paul.

Duncan, Beverly
1967 Variables in urban morphology. Urban Sociology, Ernest W. Burgess and Donald J. Bogue, eds. Phoenix Edition. Chicago: University of Chicago.

Duncan, Beverly and Otis Dudley Duncan
1968 Minorities in the process of stratification. American Sociological Review, 33:356-364.

Duncan, Otis Dudley
1955 Untitled review of Social Area Analysis by Eshref Shevky and Wendell Bell. American Journal of Sociology, 61: 84-85.

1961a A socioeconomic index for all occupations. Occupational and Social Status, Albert J. Reiss, Jr. New York: Free Press. Chapter 6:109-138.

1961b Properties and characteristics of the socioeconomic index. Occupation and Social Status, Albert J. Reiss, Jr. New York: Free Press. Chapter 7:139-161.

1969 Inheritance of poverty or inheritance of race? Understanding Poverty. Daniel P. Moynihan, ed. New York: Basic Books.

Duncan, Otis Dudley and Beverly Duncan
1955a Residential distribution and occupational stratification. American Journal of Sociology. 60:493-503.

1955b A methodological analysis of segregation indexes. American Sociological Review, 20:200-217.

1957 The Negro population of Chicago: a study in residential succession. Chicago: University of Chicago Press.

Duncan, Otis Dudley and Stanley Lieberson
1959 Ethnic segregation and assimilation. American Journal of Sociology, 64:364-374.

Earickson, Robert A.
1969 The spatial behavior of hospital patients. University of Chicago, Department of Geography, Research Paper No. 124. Chicago: Department of Geography.

Edwards, Alba M.
1938 A socio-economic grouping of the gainful workers in the United States. Washington D.C.: U.S. Government Printing Office.

Firey, William
1947 Land use in central Boston. Cambridge: Harvard University Press.

Florence, P. Sargent
1937 Economic research and industrial policy. Economic Journal, 47.

Forrester, Jay W.
1969 Urban dynamics. Cambridge, Mass.: The M.I.T. Press.

Gans, Herbert J.
1969 The Levittowners. New York: Pantheon Books.

Gini, Corrado
1914-15 Indice di omofilia e di gli indici rassomiglianza e loro relazioni col coefficiente de correlazione e con gli indici di attrazione. Atti de Reale Instituto Veneto di Scienze Lettere ed Arti, Series 8, 74(2): 583-610.

Giggs, J. A.
1971 Multivariate analysis of levels of living: the case of Greater Nottingham. Paper presented to the Insitute of British Geographers, Population Studies Section, Liverpool, September.

Gittus, Elizabeth
1964 The structure of urban areas. Town Planning Review, 35: 5-20.

1964-5 An experiment in the definition of urban sub-areas. Transactions of the Bartlett Society, 2:109-135.

Glick, Paul C., David M. Heer and John C. Beresford
1968 Family formation and family composition: trends and prospects. Population and Society, Charles B. Nam, ed. Boston: Houghton Mifflin Company. 462-266.

Glick, Paul C. and Robert Parke, Jr.
1965 New approaches in studying the life cycle of the family. Demography, 2:187-202.

Goheen, Peter G.
1970 Victorian Toronto, 1850 to 1900: patterns and processes of growth, University of Chicago, Department of Geography, Research Paper No. 127. Chicago: Department of Geography.

Goodman, Leo A. and William H. Kruskal
1954 Measures of association for cross classifications. Journal of the American Statistical Association, 49: 732-764.

1959 Measures of association for cross classification. II: further discussions and references. Journal of the American Statistical Association, 54:124-163.

Gosnell, H. and M. Schmidt
1936 Factorial and correlational analysis of the 1934 vote in Chicago. Journal of the American Statistical Association, 31:507-518.

Greenburg, Michael
1968 An analysis of socioeconomic, housing and mobility patterns in Westchester County and in Northern Bronx County through factor analysis. Unpublished M.A. dissertation, Faculty of Political Science, Columbia University.

Greer-Wootten, Bryn
1968 Cross-sectional social area analysis: Montreal 1951-1961. Unpublished paper, Department of Geography, McGill University.

Guest, Avery M.
1970 Patterns of family segregation. Urban Affairs Review.

Hagood, Margaret J. and Daniel O. Pricc
1952 Statistics for sociologists. Revised Edition. New York: Holt, Rinehart and Winston.

Harman, H. J.
1968 Modern factor analysis. Chicago: University of Chicago Press.

Harris, Chauncy D. and Edward L. Ullman
1945 The nature of cities. Annals of the Academy of Political and Social Science, 242:7-17.

Hatt, Paul K. and Cecil C. North
1947 Jobs and occupations: a popular evaluation. Opinion News, 9:3-13.

Hawley, Amos and Otis Dudley Duncan
1957 Social area analysis: a critical appraisal. Land Economics, 33:337-344.

Hemple, Carl G.
1966 The philosophy of natural science. Englewood Cliffs, N. J.: Prentice Hall.

Herbert, David T.
1967 Social area analysis: a British study. Urban Studies, 4:41-60.

1968 Principal components analysis and British studies of urban social structure. Professional Geography, 20: 280-283.

1970 Principal components analysis and urban structure: a study of Cardiff and Swansea. Urban Essays: Studies in the Geography of Wales. M. Carter and W. K. D. Davies, eds. London: Longman, 79-100.

1972 Urban geography: a social perspective. Newton Abbott: David and Charles.

Herbert, D. T. and R. J. Johnston, eds.
1976 Social areas in cities. Volume I. Spatial processes and form. London: Wiley.

1976 Social areas in cities. Volume II. Spatial perspectives on problems and policies. London: Wiley.

Hoel, Paul G.
1966 Elementary statistics. New York: John Wiley.

Hoover, Edgar M.
1936 The measurement of industrial localization. Review of Economic Statistics, 18:162-171.

Hoyt, Homer
1939 The structure and growth of residential neighborhoods in American cities. Washington, D.C.: U.S. Federal Housing Administration.

Hughes, J. W. and G. W. Carey
1972 Factorial ecologies: oblique and orthogonal solutions. A case study of the New York SMSA. Environment and Planning, 4(2):147-162.

Janson, Carl-Gunnar
1968 The spatial structure of Newark, New Jersey: Part 1, the central city. Acta Sociologica, 11(3):144-169.

1969 Some problems of ecological factor analysis. Quantitative Ecological Analysis in the Social Sciences. Mattei Dogan and Stein Rokkan, eds. Cambridge, Mass.: The M.I.T. Press, 301-341.

1971 A preliminary report on Swedish urban spatial structure. Economic Geography, 47(2):249-257.

Jencks, Christopher and David Riessmann
1968 On class in America. The Public Interest, (10):65-85.

Johnston, R. J.
1968 The location of high status residential areas. Geografiska Annaler, 48(Series B):23-35.

1971a Some limitations of factorial ecologies and social area analysis. Economic Geography, 47(2):314-323.

1971b Urban Residential Patterns. London: Bell.

Jones, F. Lancaster
1965 A social profile of Canberra, 1961. The Australian and New Zealand Journal of Sociology, 1:107-120.

1967 A social ranking of Melbourne suburbs. The Australian and New Zealand Journal of Sociology, 3:93-110.

1968 Social area analysis: some theoretical and methodological comments illustrated with Australian data. The British Journal of Sociology, 14:424-444.

1969 Dimensions of urban social structure: the social areas of Melbourne, Australia. Canberra: Australian National University Press.

Kantrowitz, Nathan
1969 Ethnic and racial segregation in the New York metropolis, 1960. American Journal of Sociology, 74:685-695.

Kitagawa, Evelyn M. and Karl E. Taeuber, eds.
1963 Local community factbook, Chicago metropolitan area. Chicago: Chicago Community Inventory, University of Chicago.

Lansing, John B. and Leslie Kish
1957 Family cycle as independent variable. American Sociological Review, 22.

Lansing, John B. and Eva Mueller
1964 Residential location and urban mobility. Ann Arbor: Institute for Social Research.

Latham, Robert F. and Maurice H. Yeates
1970 Population density growth in metropolitan Toronto. Geographical Analysis, 2:177-185.

Lee, Douglas B., Jr.
1968 Urban models and household disaggregation: an empirical problem in urban research. Unpublished Ph.D. dissertation, Department of City and Regional Planning, Cornell University.

Lieberson, Stanley
1963 Ethnic patterns in American cities. New York: The Free Press.

Lindberg, Goran
1967 Social Omgivning: En Social Ekologisk undersokning av tjugo bostadsomraden i Malmo. Sociologike Institutinien, Lund.

Lipset, Seymour Martin and Reinhart Bendix
1959 Social mobility in industrial society. Berkeley and Los Angeles: University of California Press.

Lowry, Ira S.
1960 Filtering and housing standards: a conceptual analysis. Land Economics, 36:362-370.

1964 A model of metropolis. Santa Monica: Rand Corporation (RM-4125-RC).

Mayer, Harold M. and Richard C. Wade
1969 Chicago: growth of a metropolis. Chicago: University of Chicago Press.

McElrath, Dennis C.
1962 The social areas of Rome: a comparative analysis. American Sociological Review, 27:376-391.

1965 Appendix to Chapter 3. Transportation and the new cities: a report to the automobile manufacturers association. Evanston, Ill.: The Transportation Center, Northwestern University.

1968 Social differentiation and societal scale. The New Urbanization. Scott Greer _et_. _al_., eds. New York: St. Martin's Press.

McElrath, Dennis C. and John W. Barkey
1964 Social and physical space: models of metropolitan differentiation. Unpublished paper, Center for Metropolitan Studies, Northwestern University.

Meyer, David R.
1970 Spatial variation of black urban households. University of Chicago, Department of Geography, Research Paper No. 129. Chicago: Department of Geography.

Mills, Edwin C.
1969 The value of urban land. The Quality of the Urban Environment. Harvey S. Perloff, ed. Baltimore: Johns Hopkins Press for Resources for the Future.

Morrill, Richard L.
1965a The Negro ghetto: problems and alternatives. Geographical Review, 55:339-361.

1965b Migration and the spread and growth of urban settlement. Lund Studies in Geography, Series B, Human Geography, (26).

Morrill, Richard L. and O. Fred Donaldson
1972 Geographic perspectives on the history of black America. Economic Geography, 48:1-23.

Morris, Fred B. and Gerald F. Pyle
1971 The social environment of Rio de Janiero. Economic Geography, 47(2):286-302.

Murdie, Robert A.
1969 The factorial ecology of metropolitan Toronto, 1951-1961. University of Chicago, Department of Geography, Research Paper No. 116. Chicago: Department of Geography.

Muth, Richard E.
1969 Cities and housing: the spatial pattern of urban residential land use. Chicago: University of Chicago Press.

Nam, Charles B. and Mary G. Powers
1965 Variation in socioeconomic structure by race, residence and the life cycle. American Sociological Review, 30: 97-103.

Nelson, Howard J.
1949 The livelihood structure of Des Moines, Iowa. University of Chicago, Department of Geography, Research Paper No. 4. Chicago: Department of Geography.

Newling, Bruce E.
1969 The spatial variation of urban population densities. Geographical Review, 59:242-252.

Norman, Peter
1969 A third survey of London life and labour: a new typology of London districts. Quantitative Ecological Analysis in the Social Sciences. Mattei Dogan and Stein Rokkan, eds. Cambridge, Mass.: The M.I.T. Press, 371-396.

Nostrand, Richard L.
1970 The Hispanic borderland: delimitation of an American culture region. Annals of the Association of American Geographers, 60:638-661.

Oi, Walter Y. and Paul W. Shuldiner
1962 An analysis of urban travel demands. Evanston, Ill.: Northwestern University Press.

Pedersen, Poul O.
1967 Modeller for Befolkningsstruktur og Befolkrungsudvikling i Storbyomrader Specielt med Henblik pa Storkobenhavn. Copenhagen: State Urban Planning Institute.

Pedersen, Poul O.
1967 An empirical model of urban population structure: a factor analytical study of population structure in Copenhagen. Proceedings of the First Scandinavian-Polish Regional Science Seminar. Warsaw: Polish Scientific Publishers.

1969 Spatial population processes in urban areas. Unpublished paper, Department of Road Construction, Traffic Engineering and Town Planning, The Technical University of Denmark Copenhagen.

Pocock, D. C. D. and D. Wishart
1969 Methods of deriving multi-factor uniform regions. Transactions, Institute of British Geographers, 47:73-98.

Poole, M. A. and F. W. Boal
1973 Religious residential segregation in Belfast in mid-1969: a multi-level analysis. in B. D. Clark and M. B. Gleave, eds. Social Patterns in Cities. Institute of British Geographers, London, Special Publication No. 5, 1-40.

Powers, Mary G.
1968 Class, ethnicity and residence in metropolitan America. Demography, 5:443-448.

Pyle, Gerald F.
1969 A factorial ecology of Rockford, 1960. Proceedings of the Illinois State Academy of Sciences.

Rees, Philip H.
1968 The factorial ecology of metropolitan Chicago, 1960. Unpublished M.A. dissertation, Department of Geography, University of Chicago.

1970a The urban envelope: patterns and dynamics of population density. Geographic Perspectives on Urban Systems. Brian J. L. Berry and Frank E. Horton. Englewood Cliffs, N. J.: Prentice Hall. Chapter 9, 276-305.

1970b Concepts of social space: toward an urban social geography. Geographic Perspectives on Urban Systems. Brian J. L. Berry and Frank E. Horton. Englewood Cliffs, N. J.: Prentice Hall. Chapter 10, 306-394.

1971 Factorial ecology: extended definition, survey and critique of the field. Economic Geography, 47(2):220-233.

1972a Problems of classifying subareas within cities. City Classification Handbook: Methods and Applications. Brian J. L. Berry, ed. New York: Wiley Interscience.

1972b Accounts and models for social groups within cities. Patterns and Processes in Urban and Regional Systems. A. G. Wilson, ed. London: Pion.

Robson, Brian T.
1969 Urban analysis: a study of city structure with special reference to Sunderland. Cambridge: Cambridge University Press.

Rogers, Andrei
1966 Matrix methods of population analysis. Journal of the American Institute of Planners, 32(1):177-196.

Rosing, Kenneth E. and Peter A. Wood
1971 Character of a conurbation: a computer atlas of Birmingham and the black country. London: University of London Press.

Rossi, Peter
1955 Why families move. New York: The Free Press.

Rummel, Rudolph T.
1970 Applied factor analysis. Evanston, Ill.: Northwestern University Press.

Salins, Peter H.
1969 Household location patterns in selected American metropolitan areas. Unpublished Ph.D. dissertation, University of Syracuse.

1971 Household location patterns in American metropolitan areas. Economic Geography, 47(2):234-248.

Schmid, Calvin F. and Kiyoshi Tagashira
1964 Ecological and demographic indices: a methodological analysis. Demography, 1:194-211.

Schnore, Leo F.
1965a The urban scene. New York: The Free Press.

1965b On the spatial structure of cities in the two Americas. The Study of Urbanization. Philip M. Hauser and Leo F. Schnore, eds. New York: John Wiley.

Senior, M. L.
1973 A review of the urban ecological and spatial interaction approaches to residential location modelling. Environment and Planning, 5:165-198.

Senior, M. L. and A. G. Wilson
1972 Disaggregated residential location models: some tests and further theoretical developments. Space-Time Concepts in Regional Science. London: Pion.

Shevky, Eshref and Wendell Bell
1955 Social area analysis: theory, illustrative application and computational procedures. Stanford: Stanford University Press.

Shevky, Eshref and Molly Lewin
1949 Your neighborhood. Los Angeles: Published for the Haynes Foundation by the University of California Press.

Shevky, Eshref and Marianne Williams
1949 The social areas of Los Angeles: analysis and typology. Los Angeles: University of California Press.

Simmons, James W.
1968 Changing residence in the city: a review of intra-urban mobility. Geographical Review, 58:622-651.

Simmons *et al*.
1969 The structure of land use: London, Ontario. Unpublished paper, Department of Geography, University of Toronto.

Stouffer, Samuel A.
1940 Intervening opportunities: a theory relating mobility and distance. American Sociological Review, 5:845-867.

Sweetser, Frank L.

1965a Factorial ecology: Helsinki, 1960. Demography, 1:312-386.

1965b Factor structure as ecological structure in Helsinki and Boston. Acta Sociologica, 8(3):205-225.

1969 Ecological factors in metropolitan zones and sectors. Quantitative Ecological Analysis in the Social Sciences. Mattei Dogan and Stein Rokkan, eds. Cambridge, Mass.: The M.I.T. Press.

Sweetser, Frank L. and Dorrian A. Sweetser
1968 Social class and single family housing: Helsinki and Boston. Urbanism in World Perspective: A Reader. Sylvia Fleis Fava, ed. New York: Thomas Y. Crowell, 256-266.

Taeuber, Alma F. and Karl E. Taeuber
1967 Recent immigration and studies of ethnic assimilation. Demography, 4:798-808.

Taeuber, Karl E.
1968 The effect of income distribution on racial residential segregation. Urban Affairs Quarterly, 4:5-14.

Taeuber, Karl F. and Alma F. Taeuber
1964 The Negro as an immigrant group: recent trends in racial and ethnic segregation in Chicago. American Journal of Sociology, 69:374-382.

1965 Negroes in cities. Chicago: Aldine Press.

Theodorsen, George A.
1961 Studies in Human Ecology. New York: Harper and Row.

Thurstone, L. L.
1955 Vectors of the mind. Chicago: University of Chicago Press.

Timms, Duncan
1965a Quantitative techniques in urban social geography. Frontiers in Geographical Teaching. Richard J. Chorley and Peter Haggett, eds. London: Methuen.

1965b The spatial distribution of social deviants in Luton, England. The Australian and New Zealand Journal of Sociology, 1(1):38-52.

1970 Comparative factorial ecology: some New Zealand examples. Environment and Planning, 2(4):455-468.

1971 The urban mosaic. Cambridge: Cambridge University Press.

Tryon, Robert C.
1955 Identification of social areas by cluster analysis: a general method with application to the San Francisco Bay area. Berkeley: University of California Press.

U. S. Bureau of the Census
1961 U. S. Census of Population: 1960. General population characteristics, United States summary. Final Report PC(1)-1B. Washington, D.C.: U. S. Government Printing Office.

1962a U. S. Census of Population: 1960. General social and economic characteristics, United States summary. Final Report PC(1)-1C. Washington, D.C.: U. S. Government Printing Office.

1962b U. S. Census of Population: 1960. Census tracts. Final Reports PHC(1)-7, PHC(1)-17, PHC(1)-22, PHC(1)-39, PHC(1)-43, PHC(1)-62, PHC(1)-72, PHC(1)-93, PHC(1)-122, PHC(1)-126, PHC(1)-135 and PHC(1)-156. Washington, D.C.: U. S. Government Printing Office.

1963a U. S. Census of Housing: 1960, Volume I, states and small areas. United States summary. Final Report HC(1)-1. Washington, D.C.: U. S. Government Printing Office.

1963b Methodology and scores of socioeconomic status. Working Paper No. 15, U. S. Bureau of the Census. Washington, D.C.: U. S. Government Printing Office.

1963c U. S. Census of Population: 1960. Volume II, Subject reports, families. Part PC(2)-4A. Washington, D.C.: U. S. Government Printing Office.

1963d U. S. Census of Population: 1960. Final Report PC(2)-7B. Subject report: occupation by earnings and education. Washington, D.C.: U. S. Government Printing Office.

1963e U. S. Census of Housing: 1960. Volume II, Metropolitan housing, Nos. 18, 30, 36, 56, 60, 80, 95, 114, 142, 148, 157 and 178. Washington, D.C.: Government Printing Office.

1967 U. S. Census of Population: 1960. Final Report PC(2)-5C: Subject report: socioeconomic status. Washington, D.C.: U. S. Government Printing Office.

Van Arsdol, Maurice
1957 An empirical evaluation of social area analysis in human ecology. Unpublished Ph.D. dissertation, University of Washington.

Van Arsdol, Maurice, Santo F. Camilleri and Calvin F. Schmid
1958 The generality of urban social area indexes. American Sociological Review, 23:277-284.

Vernon, Raymond
1960 Metropolis 1985. Cambridge, Mass.: Harvard University Press.

Wilson, A. G.
1969 Developments of some elementary residential location models. Journal of Regional Science, 9:377-385.

1970a Disaggregating elementary residential location models. Papers, Regional Science Association, 24:103-125.

1970b Entropy in urban and regional modelling. London: Pion.

1972 Multi-regional models of population structure and some implications for a dynamic residential location model. Patterns and Processes in Urban and Regional Systems. A. G. Wilson, ed. London: Pion.

Zelder, Raymond E.
1970 Racial Segregation in urban housing markets. Journal of Regional Science, 10:93-105.

THE UNIVERSITY OF CHICAGO
DEPARTMENT OF GEOGRAPHY
RESEARCH PAPERS (Lithographed, 6×9 Inches)

(*Available from Department of Geography, The University of Chicago, 5828 S. University Ave., Chicago, Illinois 60637. Price: $6.00 each; by series subscription, $5.00 each.*)

106. SAARINEN, THOMAS F. *Perception of the Drought Hazard on the Great Plains* 1966. 183 pp.
107. SOLZMAN, DAVID M. *Waterway Industrial Sites: A Chicago Case Study* 1967. 138 pp.
108. KASPERSON, ROGER E. *The Dodecanese: Diversity and Unity in Island Politics* 1967. 184 pp.
109. LOWENTHAL, DAVID, et al. *Environmental Perception and Behavior.* 1967. 88 pp.
110. REED, WALLACE E. *Areal Interaction in India: Commodity Flows of the Bengal-Bihar Industrial Area* 1967. 210 pp.
112. BOURNE, LARRY S. *Private Redevelopment of the Central City: Spatial Processes of Structural Change in the City of Toronto* 1967. 199 pp.
113. BRUSH, JOHN E., and GAUTHIER, HOWARD L., JR. *Service Centers and Consumer Trips: Studies on the Philadelphia Metropolitan Fringe* 1968. 182 pp.
114. CLARKSON, JAMES D. *The Cultural Ecology of a Chinese Village: Cameron Highlands, Malaysia* 1968. 174 pp.
115. BURTON, IAN; KATES, ROBERT W.; and SNEAD, RODMAN E. *The Human Ecology of Coastal Flood Hazard in Megalopolis* 1968. 196 pp.
117. WONG, SHUE TUCK. *Perception of Choice and Factors Affecting Industrial Water Supply Decisions in Northeastern Illinois* 1968. 96 pp.
118. JOHNSON, DOUGLAS L. *The Nature of Nomadism* 1969. 200 pp.
119. DIENES, LESLIE. *Locational Factors and Locational Developments in the Soviet Chemical Industry* 1969. 285 pp.
120. MIHELIC, DUSAN. *The Political Element in the Port Geography of Trieste* 1969. 104 pp.
121. BAUMANN, DUANE. *The Recreational Use of Domestic Water Supply Reservoirs: Perception and Choice* 1969. 125 pp.
122. LIND, AULIS O. *Coastal Landforms of Cat Island, Bahamas: A Study of Holocene Accretionary Topography and Sea-Level Change* 1969. 156 pp.
123. WHITNEY, JOSEPH. *China: Area, Administration and Nation Building* 1970. 198 pp.
124. EARICKSON, ROBERT. *The Spatial Behavior of Hospital Patients: A Behavioral Approach to Spatial Interaction in Metropolitan Chicago* 1970. 198 pp.
125. DAY, JOHN C. *Managing the Lower Rio Grande: An Experience in International River Development* 1970. 277 pp.
126. MAC IVER, IAN. *Urban Water Supply Alternatives: Perception and Choice in the Grand Basin, Ontario* 1970. 178 pp.
127. GOHEEN, PETER G. *Victorian Toronto, 1850 to 1900: Pattern and Process of Growth* 1970. 278 pp.
128. GOOD, CHARLES M. *Rural Markets and Trade in East Africa* 1970. 252 pp.
129. MEYER, DAVID R. *Spatial Variation of Black Urban Households* 1970. 127 pp.
130. GLADFELTER, BRUCE. *Meseta and Campiña Landforms in Central Spain: A Geomorphology of the Alto Henares Basin* 1971. 204 pp.
131. NEILS, ELAINE M. *Reservation to City: Indian Urbanization and Federal Relocation* 1971. 200 pp.
132. MOLINE, NORMAN T. *Mobility and the Small Town, 1900–1930* 1971. 169 pp.
133. SCHWIND, PAUL J. *Migration and Regional Development in the United States, 1950–1960* 1971. 170 pp.
134. PYLE, GERALD F. *Heart Disease, Cancer and Stroke in Chicago: A Geographical Analysis with Facilities Plans for 1980* 1971. 292 pp.
135. JOHNSON, JAMES F. *Renovated Waste Water: An Alternative Source of Municipal Water Supply in the U.S.* 1971. 155 pp.
136. BUTZER, KARL W. *Recent History of an Ethiopian Delta: The Omo River and the Level of Lake Rudolf* 1971. 184 pp.
137. HARRIS, CHAUNCY D. *Annotated World List of Selected Current Geographical Serials in English, French, and German* 3rd edition 1971. 77 pp.
138. HARRIS, CHAUNCY D., and FELLMANN, JEROME D. *International List of Geographical Serials* 2nd edition 1971. 267 pp.
139. MC MANIS, DOUGLAS R. *European Impressions of the New England Coast, 1497–1620* 1972. 147 pp.
140. COHEN, YEHOSHUA S. *Diffusion of an Innovation in an Urban System: The Spread of Planned Regional Shopping Centers in the United States, 1949–1968* 1972. 136 pp.

141. MITCHELL, NORA. *The Indian Hill-Station: Kodaikanal* 1972. 199 pp.

142. PLATT, RUTHERFORD H. *The Open Space Decision Process: Spatial Allocation of Costs and Benefits* 1972. 189 pp.

143. GOLANT, STEPHEN M. *The Residential Location and Spatial Behavior of the Elderly: A Canadian Example* 1972. 226 pp.

144. PANNELL, CLIFTON W. *T'ai-chung, T'ai-wan: Structure and Function* 1973. 200 pp.

145. LANKFORD, PHILIP M. *Regional Incomes in the United States, 1929–1967: Level, Distribution, Stability, and Growth* 1972. 137 pp.

146. FREEMAN, DONALD B. *International Trade, Migration, and Capital Flows: A Quantitative Analysis of Spatial Economic Interaction* 1973. 202 pp.

147. MYERS, SARAH K. *Language Shift Among Migrants to Lima, Peru* 1973. 204 pp.

148. JOHNSON, DOUGLAS L. *Jabal al-Akhdar, Cyrenaica: An Historical Geography of Settlement and Livelihood* 1973. 240 pp.

149. YEUNG, YUE-MAN. *National Development Policy and Urban Transformation in Singapore: A Study of Public Housing and the Marketing System* 1973. 204 pp.

150. HALL, FRED L. *Location Criteria for High Schools: Student Transportation and Racial Integration* 1973. 156 pp.

151. ROSENBERG, TERRY J. *Residence, Employment, and Mobility of Puerto Ricans in New York City* 1974. 230 pp.

152. MIKESELL, MARVIN W., editor. *Geographers Abroad: Essays on the Problems and Prospects of Research in Foreign Areas* 1973. 296 pp.

153. OSBORN, JAMES. *Area, Development Policy, and the Middle City in Malaysia* 1974. 273 pp.

154. WACHT, WALTER F. *The Domestic Air Transportation Network of the United States* 1974. 98 pp.

155. BERRY, BRIAN J. L., et al. *Land Use, Urban Form and Environmental Quality* 1974. 464 pp.

156. MITCHELL, JAMES K. *Community Response to Coastal Erosion: Individual and Collective Adjustments to Hazard on the Atlantic Shore* 1974. 209 pp.

157. COOK, GILLIAN P. *Spatial Dynamics of Business Growth in the Witwatersrand* 1975. 143 pp.

158. STARR, JOHN T., JR. *The Evolution of Unit Train Operations in the United States: 1960–1969—A Decade of Experience* 1976. 247 pp.

159. PYLE, GERALD F. *The Spatial Dynamics of Crime* 1974. 220 pp.

160. MEYER, JUDITH W. *Diffusion of an American Montessori Education* 1975. 109 pp.

161. SCHMID, JAMES A. *Urban Vegetation: A Review and Chicago Case Study* 1975. 280 pp.

162. LAMB, RICHARD. *Metropolitan Impacts on Rural America* 1975. 210 pp.

163. FEDOR, THOMAS. *Patterns of Urban Growth in the Russian Empire during the Nineteenth Century* 1975. 275 pp.

164. HARRIS, CHAUNCY D. *Guide to Geographical Bibliographies and Reference Works in Russian or on the Soviet Union* 1975. 496 pp.

165. JONES, DONALD W. *Migration and Urban Unemployment in Dualistic Economic Development* 1975 186 pp.

166. BEDNARZ, ROBERT S. *The Effect of Air Pollution on Property Value in Chicago* 1975. 118 pp.

167. HANNEMANN, MANFRED. *The Diffusion of the Reformation in Southwestern Germany, 1518-1534* 1975. 248 pp.

168. SUBLETT, MICHAEL D. *Farmers on the Road. Interfarm Migration and the Farming of Noncontiguous Lands in Three Midwestern Townships, 1939-1969* 1975. 228 pp.

169. STETZER, DONALD FOSTER. *Special Districts in Cook County: Toward a Geography of Local Government* 1975. 189 pp.

170. EARLE, CARVILLE V. *The Evolution of a Tidewater Settlement System: All Hallow's Parish, Maryland, 1650–1783* 1975. 249 pp.

171. SPODEK, HOWARD. *Urban-Rural Integration in Regional Development: A Case Study of Saurashtra, India—1800–1960* 1976. 156 pp.

172. COHEN, YEHOSHUA S. and BERRY, BRIAN J. L. *Spatial Components of Manufacturing Change* 1975 272 pp.

173. HAYES, CHARLES R. *The Dispersed City: The Case of Piedmont, North Carolina* 1976. 169 pp.

174. CARGO, DOUGLAS B. *Solid Wastes: Factors Influencing Generation Rates* 1977. 112 pp.

175. GILLARD, QUENTIN. *Incomes and Accessibility. Metropolitan Labor Force Participation, Commuting, and Income Differentials in the United States, 1960–1970* 1977. 140 pp.

176. MORGAN, DAVID J. *Patterns of Population Distribution: A Residential Preference Model and Its Dynamic* 1978 216 pp.

177. STOKES, HOUSTON H.; JONES, DONALD W. and NEUBURGER, HUGH M. *Unemployment and Adjustment in the Labor Market: A Comparison between the Regional and National Responses* 1975. 135 pp.

178. PICCAGLI, GIORGIO ANTONIO. *Racial Transition in Chicago Public Schools. An Examination of the Tipping Point Hypothesis, 1963–1971* WITHDRAWN.

179. HARRIS, CHAUNCY D. *Bibliography of Geography. Part I. Introduction to General Aids* 1976. 288 pp.

180. CARR, CLAUDIA J. *Pastoralism in Crisis. The Dasanetch and their Ethiopian Lands.* 1977. 339 pp.

181. GOODWIN, GARY C. *Cherokees in Transition: A Study of Changing Culture and Environment Prior to 1775.* 1977. 221 pp.

182. KNIGHT, DAVID B. *A Capital for Canada: Conflict and Compromise in the Nineteenth Century.* 1977. 359 pp.

183. HAIGH, MARTIN J. *The Evolution of Slopes on Artificial Landforms: Blaenavon, Gwent.* 1978. 311 pp.

184. FINK, L. DEE. *Listening to the Learner. An Exploratory Study of Personal Meaning in College Geography Courses.* 1977. 200 pp.

185. HELGREN, DAVID M. *Rivers of Diamonds: An Alluvial History of the Lower Vaal Basin.* 1979.

186. BUTZER, KARL W., *editor. Dimensions of Human Geography: Essays on Some Familiar and Neglected Themes.* 1978. 201 pp.

187. MITSUHASHI, SETSUKO. *Japanese Commodity Flows.* 1978. 185 pp.

188. CARIS, SUSAN L. *Community Attitudes toward Pollution.* 1978. 226 pp.

189. REES, PHILIP M. *Residential Patterns in American Cities, 1960.* 1979. 424 pp.

190. KANNE, EDWARD A. *Fresh Food for Nicosia.* 1979. 116 pp.